CONQUEST
THROUGH
IMMIGRATION

—◦◦◦—

HOW ZIONISM
TURNED PALESTINE
INTO
A JEWISH STATE

—◦◦◦—

By

George W. Robnett

Omni Publications — Hawthorne, CA 90251

Manufactured in the United States of America
Omni Publications — Hawthorne, CA 90251

IN APPRECIATION

It would be quite. impracticable to make personal reference to all the knowledgeable and gracious personalities who have given counsel and constructive criticism during the research and writing that has made this book.

To all of those who aided in this work we are deeply grateful. The wide and willing generosity to be helpful has been most gratifying.

The publishers place special importance on the Foreword by Doctor Millar Burrows who has served as visiting professor at the world-famed American University of Beirut (Lebanon), which institution has long been a great friendship-cementing influence for the United States in the Middle East.

He has also twice been a director of the important American School of Oriental Research in Jerusalem. Included in his long educational career, as listed in Who's Who in America, is his tenure as Professor of Biblical Theology at Yale University Divinity School (1934-1958); and among his several books we mention especially "What Mean These Stones?" and two separate volumes on the Dead Sea Scrolls.

Why This Book Was Written

The purpose of this volume is to deal as realistically and factually as possible with certain blurred pages of some recent and very important history. This is a studious effort by the authors to put into the record a rounded and authentic account of one of the most extraordinary political action and minority-power movements of the twentieth century — outside possibly that of the Bolshevik revolution.

It is doubtful that a more sensitive topic than the central theme of this book could have been selected since, of necessity, the subject-matter involves, in varying degree, the three most delicate issues in the whole category of human discussion — religion, race and politics.

That these are included is not a matter of the author's personal choice. These issues would be shunned if it were at all possible otherwise to explore what may well be one of the most critical phases of modern history. Let it be established at the outset that this book has the main purpose of being a factual record of certain tragically dynamic historical events.

The contents of this volume have been tediously researched, documented and written in the spirit of a truthful history-reporting job. Every reference here is considered germane to the general thesis which is to examine the Jewish-Arab conflict in Palestine and document the modus operandi involving the skillful use of politics, immigration and military action to capture and turn Palestine into a "Jewish State." This necessitates an examination of all the forces that were parties to this history-making coup — including the inglorious roles played by Great Britain and the United States. Most of the manuscript was carefully read for accuracy by authorities in the various critical fields with which it deals.

* * *

The serious study that resulted in this book was begun in 1963. It was inspired by a tour through the Holy Land countries, which brought intimate contact with the pitiable spectacle of a million or so Palestinian Arab refugees — wasting their lives in huddled camps on U.N. (mostly American) relief of around ten cents per day. These people who were once independent, self-supporting and even prosperous have been made paupers by being dispossessed of their lifetime homes and possessions — hopelessly forsaken in primitive and isolated camps, scattered around the periphery of their traditional land to which their return is forbidden.

This shocking evidence had all the earmarks of some kind of tragic injustice or political disaster, which seemingly should arrest the attention and sympathy of any individual who suddenly finds himself confronted with such distressing exposure of human catastrophe and glaring tragedy for so many people.

* * *

After talking with many of these Palestinian refugees and hearing their pathetic stories, it was only natural for an inquiring mind to ask — "How could this happen in our modern 'civilized' world?" What was the cause? Why do our people in America know so little about this human calamity for which we are partially responsible? Gradual inquiries led to more astounding revelations, all of which led irresistibly to deeper investigations. It soon became apparent that a tragically important episode of history has been largely and quite successfully swept under the carpet of time and indifference, aided and abetted by willful intent.

Out of this tedious investigation and several trips abroad has come this book which undertakes to pull back the curtains and document the forces and events that have dangerously disturbed the equilibrium of the strategic Middle East and thereby have accelerated the possibilities of another world conflagration. One of these forces not to be ignored is the Soviet-led Communist menace. The Red monster has long looked with greedy eyes for opportunities to penetrate the strategic Middle East.

The Zionist-Arab conflict aroused a fury of bitterness in this part of the world which was not overlooked by the prowling Communists, whose fondness for trouble-spots as spawning ground is notorious. Until this fertile soil of conflict and confusion was created, the deeply religious Arabs with their great friendliness for the United States presented a solid wall of resistance to Middle East Soviet aspirations. The Soviets have played both sides against the middle. Documentation on this will be presented in the later chapters.

*   *   *

Unhappily, this historical narrative is also the story of turbulence, terrorism, and resulting distress produced by the militant upsurge of relatively new forces in the highly explosive social, political and economic melting pot of a world in revolution. Revolutionary terrorism, released first by the Bolsheviks in 1917 as an aftermath of World War I (the same war that gave emerging Zionism the so-called Balfour Declaration, which document opened the road to the inevitable Zionist-Arab conflict some twenty-five years later) has spread in chain reaction and cyclonic proportions throughout the world with its evil results making jungles of American cities today. The farcical stratagems used to maneuver the Balfour document will likewise be described in special chapters of this volume.

People everywhere seem to be caught in the undertow and backlash of swift and unrelenting change which appears to be a wave of the future as a pattern for "the new social order" — change that is being forced by certain groups for what too often is a meaningless fetish for "change." This is not orderly progress — it is nothing less than Marxist revolution and everywhere in these radical movements we find dedicated Marxists in agitational action. Revolution by force and violence is completely destructive to the Anglo-Saxon theory of law and order. Politicians seem to be utterly paralyzed in their fear of minority blocs that can deliver substantial votes. This political flaccidity will be reflected throughout this book as the subservience and servility of certain "great statesmen" are revealed in the following chapters.

It is not our purpose to plead the cause of any nation or group of people other than to report the facts and let the chips fall where they may. If there is one exception to this it would be a reflection of sympathy for the homeless and destitute Palestinian-Arab refugees who have been deprived of their property possessions and citizenship rights in their

9

native homeland — and are now the helpless pawns of ruthless political insolvency.

*   *   *

We have been cautioned that forthrightness in this particular field can be a dangerous adventure. Of this hazard we are completely conscious. It is well known that where frenzied human emotions become mixed with heated political machinations, there is but little tolerance for any expressions that are less than adulation for the "righteous cause." All we can say for this volume is that its only purpose is to put certain facts of history in proper perspective and this involves the duty of tracing the roots of origin and growth.

What This Book Is All About

THIS VOLUME represents an excursion into Palestinian historiography wherein the main theses lead up to and revolve around the conflict between Zionist Jews and the Palestinian Arab-confluence.

The purpose of the following arranged chapters is to present the role of political Zionism and the other pertinent issues in the best possible sequential order for clarity and continuity to picturize a highly complicated series of events and movements of which there is very little synchronized comprehension. The first plan of text arrangement was to have Chapters I and II give short historical sketches of the two principal ethnic groups involved — the Arabs and the Jews. Consultation with the Institute's associates has changed the order to begin immediately with the axial reality of the whole theme and to add the two historical outlines as post-chapter Appendices "A" and "B". Some readers may wish to consult these two Appendices first as helpful to understanding the other chapters.

Chapter Arrangement

1. PALESTINE HISTORY —
NOT LAND OF ONE, BUT MANY PEOPLES.

During Palestine's long recorded history, the Hebrew-Israelite-Jewish ethnic complex had only a comparatively short independent occupancy. Over the centuries the country has been occupied and ruled by many other peoples. As this history is here explored, it appears by the record that the Arabs have had the longest and (up to 1948) latest occupancy.

2. ONLY FEW JEWS IN PALESTINE
FROM 135 A.D. to the 1920's.

After Emperor Hadrian completely destroyed Jerusalem and dispersed the Jews, there is but little record of them in the area until attempts were made in the 18th and 19th centuries to establish scattered settlements during the Turkish rule of the country. These consisted largely of orthodox Jews dependent upon diaspora charity.

3. ZIONISM — ORIGIN AND METHODOLOGY.

This chapter records the ferment and agitation among Jews in Poland, Russia and other East-European countries in the late 19th century which, with the leadership of early bellwethers, like Theodor Herzl, brought about the switch from traditional spiritual Zionism to political Zionist crusading for nationalistic goals.

4. THE CONTRADICTION OF BIBLE-BASED POLITICAL ZIONISM.

The question raised here concerns the moral propriety of establishing a political State on the highly tenuous doctrine of self-pleading interpretations from the Old Testament writers.

5. DO THE BIBLICAL COVENANTS GIVE PALESTINE TO THE ZIONISTS?

The question of the Old Testament "land covenants" is here examined in the light of factuality as to origin — as to the descriptions which becloud them — and as to their present day status of validity in modern day courts.

6. DOES POLITICAL ZIONISM HAVE SOCIALISTIC ROOTS?

An examination of this subject brings to light a remarkably close affiliation of Socialist and Zionist action during the early days of both movements.

7. CONTROVERSY OVER PHRASE "THE JEWISH PEOPLE" — DOES IT SIGNIFY "RELIGION" OR "NATIONALITY"?

The purpose of this chapter is to examine the controversy where certain Jewish personalities have questioned the right of the present day Zionist-Jews to posture themselves as representatives of "the Jewish people" as an all inclusive, political-binding phrase.

8. WORLD WAR I OPENS GATEWAY FOR ZIONISM. AMAZING MALCOLM STORY OF PLOT TO GET UNITED STATES INTO THAT WAR.

Revelation of an unusual document, filed in the British records, of an influential personality showing how he initiated and helped promote a "plan" whereby British strategists would work through Zionist machinery to influence America's entry into the first World War — and how it was successfully implemented with Zionist cunning.

9. BALFOUR DECLARATION USED AS KEY TO OPEN THE FATEFUL GATE.

Here is the documented history of a highly critical instrument that played a major role in the Zionist-Arab collision which brought strife, war and misery to the Middle East. A disclosure of the machinations that produced it.

10. ARABS AGREE TO FIGHT TURKS — BRITAIN PROMISES INDEPENDENCE FOR ARAB LANDS. COMPLICATIONS FOLLOW CONTRADICTORY PROMISES.

Documentation here discloses how Britain's original good intentions for the Arabs got hooked on the horns of another dilemma (the Balfour promise to the Jews) — producing the insoluble Middle East imbroglio.

11. ZIONISTS WANT BRITAIN TO HAVE MANDATE OVER PALESTINE — EXPECTING THIS TO INSURE ENFORCEMENT OF BALFOUR'S TRICKY PROMISE.

The Zionists, working through America's delegation to the Paris Peace Conference, strove busily to assure Palestine trusteeship for Britain — assuming naturally that this would implement the Balfour immigration commitment.

12. PARIS PEACE CONFERENCE. ZIONISTS GREATLY OUTNUMBER AND OUTPLAY ARAB DELEGATION.

A factual and realistic report on artful manipulation at the Paris Peace meeting where polished diplomatic strategy was used to promote the Zionist design for "right of way" in Palestine for the projected Jewish State.

13. MASSIVE JEWISH IMMIGRATION BRINGS CONFRONTATION THAT LED TO CONFLICT.

The Zionists, once they secured the Balfour commitment on Jewish immigration into Palestine, put full steam behind their plan to fill that little country with Jewish refugees from Eastern Europe. This massive confrontation inevitably brought hostile reaction from the long time Arab inhabitants.

14. TERRORISTIC "UNDERGROUND" CRUSADE TO DRIVE BRITISH FROM PALESTINE.

When British Mandate authorities tried to stop the growing Zionist-Arab conflict by minimizing Jewish immigration into Palestine, the militant Zionists started a violent crusade to get Britain out of Palestine — and out of their way.

15. BRITISH RELINQUISH MANDATE AUTHORITY TO UNITED NATIONS; U.N. IN DESPERATION ORDERS PARTITION OF PALESTINE.

After the hostility and embroilment in Palestine finally got out of hand and appeared insoluble, the British gave notice they would quit the Mandate and give the United Nations a hand at trying for a solution. The inexperienced U.N. had only one answer — which was to try the previously discarded plan to divide the country into a Jewish State and an Arab State. The experiment proved disastrous.

16. BRITISH DEPART FROM PALESTINE. ZIONISTS STAGE COUP — PROCLAIM "JEWISH STATE".

At Midnight, May 14, 1948, as British Mandate authority was relinquished, the Zionist-Jews, without waiting for the United Nations to proceed orderly with "Partition," proclaimed its own self-anointed plan for the immediate establishment of a "Jewish State" — calling it Israel.

17. PALESTINE ARABS CALL FOR HELP. NEIGHBOR ARAB STATES RESPOND — INADEQUATELY. THE 1948 WAR WAS THUS ESCALATED BETWEEN ZIONISTS AND ARABS.

When the Zionists seized State power, adding to the already developed immigration-aggression, the unarmed Palestinian Arabs, fearing total take-over, called on the League of Arab States for help. The response was too little and too late. The Zionists, heavily financed from abroad, and receiving armament from Russia, had become militarily strong and well organized.

18. TRAGIC STORY OF THE PALESTINE REFUGEES.

This is largely the story of the 1948 refugees. Panic-stricken because of Zionist "underground" terroristic acts (akin to the massacre at Deir Yaseen) Arab families, men with their women and children, began fleeing across the Palestine borders for safety. This created one of the world's most aggravating human displacement problems of modern history. The 1967 Israeli "blitz" resulted in more flights for safety, compounding the already frightening refugee disaster.

14

19. INTERESTING FACTS ABOUT SOVIETISM, SOCIALISM AND ZIONISM IN THE MIDDLE EAST.

This chapter examines the often mentioned matter of the Soviet threat in this area. The progress thus far has been made possible by the Zionist-Arab conflict. Soviet aid was first given to help Zionism establish itself as a "Jewish State" — then it helped that State defeat the Arabs in 1948 by supplying armament. Later, when the Arabs, because of this defeat, needed help, the Soviets switched aid to them. It appears the Soviets know how to fish in muddy water.

20. THE PROBLEM OF RATIONALIZING SOVIET COMMUNISM AND CERTAIN ZIONIST PHENOMENA.

The rise of political Zionism in the Jewish world has, by the record, produced a problem of rationalizing certain kinds of "liberalism" with "socialism" in its various forms. This is understandably a sensitive issue but one that has far-reaching implications — not only in the Middle East but in countries like America, where the Communist form of socialism is considered by most people to be a deadly threat. Some puzzling facts are presented here as highlights of this question.

21. HIGHLIGHTS OF THE 1967 "SIX DAY" ISRAEL EXPANSION WAR. MYSTERY OF ISRAEL ATTACK ON U.S.S. "LIBERTY".

In June of 1967, military action broke out violently again between Israel and the Arab states of Egypt, Jordan and Syria, beginning with a surprise blitz air attack by Israel jets. The causes and results of this 6-day engagement with disaster for the Arabs and large expansionism for the Israelis, are examined here briefly as this book is being prepared for press. Included is an account of the yet unexplained attempt by Israeli planes to destroy the U.S.S. "Liberty."

22. WHAT THE ZIONISTS EXPECT OF CHRISTIANS.

Many Zionist spokesmen, rabbis included among them, have been sharp in criticism of Christians for not rushing to support Zionist-Israel in its religio-nationalistic policies in the Middle East. This chapter gives a very brief summation of Zionist efforts to lay down guide lines for Christians.

15

23. HOW ZIONIST-JEWS COLLECT MILLIONS IN U.S. TO SUPPORT THE "JEWISH STATE."

The purpose in this chapter is to present reliable documentation on a most extraordinary operation conducted in the United States — a massive program of money-collection to be used for promotion and sustenance of the "Jewish State," called Israel. While this is but a brief outline of how this program is operated, it may, in some measure, be helpful to the many who have tried to understand this complicated activity.

24. POLITICAL MACHINERY AND TRENDS IN ZIONIST ISRAEL.

In researching for this volume, it became clear that very few people have any essential knowledge of the political processes that function inside the "Jewish State." Zionist spokesmen and their propaganda outlets strive to leave the impression that it is more or less a second edition of the United States and therefore should be supported by America as its indispensable conservative ally in the Middle East. This chapter undertakes to present some facts concerning the political construction of trouble-born and trouble-bearing Israel.

APPENDIX "A"

WHO ARE THE ARABS?

Arabia — the original source. Birth and rise of Mohammed — the Prophet. Birth of Islam — the religion. The great Arab conquests swept forward by religious zeal. Arab culture. The break-up of the Arab Empire. Turkish conquest of Arab lands. Arabs enter into compact with Great Britain to join in World War I to revolt against the Turks and drive them from the Middle East in return for post-war independence of the Arab countries, of which Palestine (by record of population and 1,300 years of major occupancy) was one.

*   *   *

APPENDIX "B"

WHO ARE THE JEWS?

This chapter covers five rather distinct divisions of "Jewish history": (1) The Old Testament recordings of the Patriarchal Hebrews; (2) The Old Testament story of the Israelites who proliferated from Jacob's twelve sons after thay had taken refuge in Egypt from the famines of Canaan. This epoch includes the full story of the Israelites — the 40 year trek and invasion of Canaan — wars, internecine and with other nations, and the founding of ancient Israel; (3) Next came the "Jewish period" as the exiled Hebrews in Babylon were allowed to return to Judea (Jerusalem) where, from 537 B.C. to 135 A.D., they had a turbulent and more or less vassal existence until essentially ousted by the Romans; (4) The spread throughout the world of the Jewish wanderers (Diaspora); (5) The newest epoch of Jewish history — the rise and progress of political Zionism.

Foreword

by MILLAR BURROWS

Professor Emeritus of Biblical Theology

Yale University

During the years since 1948 it has often seemed that to say a word on behalf of the Palestinian Arabs or against Zionism was merely whipping a dead horse. The eruption of war last June and Israel's occupation of what was left of Arab Palestine have made the Arabs' cause appear more hopeless than ever; but at the same time the whole question of Palestine has been brought into the open again. Perhaps it is not too much to hope that some Americans who have hitherto been blinded to the Arab side of the question by the powerful propaganda of the Zionists, and have regarded Israel only as a haven for the survivors of the Nazi horror in Europe, will now be awakened to a realization of the wrong done to the native Arab population of the Holy Land, and the still unsatisfied hope of aggressive Zionism to regain the whole area once ruled by King David.

The occupation of the whole of Palestine west of the Jordan is only the climax (so far) of a series of *faits accomplis* achieved in defiance of the repeated declarations and demands of the United Nations. In the face of the widespread conviction that the newly occupied territory and the Old City of Jerusalem should be returned to the Arabs — a view which Russia cheerfully supports, if only to embarrass us — the Israelis boldly declare that they intend to keep what they have taken, no matter what the United Nations and the conscience of the world may say.

The Arabs, never reconciled to having a new nation of foreigners planted on their land against their will, making hundreds of thousands of the native inhabitants homeless refugees, are now more bitter than ever. Their bitterness

18

against the usurpers, and against the western powers whom they hold responsible, is now intensified by a sense of frustration. A reluctant realization that they are no match for the Israelis in military power and skill is being forced upon them by sad experience, and their inability to work together effectively makes matters worse.

Israel, with a relatively small population, concentrated in a relatively small area, is united in purpose, possessed of extraordinary energy and ability, bringing to its new life the knowledge and skills gained by long residence in Europe and America, and supported financially and politically by the western nations. The Arabs, numerically far stronger, are spread over a vast area, only a fraction of which is cultivable, economically poor with the exception of the few oil-producing states, technically and culturally backward because of centuries of stagnation under the Turkish empire, and politically divided because the western powers cut up their territory into small, weak states after World War I instead of giving them the united Arab nation which had been promised. Rapid progress has been made since then, but much more over a long time would be needed to make them economically, politically and militarily the equals of the Israelis.

Under these conditions, their rankling sense of injustice and bitter frustration festers and becomes more and more a source of danger to the peace of the world. The problem of Palestine has not been settled by the success and expansion of Israel; it has been made all the more acute. It will not be settled until it is settled right; and it will not be settled right unless it is settled on the basis of justice. A reviewer of my little book, *Palestine Is Our Business,* said, "The trouble with the professor is that he thinks this problem can be solved on a moral basis." I still think so. If it is not solved on a moral basis, it will not be solved at all.

A serious aggravation of the difficulty is the common confusion of opposition to Zionism with Antisemitism. That an ardent Zionist, to whom Jewish nationalism has become practically the substance of his religion, should be inclined to equate a rejection of his position with prejudice against Jews as such is not too hard to understand; yet it can hardly

19

be doubted that this unfortunate confusion has been deliberately encouraged by some who ought to know better. The fact that many of the most devout and loyal Jews are and always have been against Zionism, and not at all convinced that the present state of Israel is a fulfilment of what the Scriptures promise, is kept so dark that few people are aware of it. Anyone who has suffered from this false identification of Antizionism with Antisemitism knows how effectively it evades and conceals the real issues. I know whereof I speak, having been called an Antisemitist because I was against Zionism, and charged with "leftish" sympathies because I was an officer of a National Committee to Combat Antisemitism! Truth and justice cannot be attained in that way.

What will have been done about Palestine by the time this book comes from the press is now quite uncertain, though one is tempted to make cynical predictions. Certainly nothing final will have been achieved: too many mistakes have been made, too many opportunities missed, and too many complicating factors are involved. The time seems ripe, however, to take a fresh look at the historical roots of the problem, and to analyze again the legal and moral issues at stake.

Mr. Robnett has done this, and in the volume here before us he presents the results of long and arduous investigation. Naturally no two writers would approach the subject from quite the same angle or view it in exactly the same way; but as one who has been deeply concerned with this tragic problem for many years I am happy to endorse Mr. Robnett's conclusions on the main issues, and to commend his careful, earnest presentation to the fair, open-minded consideration of his readers, who, I sincerely hope, will be many.
September 23, 1967

THE PUBLISHERS place special importance on this Foreword since Doctor Millar Burrows has served as visiting professor at the world famed American University of Beirut (Lebanon) which institution has long been a great friendship-cementing influence for America in the Middle East. He has also twice been a director of the important American School of Oriental Research in Jerusalem. Included in his long educational career as listed in Who's Who, is his tenure as professor of Biblical theology at Yale University Divinity School (1934-1958); and among his several books we mention especially, for archaeological emphasis, "What Mean These Stones?" and two separate volumes on The Dead Sea Scrolls.

1. PALESTINE HISTORY — NOT LAND OF ONE — BUT MANY PEOPLES

THE CENTRAL subject of this book is a small country called Palestine and for that reason some history of it should be reported here. In ancient times this territory was generally known as the southwestern section of Syria. The coastal plains of this area along the Mediterranean sea were, in the earliest days of recorded history, called the land of Canaan — and the southern part was known as Philistia or the land of the Philistines. From this comes the name of "Palestine," which sets its nascent historic status. This name has no indigenous relationship with the patriarchal Hebrews or the later Israelites. Derivation of the name rather seems to give historical prestige to the Philistines.

REDOUBTABLE PHILISTINES

The Philistines were people who, in the 13th or 12th centuries B.C., or earlier, entered (probably by sea) the rich Mediterranean coastlands, occupying the area approximately from present Tel Aviv on down to the Egyptian border beyond Gaza. Here they flourished and became the strongest opponents of the invading Israelites who, we are told in the Old Testament, entered Palestine from the opposite (Jordan river) side, bent upon conquest of the country. The battling between the two groups continued for perhaps two hundred or more years. The Philistines were finally rendered militarily impotent under the Israelite King David.

Two strange Biblical incidents make it appear that there was friendliness between the early patriarchal Hebrews and the Philistines — at least a type of cordiality. The Encyclopedia Britannica (11th edition) refers to a story of Isaac (son of

Abraham) and the Philistine Abimelech, King of Gerar, as "of great interest in its unbiased representation of intercourse, enmity, alliance and covenant." The reference obviously includes the episode where Isaac's wife became involved with Abimelech (Genesis 25). A similar experience had previously involved Abraham and his wife Sarah with this same Philistine king (Genesis 20). Later, however, when the Israelite-offspring of Abraham, Isaac and Jacob, arrived en masse to take over the country, despite these earlier intimacies between the patriarchs and the Philistine king, the Israelites and the Philistines locked horns in long and deadly warfare.

The Old Testament writers barely mentioned the word "Palestine," but identified the area as the land of Promise, land of Jehovah, land of Israel, and land of Canaan, which last term, according to the Schaff-Herzog "Encyclopedia of Religious Knowledge," is the section's oldest historical designation. Palestine, as it became known later, was, of course, a composition of what had historically been many tiny kingdoms or city-states. While much effort in later years has been exerted to associate Palestine with Jewish tradition as a sort of first mortgage lien, the area, according to some historians, was well peopled for thousands of years before the Hebrews came into history.

PALESTINE—VITAL INTERNATIONAL BRIDGE

From the earliest period of rather faithful history, deriving from often highly debatable legends, the area we know as Palestine has been a "bridge on a road" between the great antagonistic nations of antiquity — ancient Egypt at one end with Assyria, Babylonia and the whole Mesopotamian region, including Persia, at the other. Over this road, backwards and forwards, the armies of conquest have traveled, alternating with victory and defeat. On this road lies Megiddo, where a strategic pass has been the site of many historic battles — a spot which the New Testament designates as the location for the Battle of Armageddon — the final battle between the forces of good and evil.

It is because of this historic road along the coast through Palestine that this little country has for centuries been considered so important to the nations who needed this route for their armies, and this territory as buffer protection. Palestine has therefore, through the many thousands of years of its history, never, for any substantial length of time, been an independent country in the true sense, but has been continually subjected to change of "ownership."

First, it must be stated, that no satisfactory dimensional definition of early Palestine seems possible. The Encyclopedia Britannica (11th edition) states — "There is no ancient geographical term that covers all this area. Until the period of the Roman occupation, it was subdivided into independent provinces or kingdoms at different times (such as Philistia, Canaan, Judah, Israel, Bashan, etc.), but never entirely united under one collective designation. The extension of the name of Palestine, beyond the limits of Philistia proper, "is not older than the Byzantine period." Such territorial boundary definitions as were given in the Old Testament have no exactness subject to present day legal interpretations. For example, see Joshua 15:1-12.

Concerning population statistics, the 1911 Encyclopedia Britannica reports — "The inhabitants of Palestine are composed of large numbers of elements, differing widely in ethnological affinities, language and religion . . . early in the 20th century a list of no less than fifty languages, spoken in Jerusalem as vernaculars, was there drawn up by a party of men whose various official positions enabled them to possess accurate information on the subject."

BIBLE "HISTORY" OF PALESTINE

The Encyclopedia also says — "The Biblical history is a 'canonical' history which looks back to the patriarchs, the exodus from Egypt, the law-giving and the covenant with Yahweh at Sinai, the conquest of Palestine by the Israelite tribes, the monarchy, the rival kingdoms, the fall and exile of the northern tribes, and, later, of the southern (Judah) and the reconstruction of Judah in the times of Cyrus, Darius and Artaxerxes."

Being "canonical history," it is likewise priestly history — written and arranged, not by objective, disinterested historians such as we have become accustomed to today, but by ancient writers whose central purpose was to codify and dramatize a special nationalistic type of religion. This is not to criticise, but to point up a fact that must certainly be clear to anyone who has read these scriptures. This is important to mention here since the narratives and prestige of the Old Testament enter heavily into the background claims of Zionist policy. Therefore, it becomes necessary to examine the Old Testament texts and legends rather carefully in order properly to weigh the validity of such claims. That right of examination has become public domain, due especially to the involvement of Zionist activities in international politics.

The Old Testament basically and naturally concerns itself mainly with the early history of the Hebrew-Jewish people and of Palestine. With the exception of exile periods of these early people in Egypt and Babylonia, the main locale of the Old Testament writings and drama is centered in Palestine. This has created a rather wide impression that Palestine has always been a Jewish land. The books of the Old Testament which serve to leave this idea were, it must be remembered, written by Hebrews for Hebrews and dedicated to the concept of a religion for a special people (Deuteronomy 7:6 and copious other Old Testament references). This reference has only to do with clarification of a far-away (in time and space) chain of events to which the Zionists have linked their claims and whipped up a great deal of emotional sympathy among those who have been schooled in an allegorical rather than a political interpretation of the Bible. Some of these good people have not yet apparently been able to distinguish the difference in meaning between these two exegetical usages.

What was just said about the Old Testament having been written by Hebrews for Hebrews and dedicated to a special religious purpose can be paraphrased to say that the Koran was written for Moslems to interpret and promote Islam — and the New Testament was written for the same purpose for Christians and Christianity. There is, however, this difference — the Old Testament is also a major source, and in some cases the only source, of "history" for those early times.

We are concerned only with the fact that certain parts of that history have become involved in one of the great political controversies of modern international affairs — a matter of such far-reaching potentials as to awaken the concern of millions of people who, in one way or another, have been dragged into the embroilment.

With emphasis on this distinction, it should be perfectly clear that any reference made in this book to the Old Testament or to the Jewish people is by way of examining the present day Palestine situation, and is intended in no sense to reflect upon the spiritual traditions or theology of any peoples. The rather delicate question that seems to be central here, and in the minds of many people, is whether the history element of canonical or priestly weighted authorship in the Old Testament can properly be used to justify or validate mass immigration invasion with nationhood purposes (in violation of general international immigration policies) into a country that for 1,300 years has been preponderantly inhabited by other peoples.

ANCIENT ISRAEL DEAD 2,700 YEARS

Combined with the Zionist claim of a divine-covenant right to Palestine is the argument of a moral right, based upon the assumption that because the ancient Hebrews had a comparatively short-lived national existence in Palestine some 3,000 years ago, this in some way makes them heirs apparent of those ancient people, which carries with it the right to set up shop as a nation in Palestine even when that results in filling numerous refugee camps with a million or so people who, with their forebears, have lived there all their lives. This is the question, stated in candid terms, that confronts one all through the Middle East today.

If occupancy of Palestine for a short time in its long and turbulent history could be a valid claim on the part of those that have been in and out of control of that country — both before and after the Israelites — there could be many claimants with rights as valid as those of the Zionists, and some perhaps more so. There were the Canaanites — the Philistines — the Phoenicians — and many other groups there before the Israelites invaded and took over for an uncertain and troubled period. Later, there were the Assyrians — the Babylonians — the Persians — the Egyptians — the Alexander-Macedonians — and the Romans. Then followed a long list of other occupants, including the Arabs, the Turks and the Christians; but such records of long-past occupancy of any land, or by any people, are no longer acceptable by present day democratic standards as either a moral or legal basis for long-removed presumptives to arrogate to themselves the right to invade or conquer an already inhabited land. Civilization has, presumably, advanced beyond any such ancient or medieval customs.

NOTE: Recently Dean Rusk (U.S. Secretary of State) made the statement on television concerning Vietnam that "it is too late in history" for civilized nations to allow any kind of coup d'etat that destroys the homeland of any people who are well settled and established as a civilization or human domain.

The record of occupancy of Palestine should be put into clear comparative perspective, and for that purpose a brief outline of the ethnic and religious groups who, at various time-periods have inhabited and ruled this area, will be given here with adequate emphasis upon the Hebrew-Israelite occupancy period and the different peoples who followed them. With regard to the Israelites and the other nationality groups who were in Palestine before them, the reader will find greater details in final Appendix "B" — "Who Are the Jews?". Despite some slight repetition in so far as Israelite history is concerned, it seems important to make these present references in order to give clarity and sequence to the occupancy line-up.

The early Israelite Kingship was, however, but a brief incident in the long and constantly changing history of Palestine as a populated country. In the Appendix just mentioned, the story of the early Hebrews carries their history from the Abrahamic period to the time when a single family (that of Jacob) moved to Egypt to escape famine in lower Palestine, and later came out of Egypt (the Exodus) as a multitude of Israelites. These Israelites were divided, we are told, into twelve tribes, each for one of the sons of Jacob (with one exception) and after an historic 40-year trek through deserts,

26

wadis and hills, finally reached their coveted goal — Canaan. When they crossed the Jordan river into this "promised land," they proceeded with relentless vigor (as detailed in Appendix "B") to assault and vanquish the inhabitants — and confiscate lands and properties for the purpose of turning Palestine into a Nation of their own.

After a long period of fighting, they were able to take over a considerable area which they apportioned among the twelve tribes. The internecine bickering between these groups brought the development of a loose system of general community control, under what was called "the Judges." After a time, this proved unsatisfactory and a Kingship was established as the first try at creating a Hebrew nation.

ANCIENT ISRAEL KINGSHIP— SHORT INCIDENT IN TIME

This early (united) Hebrew Kingdom or nation, during its lifetime, had a series of three kings — Saul, David and Solomon. As a unit it existed about one hundred years, when dissension among the twelve tribes, after the death of the last of the three kings (Solomon), caused the nation to break into two — Northern and Southern — fragments. The total existence of the Hebrew-Israelite kingships, combining the three regimes of the united kingdom with the several kings who reigned hazardly in the northern and southern splinters (Samaria and Judea), lasted only about 400 years altogether.

During the time of the first king (Saul), there does not appear to have been much of either a unified or stable government — nor even a national capital. We are told that "Saul abode in Gibeah under a tree in Ramah . . . and all his servants . . ." (I Samuel 22:6). And again — "the Ziphites came unto Saul in Gibeah" (I Samuel 26:1).

Saul, who was selected as king by Samuel, the last of the judges of the Israelite tribes, appears, according to I-Samuel, to have spent most of his time fighting the Philistines, and trying to exterminate his son-in-law David of whose popularity he was jealous because Samuel, the first king-maker, was trying to oust Saul and put David in his place. Saul not only tried repeatedly to kill David but also tried to kill his own son Jonathan, for befriending David. Saul did have a coterie of priests slain for their kindness to David.

This was Saul, the first king of ancient Israel, who finally committed suicide by falling on his sword after a decisive defeat by the Philistines. The Old Testament reporting does not seem to leave a very impressive record of the Israelite nation throughout its first kingship. The body of Saul was recovered by some of his followers (from where the Philistines had hung it on a wall in Bethshan), and they buried it in Jabesh which was just east of the Jordan river, about fifty miles northeast of the site that became Jerusalem.

DAVID DEDICATES JERUSALEM

Jerusalem did not become the capital of the Hebrew nation until seven years after David had succeeded Saul as king. For that first seven years, David's headquarters were in Hebron, some twenty miles south of a fortified village stronghold called Jebus — capital of the Jebusites. David was having some difficulties because of jealousies among the tribes, and in order to attain tribal political unity, he decided to take Jebus by force and make it his capital — as a more neutral site. The Jebusites, for moral protection against this threatened take-over, manned their stronghold with their blind and maimed. This psychological strategy did not deter David, whose soldiers assaulted and took the town (II Samuel 5). From his palace here he ruled his kingdom. In time the place became known as Jerusalem.

Under David the Hebrew nation took better form through his aggressive conquests of surrounding territories and his better organizing ability. He consolidated the tribes and defeated the Philistines as well as Moab, Gath and other frontiers. Milman's "History of the Jews" tells us: "So far the unexampled splendor and prosperity had marked the reign of David: the remainder was as gloomy as disastrous. His own crime was the turning point of his fortunes."

David, the second king of the Israelite nation, eventually grew old and bedridden and strange attempts to revive his virility failed (I Kings 1:24). Who would be his successor?

28

We are told that David had many children with wives and concubines he took from both Hebron and Jerusalem (II Samuel 5: 12-16). One of them, Adonijah, the Son of Haggith, exalted himself, saying "I will be king," and he proceeded to take rule without his sick father's knowledge. This greatly concerned Nathan, the prophet, and Bathsheba, through whose maneuvering the son, Solomon, was put on the throne before his father's death (Standard Jewish Encyclopedia).

SOLOMON'S "GREAT SOCIETY" BRINGS END OF NATION

This apparently was good "maneuvering" as Solomon reigned with a splendid record of administration by greatly expanding commercial enterprise and instituting a vast building program, accompanied by the fanfare of a brilliant and lavish royal court. He was king for about forty years. There appears to be no certainty as to the exact years. Three Jewish Encyclopedias give him different dates of office. (1) 973-933; (2) 961-920; (3) 1015-977). The Concise Dictionary of Judaism gives high praise to Solomon's achievement, but adds: "His many foreign wives and high taxation led to the breakup of the kingdom after his death."

For quite some time before King Solomon's death, there had been strong opposition to his extravagant policies, and quickly after his death the "united" Kingdom split into two parts. The Northern section, consisting mainly of Samaria, assumed the name "Israel" even though the center of Hebrew life and culture (including the Solomon Temple and Jerusalem, the national capital since David's time) were in the Southern sector called Judah — later Judea. Relations between the two opposing districts, each maintaining its own kingships, continued to be acrimonious — and even at times warlike.

The Samarian subdivision, called "Israel," lasted until 722 B.C. when it was swallowed by the Assyrians, while the Southern sector staggered along with precarious independence until 586 B.C., when it was absorbed by the Babylonians. From that time on, for some 2,500 years, the area was under the changing control of many larger nations or empires.

When the Assyrians took Samaria (the northern Hebrew kingdom consisting of ten tribes), and the Babylonians vanquished Judah (the southern kingdom, made up of two tribes), the cream of the Hebrew population in each case was carried away and transplanted — which was an ancient policy of conquest. The "Israelites" or "Children of Israel," as the Hebrews who migrated from Egypt were variously called in the Old Testament, faded from history under those names.

Those who had been taken to Babylonia became known in Biblical literature as the Exiles, while the ten tribes taken from Samaria by the Assyrians were apparently "absorbed in the nations among whom they were planted," says the well known scholar and excavator of the ancient Palestine town of Gezer, Professor R. A. S. Macalister, in his book "History of Civilization in Palestine." Some of them doubtless eventually joined the Exile colony in Babylonia, while others were gradually assimilated in other parts of the Assyrian empire.

But what about the Samaritans who were not carried away by the Assyrians — as only the selected "cream of the crop" were taken. In the January 1967 issue of the National Geographic magazine, Howard LaFay, in an interesting article titled "Where Jesus Walked," relates that there are about 230 descendants of this remnant of the ten tribes still living in the city of Nablus at the base of Mount Gerizim. He says the Samaritans have for some 3,500 years regarded this as "the" sacred mountain (where they have worshipped for most of that time) and this was one of the religious differences that split the Samaritans from the Judeans whom they called "Jews" (St. John 4: 6,7,9). "Bitter enmity sprang up between the Jewish factions," writes Mr. LaFay, "each convinced that it alone worshipped Yaweh in the true tradition."

This has been a quick thumbnail sketch of the early Hebrew kingdoms in Palestine. It is difficult to resist the temptation to explore their period in greater depth with some of the interesting documentation available on the people and conditions that prevailed in Palestine at that period of history, but both space and topic design rule that out for this particular volume.

* * *

ASSYRIANS, BABYLONIANS, THEN PERSIANS OVER PALESTINE

Very soon after the Israelites of Judea had been carried off to Babylon, a new star began to shine in the Mesopotamian region that boded ill for that ancient nation on the Euphrates. A man named Cyrus was rising to leadership by putting the Persians and the Medes into a nascent empire of his own. In less than fifty years after the Jews had been carried to Babylon, Cyrus, as head of the new Persian empire, conquered Babylon, thereby increasing his empire greatly.

The Exiles in Babylon had become so bitter toward their Babylonian captors that they welcomed Cyrus as the "Lord's Anointed" with God, as quoted in Isaiah, saying: "He is my shepherd, and shall perform all my pleasure . . ." After Cyrus had consolidated himself in Babylonia he, according to the Old Testament, issued a decree which permitted the Jewish exiles to return to Jerusalem.

There probably were several reasons for this generosity. First it was the policy of Cyrus to be tolerant toward the religious practices of his captives. Although he apparently worshipped the Persian God (Ahura-Mazdah), he rebuilt in Babylon the shrine of Marduk (chief Babylonian deity) and proclaimed widely to the Babylonians how gloriously Marduk welcomed him as the new ruler. It was in line with that policy that he offered to let the Exiles return to Jerusalem to rebuild their Temple, with an offer of financial aid — of which we hear no more in the records.

Cyrus may have had also some very practical reasons for letting the Exiles who were now praising him so highly, return to Jerusalem which, combined with Syria and Phoenicia, had been joined to Babylonia as one large satrapy. The Palestine area, as already stated, was buffer territory at the point where Asia meets Egypt — and this country of the Nile was always "an apple of the eye" for emerging Asian empires.

The King of Egypt, at that time, was Amasis who had been in alliance with Croesus, the legendary and fabulously rich king of Lydia. Croesus had already been conquered by Cyrus. There was but little question that Egypt would soon be the target of the crusading Persian king, and it would be natural for Cyrus to prefer a friendly population in Palestine through which his armies would have to pass to reach the country of the Pharaohs.

SOME JEWS ALLOWED RETURN TO JERUSALEM

From a true historical sense, it perhaps should be stated that the story about Cyrus returning the Exiles to Jerusalem is based upon the reporting of the Old Testament writers. Strangely, Herodotus, the great historian whom Cicero called "the father of history," lived very close to the time of Cyrus and wrote intimately about him and his reign, yet he does not mention the Hebrews. It would seem, from this omission, that he had never heard of them — or at least did not regard them of historical importance.

At any rate, according to the Old Testament (principally the book of Ezra), some of the Hebrew Exiles, who were beginning to be called Jews, did return to Judea and after years of great difficulty, including opposition from the Samarian Jews who had not been exiled from Palestine, succeeded in completing a new Temple (about 516 B.C.), many years after the death of Cyrus.

This second Temple idea did not have as great a psychological or religious affect upon the people as did the first one, built during the glamorous reign of King Solomon. After the first Temple was built and until it was destroyed (586 B.C.) when the Judeans were exiled to Babylonia, the Temple had been the one center of all Hebrew worship — except for certain early High Places which had finally been abolished by Josiah, the king of Judah from 637 to 608 B.C. It might be worth mentioning again that Josiah was the ruler who was frightened into cleansing the temples of the wide idolatry that had developed among his people, when he was shown a document, miraculously discovered, which threatened dire punishment for those who failed to preserve the Mosaic code of the priestly establishment. This seems to be about the first of temple literature.

32

After the destruction of the first Temple and during the long Babylonian exile, the Jewish people learned to assemble in groups for religious purposes, without benefit of the sacred Temple with its "Holy of Holies." Out of this and a developing Diaspora, there gradually evolved the institution known as the Synagogue. This was also an important period in early evolutionary development of the Old Testament literature.

NOTE: Any attempt to examine early Biblical literature would require a volume unto itself. So little of fact seems to be known about this that it may be helpful to point up a few highlights here concerning the finalization of the Old Testament. The British biblical scholar, Dr. Hugh J. Schonfield, explains that in the earliest primitive days of religious communication, the very "art of writing was regarded as of divine origin." He also states — "the ancient royal and hieratic libraries of the Middle East" contained a variety of writings covering many subjects. An example of what he means would presumably include the Egyptian Book of the Dead. In his Mentor book, "The History of Biblical Literature," Schonfield conjectures that by the time of the Hebrew kings (roughly 1000 B.C. to 586 B.C.), these people must have used considerable writing in some form, but that most all of it may have been lost when the tribes were exiled.

Schonfield concludes that none of the books of the Old Testament could have been thought of as "canonical" before 400 B.C. Somewhere between that date and 250 B.C. the art of Biblical writing and codification seems to have materially improved. Worship was enhanced under the guardianship of the scribes and rabbis.

The eminent British scholar and archaeologist, Dr. H. R. Hall, in his "Ancient History of the Near East," in discussing David's time, says: "Learning was probably unknown. Scribes existed but it is uncertain what script they used, as we do not know whether the Phoenician or Aramaic alphabet (which had probably already been devised) had yet spread to southern Palestine" (p. 429).

In worship, the reading of the Law always came first — then the Pharisees began reading from the Prophets. The reading of a book in worship gave it a sacred status. "What determined the inclusion of any book in the Hebrew Bible," says Schonfield, "was whether it was agreed it should be publicly read in the synagogue."

There was much discussing and arguing in those days among the rabbis as to what was considered sacred and what was considered secular. For instance there was wide feeling that Ecclesiastes and the Song of Solomon were too secular. Much of this argument was settled by the Synod of Jabneh. Jabneh was the little coastal town, south of Jaffa, called Jamnia in Greek, where the Sanhedrin was reconvened after the destruction of the Second Temple by the Romans in 70 A.D.

The problems of the early Hebrew writers "were very different and inevitably so" from later writers, says E. E. Kellett in his book "A Short History of the Jews" (Routledge & Sons, London). "They had few authentic documents to work upon," he says, and "for many of their facts they had nothing better to hand than vague oral tradition." Referring to the author of the "Book of Judges," Kellett says, "Writing, probably, not earlier than 600 B.C., he was dealing with events of four or five hundred years before his time, and he had no material for checking his materials . . . worse, he had his theory to prove." That theory, Kellett indicates, was that "every disaster suffered by the Hebrew nation was due to a desertion of the national God Yahweh — and of Yahweh as the coterie understood him." Kellett goes on to explain how the conceptions of Yahweh changed over the long stretches of time, as he gives a general examination of the scriptures.

*   *   *

A matter of interest concerning the split of Israel into North and South kingdoms is their disagreement on sacred literature. Maurice Simon, in his book "Jewish Religious Conflicts," (Cecil Roth, editor — England), explains that the Samaritans only accepted the Pentateuch writings (first five books of the Old Testament) and regarded Mount Gerizim as the proper place of sanctuary — as already noted. The Judeans, on the contrary, began to expand their sacred literature, "the texts and arrangements of which," says Simon, "led to a sharp conflict between the Judeans and the Samaritans . . . This was the first broadening of the original religion of Torah as propounded by Ezra, and the first step in the metamorphous into the Rabbinism of later generations."

In his book "The Bible Today," Professor C. H. Dodd (University of Cambridge Press) tells us that "the books of the Old Testament, as we know them, were composed in the period starting with the great prophets Amos, Hosea, Micah and Isaiah" (8th to 5th centuries B.C.). It was the work of these prophets, he says, that "influenced the character of the canon."

The question is often asked — "How was the Bible put together — and decided upon as sacred?" Any answer to this requires long and tedious research and even then cannot be fully satisfactory. Our examination here concerns only the Old Testament. The New Testament is not germane to the topic.

W. Robertson Smith, Professor of Aramaic, University of Cambridge, in a 450-page book, "The Old Testament in the Jewish Church," was unable to give any short, concise answer to this question. William Barclay, a British co-editor of a series of "Bible Guide" books, wrote "The Making of the Bible," which undertakes to tell the story of the "Formation of the Canon." Dr. Barclay (University of Glasgow) makes a valuable contribution to this question about which so many know so little. In a book titled "How Our Bible Came to Us" (Oxford University Press), H. G. G. Herklots presents well the story of how the Bible was put together. "Biblical Archaeology," by Dr. G. Ernest Wright, is also 200 pages of incalculable documentation.

When one searches through all the scholarly effort that has been devoted to philological and archaeological research into the background of Biblical writing, there still remains much vacuum for those inquiring minds who want facts. The purpose here is only to throw as much light as possible upon the source and character of the patriarchal land-covenants whose lengthening shadows today darken a land that has known little but trouble for thousands of years — the Holy Land.

In the light of so many thoughtful and varied opinions — and the many uncertainties of fact and substance — the question has been asked as to how extensively the early Biblical writers may have been swayed to adjust legend and history to sacradotal purposes. The average individual often finds it difficult to equate many of the written passages with reality — and there are other questions that arise when only about two years of the proclaimed

It should be explained, perhaps, that the opportunity granted the Babylonian Exiles to return to Jerusalem did not arouse the expected enthusiasm predicted by the priestly leaders. In Babylon, many of the Exiles had, in their natural way, become prosperous — and had developed a vibrant cultural community, out of which concentration of Judaic scholars there later evolved the voluminous Babylonian Talmud as a Rabbinical guide for. Judaism. Only a moderate percentage of the Hebrews, exiled in Babylonia, chose to return to the arid and desolate precincts of Jerusalem. These earlier off-spring of the ancient Israelites did not seem to have as much interest in Palestine as do the Zionist leaders of this age. These later crusading leaders, according to some critics of political Zionism, have shown great astuteness in making artful capital out of a tenuous bloodstream presumption, which stream must have thinned mightily through intermarriage and wide intermixture (such as the Khazar conversion in the 8th to 10th centuries A.D.). A 3,000 year run of a bloodstream must, in the nature of things, produce some major inheritance uncertainties.

To this question of racial purity, reference may be made to the words of the noted Jewish historian, Professor H. Graetz, in his several volume "History of the Jews." He mentions the case of testimony before the college of the Sanhedrin (of which Gamaliel was then president — early in the first century) where a heathen of Amorite descent came before the meeting to ask if he could be legally accepted as a proselyte. Gamaliel rejected him, using the authority of the "written law," which said, "Moabites and Amorites may not be received into the congregation of God, even in the tenth generation." On this he was successfully challenged by Joshua ben Chananya, who claimed that that part of the law no longer applied because "through the aggressions of their conquerors, all nations had become mixed together and confused beyond recognition." Since that decision, nearly 2,000 years of human history have further confounded the blood-stream

35

purity question through intermarriage and integration — thus clearly invalidating the claim of lineage inheritance of Palestine.

*   *   *

TEMPLE REBUILT—IDOLATRY PERSISTS

After the Temple was finally rebuilt in Jerusalem by those who did return from Babylon in 538 B.C., instead of the expected revival effect there followed a spiritual deterioration involving pagan tendencies that greatly distressed the priestly leaders who, according to the Old Testament, were forever busy, during those many centuries, trying to keep their people from the luring ways of the Golden Calf.

The authors of the Book of Ezra tell us how he (Ezra), while employed by the Persian government, learned of this sad state of affairs and sought leave to go to Jerusalem to help revive the faith. By Persian permission, Ezra and Nehemiah journied to that city and, according to the authors, succeeded in refreshing an interest in Torah by establishing a rigid system of Mosaic law. Here, with Ezra, we begin to get acquainted with the foundations of the Pentateuch and the beginning of what we know today as organized Judaism.

From that time, say Bailey and Kent in their "History of the Jewish Commonwealth," religion became less a matter of the heart and more strictly a system of detailed rules and laws governing religious rites. These authors further comment that Ezra may have been an historical figure but that modern scholars are inclined to feel that the wide reforms and the introduction of laws credited to him are more apt to have been the work of many reformers, working over a period of two centuries, the results of which were finally put into form by the priestly writers under the name of Ezra. There is considerable belief that the same authors also prepared the book of Chronicles. The last two paragraphs of that book and the first two of the Book of Ezra, in some Bibles, are identical, indicating that these two books represent a separation of what was originally a single book.

There is no inference in these references that the Old Testament does not offer sagacious counsel and penetrating

36

judgments on human character and action — just as do many other writings before and since. References to it here are in the framework of the authority and reliability of its writers in pressing a priestly-secular line by reporting so vaguely on matters such as the land covenants which dated hundreds of years before the writers were born.

This post-Exile revival of Jewish community life in Jerusalem was by no means a reinstitution of a Jewish kingdom. The area at the time was strictly a Persian satrapy. The great Middle East Egyptologist and historian, the late Dr. James H. Breasted (creator of the famed Oriental Institute at the University of Chicago), in his book "Ancient Times — A History of the Early World" (Ginn and Company), points out that instead of anything similar to the old kingship, there was instituted for the Jews of Palestine (under the guardianship of Persian overlords) a system of partial autonomy whereby the Jews had their High Priest who was their highest ecclesiastical official. He served as chief ministrant in the Temple and presided over a 71-member Sanhedrin which was an adjudicating court but, under later Roman rule, had no authority to impose the death sentence.

NOTE: It was this arrangement of authority where the High Priest and the Sanhedrin could arrest, prosecute and demand — but not actually carry out execution — that has created the historical confusion around which the argument of responsibility for the crucifixion of Christ has developed.

The High Priest office and the Sanhedrin continued as a system of local rule for the Jews, beginning soon after their return to Jerusalem from Babylonia (early in the 5th Century, B.C.) and largely ending with the destruction of Jerusalem by the Romans in 70 A.D. During that time they were under various overlord nations — Persia — Alexander's empire with its Hellenistic successors — and finally Rome. Among the Roman supervisory officials, for instance, were consuls, proconsuls, procurators, ethnarchs, governors — and even a king (Herod), who was appointed by Rome.

The most interesting period of this stretch of post-exilic Jewish semi-independence came during the Syria-Palestine rule of the Seleucide dynasty (one of the inheritors of Alexander's empire). For the Hebrews, this was the turbulent time of the Maccabean revolt — the rise of the Hasmonean dynasty — and it was in this general period that party conflict developed between the Saducees and the Pharisees. This post-Exilic period is sometimes referred to in Jewish literature as the Second Commonwealth. But while all of this would be interesting to explore, it is not especially germane to the thesis of this book, and therefore must be excluded. Our purpose is merely to give an account of how Palestine has been occupied and ruled during the last several thousand years, to simplify a comparative perspective.

The Hasmonean dynasty, during which the Jews enjoyed considerable freedom in Judea, finally broke up through quarrels among the leaders and political-party groups. The Roman general Pompey took advantage of this internecine wrangling and occupied the territory in 63 B.C. in the name of Rome. The Roman-control line over Palestine continued from that time on for several hundred years, telescoping into Christian-Byzantine influences. It was during this period (325 A.D.) that the Roman Emperor Constantine accepted Christianity for Rome and had the Christian shrines and the Holy Places in Jerusalem located and dedicated with appropriate buildings and symbols.

In 614, the Persians, under King Chosroes II, took Jerusalem from the Byzantines. In 638, the great Moslem Caliph Omar conquered Jerusalem in the fast-moving Arab conquest. In 1070, the Seljuk Turks moved in and were in control only until 1099, when they were driven out by the Christian Crusaders. "The importance of the Crusades in the cultural history of Western Europe," says George E. Kirk in his "Short History of the Middle East" (Praeger), "can hardly be overestimated for their effects in throwing open the windows of men's minds to the influence of the Middle East, whose level of civilization was still far higher than that of the West."

The Christian Crusaders ruled the "Kingdom of Jerusalem" from 1088 until 1187 A.D. — about 100 years —and, for illustration, approximately the same length of time that a united Kingdom of Israel existed under its three kings, Saul, David and Solomon, about two thousand years earlier. The

Christian Crusaders were driven out in 1187 by the Moslems under their celebrated leader Saladin. During the Moslem reign, many Jews returned to the vicinity, and under Moslem protection established a Jewish community. How times have changed! It may be pointed out here that Jews who had difficulties in unfriendly countries, during medieval times, often found cordial welcome and asylum in lands controlled by the Arabs.

In 1244 the Mongolian Tartars moved into Jerusalem, and in 1260 were ousted by the Egyptian Mamelukes (a Moslem branch), both of which had short periods of occupancy. In 1516 the Turkish Sultan, Selim I (the Grim) conquered Jerusalem. He was succeeded in 1520 by his son, Suleiman (the Magnificent). With the exception of about ten years (1831 - 1841), when Mohammed Ali (an Albanian Moslem who, out of the confusion following Napolean's abortive trip to Egypt, had made himself dictator of the country of the Nile) invaded and occupied the Palestine area for some ten years, the Turks ruled all that part of the Middle East until 1917, when they were driven out by the British, aided by the Arabs. The British then ruled Palestine, under a League of Nations Mandate, until 1948 when intolerable circumstances created by the Zionist-Arab conflict forced them to abandon their authority. (See Chapter XIV.)

The Turks were in control of the Palestine area for approximately 400 years which, by comparision, was about the same length of time the Hebrew kings of ancient Israel (including those of Samaria and Judah after the united kingdom broke up) ruled it.

It would therefore appear that the early time-span of Hebrew domination of Palestine, when compared with the time-periods of other peoples who lived in and ruled this territory, gives little or no credence to the fanciful assumption of "prior occupancy rights" which have been so widely and unquestionably accepted by the Christians who aided and abetted the aggression that put hundreds of thousands of former Palestinian Arabs (many of them Christians) in desolate refugee-camps where they are today, helplessly abandoned on meager charity as "the forgotten people."

NOTE: Reference here is to the Palestinian Arab refugees who were torn from their homes and homeland in the 1947-48 military confrontation of Zionists and Arabs. (See Chapters XIII and XIV.)

The comparatively short early period of Hebrew occupancy of Palestine has been dramatized to the Christian world so well, especially through the Old Testament being incorporated with the New Testament, that many religious people — especially those who know little about the history of Palestine — have, it appears, accepted these self-asserted Zionist rights without examining them in depth. The facts, as we have explored them here, do not appear to give the Zionists of today any greater rights in Jerusalem and Palestine than those of Christians — the Arabs — or some of the others who have had long occupancy in this area. Beyond this is the total question of legality of any such hereditary rights as those assumed by the present day Zionists.

*   *   *

JERUSALEM — KEY TO PEACE IN MIDDLE EAST

THIS CHAPTER — and the one that follows — are heavily weighted with evidential facts to show that Jerusalem (and this could perhaps well apply to Palestine as a whole) has such a well documented history of widely distributed international genealogy and religious background as to validate its proper status as an international geographical entity — and was so characterized by the United Nations in its Partition Resolution of November 29, 1947.

There is not only the evidence of history to recommend this "international zone" status but there is also the legalistic stipulation of the United Nations Resolution for whatever that may be worth in the court of World Opinion. Such an arrangement would require the polarization of world sentiment around the idea of an "international Jerusalem" to be placed under control of a well constituted form of government, originating perhaps out of some kind of perpetual mandatory to the constituted high authorities of the three great religions which have a background of religious relationship with Jerusalem and its environs. This arrangement would not be easily accomplished but it could be a pattern that would give some promise for peace to replace strife and war in and around the Holy City. This accomplishment would require pressure from the great powers who otherwise are being steadily led toward disastrous confrontation.

2. ONLY A FEW JEWS IN PALESTINE FROM 135 A.D. to 1920's

FOR CONSIDERABLY more than a thousand years after the Roman dispersion, the Jewish population in Palestine, with the Jerusalem area as its strategic center, was negligible. Among the earliest reports from this vicinity is that of Moses Maimonides (Moses ben Maimon), the veteran Talmudist, who as a boy with his parents left Cordova, Spain, and after a tempestuous journey reached the Palestine port of Accho (later Acre), after which they made their way to Jerusalem for a day or so, then to Hebron — and on to Egypt for residence in Old Cairo. Later he chronicled that there were at that time — about 1165 A.D. — only two Jewish families in Jerusalem. This would have been while the Christian Crusaders were occupying Jerusalem.

When the Sephardic Jews were expelled from Spain in 1492 (during the reign of Ferdinand and Isabella), some of those expelled found their way to Jerusalem, and in that general period of time, the Jewish population of the vicinity grew to about 5,000. It is estimated that by 1900 this number had increased throughout Palestine to around 35,000 — largely concentrated in Jerusalem, Hebron, Safed and Tiberias — the centers claimed as sacred to Jewish tradition. By that time, the Jewish population was about equally divided between the Ashkenazim (Yiddish speaking) and the Sephardic (Oriental or Spanish type).

A slow colonization of Jews in Palestine did begin in the latter part of the 19th century — while that area was under Turkish rule. The colonizing effort before World War I, according to the ESCO Foundation report, can be divided into three periods: Up to 1900, seven small colonies were

41

founded, devoted mainly to grape and orange growing, and supported by the Rothschild administration. From 1901 to 1907, several small colonies were set up in Lower Galilee — supported by funds from Baron Edmund de Rothschild. From 1908 to the outbreak of World War I (1914), a limited colonization was carried on by the struggling Zionist organization, which resulted in several small agricultural colonies with an approximate population of 12,000.

It is interesting to learn how the "Return" Jewish immigration community (mostly in Jerusalem) was supported up until at least 1920 — when the increasing influx was estimated at around 100,000. The individual livelihoods of these Jewish immigrants came from what was called the Halukkah. This represented funds collected for them from other Jews all over the world. It was a well organized system with "salesmen" known as Messengers of Charity who traveled through the various countries — such as the United States where there were many wealthy Jews — soliciting and gathering money which was carried back to be distributed through the Jerusalem Rabbi hierarchy. This, of course, made all the Jewish population dependent upon the good graces of the Rabbis, which caused continuous "murmuring."

It appears that at least ten percent or more of the Jewish population of Jerusalem in 1889 must have been Rabbis. In that year the American Consul in Jerusalem sent a report to the U.S. State Department containing an illuminating description of the bickering and quarreling over the Halukkah funds. Part of his report is reprinted in "The Realities of American-Palestine Relations," a book by Dr. Frank E. Manuel (Public Affairs Press). It reads:

"Recriminations between the head rabbis and the members of the various congregations are incessant and prolific of the most acrimonious feuds. The chief accusations are that the Rabbis made an improper use of the fund, expending it upon themselves, their families, relatives and friends to a large extent, and using favoritism generally in its distribution . . . There are about 200 synagogues in Jerusalem, and there are thousands of Rabbis, the majority of whom are far from being what they ought to be." (p. 96)

A few years later, the number of "American Jews" in Jerusalem had risen to around 1,000, all of whom had become very discontented with the handling of the fund. They started to form an independent organization so they could get the direct benefit of the money coming from America. This rebellion having to do with the money that came from rich America was like an earthquake to the Rabbis who directed the fund. Bitter words were poured on the "American" Jews who had been born in Poland or some other east European country and had lived only a few years in America — and complaints were filed, making it somewhat difficult for the Messengers of Charity when they went out to solicit. Finally the "Americans" did get a separate arrangement.

Prior to the report just mentioned, another Consul, Lorenzo Johnson, had sent the State Department a report in 1868 complaining that the Jews in Jerusalem lived in idleness, sustained by contributions from America and Europe. The learned among them studied only the Talmud, he reported. This Halukkah fund was no pigmy business. In 1874 American Consul Willson, according to Dr. Manuel, reported that the Jerusalem Jews received from eight to ten thousand pounds sterling a month from communities throughout the world.

* * *

PALESTINE AT OUTBREAK OF WAR

World War I broke in 1914. Turkey soon joined Germany. Palestine — and most of the Middle East — were within the Turkish Empire. At the outbreak of war it has been estimated that about half the Jews in Palestine were immigrants from Russia — a gradual accumulation of the "settlement" programs (both old and new) already described. This created a problem since Russia was joined with the Allied side — and now a war enemy of Turkey. President Wilson had induced Henry Morgenthau, Sr. to accept the post of Ambassador to Turkey. He had made a tour of the Palestine settlements and although himself an outspoken anti-Zionist, had indicated admiration for the new (Zionist) settlements. This was believed by' some to have been a performance of diplomatic politeness and duty. In his book "All in a Lifetime," Mr. Morgenthau said that the Old Testament prophets who proclaimed that Zion should be returned to the Jews meant this symbolically only. He further gave a stinging denunciation of Zionism as holding no benefit for Jews as a people. "Zionism looks backward," he declared, "not forward."

*　　*　　*

Now, with World War I, how could these settlements be saved — especially those of the Russian Jews? Morgenthau sent a dispatch to Secretary of State Lansing that the Turkish Government had decided not to expel the Russian Jews in Palestine but to allow them to become naturalized Ottoman subjects. The facts were that in the early part of the war, the Turkish Government was so busy with military and other problems that it could pay little attention to the Palestine settlements. After all, at least half of the Jews in Palestine were paupers and dedicated religionists and not any immediate threat to the Turkish war efforts. But for the Zionists — and others who were not Zionists (nor even Jews) — there was the humane problem of getting food to these immigrant settlers through the war blockade.

The responsibility for this job fell largely on America. Justice Brandeis and Rabbi Stephen Wise were busy making this America's problem. Zionists and non-Zionists in the United States collaborated in this humanitarian task and since the Jewish Relief Committee was unable to charter commercial ships, U.S. Government vessels were pressed into service — the first being the U.S.S. Vulcan. Rabbi Wise and Brandeis then began pressuring Secretary of State Lansing to help get petroleum to the settlers for the pumps in their orange groves.

The World Zionist organization had, by the time of the first World War, become large enough to have financial deposits in the major cities in Europe and the United States but the war had quickly complicated the transfer of funds to Palestine and made the situation there all the more precarious. In other words, the Zionist resettlement program in Palestine had added just another headache to the war situation. By the fall of 1916, the United States had become the main source of support for the Jews (Zionists and all) in Palestine.

The Turkish Government soon changed its mind about the Russian Jews in Palestine and ordered both internment and mass expulsion. Many of them were taken to Alexandria, Egypt; and Alexandria again, as in the early Philo period, became heavily colonized with Jews. In his documentary report, Dr. Frank Manuel states that "The Jews in Palestine . . . fared better than any other minorities in the Ottoman Empire because of the peculiarities of the Jewish dispersion throughout the world and the economic resources available for aid from the neutral United States."

The report went on to explain how the small Jewish minority then in Palestine was kept alive during four years of war blockade which cut it off from Halukkah (foreign welfare), which had to stop at the outbreak of war. The "old settlement," often going hungry, would have perished but for a relief organization maintained by Jewry outside Palestine. (The reference to the "old settlement" was to pre-Zionist immigrants.)

BEST LANDS SOUGHT

The "new settlements" included some rich coastal orange grove and produce lands which had been acquired quietly by the Zionist Organization, to implement the new immigration policy which, even then, was widely criticized by the Palestinian Arab inhabitants as a program of intended conquest by preponderant infiltration through immigration. The purchases in some instances were made from absentee landlords living outside Palestine — and others were from struggling farmers who grasped the chance to get money for their land.

During World War I, these new Zionist settlements, that had moved in to compete with the predominant Arab citrus growers, lost their European markets, and according to the report could not have survived without outside diaspora help. It seems clear from the record that the Jewish State, founded upon a base of mass immigration which in turn has been piled upon earlier insecure "settlements," has not been able to stand on its own economic legs. It continues to require a vast inflow of money from United States sources and no end to this is in sight.

It would be tiring, and unnecessary to the purpose of this book, to undertake great detail here concerning the Zionist program in Palestine as it was wearily developed from World War I on to World War II, except to give important highlights. The great Zionist political accomplishments during and immediately after the first war were the Balfour Declaration (commitment) and the supplemental British Mandate. The Zionists had hoped that these two devices would smooth the road for rapid advance, but actually progress was slow and tedious until unexpected and astonishing events exploded out of World War II.

Population figures concerning the Jewish people have always been difficult to authenticate — from Bible times down to the present. One fairly reliable source estimates there were about 60,000 Jews in Palestine in 1920, with some 500,000 Arabs and about 70,000 Christians.

Beginning in 1922, an effort was made to take a population census and this helped, over a nineteen year period, to make possible the following estimates by years during that time. These statistics are reprinted by permission from a highly reliable and informative capsule story of the Zionist-Arab conflict. It is a 60-page paperback book titled "Decisive Years in Palestine: 1918-1948," prepared by Dr. Erich W. Bethmann, Director of Research and Publications, American Friends of the Middle East, Inc.; 1607 New Hampshire Avenue, N.W., Washington, D.C. 20009 (price 50 cents).

Year	Muslims	Christians	Jews
1922..........	589,177	71,464	83,790
1923..........	609,331	72,030	89,660
1924..........	627,660	74,094	94,945
1925..........	641,494	75,512	121,725
1926..........	663,613	76,467	149,500
1927..........	680,725	77,880	149,789
1928..........	695,280	79,812	151,656
1929..........	712,343	81,776	156,481
1930..........	733,149	84,986	164,796

While the combined Muslim and Christian population, that is the Arab population, of Palestine increased in these eight years by natural growth from 660,641 to 818,135, or about 23 per cent, the Jewish population increased, largely through immigration, from 83,790 to 164,796, or almost 100 per cent.

The figures for the subsequent ten-year period show an even more striking contrast between the growth of the Arab population and that of the Jews:[21]

Year	Muslims	Christians	Jews
1931..........	759,700	88,907	174,606
1932..........	778,803	92,520	192,137
1933..........	798,506	96,791	234,967
1934..........	814,379	102,407	282,975
1935..........	836,688	105,236	355,157
1936..........	862,730	108,506	384,078
1937..........	883,446	110,869	395,836
1938..........	900,250	111,974	411,222
1939..........	927,133	116,958	445,457
1940..........	947,846	120,587	463,535

Thus the Arab population grew from 848,607 to 1,068,433 in this ten-year period while the Jewish population grew from 174,606 to 463,535 which means it more than tripled, and by 1940 constituted about 30 per cent of the population of Palestine. It should be added that the immigration of Jews into Palestine was accompanied by an impressive import of Jewish capital, estimated at nearly 80,000,000 Palestine Pounds,[22] or 400,000,000 dollars, by the end of 1936.

---

[21] *Ibid.*, Vol. II, p. 665.
[22] *The Political History of Palestine under British Administration, op. cit.*, p. 15.

3. ZIONISM — ORIGIN AND METHODOLOGY

ZIONISM is an "ism" latched on to the word Zion. Zion is mentioned several times in the Bible — usually referring to what the Bible authors called Mount Zion, or the site of what gradually became known as the "city of David." This was originally the small village of Jebus which, for strategic reasons, David seized and converted into his capital of ancient Israel. Historian Graetz says it was at some time given the name of "Jerushalayim" which in later translations took on the spelling of Jerusalem.

The word Zion seems to derive from the legend of David bringing the glorified and portable "Ark of the Covenant" (an ornated chest) with much fanfare, on a bullock-drawn cart for a short trip from Kirjath Jearim (where it had been stored for 20 years after being recovered from the Philistines) to his new capital — Jerusalem. This apparently had a salutary political effect in sanctifying David as king. The term "Mount Zion" in some way became attached to one of the Jerusalem hills where the Ark was supposedly deposited by David as a shrine.

In Maccabean times, says the Standard Jewish Encyclopedia, this site was identified as (Solomon's) Temple Hill in opposition to the Hellenistic quarters on Acre Hill. Josephus, the ancient Jewish historian, identified Zion with what he called the Upper city. Its previously accepted location, as on the eastern hill (Lower city), was then soon forgotten. Later, after the Crusader's period, Mount Zion became identified with the hill outside the Old City where the Tomb of David is now shown. The Bible's reference to David's burial place is only that he was buried "in the city of David." (I Kings: 2,10)

The word "Zionism" is now hybrid terminology, used by political Zionists to capitalize the ancient word Zion, with its reverent attachment to ancient Israel and King David. The Zionists seek to capture the halo and Biblical prestige of David because it was he who, after many battles and subjugations, consolidated the Israelite tribes into one of the many "come and go" nations that have long been buried under the shifting sands of time, in what we now call the Middle East.

There is one major unanswered question that seems to rise out of what appears to be Old Testament approval of invasion and conquest by the early Israelites in their purpose to create a Hebrew nation. There are those who ask if this divine authority flows on to give Old Testament validity to the conquest-purposes and political tactics of present-day Zionists when nearly 3,000 years of world advancement calls loudly for a modus operandi based upon recognition of "law and order" procedure.

NOTE: Zionism, as a word, seems to have been coined by Nathan Birnbaum (Mathias Acher) in 1886, who used the term in his early writings which emphasized "Jewish nationalism" some ten years before Theodor Herzl published his book "Der Judenstaat" (The Jewish State). To Birnbaum, however, should go some credit for perceiving the built-in-perils for the Jewish people in the kind of religious nationalism toward which Herzl and his brand of Zionism were trending. Although he had become the first secretary of Herzl's World Zionist Organization, he early separated himself from this movement — opposing the belief that a nationalist settlement of Jews in Palestine would solve their particular problems.

Birnbaum then began to advocate a cultural and political autonomy for the Diaspora (the Jewish communities throughout the world) which seems to have been the advocacy of an amorphous Jewish nationalism mixed in some way with religious identity. Like many others who have followed him, he could not quite break with the old traditional orthodoxy of religious nationalism to the point of recognizing the nature of the newer world relationships where religion and brotherhood flourish better under the kind of assimilation that recognizes but one national loyalty — and that is for the one country of which each is an accepted citizen.

It is astonishing how little the average non-Jewish American knows about the movement called ZIONISM — particularly when it has played so large a hidden role in U.S. politics and Government action. The first look will be at political Zionism's earliest days. Theodor Herzl (1860-1904, Hungarian born) is generally regarded as the "father" of organized

Zionism because of his 1896 book "Der Judenstaat," and also because it was he who called the first organizational meeting at Basle in 1897.

MOSES HESS—ALSO ZIONIST PATRIARCH

It is important, however, to mention that before Herzl's book, there was a somewhat similar one by Moses Hess (German leftist) strongly advocating Jewish "statehood." In 1862, he published "Rome and Jerusalem" wherein he said — "That which the Jewish people were not able to obtain as individuals the people can secure as a nation."

"Judaism is no passive religion," he wrote, "but an active knowledge, which is organically related to Jewish nationalism. Judaism is, above all, a nationality . . . It is a nation . . ."

He suggests that people may wonder why the modern belief of immortality "is not taught in the Old Testament." His explanation is that if "Moses and the Prophets had believed in another life in the Christian sense, they would have spoken of it as did the writers of the New Testament . . . The idea of immortality made its appearance among Jews when they began to feel the coming of the first national decline."

"The pious Jew," continues Hess as an early evangelist for Zionism, "is before all else a Jewish patriot. The 'newfangled' Jew who denies Jewish nationalism is not only an apostate, a renegade in the religious sense, but a traitor to the people and to his family" (p. 27). Rabbi Maurice J. Bloom, on the fly leaf of his translation of the Hess book (Philosophical Library, Inc., New York, publishers) explains that Hess goes so far as to "suggest that if Jewish nationalism should be incompatible with Jewish emancipation in any country, the latter should be rejected."

These few quotes from an early and zealous evangelist for Zionism (together with others to follow from Herzl's pen) are presented to show the emphasis placed on the "nationalism" of Judaism as post-dispersion spiritual Zionism began to give way to political Zionism. This early literature reflected an extremely chauvinistic disposition as it expounded its plea for ultra-Jewish nationalism.

In examining the development of political Zionism, more attention must be given to Theodor Herzl than to Moses Hess or Leo Pinsker (Russian) who in 1882 wrote a pamphlet "Auto-Emancipation" calling upon Jews as a "nation" to return to a national consciousness and look forward to a future of territorial independence. He also said that Jews, in the nations where they reside, form a distinct element which cannot be well digested by any country. He placed emphasis on the problem of a "nation" (as the Zionists think of "the Jewish people") living within any non-Jewish nation. As a matter of fact this same idea has been emphatically expressed by Ben Gurion, one of the top leaders of present day Zionist Israel.

The most important of all the early literature, however, was the book by Herzl "The Jewish State." When he first wrote it he called it "An Address to the Rothschilds" but in 1896 it was published as "Der Judenstaat." This book is highly important for students as in it Herzl lays down the first blueprint for a new Jewish nation — and it is followed by Herzl calling together at Basle the first Zionist Congress for the distinct purpose of bringing a "Jewish State" into existence.

He began the book by saying — "The idea which I have developed is a very old one: it is the restoration of the Jewish State." Toward this end, he says, "Everything depends upon our propelling force." There are those who have felt the impact of this new "propelling force" and agree that it combines an inexorable political determination and Messianic impatience into what at times some have regarded as "driving imperiousness."

In "The Jewish State" Herzl says that it would be stupid to deny that the Jewish question exists as a hang-over from the Middle Ages of which "the modern civilized nations, with the best will in the world, cannot rid themselves . . . The Jewish question exists wherever Jews are to be found in larger numbers. Wherever it does not exist it is brought in by immigrating Jews."

"We move naturally toward those areas where we are not persecuted," says Herzl; "our appearance in those areas is followed by persecution. This is true, but it must remain true, even in highly developed countries — France proves it — as long as the question is not solved politically. The poorer Jews are bringing anti-Semitism into England; they have already brought it into America."

NOTE: While this was intended by Herzl as argument for setting up a (ghettoized) Jewish State it insinuates a blame upon non-Jewish people for the 'persecution' of Jews which is now featured and publicized as 'anti-Semitism'. In researching this charge, which is even more widely used today than in Herzl's time, we found widespread resentment among non-Jews for what some of them frankly say is an unjust age-old custom of always blaming someone else for public reaction to personal habits and manners that may be causing the trouble. "It just isn't according to human nature," said one noted New York writer, "that all the nations of the world — down through the ages — would select one and the same race or group of people for 'persecution'. There is no such thing as a one-way street where one individual or group is always right and everyone else wrong in human relationships. It could be that this charge of 'persecution' has become something of an obsession and has developed into a sort of 'open sesame' profession."

The present day importance of Herzl's writings is well stated on the jacket of the latest edition of his book "The Jewish State" (American Zionist Emergency Council, New York, 1946) where it says of him: "A noble vision of a Jewish journalist in 1896 is now not only the political program of the Jewish people but also a major issue in international politics. Herzl's Judenstaat was primarily responsible for all Jewish achievements in Palestine. The sweat, blood and idealism invested by Jewish colonists in Palestine were largely of the vision of Judenstaat."

Another statement (in the book's Introduction) shows how Zionism has grown from a small cell to a giant organism. "With the advent of Herzl," it states, "Zionism was no more a matter of domestic concern only. It was no longer an internal Jewish problem only, not a theme for discussion only at Zionist meetings, not a problem to heat the spirit of Jewish writers. The problem of Jewish exile now occupied a place on the agenda of international affairs." This is not quite correct. Zionism became an issue in "international affairs" under the hard-driving political astuteness of Chaim Weizmann who followed Herzl as its miraculous genius and super-extraordinary leader.

The Herzl book which was quite a detailed and comprehensive blueprint for establishing a Jewish State (or Nation) cannot, for lack of space, be examined in its fullest minutiae here — nor would that be particularly useful as the whole matter of Zionist organization and plans underwent changes at the various Zionist Congresses (six in all) held during Herzl's administration. It is a pragmatic political movement, and with the exception of its goals of nationalism and expansionism, changes continue as exigencies and expediency demand. A main suggestion in Herzl's original plan, however, was to form a "Jewish Company" to raise money through stock-selling with which to purchase land and meet other needs. He suggested a minimum capitalization of a thousand million marks which would have amounted to about 50,000,000 pounds, or $200,000,000.

* * *

THE "WORLD ZIONIST ORGANIZATION" (WZO) was created at the 1897 Basle meeting called by Herzl where he was made president. In his diary he wrote: "This day I have created the Jewish State." Twenty-five years later (1922), under Weizmann's leadership, the Zionists in engineering a Palestine "mandate" for the British succeeded in having included in the mandate document references to "a Jewish agency" to represent the Zionist-Jews in Palestine, in promoting "public works" and seeking concessions from the Mandate authorities. There was no hint that this innocent-sounding "Jewish agency" was to become the alter ego of the powerful World Zionist Organization — which it soon did.

It is interesting in retrospect that Herzl did not pin-point Palestine as a land-objective in his plan. The reason, of course, was that the Middle East (including Palestine) was at the time under the hard and fast control of the Turks. Herzl tried to buy the right of immigration for Jews into Palestine by offering money to help the badly indebted Turkish economy, but the Sultan rejected the plan.

As the next best potential for eventually getting into Palestine, the Zionists (under Herzl) considered the area of El Arish — a wadi desert section bordering Palestine in the edge of Egypt. In 1903 the Zionists sent a Commission to examine El Arish but dropped the project when the British viceroy for Egypt refused permission to allow irrigation of the arid section from the river Nile.

The British did, however, at the time, offer the Zionists the right to immigrate into the Uganda territory in British East Africa, which proffer the Zionist leaders rejected. They did regard this gesture as something of an advance for their cause in the sense that it was the first official recognition of their asserted nationality status.

Herzl's importance to the Zionist movement was more as a dreamer and propagandist than as an organizer and builder. He might be called a sort of Messianic rhapsodist. He kept voluminous notes of his efforts and ideas. These notes have lately (1962) been published in a 500-page book as "The Diaries of Theodor Herzl" (Grosset and Dunlap, New York). His "diaries" are heavily weighted with impassioned nationalistic pleadings and ad hominem polemics.

"We are one people," he writes, "Our enemies have made us one . . . Distress binds us together, and thus united, we suddenly discover our strength . . . Yes, we are strong enough to form a State. We have no flag and we need one . . . The very impossibility of getting at the Jews nourishes by day and hour among the nations; indeed, it is bound to increase, because the cause of its growth continues to exist and cannot be removed." His writings, while loaded with more of the same immemorial lamentations about enemies and persecutions do not match the more succinct rhetoric of Moses Hess.

HERZL'S BACKGROUND

Theodor Herzl was born in the Hungarian city of Pest, which was united in 1872 with the town of Buda (across the river Danube from each other), and since that time known as Budapest. His parents were well-to-do Jewish people who moved to Vienna when young Herzl was eighteen. His father was a banker. The youth, after studying law at the University of Vienna, engaged in journalism and special writing in that city. He became fairly well known as a playwright. In 1891 he took up residence in Paris as a journalist on a paper called the Neue Freie Presse (New Free Press). This plunged his interest into the maelstrom of French political turmoil in a country where anti-Semitism was wide-spread.

In December of 1894 the notorious anti-Jewish Dreyfus trial began — which stirred him deeply. It was not long until he had become completely obsessed with what he regarded as the need to find a solution to the age-old controversial status of the Jews. Finally his thinking crystallized into the thesis published as "Der Judenstaat." The next year (1897) he called the meeting at Basle which brought together a number of pro-Zionist Jewish leaders from various countries to discuss and start organizational plans to bring about his dream of a Jewish nation.

In the early days of the movement there was considerable opposition to political Zionism among prominent Jews who had become well entrenched in the life of the countries where they live — principally France, England and the United States. They viewed the potentials of a "Jewish nation" with great apprehension, for several reasons. Herzl's obsession over "anti-Semitism" caused him to believe that one of the best ways to eliminate this malady would be to have a Jewish nation which would, he hoped, attain international dignity and power. The Jews who opposed this plan (of which there are still some important ones — notably the American Council for Judaism members) have insisted that the status of the Jewish people be distinctively known as a religious grouping — and not as a "nation." (See Chapter VII covering this subject.)

After the Zionist movement was officially launched at Basle, Herzl spent much of his time (in silk hat and formal clothes) contacting or trying to contact important world political dignitaries — without too much success. Palestine was then under Turkish rule.

PASSING OF HERZL
BEGINNING OF WEIZMANN

Herzl died on Sunday, July 3, 1904 at a mountain health resort (Edlach) near Vienna. In August, 1949, after the new State of Israel had been founded, the Zionists brought

Herzl's body to Palestine by plane to the Lydda airport. It was then taken to nearby Tel Aviv where it lay in state for one day and then was conveyed over the winding road that leads from Tel Aviv to Israeli-Jerusalem, where it was buried on a hill as a shrine in tribute for his work and leadership as the father of modern Zionism.

Organized Zionism, as we know, did not die with Herzl. A new and faster moving star was rising over the Zionist movement in the person of Dr. Chaim Weizmann, a chemist from Russia. Weizmann had been active in Zionism long before he migrated to England in 1904 — the same year that Herzl died. His success as a chemist had apparently not been notable. He first tried his luck in Switzerland where, as a small-time chemist, he found slow progress. Steeped in Zionism, as he was, he sensed England as having greener fields for his broader aims.

In explaining his move to London in his autobiography, Weizmann wrote — "My position in Geneva and my income from my patent were both petering out." Moving to England, his greatly improved status as a Zionist leader was displayed in a 1918 photograph of him (in his book) which shows him elegantly dressed in the best British "statesman" style — stovepipe silk hat — velvet collared top coat — Chamberlain type collar and tie — and stylish cane. When he first moved to England he was able to secure a partial lecturing arrangement, as a chemist, with the University of Manchester — and to have the part-time use of a small laboratory at the University for experiments.

His major interest and application, as shown by his record, was to build a Zionist foothold in Britain as the country that, due to her then Middle East involvement, could most help the Zionist goal. Christopher Sykes, in his "Two Studies in Virtue," indicates that Weizmann's move to Britain was motivated by his ambition to get closer to leading British statesmen as the only hope, at that time, of developing any kind of a Zionist entree into Palestine.

He was thirty years old when he took up residence in the industrial city of Manchester, England. In his autobiography he explains that — "None of the men in Manchester had so much as heard of Zionism before they met me." But wherever Weizmann went Zionism soon became an animated issue. He made it his business to know more and more important people and to let them know about Zionist hopes — for Zionism, not chemistry, was now his practicing profession.

Weizmann was in truth much more than a chemist. He had the full calling of an astute and skillful politician — a combination of polished talents that was to outmatch the brilliancy of England's World War I statesmen in the field of maneuverable diplomacy, for which British political leaders had so long been distinguished. There was probably no other Jew of the time who could have accomplished for the Zionist movement what Weizmann did.

He was quick to perceive the importance of developing sympathy for the Zionist cause among British political leaders — at first because of Britain's commanding status in Egypt — and later when World War I broke, he understood better than any of the others that Zionism's only hope, so far as Palestine was concerned, was to place all bets on the British. It was not so much what Zionism could do for the British as what the British could do for Zionism in Palestine.

Leaning heavily upon the traditional plea of "Jewish persecution" and the Biblical implications of ancient Zion, Weizmann realized that Christian statesmen could more readily be persuaded to give sympathy and aid to his plans than would the more important Jewish leaders in Great Britain — at that time. In fact he soon learned that it was as easy to work this angle in America as in England.

The term "Gentile Zionism" became a rather widely used figure of speech to describe the enthusiasm of some non-Jews who were said to have been attracted, to a considerable degree, by the belief that the Zionist movement was in some way synonymous with the new wave of "Liberalism." Those who contradict this similitude contend that the better example of liberalism is by those Jews who assimilate in the countries where they have settled and intend to live — with no other nationality influences to bother them. In those days there were many outstanding Jews who were of this mind. There was heavy opposition to the Weizmann plans and Zionist ideology among substantial Jews in England. Time and growing pressures, however, have obviously had their compelling effect.

WEIZMANN MOVES FORWARD RAPIDLY

Zionist Weizmann, after moving to England, wasted no time. By 1906, through a mutual Jewish friend, he arranged to meet Arthur James Balfour who, later as Minister of Foreign Affairs of His Majesty's Government, signed the highly controversial "Balfour Declaration" which had been largely prepared and finally approved by top-ranking Zionist leaders in both England and America. In the United States the master-minding in this operation was in the hands especially of Justice Louis Brandeis, his protege Felix Frankfurter, and Rabbi Stephen Wise. (See Chapter IX)

All of this procedure on the part of Weizmann and his colleagues took time and tedious diplomacy. It required some ten years after Weizmann first met Balfour before British statesmen finally succumbed to Zionist (and war) pressures and hesitatingly granted the appeasing document known as the Balfour Declaration.

Weizmann's first meeting with Balfour was arranged through Charles Dreyfus, a pro-Uganda Zionist, who set the meeting hoping that Balfour could sell the Uganda-site to Weizmann. They met in the old Queen's Hotel in Piccadilly where Balfour, then engaged in one of his early political campaigns (1906), had his headquarters. One of the first questions Balfour asked, according to Weizmann, was why he was so obstinately opposed to the British proposal of a homeland for distressed Jews in Uganda — an offer which Balfour had supported.

Weizmann's reply was most interesting. In his autobiography, "Trial and Error," he says he explained to Balfour, in his then hesitant English, that Zionism was a spiritual movement and that "nothing but a deep religious conviction expressed in modern political terms could keep the movement alive, and that this conviction had to be based upon Palestine and on Palestine alone. Any defection from

Palestine was — well, a form of idolatry . . . The Jewish people would never produce either the money or the energy required . . . unless that land were Palestine. Palestine has its magic and romantic appeal for the Jews; our history has been what it is because of our tenacious hold on Palestine."

Here was a case where the Weizmann establishment was urging a "homeland" as an asylum for the suffering Jews of Europe, where presumably they could be free to lead their own lives. Weizmann was asking for this, he said, on behalf of the Jews of the world — but these Jews, according to him, would not put up the money necessary to make a home for their troubled brothers in any place but Palestine. After Weizmann's explanation became known, there were those who charged that the "Palestine idea" was cut to pattern more for the Jews who were putting up the money than for the Jews who needed a homeland — and that it had a meaning far beyond "a homeland for suffering Jews." Palestine has always been a sought-for prize by kings and pharaohs for the power and prestige it gives its ruler as a bridge between Asia and Africa.

Weizmann, in his talk with Balfour, referred to "our tenacious hold on Palestine." This is difficult to rationalize with the facts of history. The records are clear that anything which could be called Hebrew or Jewish statehood in Palestine was of comparatively short and troubled duration — only a few hundred years among the thousands of years of Palestine history. It could hardly be called a "tenacious hold."

NOTE: Ancient Israel was established as a nation (deriving from a group of federated Israelite tribes) under Saul as its first king sometime in the eleventh century B.C. — estimated by the New Jewish Encyclopedia as 1028 — and by the Jewish historian Graetz as 1067. It was a very loose "nation" until consolidated by David as Saul's successor. David was in turn succeeded by his son Solomon who, according to the same mentioned Encyclopedia, ruled from 973 to 933 B.C. After Solomon's death, internal turmoil split the nation with only the northern section (Samaria) retaining the name "Israel". It was destroyed by the Assyrians in 722 B.C. — and that was the end of Israel as a nation. The southern province with the tribal name of Judah (called Judea by the Romans) survived only another 135 years until taken over by Babylonia's Nebuchadnezzar in 588-587 B.C. Jews continued to live in and around Jerusalem until they were dispersed because of their rebellion under the Romans — first in 70 A.D. by Titus and finally by Hadrian in 135 A.D.

Weizmann was the master political strategist with typical ingenuity for sensing opportunity. He writes that when World War I broke, he and his wife were in Switzerland on a short vacation but realizing the importance of the war outbreak he managed, as quickly as possible, to return to England. There he sought out his close Zionist friends and "talked over the great possibilities now opening . . . I went about with my hopes, waiting for my chance. It came soon."

At a party in Withington he met C. P. Scott, the noted editor of the liberal Manchester Guardian whom he knew "to be sympathetic with Jewish ideals." With Scott he grasped the opportunity to pour out his heart on the Jewish question. "I told him of my hatred for (Czarist) Russia, of the internal conflicts of the Jews, of our universal tragedy, of our hopes and aspirations for Palestine . . . He listened intently, and said, 'I would like to do something for you. I would like to put you in touch with the Chancellor of the Exchequer, Lloyd George' — and then he added, 'You know you have a Jew in the Government, Mr. Herbert Samuel'."

Scott did as promised and introduced Weizmann and his top Zionist strategy colleague, Nahum Sokolow, to both Lloyd George and Herbert Samuel, the latter being the first professing Jew to become a member of the British Cabinet. This meeting was a crowning achievement for the Zionist strategists. A short time before this propitious acquaintance-contact, Weizmann had laid some groundwork for Zionist post-war possibilities in a letter to C. B. Scott, which read in part as follows:

"Don't you think that the chance for the Jewish people is now within the limits of discussion at least? . . . We can reasonably say that should Palestine fall within the British sphere of influence, and should Britain encourage a Jewish settlement there, as a British dependency, we would have within twenty to thirty years a million Jews out there, perhaps more; they would develop the country, bring back civilization to it and form a very effective guard for the Suez canal" ("Trial and Error").

Weizmann was gradually putting his program into a realistic mosaic. With Sir Herbert Samuel, a co-religionist and now a Weizmann colleague in the British cabinet, and with Lloyd George showing great friendliness, there was reason for high elation on the part of the Zionists — all depending, of course, on ultimate victory for Britain against Germany and the Turks who had become a German ally — and who dominated the Middle East, including Palestine. If Britain could drive the Turks from that area then the chances for the victory of Zionist aims would be excellent.

Sir Herbert Samuel went so far in his enthusiasm as to issue an official memorandum titled "The Future of Palestine," arguing for British annexation of that little country and predicting an "ingathering" there of three to four million Jews —and did it with such fervor as to elicit an expression of amusement from even Weizmann.

Not all British statesmen were mesmerized by Weizmann's articulate dexterity or Samuel's over-flowing infatuation for Zionism. For instance, the distinguished Lord Asquith's impression of Samuel's Utopianism was jotted into his diary (January 28, 1915) — "I have just received from Herbert Samuel a memorandum headed 'The Future of Palestine'. He goes on to argue at considerable length and with some vehemence in favor of the British annexation of Palestine . . . He thinks he might plant in this not very promising territory about three or four million European Jews . . . It reads almost like a new edition of 'Tancred' brought up to date . . . I confess I am not attracted to this proposed addition to our responsibilities, but it is a curious illustration of Dizzy's (Disraeli's) favorite maxim — 'Race is everything' . . ." Prominent among others who gave cold reception to the poorly veiled Zionist plan to capture Palestine through mass immigration were Lord Bertie (then Ambassador to France) and the distinguished Lord Reading.

It was Asquith's belief that Britain should help replace Turkish rule in the Palestine area with the Arabs who lived there (and had done so for centuries) — and who were then Britain's trustworthy friends. It was to the Arab bloc of the Middle East that Britain was looking at that time for crucial help to oust the Turks from the territory.

An unpredictable turn of war-time events, however, brought the Premiership resignation of the Honorable Mr.

61

Asquith in December, 1916, a little less than two years after he made his diary entry about Samuel's plan. As a result of this political war upheaval, the Second British Coalition Government was formed. Luck was with the Zionists. Their friend Lloyd George became Prime Minister and another Weizmann convert, Arthur James Balfour, was appointed Foreign Secretary to succeed Sir Edward Grey.

NOTE: Edward Viscount Grey is remembered especially for this observation as, on August 6, 1914, he gazed from his Foreign Office window: "The lights are going out all over Europe; we shall not see them lit again in our lifetime."

Things were going well for Zionism whose activists were by now numerous and busy as bees. Nothing succeeds like success and the Weizmann genius for selection and timing was on target — he had been cultivating the right men. The Arabs at that time (first World War), unfortunately for them, had no propaganda agents at work in America or Britain — no voting blocs in those countries —no far-flung wealth to call upon. They were poor people, seeking freedom from Turkish rule in the country of Palestine where they were the dominant populace. At that time they numbered approximately 660,000 (75,000 of which were Christians) while the Jewish population was roughly only 71,000. (See Palestine population chart — Chapter II.)

One of Weizmann's big tasks was to create a propaganda-impression among British statesmen that Jews everywhere were predominantly behind the Zionist movement, which of course, was not at that time anywhere near true. The political power of the Zionists in British high places was, however, under the Weismann charm, increasing enormously — but he was having plenty of trouble with some of the prominent British Jewish leaders. Just a few of the jottings in Weizmann's autobiography emphasize this Jewish opposition: "Old Leopold de Rothschild," he writes, "whom I never met, was like his wife, furiously anti-Zionist and remained so to the end. Sir Philip Magnus who was also anti-Zionist in his views, was interested for a time in Palestine colonization as pure philanthropy."

WEIZMANN CRITICAL
OF ASSIMILATED JEWS

Referring to lack of interest in Zionism by "assimilated Jews," Weizmann wrote: "They looked upon it — Lucien Wolf, for instance, — as a primitive tribalism. They felt themselves, when they were men of an ethical turn of mind like Claude Montefiore, called upon to 'rescue' Judaism from Zionism . . . It was a pleasure to find among some of the Rothschilds a generous degree of sympathy, it was correspondingly difficult to put up with the blind, immovable and utterly unprovoked hostility of the 'pure' philanthropists in a matter which, on their own showing, was actually none of their business.

"I wrote to Sacher and Simon in December 1914: 'The gentlemen of the type of Lucien Wolf have to be told the candid truth and made to realize that we and not they are masters of the situation, that if we come to them it is only and solely because we desire to show to the world a united Jewry . . . If anyone of their tribe had done the amount of work I did for the University there would be no end of trumpet blowing. Starting with nothing I, Chaim Weizmann, a Yid from Motelle and only an almost professor at a provincial university, have organized the flower of Jewry in favor of the prospect' . . ."

In the same paragraphs, Weizmann said: "Then there were of course, Israel Sieff and Simon Marks, with whom I became increasingly intimate, and whose collaboration became more and more important." To these two ardent and vigorous front-line workers for Weizmann and Zionism was added keen, intellectual Harry Sacher, journalist and budding lawyer.

The three were tied together by close intermarriage. Sieff (who later was politically rewarded by being made "Lord Sieff") was married to the older sister of Marks, while Sacher married his younger sister; and Marks in turn was married to Sieff's sister. Sieff and Marks were partners in "Marks and Spencer," a chain of bargain-stores then growing up throughout England, which had been started by Marks' father as Marks and Spencer's Penny Bazaars.

NOTE: Mr. Sieff was active in the United States in 1942, advising the New Dealers on "planning". He was head of the left-liberal British Political and Economic Planning Commission (PEP).

Sacher, who later "built up a big legal practice in Palestine" was, at the time of Weizmann, writing for the Manchester Guardian, which liberal paper became an important cog in Weizmann's propaganda drive. Weizmann wrote — "Harry Sacher, as leading writer on the Manchester Guardian, was an excellent link with C. P. Scott." Scott was the editor. "It was Sacher," said Weizmann, "who put me in touch with Herbert Sidebotham, the prominent journalist and publicist who was associated with the Manchester Guardian and later with the Sunday Times." The Zionists, from the first, have placed great store on the influence of newspapers and other kinds of communications media in their climb to power.

"In 1916," wrote Weizmann, "Herbert Sidebotham, then of the Manchester Guardian, helped us found the British Palestine Committee, which played an important role in the moulding of public opinion in our favor." The British Palestine Committee was organized largely to bring non-Jews into the Zionist program — and it was quite successful in the way it worked. It published a magazine called "Palestine," with overriding emphasis on how a Jewish Palestine would benefit Great Britain by serving as a "friendly and cooperative bloc" to protect the British life iine to Egypt and the far-East. This was Herbert Sidebotham's line of argument and it strangely swayed leaders like Lloyd George, Balfour and many others.

As an illustration of how this propaganda-combination was working, there appeared in the Manchester Guardian (November 22, 1915) an editorial written by Herbert Sidebotham (one of the most ardent of the converted pro-Zionists) arguing that with the loss of Turkey as an English ally (Turkey had just allied itself with Germany) "the most vital spot in our communications with the East would be exposed to attack from the land, an attack from which the most pow-

64

erful navy could not possibly secure us." The editorial then proceeded to capitalize this projected danger by suggesting that a buffer state be established in Palestine as a means of protecting the Suez Canal and Egypt — and "the only people capable of forming such a State was the Jewish nation."

Harry Sacher (already mentioned as one of a trio of ardent young Zionist collaborators) brought the editorial to the immediate attention of Weizmann, and Sidebotham "was asked to prepare a comprehensive memorandum elaborating on the idea." This was done — and in February of 1916 it was submitted to key British officials. One purpose of this, according to Sidebotham's notes, was to counteract the trend at that time of the official British leaders to favor a policy that would substitute the Palestinian Arabs for the Turks as dominant in that area.

Sidebotham urged an alternative: the reconstituting of the Jews as a large self-sustaining State extending over the whole of Palestine — "a modern State such as could ultimately . . . form a self-sufficing State as a British Dominion . . . and tender voluntary help to the Empire in its trials" (Esco Foundation for Palestine Report, p.81).

In retrospect this pro-Zionist line of argument appears little· less than ludicrous. In 1937 (twenty years after the Balfour Declaration) Sidebotham and his Zionist friends published a book titled "Great Britain and Palestine." This was in the nature of an apologete attempting to explain why the whole beautiful picture of Zionist and British friendship and cooperation in Palestine had turned so sour. The blame, of course was, as always, on the other fellow. The reflection of fault was cast on the Arabs and the British. It would be interesting to have the opinions of Mr. Lloyd George and Mr. Balfour, if they could speak from the grave today.

In the light of what has happened in the Middle East since the first world war, it is interesting to take another look at that Sidebotham-Zionist editorial strategy appeal to British statesmen (especially members of the War Cabinet) which urged them to turn away from the growing interest toward recognition of Arab supremacy in Palestine — and instead open the doors for mass Jewish immigration into that country. The argument was that the Zionist-Jews would be more helpful to Britain than would the "backward" Arabs.

ROMANTICISM THAT FAILED

This charming theory was swallowed by the Lloyd George-Balfour government and soon emerged in the Zionist-pressured, ambiguous Balfour Declaration. (See Chapter IX for details on Balfour Declaration.) The Zionists immediately interpreted this ill-born document publicly as license for mass-immigration of Jews into Palestine. To attempt some legal validation for the document, the Zionists then exerted themselves to have the League of Nations give Great Britain a "mandate" over Palestine. Gradually, as British authority sought to restrain Zionist immigration excesses, the beautiful picture of friendship for Britain which the Weizmann crowd had painted to get the Balfour document, began to fade. The Zionists, as time passed, became more and more restive under British rule. By the early 1940's, a revolt-movement against the British by the Zionists was well under way — much as earlier Jews had revolted against Roman authority. This gradually became an organized "underground" rebellion to harass and oust the British entirely from Palestine. The amazing story of this "underground" revolt and the Zionist "war of liberation" is revealed in Chapter XIV.

By 1947-1948, Lloyd George, Balfour and other British statesmen who had been swayed to help give Zionism its foothold in Palestine, had passed beyond responsibility or accountability. Succeeding statesmen had to face the increasing raucous music. Among these troubled men were some who believed they could have been spared this ordeal of ignominy (being pushed out of Palestine in 1948) if Asquith's advice (in 1916) had been followed. His counsel was to place British hopes and interests in Palestine with the resident Palestinian Arabs who had been there as the dominant population for centuries — and were recognized as trustworthy friends of the British.

Also involved in that consideration was the agreement-promise of postwar independence for the Arab states (from

66

which Palestine was not excluded), made in solemn compact by British statesmen (see note below) to King Hussein in return for Arab help to drive the Turks from the Middle East. That aid was adequately given, and with the help of the famous "Lawrence of Arabia," the Arab revolt was carried out, resulting in the Arab capture of such strategic key points as Aqaba, Damascus and others that materially helped drive the Turks from the Middle East. The Arabs were dumfounded and bitterly disappointed when they later learned about the Balfour Declaration with its essential promise of Palestine to the Jewish Zionists — a promise that they felt would inevitably lead to the conflict that mass immigration would bring.

NOTE: Concerning the foregoing reference to Britain seeking aid from the Arabs in her desperate war with the Turks, negotiations had begun in 1915 between Britain's Sir Henry McMahon, High Commissioner for Egypt, and King Hussein of the Hedjaz, Shereef of Mecca and the recognized Arab leader of the time. The complete exchange of correspondnce is contained in the book "The Arab Awakening" by the late eminent journalist, George Antonius. This exchange set forth the qualifications and stipulations requested by King Hussein and Great Britain's final acceptance of them as contained in McMahon's letters of 1915 and 1916, amounting to a binding engagement on the part of Great Britain. It recognized the Shereef of Mecca (King Hussein) as the accredited spokesman of the Arab people and accepted them as a negotiating body. The terms were as plain as was its validity.

In return for the aid of the Arabs against the Turks, Britain guaranteed a postwar independence of the Arabs within the frontiers designated by King Hussein. Britain had made certain reservations of "portions of Syria lying to the west of the districts of Damascus, Hama, Homs and Aleppo" which could not be called purely Arab but there was no reservation placed upon the northern coastal district of Syria and no reservation whatever on the southern sphere known as Palestine. Palestine for some 1,300 years had been predominantly Arab.

There are those also who think that if British policy had continued the way it was veering at the time the Sidebotham-Weizmann editorial strategy was introduced — that is with the Palestinian Arabs instead of the Zionists getting Britain's favor as the continuing resident-dominance in Palestine — the road ahead might have been smoother for the British.

For one thing, they say, Britain would have been spared the pressure-harassment of the powerful U.S. Zionist bloc which began with a Palestine inspection trip by Justice Brandeis who, not finding things to his liking, made a hurried trip to London demanding changes in British rule in Jerusalem, which demands were quickly and obediently met — with not too much enthusiasm from the British officers in Jerusalem. This harassment continued and grew in proportions until it reached its final stages in the Zionists' drive to challenge Britain's authority in Palestine, as is graphically told in great detail by the Zionist underground leader Menachem W. Begin in his book "The Revolt" (See Chapter XIV).

Another "cross of thorns" for Britain to wear during her years of anguish in trying to administer her Palestine-mandatory responsibility (especially from 1945 to May 1948) was the irritating "advice interference" (sans responsibility) by the Zionist infiltrated and influenced American New Deal government. Finally, unwilling to carry the thankless burden in Palestine any longer, Britain threw in the sponge and withdrew her costly administrative forces — much to the delight of the Zionists, but sadly for England it was the beginning of the end of her influence and rights in the important Middle East — and undoubtedly a beginning factor in her general Empire retrogression.

The exit of Great Britain as the ruling authority in Palestine was the green light for the Zionists to take over and set up their own self-anointed government. That story is told in Chapter XVI.

*   *   *

HOW LONG THE ARMS OF POLITICAL ZIONISM

This present chapter has been a short review of political Zionism as a movement, mainly directed to its central objective — the conquest of Palestine to reestablish a Jewish Nation for its political advantages. It has become clear, however, that political Zionism has a much greater built-in reach than its originally declared purpose of seeking a "homeland" for distressed and indigent Jews.

It will not be the purpose here to explore in depth the far-reaching effects of Zionist politics in anchor-countries like the United States and Great Britain (where Zionism cut its political teeth) — nor to offer prophecy as to its eventual consequence for Jews and the Jewish image throughout the world. One knowledgeable observer has indicated that if it should, like certain other political "comets" we have recently seen, feed upon extravagant and arrogant ambitions, it could bring repetition of the age-old disasters with which Jewish history seems to have special rendezvous.

There are those who fear that these succeeding Palestine-crises have all the ingredients that make for long-reaching trouble in the Middle East. This concerns not only Jews (Zionists, non-Zionists and anti-Zionists) and Arabs — but the citizens of nations who could be dragged into an international conflagration through the nationalistic adventures and machinations of political fledglings passionately engaged in trying out their newly sprouted wings. Those countries which may be especially vulnerable to this danger, with much to lose and nothing to gain, should, in the opinion of many worried by-standers, adhere closely to the test of single-loyalty and be eternally alert to pitfalls in our present dangerously disturbed world.

There are still in America some prominent Jews who are unhappy about the effect that Zionism has already had upon the Jewish image — Jewish culture — the Jewish religion — the Jewish character — and the further shadows it throws over the future. One of these is a distinguished Jewish citizen of California named Moshe Menuhin, whose recent and most extraordinary book of dissent and protest is titled "The Decadence of Judaism in Our Time" (Exposition Press, New York). Besides being widely known for his own achievements, he is the father of the internationally celebrated violinist Yehudi Menuhin, whom he excludes from any responsibility for the book and its theme.

Mr. Menuhin is a highly substantial citizen with what seems clearly no other purpose in writing his book than to express his concern, as a Jew who believes in prophetic Judaism, with what he regards to be the erosion of traditional Judaism by a gradual merging of Statehood with Godhood, through the prostitution of a misconstrued ancestral religious concept.

"To stultify, brainwash, and inoculate the amorphous body of world Jewry with the virus of secular, rampant 'Jewish' political nationalism," writes Mr. Menuhin, "Jewish education for ALIYAH ('ingathering of the exiles' through immigration into Israel) under the pretense of spiritual and religious immunity or liberty has been instituted everywhere. This, in turn, has been undoing the normal and natural processes of the integration and evolution of the Jew into the new order of universalism and brotherhood. Cultural isolation, hidden behind the much abused expression 'cultural pluralism,' has been self-segregating the Jew from the Gentile in America, England, France and elsewhere in the free world, to prepare him for Aliyah.

"Advancing, evolving, universal and spiritual Judaism," states Mr. Menuhin, "which was the core of the Judeo-Christian code of ethics, is now becoming the tool, the handmaiden of 'Jewish' nationalism, so that the ethical injunctions Thou shalt not kill, Thou shalt not steal, Thou shalt not covet have been transformed into the unethical, primitive and tribalistic 'Covenant of the Chosen People' and 'Israel First'."

Reference to this book is made here for two particular reasons: (1) Mr. Menuhin is clearly a scholar of Jewish history, enabling him to present an unusually valuable commentary on ancient and modern life and tradition; (2) the book is a singular example of feeling and courage, which is rare today among the hushed voices of those who secretly fear political Zionism. There are only a few who have the courage to speak out. Another was the voice (in a Tel Aviv hotel lounge) of a Jewish woman from South Africa who, greatly influenced by the golden stories she had heard about the new Israel, had brought her 20-year-old daughter to see the great Zionist miracle. She said she had been there for three weeks and the sooner her tour was ready to leave the better she would be pleased. "I came here because I had heard so much about this being a great revival of the true spirit of our Jewish religion — but I do not find it. What I do see is a veneer of tinsel — and hands out to get my money." (The last point was made with emphasis, April 17, 1966).

Wide-range research and interrogation have disclosed that there is much suppressed feeling on this general subject. It appears that one reason there is not more critical expression is not that it does not exist — but rather, on the part of non-Zionist Jews is the fear of group-disapprobation and ostracism.

Critics like Alfred Lilienthal and Moshe Menuhin as Jews can speak out without being charged with "anti-Semitism" — the most lethal weapon in the arsenal of the professional "anti-defamationists" but the arsenal contains other types of punishment for them, as they can testify.

70

When the late Dr. John Beaty, distinguished scholar and professor, published his critical book "Iron Curtain Over America," all the weapons of torment were unleashed upon him with fury unrestrained by the "gentle" myrmidons of the new order — even though his book was highly praised by many great Americans, including General Albert C. Wedemeyer.

When political action can be enshrouded with religious coloration, its functionaries are provided with a sacrosanctity that puts a fascist-like embargo on all dissent. There are both Jews and non-Jews who regard the tremendous upsurge of political Zionism as an extremely grave threat to the widely acclaimed ideal of church and state separation. The test of any project or ideal is — can it stand the bright light of close inspection? Attempts to suppress objective and honest criticism are not representative of the democratic ethic, nor of the "American way of life." They are communistic in conception and fascistic in application.

4. THE CONTRADICTION OF BIBLE-BASED POLITICAL ZIONISM

The rise of political Zionism has placed before the world a number of highly interesting questions, and foremost among them is the riddle of whether Zionism is a political or a religious movement. (See Chapter VII for "the Jewish people" controversy.)

In the days when the Old Testament was written, and up through the Middle Ages, it certainly was not uncommon for State potentates to pose as having divine status. It was out of the profanation of equating God with King or State that the theory of "separation" of State and religion arose which, as is well known, is a widely applied Constitutional stipulation in some countries, as in the United States.

One question that arises, so far as Zionism and the new "Jewish State" is concerned, is a strange phenomenon whereby more Zionist-oriented Jews live in countries where the sentiment against religious-based Statehood is strong and rigid than there are Zionists living in Israel. Rightly or wrongly, this has within it for many the seeds of suspicion as to dual loyalties. While Israel is widely regarded as an Old Testament based State, this is not to say that as a State it is more religious than political. But the illusion is promoted that Israel represents the rebirth of the religion of the ancient Jews. It is this illusion, some say, that brings money into the support of Israel from religious Jews in other countries. It is this apocryphal image that has brought thousands of pilgrims to Israel to see the great religious revival, but, as the Jewish lady from South Africa explained to a hotel lobby group in Tel Aviv — "I came purposely to see this rebirth, but I did not find it."

As to the citizens of present Israel, we have talked with some Polish Jews there who say they are not Zionists. One driver (from Jerusalem to Tel Aviv) with whom this was discussed, seemed confused over the question but stoutly said he was not a Zionist. He did not seem to be one of the Jews who Weizmann and other Zionist leaders claimed were burning with zeal to "return to Zion" because Abraham and the Israelites had been there. His main urge, at the time of his migration, was to get safely out of Poland.

BIBLE SCHOLARS DISPUTE POLITICAL ZIONISM

In a booklet containing appraisals of "Israel, According to Holy Scriptures," by seven foremost Bible scholars, Professor Alfred Guillaume, Professor of Old Testament Studies, University of London, gives devastating refutation to the Zionist claims that Palestine belongs to "certain people" because of self-pleading interpretations by Zionist leaders of abstruse wordings in the Old Testament.

The well known Jewish Rabbi, Dr. Elmer Berger, in this same collection of opinions, points out that there have always been two main schools of thought among Jews as to the meaning of the "return to Zion" doctrine — one stressing the nationalistic and the other advocating the universal interpretations of Jewish faith. He quotes two significant clauses from a declaration by a group of distinguished Reform rabbis, meeting in Pittsburgh, Pennsylvania, in 1885, "in what," he says, "is still the classic statement of this protestant or Reform Judaism (as it is known in the United States)":

"4. We hold that all such Mosaic and rabbinical laws as regulate diet, priestly purity, and dress originated in ages and under the influence of ideas entirely foreign to our present mental and spiritual state. They fail to impress the modern Jew with a spirit of priestly holiness; their observance in our days is apt rather to obstruct than to further modern spiritual elevation.

"5. We recognize in the modern era of universal culture of heart and intellect the approaching of the realization of Israel's great Messianic hope for the establishment of the kingdom of truth, justice and peace among all men. We consider ourselves no longer a nation, but a religious community, and therefore expect neither a return to Palestine, nor a sacrificial worship under the sons of Aaron, nor the restoration of any of the laws concerning the Jewish state."

Despite the charges of false arrogation against the Zionists, the facts remain that present day Zionism has been promoted as a Bible-based "Return" movement. From the loud and far-flung outcry and outpouring of approval of Jews, especially in the United States, over the 1967 6-day battle between Israelis and Arabs, the concept of an Israel-Bible affiliation seems to be well accepted and widely approved. Some may question, as they do, whether this enthusiasm is an effervescence of religious or racial-nationalism feeling; but whatever its source, it affords no solace or comfort for over a million uprooted Palestinian refugees rotting away in squalid camps.

A strange anomaly of this is that there are numbers of Fundamentalist Christians in America who welcomed the Israeli 1967 blitz victory as "a working out of prophecy" — even when thousands of Christian Arabs were the refugee-victims. Riding two horses, each going its own way, is not only an act difficult to perform — it is also one difficult to explain.

In summary on the nature of Zionism, the following statements expressing both Jewish and Arab views are presented for consideration.

THE ZIONIST VIEW

"The aim of Zionism," as described in Volume II of "Who's Who in the State of Israel," edited by Alexander Aurel-Ariely, Tel Aviv, Israel, "is the redemption of the Jewish people and its land, the revival of its state and language, the implanting in Jewish life of the sacred treasures of Jewish tradition. These objectives are to be attained by the creation of a Jewish majority in Palestine on both sides of the Jordan, the up-building of a Jewish State on the basis of civil liberty, social justice in the spirit of Jewish tradition, the return to Zion of all who seek Zion, and the liquidation of the Jewish dispersion."

This rationale contains three interesting implications: (1) "The aim of Zionism is the redemption of the Jewish people and its land . . .", meaning Palestine — which, throughout

74

its history, has been occupied by many peoples besides Jews. (2) The purpose of Zionism was to "redeem" Palestine by massive immigration into a predominately Arab country "on both sides of the Jordan" to bring about a "Jewish State." "Both sides of the Jordan" would imply there is still unfinished business. (3) "The return to Zion of all who seek Zion, and the liquidation of the Jewish dispersion." This last point has been stressed by Ben Gurion and would seem to mean a centralization of Jewish world authority in Israel," with hegemony over all Jews "who seek Zion" and Jewish communities throughout the world.

In the Introduction to a book titled "Zionism — Problems and Views," edited by Paul Goodman and Arthur Lewis, Dr. Max Nordau (distinguished European Jewish writer, critic of religions, early Herzl Zionist) says: "There is nothing vague or hazy about the tenets of Zionism . . . The Jews form not merely a religious community but also a nation . . . Zionism has no meaning for Jews who favor the melting-pot theory. It is the ideal of those who feel themselves to belong to a Jewish nation . . ."

Max Bressler, prominent and ardent Jewish leader, writing on "Zionism Today" in the Chicago Jewish Sentinel (April 19, 1956), stated that "It was Herzl's idea that Zionism is more than the founding of a Jewish State. Zionism means the regeneration of the Jewish people throughout the world." Now that the Jewish State has been founded, Bressler believes, the next big task of the World Zionist movement is to promote Jewish education for every Jewish child to bring personal identification of the American Jew with Israel and what it stands for.

Assimilation, he contends, is sapping Jewish vitality and there is no time to lose in a drive to bring about "Jewish regeneration" through Zionism. Mr. Bressler, writing on "Who Is a Zionist?" in the Sentinel (April 26, 1956), says that every Jew has a stake in the land of Israel, and the aim of the Zionist movement is to stress the importance of the sources of world Jewry for the Jewish Homeland (Israel).

THE ARAB VIEW

From an Arab booklet, "Palestine: Questions and Answers," prepared by the well known Arab authority, Sami Hadawi, in answering the question "What Are the Principles of the Zionist Movement?", writes:

"The Zionist movement is a political philosophy which preaches that the Jews are one people and one nation requiring its own land, to which all Jews must eventually return. Zionism thus spurns the concept of fellowship among Jews and seeks to endow them with national attributes. For those Jews who choose not to be ingathered, Zionism attempts to thwart their civic, cultural and social integration in lands outside of Israel in order to attach them to a nationhood of Jews . . . Though they (Jews) live in many countries, they are considered in the Diaspora and are supposed to be longing to live in Eretz Israel alone."

"The basic issue," also states this booklet of Arab opinion, "in the Palestine question is the uprooting and dispossession of an entire nation in order to make room for alien Jews, from all parts of the world. Whereas some of these Jews were hapless victims of terror and injustice, the majority are pawns in a movement of political and totalitarian oppression. They have been herded into Palestine in order to fulfill the political aspirations of a major ideological movement — Zionism."

OTHER STATEMENTS

Frank Chodorov, noted Jewish journalist, writing for Human Events (March 10, 1956), refers to Rabbi Elmer Berger's anti-Zionist book "Those Who Know Better Must Say So" (American Council for Judaism), as being dedicated to the concept that "Judaism is a religion, nothing else, and that Americans who are of that faith are Americans, nothing else." "But," Chodorov goes on, "to the well organized and highly financed forces of Zionism, the position taken by Dr. Berger and the A.C.J. for Judaism is anathema, for they hold that Jews throughout the world, no matter what citizenship they hold, and even though they be agnostics or atheists, owe first allegiance to the nation of their Biblical forefathers. That is, they maintain that Judaism is not a religion but a political entity to which the members of the race are tied by blood and tradition to the end of time."

The New York Times (June 15, 1952) carried an extensive story about a meeting of 2,000 Zionist delegates in New York where they received a cablegram from Israel's Prime Minister, Ben Gurion, and other high-ranking Israel leaders, urging that "the Zionist movement must take the lead in forming a 'partnership' between American Jews and Israel. It is now," the Prime Minister was reported as saying, "the mission of the Zionist movement to mold this partnership and lead it. This is particularly imperative in the greatest Jewish community of our time (meaning the United States). It is therefore essential to strengthen the Zionist organization, unite the entire Zionist movement in America, intensify Zionist education among the masses and inspire youth." Among other delegates quoted by the Times was Benjamin G. Browdy, retiring president of the Zionist Organization of America, as saying — "If American Zionists neglect the American Jewish Community, leaving it to the care of others, the future Jewish generations of America may bear little resemblance to all that we hold dear and devoutly hope for."

The Honorable Henry Morgenthau (distinguished from his son, Henry Jr., of the Roosevelt New Deal) said in his book, "All in a Life Time" (Doubleday & Company), "Zionism is the most stupendous fallacy in Jewish history . . . Where it is not pathetically visionary, it is a cruel playing with the hopes of a people who have had long miseries." He went on at great length to express his aroused feelings of great apprehension for what political Zionism would lead to. "Zionism," he said, "is based upon a literal acceptance of promises made to the Jews by their prophets in the Old Testament that Zion would be restored to them," and he explains that of course the prophets were speaking symbolically — and only with "spiritual meaning." "Zionism," he also said, "is a surrender, not a solution."

The late William Zukerman, widely known editor of the Jewish Newsletter, said that "the establishment of a Jewish State was the primary but not the (real) aim of Zionism.

Another aim was the awakening, in Jews, of the consciousness that they are a nation . . . The Zionist movement, therefore, now has another great task before it: to Zionize the Jews, to imbue them with a love for Israel as their national home and centre; to spur them above all, culturally and spiritually."

NOTE: The foregoing quotations were included in the text of this book prior to the June, 1967 flare-up of war between the Jews and the Arabs. After the extension of land-conquests of Palestine in this latest war, it seems hardly necessary to add further observations concerning the aims of the Zionists in Palestine and the Middle East.

---

* * *

"THE ZIONIST ILLUSION"

It is doubtful if any more interesting and scholarly analysis of political Zionism has been made than that written by Dr. W. T. Stace (Professor of Philosophy, Princeton University) which appeared in the Atlantic Monthly (February, 1947). This was at the crucial time when the confrontation between the native Arabs of Palestine and the immigrating Jews was almost at an exploding point. It was just before the British mandatory in Palestine, reeling from constant attacks and interference from the Zionist "underground," retreated from the intolerable situation and informed the United Nations that they (the British) would relinquish their mandate-authority and all control of Palestine at a date set as May 15, 1948. This, of course, was precisely what the Zionist "war of liberation" had been directed to accomplish.

Dr. Stace, in his informative article, stated that the whole case of the claim by the Jews for special rights in Palestine was based upon five assumptions, which he listed as follows:

1. The claim that Palestine was a Jewish land in ancient times;

2. That Palestine has for the Jews a special and peculiar religious meaning;

3. That in 1917 the British Government sanctioned (through the so-called Balfour Declaration) the right of the Jews to have a "homeland" in Palestine;

4. That the "homelessness" and "long suffering" of the Jews was a just reason for the mass immigration of Eastern European Jews into a country that had been predominantly occupied by other peoples for some 1,300 years;

5. That the Jews, who had already immigrated to Palestine, had brought considerable improvement to the industry of that country.

Professor Stace, after listing (as above) the five claims upon which the Zionists have laid claim to Palestine, offers some pertinent observations on each of these claims as to its validity. Here is a brief summary of the Stace analysis:

1. Only through long possession, says Dr. Stace, does any grouping of people come into legal national possession of the land they occupy. Their generations must have grown from the land. Having been the predominant occupants of Palestine for hundreds of years until the families, the homes, the villages and the institutions were mainly Arabic, the Arabs had a perfect right to resist the mass immigration of foreigners which the Zionists, aided improperly by certain pro-Zionist public officials in Britain and in America, were pressing upon them. Dr. Stace calls upon the precedent, established in law, known as "prescription." The dictionary says that in law this word means the acquirement of title or right to something through its continued use or possession over a long period. Actually, he contends, the Arabs have a better time-title to Palestine than Americans do to America by several hundred years.

2. As to any rights that might belong to Zionists in Palestine on a "peculiarly sacred religious" consideration, Dr. Stace questions whether any such claim on behalf of mass immigration would be allowed by any country in the world. If this were a valid claim, then Christians from other countries could move into Palestine en masse just as properly as could the Jews — for Christians also have a "peculiarly sacred religious attachment" to that land.

79

3. The third Zionist claim mentioned is founded upon the so-called Balfour Declaration, where a few pro-Zionist British statesmen, at a certain expedient time, made a vague promise of "favouring" a homeland for the Jews in Palestine. Dr. Stace disposes of the Balfour document (as most thinking people have by now) as a worthless and reckless venture in politicking. (The Balfour matter is examined in Chapter IX.)

4. The fourth Zionist "claim" for a massive "ingathering" of Jews into Palestine was that of "homelessness" and long suffering," which Zionist Weizmann used most effectively in swaying high British and American officials to a posture of Zionist sympathy. Dr. Stace grants the propriety of deep feeling of pity and shame for the historical plight of Jews (and all peoples) whenever and wherever they may have suffered, but he asks what possible responsibility could be assessed against the Arab population of Palestine for the Roman dispersion of two thousand years ago — or the pogroms and other injustices to Jews in their erstwhile major habitats of Poland, Russia and other countries? The fact that an individual may be homeless does not give him the right to intrude and make himself at home with John Doe or Henry Smith, neither of whom had done him any wrong.

5. Another argument advanced by the Zionists, according to Dr. Stace, is the claim of "general improvements and progress" accomplished in Palestine by the Jews who had already reached the country through immigration "permitted" by the Balfour statement. "The hole in this contention," says Dr. Stace, "is that it could be used to justify almost any aggression whatever" — especially by a more prosperous nation that had ambitions to grab a less prosperous one. This would give the rich advantages over the poor. Without further extending this review of scholarly reasoning it is submitted as lucid weighting of fallacies against fact and logic.

5. DO BIBLICAL COVENANTS GIVE PALESTINE TO THE ZIONISTS?

The basic tenets upon which the Zionists have founded their claims to historic rights in Palestine are: (1) certain Old Testament references to land "covenants" from God to Abraham and his seed; (2) an hereditary theory or assumption of "ancestral occupancy," which claim is predicated upon the ancient history of an Israelite nation that once in the foggy past existed for a limited period in Palestine; and (3) a document called the Balfour Declaration which the Zionists enticed from the British leaders in 1917 to "legalize" their Palestine rights. The Balfour deal was skilfully used until no longer needed and then given a quiet burial.

Coincidental with these tenets — especially the first two — is the implied assumption that the present day Zionists have a direct ethnic or bloodline consanguinity with the ancient patriarchal Hebrews (who lived presumably some three thousand, eight hundred years ago) and likewise with the later Israelites who antidate our present period by some three thousand years. It was the Israelites who first invaded Palestine and conquered the Canaanites by force and violence (as related in the Old Testament, Joshua 6: 21, 22, 23) — a violent act that was sanctified several hundred years later by the Old Testament writers with scriptures that were later canonized.

Any examination of the Hebrew biblical covenants brings us immediately to the Old Testament scriptures — and the authors — as they are the only historical source of documentation and the only corridor of discussion through which the status of these particular covenants may be approached and appraised.

81

WHO WERE THE AUTHORS?

Mention of the Hebrew Bible (Old Testament) and the land-covenants necessarily and unavoidably opens the door to the "sacrosanct" question, inter alia, as to when and by whom were the scriptures (as later canonized) written. It is not the purpose here to enter into any lengthy or detailed exploration of this enigmatic and apparently impenetrable subject about which the most learned scholars can only hazard guesses and speculations. The old and commonly accepted beliefs that the use of certain names like Moses, Joshua and prophets such as Ezekiel meant that certain books in the Old Testament had been written by such named personalities have been yielding slowly to the massive accumulation of facts which science and archaeology have put into the record.

In a book titled "The Growth of the Old Testament" published in America as one of the excellent Harper Torchbook Series (originally published by Hutchinson & Co., Ltd., London), the author, H. H. Rowley, says — "the tradition that Moses was the writer of the Pentateuch (first five books of the Old Testament) has been largely abandoned by modern scholars." Concerning Joshua he says that while Jewish tradition "as recorded in the Talmud, attributes the book (Joshua) to the hand of Joshua" this is today rejected "no less decisively than the Mosaic authorship of the Pentateuch."

He also tells us that while down through the years the book Ezekiel was regarded generally as having been authored by that prophet-priest, this theory has, during the last twenty years, "found a long succession of challengers." There are many more examples of the preponderant voice of scholarship as it has been developing under the pressure of modern research. In the matter of the land-covenants authorship is a highly important matter.

TOUCHY—BUT RELEVANT SUBJECT

By its very nature any subject dealing with "Biblical questions" has become highly sensitive and its introduction here is only for comparative historical purposes. In examining first the question of the covenants (before taking up the other two mentioned tenets in separate chapters) the discussion will be limited to the most salient documentation as recorded in the Hebrew Old Testament which, as previously stated, is the only source of information on the early Hebrew story.

The narrative begins and centers around a legendary person first called Abram, which name was later changed to Abraham. He was the first person identified with the so-called land-covenants by the Old Testament writers. The identity of Abram (Abraham) is examined in some detail in "Who Are the Jews?" (Appendix "B") and reference to him here will be only to place him in posture for discussing the covenants.

Abram, we are told in the Old Testament, was a native of the ancient Mesopotamian (Sumer-Babylonian) town of Ur of the Chaldees which was located several miles up-river from the mouth of the Euphrates. Archeologists have determined from the excavation of ruins in this area that about the estimated time of Abram (in the neighborhood of 1800 B.C.) there was violent revolution and wide devastation in that part of the world.

About that time, and possibly because of the social and political upheavals, Abram's father Terah took his family (including Abram and his wife Sarai — later to be known as Sarah) and departed for other regions. They stopped and sojourned at a place called Haran, a few hundred miles up the Euphrates. It was there that Terah died.

It was there also, according to the Old Testament (Genesis 12:1) that the Lord appeared to Abram and told him to "Get thee out of the country, and from thy kindred, and from thy father's house unto a land I will shew thee." Abram was then 75. Accompanied by his wife Sarai (they had no children as yet), his nephew Lot whom he had adopted, and Lot's wife, they all moved down toward Canaan, traveling through Damascus and Shechem. When Abram reached Canaan we are told (Genesis 12:7) that the Lord appeared again unto him and said — "Unto thy seed will I give this land" but no description of the land is stated — neither a reason for the giving.

Abram was apparently a passing stranger in the land —
a wandering nomad of the times who had never been in this
area before —and yet, according to the Old Testament authors who wrote about Abram some thousand years after
his time, he (Abram) was told, without apparent reason or
qualification, that "this land" which was already long inhabited by Canaanites and others, would belong to his seed
forever.

ABRAM ABANDONS HIS COVENANT

Abram, however, did not find Canaan, then barren in
an extreme state of famine, to be exactly what the Bible
writers later described as a "land of milk and honey." He
quickly moved on to the inviting Nile-fertility of Egypt
where food was plentiful. While sojourning there we are
told (Genesis 12:11-20) of a strange and exceptional experience in the irregular conduct of Abram and his wife
Sarai with the Egyptian Pharaoh. Later Abraham, with Sarai,
departed from Egypt (at the Pharoah's request) "very rich
in cattle, in silver and in gold," which condition of affluence
was not indicated when he entered Egypt to escape the famine in the land that the Old Testament writers later say had
been covenanted to him.

This particular reference to Abram is made as pertinent
here because in our research concerning the history of the
land-covenants, many people have expressed serious difficulty
in equating this strange affair engaged in by the patriarch
and his wife with the reported close relationship between
him and the Lord. The perplexity in understanding this cov-
enant-relationship is compounded by a somewhat similar episode between Abram, Sarai and Abimelech (King of the
Philistines) after Abram and Sarai had been ordered out of
Egypt and had traveled back to the Canaanite city of Gerar
(Genesis 20). Despite this enigmatic reporting, there is the
further emphasized impression that Abram (or Abraham)
was so much a favorite of the Lord that he was repeatedly
singled out from all men that were, or had been, to be rewarded with special land-grants for himself and his eternal
and unpredictable "seed."

COVENANT CONFUSION

Abram and his wife, after leaving Egypt perforce, returned to Canaan. Here he and his adopted nephew Lot (who had been with him on the long trek from Mesopotamia) decided to separate and each go his way. After the separation the Old Testament writers report that the Lord again came to Abram (now sojourning in Canaan) and said: "Lift up now thine eyes, and look from the place where thou are northward, and southward, and eastward, and westward: for all the land which thou seest, to thee will I give it, and to thy seed forever."

Presumably there was no language-barrier between Abram and the Lord and several hundred years later it seems to have been easy for the Scripture writers to put the Lord's exact words into Hebrew — although it is not known what language Abram spoke or understood. He had migrated from the ancient land of Sumer-Babylonia where archaeological excavations show that clay tablets were used (mostly by royalty) for a primitive cuneiform type of writing.

With full charity for the writers who prepared these records several centuries after the time-slots of the events, this is not the only problem that they left unanswered. There is also the question of unintelligible ambiguity of the land descriptions as given in the various covenants. In the one quoted above, for instance, the question arises as to how far could a man well past 75 see with hills in almost every direction limiting his vision.

Then quickly following this (after one short paragraph) the Old Testament writers give another rather confusing land-covenant description. The Lord tells Abram (Genesis 13:16) — "Arise, walk through the land in the length of it and the breadth of it; for I will give it unto thee." Anyone who has traveled in Palestine — and even those who have not — can easily see how vague and indefinite is this specification. These strange descriptions do not seem to have bothered the Zionists who have based their "rights" upon them. And no one else has seemed to give it a second thought.

Moving on to Genesis 15:18, the land-covenant descriptions appear to become even more confounding. "In the same day," reads this passage, "the Lord made a covenant with Abram, saying, Unto thy seed have I given this land, from the river of Egypt unto the great river, the river Euphrates," to which is added the names of several people-groups occupying some of the land involved — the Kenites, Kenizzites, Kadmonites, Hittites, Canaanites, Perizzites, Amorites, Jebusites — and a few other tribes who, in the main seem to have been in the way of the Israelite conquest. Consequently it appears the writers conveniently "covenanted" them to the "seed" of Abram.

This may have satisfied the purpose of some wishful thinking writers and redactors of some twenty-five hundred years ago who were then attempting to write about long past legendary events. But antiquity in every field is being evaluated today by scholars and realists in the light of modern research and advanced learning. The world is no longer considered as flat. It is not improper to take note here of the emphasis these early writers put on Abram's "seed" as the inheritors of the land-covenants. First this became a blessing for the Israelites and now a windfall for the modern Zionists.

When Abram was 90 years old, we are told (Genesis 17) that the Lord covenanted with him again with promises to multiply his seed and also told him that henceforth his name was to be Abraham instead of Abram. The purpose of this change is not made clear but the writers do quote the Lord as saying: "And I will give unto thee, and thy seed after thee, the land wherein thou art a stranger, all the land of Canaan, for an everlasting possession; and I will be their God." There are those who see in this a priestly polemic to the errant or backsliding Hebrews of that day — holding out the material reward that they could be the inheritors of land if they would follow the God of Abraham as their God. As the Old Testament writers moved into Israelitic narratives, the God of Abraham was clarified as the God of Israel.

We begin to get a clearer picture of how the land-covenants fit into the narrative pattern as a nationalistic meaning emerges when the writers report that the Lord talks with Moses and instructs him to take the Israelites to the land of "milk and honey" (a strange description) which He had

86

sworn to the three patriarchs that He would give to their seed. And to make the entrance easy for the Israelites, the Lord promised to send an angel in advance to drive the Canaanite, Amorite, Hittite, Perizzite, Hivite and Jebusite inhabitants from the land (Exodus 33: 3-7). This was more than 600 years after He had covenanted all these people to Abram.

Apparently this cooperation did not materialize as the Israelites had a long, hard and often discouraging struggle of some two or three hundred years before David smashed most of the opposition. When the Israelites crossed the Jordan and attacked Jericho they apparently did not have any cooperation from an angel for they used the sword utterly to destroy "man and woman, young and old" sparing only Rahab the harlot (Joshua 6: 17-25).

OLD TESTAMENT—BIBLE OF ISRAEL

In No. 2 of a series of twenty-two books called "Bible Guides" (of which the General Editors are Dr. William Barclay of Glasgow University and Professor Frederick F. Bruce of the University of Manchester), the author, Professor Bernhard W. Anderson (Professor Biblical Theology, Drew University), gives a comprehensive interpretation of Genesis in which he says: "The purpose of the Book of Genesis is to give the opening of the story of the formation of Israel." In other words, it is the foundation of a theme-purpose that runs throughout the Hebrew Bible (Old Testament).

To catch a sense of the meaning of the Biblical land-covenants one must be somewhat familiar with the continuity of the Old Testament story as its ancient writers formulated it to serve the priestly purpose of the Hebrew-Israelite people — at a certain time in history. Unfortunately very few people today have the time or interest to study this book or to learn any substantial facts concerning its historic background. It is no criticism of its intrinsic value to point out that its theology is heavily burdened with historical narrative in the sense that its main theme is the story of a particular people as the writers envisioned them — and of God's relationship with them. This particularization, incidentally, is

87

a major distinction between the Old and the New Testaments. For this and other reasons there was considerable objection and opposition among the early Christian leaders as to combining the two into one general Bible.

What was known first as the "God of the Fathers" (of Abraham, Isaac and Jacob), as already stated, later became the "God of Israel" through what Professor Anderson calls the greatest incisive event in Israel's historical experience — the exodus of the Israelites from Egypt to Canaan to become a nation. "Israel's purpose," says Professor Anderson, "was to confess the meaning of the event of the Exodus which was the source and origin of her life and to follow that meaning back to the beginning, using various popular traditions that were available."

TRAIL OF THE COVENANTS

This appears to be the grand theme in the meaning and purpose of the Old Testament writers. It is the event used to introduce the "God of Moses" which some writers have called a monolatry concept (a God for a particular people) — not monotheism as we know it today. However this concept took a gradual change — beginning in the time of the prophets and becoming more emphatic with the dawn and growth of Christianity.

The story of Moses and the Israelites (from the Exodus through the conquest of Canaan to the formation of the ancient nation called "Israel"), we are told by scholars, is the life blood of the priestly theme of the Old Testament writers. Not only are the land-covenants to Abraham carried through to connect with Moses and the Israelites to justify the first "Israel," but in our present day the "covenant theme of inheritance" has been used by modern Zionists again to defend their recent conquest of Palestine.

Many questions arise in researching the subject of the land-covenants of the early Hebrew patriarchs when this subject is examined under the microscopes of reality. Among the questions encountered are: (1) the matter of the writers having any reliable records that could possibly have survived a thousand years when even today the nomads of the deserts cannot keep records that endure the rugged elements and nomadic living for more than a few months under the best conditions; (2) the stumbling indefiniteness of the covenant descriptions lends to them an obvious status of incredibility; (3) the confrontation projection under which the covenants were reputedly given appears so highly imaginative as to place a heavy burden on rational thinking. These and other questions, such as belief and faith in some reported traditions, arise to confront many people whose sincerity is beyond question. There is also the bothersome problem that comes with trying to stretch these extraordinary covenants to present day Zionists where ancestral lineage may, to a large degree, be highly questionable.

ABOUT THE SCRIPTURE WRITERS

There is also the legitimate question of how far the Old Testament writers were swayed by their priestly zeal to adjust history and legend to sacerdotal purposes. The story of Moses, for illustration, has many bewildering and admittedly fanciful facets involving his reported dealings with the Egyptian Pharaoh and likewise his amazing experiences on the forty-year trek to fulfill the land-covenant "promises." A remarkable part of this basic scriptural story is that the Hebrew writers skipped all but two or three of the forty years attributed to the Exodus journey. The Standard Jewish Encyclopedia says — "The Bible is silent on events between the 2nd and 39th year of the Exodus."

Part of this forty-year journey is indicated as having touched the rugged desert section known as the Negev, now the southern part of present Zionist Israel but which was never a part of the ancient Israelite kingdom. With certain relevancy to the proclivities of the B.C. Bible authors, mention may well be made here of the most important book yet written about the rough and arid land of the Negev. The book is titled "Rivers in the Desert" and the author is Dr. Nelson Glueck, president of the Hebrew-Union Jewish Institute of Religion, Cincinnati (Grove Press —Evergreen Encyclopedia, Vol. 5).

Dr. Glueck is not only an outstanding Bible authority but is a highly distinguished archaeologist who has spent much time in Biblical-archaeological research — especially in the Negev. By "rivers in the desert" he refers to the profusion of usually dry wadies (ravines or desert water courses) that furrow the arid, hot, shaggy Negev country where the ancient Nabataean tribal-civilization eked out a living some 2,000 years ago. Their capital was the nearby famous rose-red, cliff-carved city of Petra which is reached by a rugged hour's ride on a donkey or horse down a high-walled, narrow defile, a natural formation that served the Nabataeans as an excellent fortification.

Dr. Glueck's work in the Negev has produced substantial confirmation of numerous Biblical sites as well as uncovering much heretofore unknown information about the early Nabataeans — also his investigations have thrown more light on the problematical itinerary of Moses and the Israelites.

This distinguished archaeologist and Bible authority, in discussing Biblical history and content, puts his finger on one of the bothersome problems of early Biblical composition by explaining that there were hundreds of communities (some highly important where he has excavated) which were passed over without mention by the Old Testament authors because — "for one reason or another the tales connected with them were not woven into the tapestry of theologically colored text of Sacred Writ."

He says further that whole districts and places of great importance were ignored in Scriptural writing and even important persons were passed over or given but slight attention. He illustrates this with the example of King Omri who, he feels, was one of the "most capable rulers ever to sit on the throne of Israel and yet the Bible editors dismissed him with curt mention" — apparently because he was not favored by those who were shaping ecclesiastical policies.

While the Bible writers largely ignored King Omri, they glorified King David regardless of his carnal conduct with Bath-sheba, wife of Uriah (II Samuel 11: 2-6) and other profane acts. But, according to the Standard Jewish Encyclopedia, "in the course of time he became a religious symbol and the Jewish messianic hope was attached to his descendants."

Dr. Glueck observes: "He (David) and his household were become Jehovah's chosen instrument" and no detail was too small but to "be included in his spiritual biography whether it portrayed him as good or bad." That David was an amenable and important figure in the priestly program of the Old Testament period is evident when its authors have him saying — "Wherefore, thou art great, O Jehovah God, for there is none like Thee, neither is there any God beside Thee . . ."

The Bible writers, says Dr. Glueck, appear to have been interested in important Negev Bible history "only insofar as it figured in the lives of the elect of the Lord from the time of Abraham on." He indicates further that those ancient editors based their interest on individuals for scriptural inclusion on the degree of their "sub-servience to the will of God, however errant on occasion they might prove to be."

Dr. Glueck has been quoted not alone because of his stature as a Bible authority but also for his bold honesty in stating facts as he finds them. An article by him appeared in the New York Times Magazine (Sept. 26, 1960) which within itself was a highly enlightening "short course" in Bible history. From it is taken this excerpt:

"The Old Testament," he wrote, "was the work of approximately a thousand years of continuous writing. Prophets and priests, kings and shepherds, the perceptive and the perplexed contributed to it. What they wrote is for the best part cloaked in anonymity or ascribed, with a passion for selflessness, to famous predecessors — as those psalms written centuries after the death of David and Solomon were attributed to them. Some Biblical books are an overlay of materials by so many hands that it is almost impossible to think of them in terms of authorship.

"Every Biblical book (in the Old Testament) whether it had been originally the work of one or several hands, underwent centuries of repeated revisions by anonymous writers. To illustrate their theme, the writers of the Bible employed preachment and prediction, histories, geographical descriptions, universal biographical sketches and compressed genealogical tables. They adapted pagan myths; many of the best known Biblical stories — the Creation, the Flood, Joseph and his brothers — have earlier Sumerian, Assyrian, Babylonian, Ugaritic, and Egyptian counterparts."

*   *   *

Nothing written or quoted in this book should be construed in any way as reflection or criticism of any religious belief, faith or practice. In its finality the essence of religious faith is a dedicated belief in a very personal religious ideal — and in a Supreme Universal Force. Into religious conception, doctrine and dogma writers of scripture have often intertwined threads of history that have been more confusing than helpful as time and scholarly enlightenment have opened new thresholds of understanding.

It is certain aspects of scriptural history — and not theology — that we are examining here in relation to the Biblical land-covenants and their misplaced application in Palestine today.

Facsimile page of the First of the Book of Psalms from the Gutenberg Bible.

6. DOES POLITICAL ZIONISM HAVE SOCIALISTIC ROOTS?

It is fascinatingly amazing how little the average non-Jewish citizen knows about the movement called Zionism — particularly when it has played so large a role in United States politics and Government actions. One purpose of this book is to examine some of the facets of the movement's history about which people seem to know so little.

Most of the books available in dealing with Zionism appear to have been written by authors who, for understandable reasons, have overlooked some aspects of the subject that are needed for a full projection. One of these is the background consanguinity of Russian socialism and Russian Zionism. Strangely, the "nationalist" strain in Zionism did not seem to bother the socialist ideologists too much. Nationalism and Socialism are not theoretically compatible — but in the case of political Zionism, it did not seem to matter.

Historians seem to be in general agreement that Moses Hess laid down the first recognized call for political Zionism in his book "Rome and Jerusalem," published in 1862. Hess is otherwise referred to in this volume, but here certain documentation will be given to show the early grafting of socialist and Zionist roots.

In a "foreword page" of the Hess book, Rabbi Maurice J. Bloom says that "Moses Hess was an early apostle of European Socialism and a friend and collaborator of Karl Marx." He explains that they afterwards went their separate ways because Hess wanted to mingle his socialism with a bit of spiritual Zionism. Socialism has always had its differing branches.

The New Jewish Encyclopedia says Hess "shared the views of Marx and Engels." The Standard Jewish Encyclopedia says of Hess — "He joined other left-wing Hegelians in founding the Rheinische Zeitung of which Karl Marx became editor." The same Encyclopedia describes the Moses Hess book, "Rome and Jerusalem," as "the first Zionist classic."

In a book titled "Zionism," Professor R. J. H. Gottheil, then professor of Semitic Languages at Columbia University, described Moses Hess as "a propagator of Proudhon's anarchistic ideas" (p. 36). He also states — "it is interesting to note that Moses Hess, a staunch worker in the Socialist cause, was a prophet of modern Zionism" (p. 168). Proudhon, incidentally, was a well known French Socialist of the 1840 period, who wrote an essay titled "What Is Property? Theft." This treatise described his social philosophy.

TYPICAL REVOLUTIONIST CONFUSION

The denial of property virtues by Proudhon, says Arnold Whitridge in his illuminating documentary on the Revolutions of 1848,"was followed by an equally emphatic rejection of God." It was during this spate of rebellious activity throughout Europe that Marx tried to work with Proudhon but this became impossible because of their divergent opinionated personalities in the hard-core profession of "changing the world."

Incidentally, and with no particular relevance to our special subject, Proudhon, with all his revolutionary avidity, possessed a streak of particularized idealism which, in the same general way as with Hess, made it difficult to work closely with Karl Marx — the bitter revolutionist with undeviating goal. Proudhon wrote a book titled "The Philosophy of Poverty" which Marx answered with a treatise on "The Poverty of Philosophy." This reference to revolutionists is mainly a passing note on the social and political ferment during the period when political Zionism was taking root.

It perhaps should be explained that the book by Moses Hess ("Rome and Jerusalem") is a compilation of twelve letters he had written to a "disturbed" friend and had published in booklet form in 1862. In his third letter, Hess

94

wrote: "The Jewish notion of immortality is inseparable from the national belief in the Messiah." He quoted several of the early rabbis to make his point — with Rabbi Jochanan (Johanan) saying: "All prophets speak of the Messianic Kingdom." He also refers to the law of solidarity — "All Israelites are responsible for one another."

Hess further expounds his interesting thesis by saying — "The Jewish religion is primarily Jewish patriotism." He thus brings up to the nineteenth century the Israelitish thinking of some three thousand years before. He gives an interesting analysis in his sixth letter. "Jewish life," he says, "never was in any way spiritualistic." Neither, he contends, were the early Christians. "When this sect finally did become spiritualistic in Christianity, it disappeared from Judaism altogether."

In the Diaries of Theodor Herzl, there is reference to Moses Hess as — "adventurer in the world of ideas, who became in turn Spinozist, Hegelian, anarchist, communist (he worked at Marx's side for three years) — and socialist . . . He ended up . . . as one of the first exponents of political Zionism." Hess was the first generally recognized intellectual designer of the present Zionist movement — and the record is quite clear as to his socialist-involvement.

*　　*　　*

HERZL AND THE JEWISH STATE

The next of the early important Zionist prescriptions was the book by Theodor Herzl, called "Der Judenstaat" or "The Jewish State." Herzl is called the father of Zionism, not only because he wrote this Zionist "bible," but also because he called the first meeting to organize modern Zionism and labored diligently for seven years (until his death) to promote the organization and its goals. His work is described in Chapter III.

Here it is necessary only to mention the book as an ideological foundation-stone of the Zionist movement, with its grand over-all obsession concerning "anti-Semitism" and his belief in "a Jewish State" as the Jewish solution. "The Jewish question," he writes, "exists wherever Jews live in perceptible numbers. Where it did not exist, it is carried by Jews in the course of their migration . . . unfortunate Jews are now carrying the seeds of anti-Semitism into England; they have already introduced it into America."

Herzl here pictures either a dreadful condition or manifests a psychotic hallucination. He poses a status of affairs which agitated and inspired his thinking from the days of the famous French Dreyfus case. His solution was the exclusiveness of Jewish isolationism in a national sense, rather than a full adjustment to a world that has vastly changed since the days of the storied Moses.

It is recorded that he was much impressed by reading Eugen Duhring's stirring book of the period — "The Jewish Problem As a Problem of Race, Morals and Culture," and other Semitic recoil literature that followed the Middle Ages and the French Revolution. It is an accepted axiom that a person can concentrate sufficiently on an issue until it becomes a part of his being. Into the roots of Zionism clearly went the fertilization of both European socialism and a haunting obsession with an enigma called "anti-Semitism."

Herzl's forte was painting word pictures with high emotional overtones. His mission was to light the fuse. His "Diaries," which have been published in a 500-page book, are loaded with impassioned pleadings and ad hominem arguments. "We are one people," he says, "our enemies have made us one in our own despite . . . Distress binds us together, and thus united, we suddenly discover our strength . . . Yes, we are strong enough to form a State. We have no flag, and we need one . . . The very impossibility of getting at the Jews nourishes by day and hour among the nations; indeed, it is bound to increase, because the cause of its growth continues to exist and cannot be removed." These are examples of Herzl's Zionistic thinking.

EASTERN EUROPEAN SOCIALISM AS A MOTIVATING FORCE

The early period of social ferment and unrest in the Russo-Polish area (the source of modern Zionism) which stemmed largely from the heavy concentration of Jews in that sector, has been well described by one who grew up in that environment. He is A. L. Patkin, who wrote a book titled "The Origin of the Russian-Jewish Labor Movement" (published in London and Melbourne). Patkin was born in Tetarck (about 1890) and his book, published in 1947, is a comprehensive coverage of the rise of Socialism and Zionism in Russia.

According to the book's jacket, the author was a member of the Underground Revolutionary Movement in Russia from his early youth. He engaged in propaganda among Jewish workers — was arrested many times and served time in a Polish prison. When Lenin's Communism became dominant in Russia (1917), splitting the Social-Democratic movement into two factions, viz. Bolsheviks (the Marxist-Leninist Communists) and the Mensheviks (the old Socialists), Patkin decided it was the better part of valor to get out of the country. He apparently found no difficulty in merging his socialist background into nationalistic Zionist activity. When he wrote his book he was editor of "The Zionist" — a publication of the Australian-New Zealand Zionist Federation.

In the book's introduction, Patkin describes the various forms of early Socialism resulting from clashes and splits of the socialist doctrinaires, such as the Kautsky-Bernstein controversy, the Marx-Lassalle separation, the Marx-Fabian split, the Stalin-Trotsky feud — and on ad infinitum. In analyzing the socialist movement, he explains that as soon as it (socialism) "descends from the theoretical plane to practicalities," it must adjust to the particular mores of the working class, because "it is they" who are the backbone of the socialist movement.

"Jewish Socialism," he says, "is a mass labor movement that was born in September of 1897 — and its theoretical foundation is the same as that of Russian Socialism which is the Marxian "Plekhanov-Kautski pattern." "Marxism is its shell but its kernel is Jewish Socialism;" says this well grounded authority. "Jewish Socialism," he says, "had two explosive elements — misery and intellectual doctrine."

THE INFLUENCE OF THE JEWISH BUND

The Jewish socialist movement in Lithuania, Poland and Russia was part and parcel of the "General Federation of

Jewish Workers" of these three countries — otherwise referred to in the Standard Jewish Encyclopedia as the Jewish Socialist Party. Patkin identifies the Jewish Bund as a creation of the early European Social-Democrat (socialist) movement. The Social-Democrats in Russia (as already mentioned) were split by Lenin into the Bolsheviks and the Mensheviks. The Bund (Jewish Socialist Party) was first a Social-Democrat movement, but was gradually drawn into the Bolshevik (Communist) Party structure. The Ukraine Bund joined the Russian Communists in 1919 (the year the Comintern was formed in Russia to organize Communist tentacles throughout the world). The Russian Bund joined the Bolsheviks in 1920 and the Polish Bund "joined up" in 1939 — the year that Hitler attacked Poland.

*　　*　　*

The January, 1963 issue of Commentary (the highly readable Journal of the American Jewish Committee) carried a review of a book called "The Soviet Revolution, 1917-1939," by Raphael R. Abramovich. This gentleman was born in Latvia in 1880 and, according to the review, "was a leader of the Bund — the organization of Social Democratic Jewish Marxists in Russia, who opposing both religion and Zionism, worked within the Socialist movement for autonomous nationality for the Jews." While there were personality differences, they were both working for the same common goal — nationalism and a Jewish State.

Abramovich's book on the Soviet Revolution is a first-rate, first-hand account of the villainy of dictatorship which was the inevitable culmination of movements and activities which, in the beginning, were helped by gullible people who had only freedom and better life in mind — but were unable to perceive the destiny of political action that seeks to benefit self by taking forcibly from others. Abramovich was caught up in the toils of these forces — and sentenced to death. To friends he owes his escape from this sentence and his opportunity to review the horrors of one of the twentieth century's great tragedies.

It is generally accepted that mass immigration into Palestine was the beginning of the trouble that has racked that country for the last thirty years — but there are authorities who point out that in addition to immigrant numbers, there is also the factor of source-influence. Most of these immigrants were from the Russo-Polish area which for 200 years or more had been a cauldron of social ferment.

The content of this chapter gives some indication of the agitational culture that must have been part of the emotional luggage some of these immigrants carried with them out of the way of life from which they had come. The glorified theory of the "melting pot" has not worked too well anywhere — and it didn't work in Palestine. Now that the immigrants have it all their own way in Palestine, it does not appear that the mixing of the East-European "isms" in the Knesset is producing the Utopia that has been so beautifully advertised as the solution of the "Jewish problem."

7. CONTROVERSY OVER PHRASE— "THE JEWISH PEOPLE" DOES IT SIGNIFY "RELIGION" OR "NATIONALITY?"

Many Americans, some say too many, think of Zionism as some unimportant, ephemeral, far-removed, ideological affair which involves only the Jewish people — and only a segment of them at that. Consequently they are disposed to dismiss the "far away" subject as much ado about nothing, so far as they are concerned.

There are, on the other hand, some thoughtful Americans who do not regard Zionism as unimportant, ephemeral and far-removed — and among them are a number of substantial American Jews. It is naturally true that in this general grouping there are variations of motivation, but there is enough common cause to give each and all of them a genuine sense of apprehension as to present and future consequences.

NATURE OF DISPUTE

The central theme of the dispute between Zionist and anti-Zionist Jews concerns the use and meaning of the term "the Jewish people." The Zionists have boldly and unconditionally taken possession of this particular phrase as a kind of ancient birthright, giving them (the Zionists) the covenanted authority to speak and act in the name of all Jews. There are still in the world some responsible anti-Zionist Jews who object vigorously to this arrogation of Jewish leadership.

There are those who believe that the historic individuality of the Jew does not destine him to be herded into either a nomenclature or a nationalistic corral. Those who regard themselves as a "religious grouping" rather than "a nation," if we understand their position, object to political Zionism not only because it is casting a sinister shadow over the freedom of spiritual life but also because, taking history as a guide, they fear political-nationalism as a grave threat to the future of the Jewish people's image among the other peoples of the world.

Some already see portentous evidence of this danger. The political stride of Zionism (as a movement of power) has a measurement of approximately thirty years. Those years have been filled with the. kind of turmoil that inevitably creates bitterness of feeling among men —dislike and suspicion that belies the spirit of brotherhood which presumably is the very heart of religion. There are responsible Jews with deep Judaic roots, like Mr. Moshe Menuhin of Los Gatos, California, who has given vehement expression in his book "The Decadence of Judaism in Our Time" to his fear of what lies at the end of the road that Zionism is traveling. A quotation from Mr. Menuhin's book appears in Chapter III.

Mr. Menuhin has told of the difficulties he has experienced in selling this book. In a ten-page magazine article (later published separately as a tract), he goes into great detail to explain the agonies and travail of those who seek to dissent from the present rushing current of the Zionist movement.

"I knew," he writes, "that the Zionist machine was devious, omnipresent and seemingly omnipotent. But I still was not prepared for what did happen: in a very short space of time after the publication of my book, a nationwide assault — invisible, underground and highly organized — stopped my book in its tracks, stifled every move I made and left me isolated, crushed, and my character assassinated in the American Jewish sphere." (Mr. Menuhin's publishing venture was badly hurt but not destroyed. The efforts to suppress and defame that hurt also helped him. The sale of the book increased as the efforts to detract and suppress became known.)

There are those with rationalism stronger than emotionalism who fear that the characteristic of suppression — the reckless dogma of rule or ruin — can easily become a Frankenstein to destroy the spiritual traditions of Jewish life that make it compatible with other religions. The marriage of religion with political nationalism, it is feared, may produce succeeding generations where the lust of political conquest will completely overshadow interest in religion.

NOTE: It may be mentioned here that the agencies of suppression described by Mr. Menuhin are not just the concern of anti-Zionist Jews. Every day a wider consciousness is growing among non-Jews that there is an invisible gestapo operating to make record of their opinions and retaliate with defamation and suppression through a so-called "anti-defamation" apparatus that is rapidly becoming one of the greatest threats in the United States to the future compatibility of Jews and non-Jews. This is because, as this apparatus extends its activities of invisible control over the thoughts and actions of everyone, the wider becomes the understanding of this menace. Millions of dollars are collected and used to create a national fear-complex by using tactics of suppression and retaliation against those who dare dissent from forces that have suddenly found new wings of power. The misnamed "anti-defamation" apparatus that has grown up contemporaneously with Communism and Zionism (and operates also in an underground way) is a dangerous, double-edged sword. Unfortunately, its big-money sponsors have no communication-contact with the unfavorable volcanic consensus the spy technique is generating. What is the value of temporary suppression, some people are asking, if it is only building angry pressure for later explosion?

An unfortunate by-product of this now widely understood muzzling control (so evident in the United States during the 1967 Israel-Arab six-day war) is that many are disposed to equate the Zionist-complex with Jewry in general. If this was not the studied intention of the Zionist activity-mechanism, the results were most convincing to the widespread public. This is just another problem that anti-Zionists face in a world of confusing directions.

Another wide-spread misconception among many people is that the Zionism in action today is a religious movement that not only derives from the Old Testament, but is more or less the equivalent of the Judaism of the temple and synagogue. The early high priests of organized Zionism (Moses Hess, in his "Rome and Jerusalem," and Theodor Herzl, in his "The Jewish State") by implication and references to ancient Jewish religion, laid a foundation of tradition which has clung to Zionism's image, even though political Zionism has long since shed the wings of angels.

WILL RELIGION MIX WITH POLITICS?

Anti-Zionist Jews contend that present day Zionism is a political movement in a most flagrant form — nationalism.

They charge that this nationalism is a graftage that has been promoted mainly in the name of "the Jewish people," some of whom, at least, do not approve and do not wish to be excommunicated by the professional Zionists from their belief that "the Jewish people" has the meaning only of a religious and social congregation. They do not believe that nationalism and religion can be mixed any more successfully than can oil and water.

Some of them have taken a close look at history and have found that such efforts at mixing have been tried over and over, and that all such experiments can now be catalogued in the ruins of empires. We sense that they do not believe that anything in the nature of permanent nationalism can be established at the cost of generating the mistrust and hatred of vast numbers surrounding them, as well as numerous others scattered throughout the world. These fears they entertain especially in the interest of their religion.

In America, the one anti-Zionist Jewish organization (The American Council for Judaism) has, for the last twenty years or more, been locking horns with the Zionist apparatus. The central issue has been the Zionists' political doctrine of "nationalism." The issue became militantly devisive when the Zionists boldly mandated themselves as the avant-garde and the voice of "the Jewish people." When the Zionists revealed through high official spokesmen, that the movement had an inherent propensity to issue guide-lines and make decisions involving the Diaspora (Jews outside Israel), indicating these Jews, in all countries, were regarded more or less as subject people, this, to some Jews, was regarded as objectionable and perilous.

As early as 1918 there were some anti-Zionist Jews in America trying to organize opposition to the Zionist plans (as they were beginning to show their political purposes) but the attempts at organization were delayed and essentially stifled by cautious Jewish leaders whom Rabbi Elmer Berger, of the now active anti-Zionist American Council for Judaism, described in a 1958 Review release as "non Zionists" or neutralists. Dr. Berger named two periods of "crisis" when opposition could have been effective. One was the time of the Balfour coup (1917-1918) and the other was in 1925-1929 when the Zionists were in deep financial trouble. Both opportunities were lost because of the "wait-see" attitude of kindly and cautious non-Zionist neutralist leaders.

WEIZMANN—MASTER IN FINESSE

Dr. Chaim Weizmann, the astute strategist and leader of Zionism, knew well how to deal with neutralists, as indicated in the following quotation from his autobiography, "Trial and Error":

> "Then, as later, those wealthy Jews who could not wholly divorce themselves from a feeling of responsibility towards their people, but at the same time could not identify themselves from the hopes of the masses, were prepared to dispense a sort of left-handed generosity, on condition that their right hand did not know what their left hand was doing. To them the university-to-be in Jerusalem was philanthropy, which did not compromise them; to us it was nationalist renaissance. They would give — with disclaimers; we would accept — with reservations."

During the first World War, in the favorable climate produced by that conflict, the Zionist political machine gradually developed powerful prestige momentum and sweeping influence, by combining political astuteness and emotional fervor into a quite compelling activist combination — all of which is well described in other chapters of this book. During this time, there were substantial Jewish leaders like Sir Edwin Montagu in England and Henry Morgenthau, Sr. in the United States, who expressed vigorous passive resistance to the developing Zionist plans; but this inactive opposition did not interfere with the hard-hitting work of the Weizmann Zionists in fastening their designs on a nationalistic right-of-way into Palestine, with the help of easily swayed statesmen in both England and the United States.

The advent of the Zionist movement, with its "nationhood" purpose, was in essence a revival of the old troublesome question of "race." For centuries the word Jew was widely understood to signify race. In public libraries today, we find many books written by both Jews and Gentiles who have quite casually and regularly made references to the Jewish "race." In fact, this seems to have been quite a common practice until some thirty or forty years ago. A change gradually developed in the use of this designation as immigrant Jews began to shed their old-country stereotypeness and assimilate into the social milieu and national consciousness of their adopted country (referring here to the United States) and to accept its unique obligations and responsibilities.

Then, as the somewhat bothersome question of "race" began to fade, there burst upon the world with explosive effect a new sort of Messianic force among the Jewish people, called Zionism. Its battle cry was Palestine — its underlying objective was "nationhood," which in essence reintroduced the old "racial" issue by the innovation of a new twist in the use of words. The new angle was a semantic dodge to avoid the category of "race" while, at the same time, engendering a racial consciousness of cohesion by putting all Jews into one ethnic package called "the Jewish people." The rallying call of "Zionism" sounded a mythical symphony of Old Testament convenants; and the semi-secret goal was to imitate the ancient Hebrews who once, some three thousand years ago, maintained, for a limited time, an unstable nation called Israel.

NOTE: Even top historians find it difficult to recall or imagine any diplomatic coup that could equal or surpass the maneuvering dexterity and political cunning with which the clever Zionists brought their Palestine design from the drawing table to statehood maturity. The story can only be grasped by close study of every move and facet of the record.

First, the all-encompassing term "the Jewish people" was coined and used to influence all Jews toward a consciousness of being part of the new Zionist statehood movement. (2) The Zionists identified themselves with this "Jewish people" concept as a "juridically recognized political and ethnic entity" and put teeth in this claim (even though they were false teeth) by pressuring the British government into the Balfour Declaration commitment. Into this commitment, the Zionists engineered "the Jewish people" wording, and capitalized the accomplishment as "recognition" of their "legal status." (3) Later maneuvering succeeded in getting "recognition" of this verbiage-status from the newly organized League of Nations, by getting this self-same wording ("the Jewish people") included in the Palestine Mandate given to Great Britain. (4) The Brandeis influence in Washington, operated to encourage the Wilson government to sign a 1924 covenant, which, even though the United States did not ratify the League of Nations, was a preliminary act to be capitalized. (5) All of this manipulation is now a "dead letter," but it served well its advancing purpose up to the critical period of 1947-1948 when the United Nations replaced British authority in Palestine. The U.N. (with vigorous Zionist support) then ordered "partition" of Palestine with one section to become "a Jewish State," which was the final "legal" recognition for which the Zionists had been tirelessly working. (6)

From here on, the Zionists were by now strong enough (with the financial support coming from within the United States) to complete the design.

* * *

In relation to the Zionists' effort in seeking Jewish co-identity, Dr. Max F. Baer, national director of B'nai B'rith Youth Organization (Washington, D.C.), quoted in the Chicago (Jewish) Sentinel, July 20, 1967, said:

"The fortitude and achievements of the Israelis are doing more to give American Jewish youth a feeling of identity as Jews than all of the educational programs sponsored by synagog and other American Jewish organizations. Israel may have accomplished more than the American Jewish community is willing to do to prevent our young people from disappearing in the open American society."

Dr. Baer then went on to emphasize the obligation of American Jewish institutions to "capitalize on the pride of Jewishness which has swelled the hearts of young Jews because of the startling achievements of the Jewish state."

OPPOSITION FINALLY TAKES FORM

Zionism forged ahead with its design, making highly strategic progress, while essentially no effective or organized opposition was offered. Finally, in 1943, a number of substantial American Jews headed by Lessing J. Rosenwald, son of the late Julius Rosenwald, noted philanthropist and one time head of Sears, Roebuck and Company, formed the American Council for Judaism, with main offices in New York and regional offices in other cities.

This organization is cited here because it is the only organized force offering any opposition to the hard-riding Zionist movement, and therefore is an integral part of the story of Zionism. It is cited also because it has contributed substantially to a better public understanding of the Zionist movement, with two particular accomplishments included in this report.

One of these is its work that helped to bring about the U.S. Senate Foreign Relations Committee inquiry into the Zionist-Jewish money-collecting apparatus in the United States, which is described in chapter XXIII. The other especially important achievement of A.C.J. was to get from the United States government a clarification of the Govern-

106

ment's official position vis-a-vis Zionist Israel as "a Jewish State."

U.S. STATE DEPARTMENT DEFINES STATUS

"For nearly 21 years," writes Clarence J. Coleman, Jr., president of A.C.J., in one of its publications, "the American Council for Judaism has petitioned the U.S. Government to clarify — on behalf of Americans of Jewish faith — its position in respect to this fundamental, legal-political concept of 'the Jewish people'."

Finally, on April 20, 1964, Phillips Talbot, Assistant Secretary of the U.S. Department of State, addressed a letter to Rabbi Elmer Berger, Executive Vice President of the American Council for Judaism, in which he reviewed the A.C.J. appeal and otherwise stated:

"The Department of State recognizes the State of Israel as a sovereign State and citizenship of the State of Israel. It recognizes no other sovereignty or citizenship in connection therewith. It does not recognize a legal-political relationship based upon the religious identification of American citizens. It does not in any way discriminate among American citizens upon the basis of their religion. Accordingly, it should be clear that the Department of State does not regard the 'Jewish people' concept as a concept of international law."

It is notable that this statement very carefully avoids any reference to possible commitments to the State of Israel as a sovereign entity. As the June, 1967 flare-up began to threaten war between Israel and the Arab states, many Americans were surprised and alarmed to learn of the several so-called protection commitments allegedly made to Israel by spokesmen for the United States. They are too numerous to list here, but such startling possibilities can be a nightmare to the common citizen when he contemplates the unknown perils to his nation that are possible in the smoke-filled rooms of secret diplomacy.

Considering for a further moment the statement by Assistant Secretary of State Talbot, it is interesting to note Israel's reaction to it. On May 10, 1964, the Jerusalem Post (regarded as the paper voicing Israeli government opinion) declared that the Talbot letter was "perfectly proper from the U.S. standpoint," but added:

"It does not diminish the fact that the U.S. Government recognized the existence of the Jewish people at the time when the League of Nations Mandate for the creation of the Jewish National Home in this country was given to Britain, and that its present recognition of Israel as a sovereign State, and of Israel citizenship, which derives its legal basis in part from the Balfour Declaration, is ultimately also based on the recognition of the existence of the Jewish people as a national unit."

VOICE OF ISRAEL

Ben Gurion, who followed in the steps of Chaim Weizmann as builder of the new Israel, was quoted in the Jerusalem Post (July 19, 1957) as saying: "I am a Jew first, and an Israeli only afterwards, for in my conviction the State of Israel was created for and on behalf of the whole Jewish people, though from now on the future of the Jewish people depends upon the survival, growth and consolidation of the State . . . It is only in Israel that Jews are free as men and as Jews. Only in Israel does the Jew achieve spiritual integrity; only here can he be a Jew and a man naturally without barriers or cleavages."

In 1961, Ben Gurion, the stormy petrel, stirred a furor among world Jewry when he made a speech before 500 delegates attending the 25th World Zionist Congress in Jerusalem (Israel) when he (according to the National Jewish Post and Opinion — January 6, 1961) "labeled all Jews who ignore the call to migrate to Israel" godless and appealed to them to send 100,000 youths to study in Israel.

* * *

For the record it may be well to explain the modus operandi by which the American Council for Judaism is classified as an anti-Zionist organization. Its main principals of purpose are listed as:

(1) to sustain recognition of Judaism as a religious faith only and that its institutions should in no way have political inference or attachment; (2) that the members of A.C.J. reject the Zionist concept that all Jews must inherently and automatically have political relationship with the nationalism of the foreign State of Israel; (3) that they (members of A.C.J.) strive to offset all efforts to establish Jews in the United States as a segregated, identifiable Israel-oriented political collectivity, separate and apart from their fellow Americans of other faiths; (4) that they are committed to the basis and demonstrable fact that no Jew, no group of Jews and no Jewish organization can speak for or represent all Jews.

It is difficult to understand why a program of this kind

should be objectionable to any American of any religious affiliation, yet the record shows that the Council, for sponsoring this program, has been repeatedly attacked by various Jewish publications as well as by Zionist and pro-Zionist individuals and organizations.

NOTE: What has been said here about the American Council for Judaism is strictly in the nature of reporting — and without the knowledge of the Council. This book is written with honest intentions — and with no favors asked or granted from any source.

AMERICAN CITIZENSHIP—A PRIVILEGE

It was to the United States that millions of Jews have come, seeking haven and opportunity. They surely did not come to remold our "American way" which lured them here — or to live as a separate ethnic community with divided loyalties. They came, and were received, in the spirit of purpose, which it was believed they had in coming. It was believed they came to assimilate into American society and culture and be accepted as citizens dedicated to the ideals for which America is widely known.

They came to become American citizens, it is hoped, in the fullest sense of devotion and loyalty — or otherwise why would they have come? Surely they did not and do not come to be badgered into playing a role of dual-loyalty where they would be responsible to the ideologies and whims of a foreign nation — especially one that cannot even support itself independently.

The great majority of American citizens are so deeply rooted in their country's traditions that they have no desire to make a fetish of the fact that some former forebear was an immigrant. Most citizens are glad that they are in the United States — and very few are leaving to adopt any other country. Most of them are proud to call themselves just plain American citizens and let it go at that — for in no other country do the citizens, as a whole, enjoy such prosperity and opportunities as they do in their own land — and they know it!

"Breathes there the man with soul so dead who never to himself hath said" I am glad I can call America my own.

8. WORLD WAR I OPENS GATEWAY FOR ZIONISM. AMAZING MALCOLM STORY OF SCHEME TO GET UNITED STATES INTO THAT WAR.

One of the most revealing documents reflecting light upon the plan that largely produced the Balfour Declaration and helped get the United States into World War I rests quietly in the well guarded files of that great reliquary of historical records and exhibits known throughout the world as the British Museum.

The title of that document is "Origin of the Balfour Declaration — Dr. Weizmann's Contribution" and the author is the late Mr. James A. Malcolm who has been described by the late Mr. Wickham Steed, editor of the London Times, as "a prominent British-Armenian whose family had been British for several generations — a Balliol (Oxford) man who was a Government official with topmost contacts." Mr. Malcolm, several years after the war, prepared this typewritten account and filed it in the British Museum for posterity. We were granted the privilege of copying it in the Museum's copying room. The document explains why and how Malcolm had become interested in the Zionist cause and how it fell to his lot to start the negotiations that culminated in the Balfour Declaration — and incidentally in making the right contact with American Zionists to bring the United States into the picture.

In referring to his own background, he explains how his family of Armenian stock had settled in Persia long before Elizabethan days — and for at least two centuries had been engaged in shipping and in commerce generally. This meant that they had long been identified with British interests in Persia and areas of the Persian Gulf and Indian Ocean. Their family agents in Baghdad had been the important David Sassoon who had originally hailed from Sasoun in Armenia and the Sassoons had once sought refuge in the Malcolm home from the hostile Pasha of Baghdad. "For many decades the Jews in Southern Persia always looked to our family for protection. We also sometimes acted as agents for Sir Moses Montefiore, who sent us money for distribution amongst the indigent members of the Jewish community. This was done by our cashiers who were all Jews and who had full charge of all the cash resources of our firm."

Later, as a boy, when he was sent to England for his education, Malcolm was placed under the guardianship of Sir Albert (Abdalla) Sassoon in London and this brought him into contact with many Jewish friends. Through these he heard about the projected Jewish settlements — then mentioned as probably in Palestine, El Arish, Argentina or Kenya. "Of course," he writes, "I had read Byron, George Eliot and Oliphant about the Jews." His father, Malcolm explains, had told him that Jews, wherever they were, never failed at Passover to drink to "next year in the land of Israel."

At some length Mr. Malcolm relates his many official contacts and appointments which are of no special interest here other than to distinguish him as a man of wide acquaintanceship and high official standing — a man of genuine importance in British circles. Prior to World War I he had become acquainted with some of the most active political Zionists and seemed to understand well the potential force of that movement which held considerable of his sympathy.

Among his high British official friends was Sir Mark Sykes who, at the time in question, was Assistant-Secretary to the British War Office — and who also was a wide-range liaison man among numerous high British officials who had important obligations in the war effort. For some time Sir Mark had been trying to make contact with an influential consensus of German-American opinion in the United States to determine its vulnerability and potential usefulness in

111

bringing America into the war on the side of Britain against Germany.

"During one of my visits to the War Cabinet Office in Whitehall Gardens," writes Mr. Malcolm, "in the late autumn of 1916, I found Sir Mark Sykes less buoyant than usual. As I had known his family of old and our relations were unrestrained, I enquired what was troubling him. He spoke of military deadlock in France, the growing menace of submarine warfare, the unsatisfactory situation which was developing in Russia and the general bleak outlook."

BRITISH EAGER FOR AMERICAN INTERVENTION

Malcolm, in his written report, tells how the British Cabinet was anxiously seeking and hoping for United States intervention. He asked Sir Mark what progress on this was being made and the reply was "Precious little." Sir Mark told him that he had thought of enlisting the substantial Jewish influence in the United States but had been unable to do so since reports revealed "a very pro-German tendency among the wealthy American Jewish bankers and bond issuing houses (nearly all of German origin) and among Jewish journalists who took their cue from them."

Sir Mark told him that two missions which had been sent to the United States from France and Italy had both failed to make any headway and he was quite puzzled and disappointed. It seemed that the Jewish indifference was largely caused by their bitterness toward Czarist Russia. Malcolm states that he asked Sir Mark what efforts had been made to win over the Jews in America and he answered that the main argument had been that the Allies would eventually win and it would be better to be with the winning side.

"You are going the wrong way about it," Malcolm told him. "The well-to-do English Jews you meet and the Jewish clergy are not the real leaders of the Jewish people. You have overlooked what the call of nationality means. Do you know of the Zionist Movement?" Sir Mark admitted ignorance and Malcolm says he explained its nature and possibilities to him and emphasized his argument by adding — "You

112

can win the sympathy of the Jews everywhere, in one way only, and that way is by offering to try to secure Palestine for them.

"Sir Mark was taken aback and confessed that what I had told him was something quite new and impressive. He would talk to me again about it." A few days later the subject came up again and Sir Mark said it was most intriguing but that there were stumbling blocks which he did not explain; but Malcolm says he learned later about the existing Sykes-Picot treaty with France and Russia. This, incidentally, was a secret agreement that had previously been executed by Sir Mark Sykes and M. Picot of France whereby Turkish territories in the Middle East were, after the war, to be divided into three zones of influence — British, French and Russian. Palestine was to be divided between France and Britain. The Jews had not been mentioned at all and clearly were not intended to be beneficiaries in any way. More particularly the treaty was being kept secret from the more involved Arabs.

Not knowing about this treaty at the time, Malcolm suggested to Sir Mark that he discuss his proposal to build up a promise of Jewish nationalism in order to get their cooperation in influencing America into the war. Sir Mark promised to talk it over with Lord Milner, an influential member of the War Cabinet. Later he reported to Malcolm that he had discussed the matter with Lord Milner and that he in turn was greatly interested in the idea — but did not see how it would be possible to promise Palestine to the Jews.

Malcolm then pointed out what seemed to him the only way to achieve the desired result and in doing so explained that "one of President Wilson's most intimate friends, for whose humanitarian views he had the greatest respect, was Justice Brandeis, of the Supreme Court, who was a convinced Zionist."

ZIONIST ANGLE AROUSES INTEREST

Sir Mark was extremely interested in this new aspect presented to him by Malcolm and promised to check into it further. Later he told Malcolm that he could see no possibility of the Cabinet adopting it. When asked why not, Sir Mark explained that Britain could not act without the consent of her allies and he was sure they would not go along with the proposal. (In the background as hindrance, of course, was the secret Sykes-Picot treaty.)

Malcolm writes — "I then suggested that if the object was to secure United States help, surely the Allies would agree if he could obtain from the War Cabinet an assurance that help would be given toward securing Palestine for the Jews. It was certain that Jews in all neutral countries, especially the United States, would become pro-British and pro-Ally." Sir Mark then promised to put the question to Lord Milner again and in about a week Sir Mark reported back to Malcolm that Milner had talked with his colleagues again and the idea pleased them. They suggested that, without committing themselves, Malcolm open negotiations with the Zionist leaders. Malcolm protested that he could not go to these leaders empty handed but would be willing to do so if he could be sufficiently sure of the Cabinet's intentions to be able to say to the Zionists — "If you help the Allies, you will have the support of the British in securing Palestine for the Jews.

"This appealed to Sir Mark as eminently reasonable but he saw difficulties. France would have to be persuaded to support the idea of Palestine for the Jews. Then there was the Vatican (Sir Mark himself was a Catholic) which would oppose my scheme which meant placing the Christian Holy Places under Jewish control. I replied that these difficulties must be overcome if the Allies wanted the help of the United States."

Sir Mark then raised the question of how some Jews were apathetic as to Palestine and others were actually opposed to it. To this objection Malcolm replied: "That is because you have not met the other kind of Jews, who are remarkable types and intensely interested in the idea of Zion. There are tens of thousands, perhaps hundreds of thousands, of such Jews. The wealthy Jewish bankers of London are completely out of touch with them." Sir Mark agreed to put this suggestion to the Cabinet and "a day or two later" he reported back that the Cabinet had agreed to his suggestion and "authorized me to open negotiations with the Zionists."

"Remembering my conversations with L. J. Greenberg, Editor of the 'Jewish Chronicle,' I wrote him at once. I told him that from information in my possession I was sure the time had arrived when Jewry should cease 'sitting on the fence' and come down definitely to the side of the Allies and use all their influence especially in the U.S.A. to secure an Allied victory. The Jews wanted Palestine and now was the chance to get it. Such an opportunity would hardly recur and it was the duty of every Zionist to act quickly. I concluded by asking him if he could enable me to meet the leaders of the Zionist Movement. Greenberg replied in an enthusiastic letter, inviting me for a discussion."

ZIONISTS SEE BIG FUTURE OPENING

After Malcolm told Greenberg of the situation and the favorable prospects, Greenberg offered to arrange a meeting for him (Malcolm) with Dr. Weizmann. The meeting was arranged at Weizmann's home in Addison Road. At this meeting present with Weizmann were his closest associate, Nahum Sokolow, and a few other Zionist leaders. Weizmann, a chemist, was at the time working in London on explosives for the Admiralty. Weizmann was keenly interested and asked when he could meet Sir Mark Sykes. Malcolm called Sykes from Weizmann's home and an appointment was arranged for the very next day — Sunday.

For some reason Weizmann was unable to attend that first meeting but Sokolow, Greenberg and other Zionists were present and after this and other meetings the Zionists were satisfied that the British promise was reliable. "The first step," writes Mr. Malcolm, "was to inform Zionist leaders in all parts of the world of the compact and Sir Mark said they would be given immediate facilities for cables to be sent through the Foreign Office and War Office, through the British Embassies and Consulates. A special detailed message was at once sent to Justice Brandeis in cipher through the Foreign Office. Further talks were held in various Government departments, at which Dr. Weizmann was present. All of these conversations took place with the knowledge and approval of Sir Maurice (now Lord) Hankey, Secretary of the Cabinet."

Out of these talks, Malcolm explains, there came a general understanding which he called a "Gentlemen's Agreement" to the effect that "the Zionists should work for active Jewish sympathy and support for the Allied cause, especially in the United States, so as to bring about a radical pro-Allied tendency in that country and that the British Cabinet would help the Jews to gain Palestine for this. The negotiations were now carried on in Sir Mark's room at the Foreign Office to which the matter was referred to the War Cabinet for action."

A new movement had entered the war. Jews everywhere were pressured with emotional propaganda based upon the implied promise they were to get Palestine. Malcolm relates one case of a group of Jews in Persia who were at the point of embracing Islam (Moslem faith) and quickly changed their minds because of this promise. The Zionist Movement was being stimulated and organized in all Jewish quarters.

Britain, confronted with the exigencies of war, was now playing with two hot potatoes — conflicting promises to the Arabs on one hand and to the Zionists on the other. Sir Mark, worried about this, asked Malcolm to give the Arabs a hint of the new Zionist strategy. Accordingly he had an interview with General Haddad Pasha, the London representative of the then Arab leader Sherif Hussein. Other high Arab officers were also present. They were not pleased with the inkling Malcolm gave them. "They did not want Jews to go to Palestine, which was an Arab land," comments Malcolm. They did not, of course, realize that this was to mean a mass immigration with a final take-over, and gradually accepted with sòme reluctance the picture Malcolm painted of the importance of having United States' participation.

FRENCH JEWS WERE ANTI-ZIONIST THEN

During the period of developing this new phase of the war, much back-room conference work was necessary to conciliate and break down resistance. The bothersome Sykes-Picot treaty still hung over the "Palestine promise" to the Zionists. Under this treaty Britain and France were to divide Palestine. "All the leading Jews in France," writes Malcolm, "were anti-Zionists and scoffed at the idea that any appreciable number of Jews would ever want to go and settle in Palestine. Picot was told by them that Zionism was only an idealistic obsession of a few Eastern European Jewish fanatical nationalists who themselves would never go to Palestine." Malcolm explains that it took a great deal of cogent argument which he "happened to have" to get any cooperation from the French Jews. Malcolm went to Paris and had conferences in an attempt to mollify and convince the leaders — but there were strong anti-Zionist French Jews like Professor Sylvain Levi who made the French situation difficult.

In December of 1916, Prime Minister Herbert Asquith, who had not been favorable to the Zionist deal, resigned and Lloyd George became Premier. "This change was beneficial to the Zionist cause inasmuch as Asquith had been definitely unsympathetic whereas Lloyd George . . . was naturally predisposed to understand the Zionist Movement," writes Malcolm. "Sir Mark Sykes and I," he continues, "were greatly helped in gaining his support by Philip Kerr (later Lord Lothian), who was Lloyd George's Secretary and whose guidance in such matters he generally followed."

In the earlier days of the Zionist-Palestine plan there was a great deal of opposition from substantial Jewish citizens in England, but the main stumbling block in this early stage seemed to be the Jewish opposition in France where Malcolm had been using his best charm and argument — and without much effect. It was decided by the British Foreign Office, he recorded, that he should accompany the top Zionist official at that time (Nahum Sokolow) to Paris to insure his getting an audience with officials at the Quai d'Orsay. The conference was finally arranged in Paris but the important Jewish organization (Alliance Israelite) had caught wind of the brewing plan and tried unsuccessfully to prevent it.

117

From the Paris conference Sokolow went on to Rome with Malcolm, seeing that he took with him "the indispensable frock coat and silk hat." There he got assurance from the Pope that the Vatican and the Jews would be good neighbors in Palestine. Sykes and Malcolm made elaborate arrangements for other important prestige meetings in the process of lining up this deal which promised to Jewry (especially the Jews in the United States) that if they helped to bring America in and created a sufficient world pressure group they could have Palestine. "All of these steps were taken," writes Malcolm, "with the full knowledge and approval of (U.S.) Justice Brandeis, between whom and Dr. Weizmann there was an active interchange of cables."

STRATEGY WORKS—AMERICA ENTERS

"The work was making satisfactory progress in the spring of 1917" — the United States at that time entered the war. Sir Mark, says Malcolm, was very confident that the Government's promise to the Zionists would be publicly confirmed at an early date. This, however, did not happen. During 1917 there were serious setbacks for the Allies in the war and there were other problems. One of these, Malcolm learned, was that a member of the British Cabinet "was working with all his might to prevent the promise being (officially) given" — and that man was an important Jew in British affairs — Edwin Montagu, Secretary for India and the son of Lord Swaythling (the banker). Further opposition was coming from the Jews of France where "nearly all the leading Jews, with the exception of Baron Edmond de Rothschild, were bitterly opposed to the pro-Zionist declaration of M. Pichon." One reason for this was that the French Jews — largely prominent and well assimilated — feared that a Jewish "homeland" in Palestine would affect their political status in France.

More opposition came in the action of a group of substantial Jews in England headed by Claude Montefiore (President of the Anglo-Jewish Association) and David Alexander, K.C. (President of the Board of Deputies) who, "acting through" Lucien Wolf of the Conjoint Foreign Committee, published a long statement in the London Times "protesting against the reported intention of the Government to adopt a pro-Zionist policy in regard to Palestine."

This was quickly answered by the Chief Rabbi of the British Empire, Dr. Hertz, and was followed with a pro-Zionist editorial written by Wickham Steed, editor of the Times, who, like Lloyd George and A. J. Balfour, had apparently become persuaded that the Zionist angle had power in America. The Zionists obviously had found the "golden key." The fight between the two factions over the Zionist question continued heatedly for some time with the pro-Zionists organizing to put pressure and persuasion on members of the Board of Deputies and other important British leaders.

The Palestine "announcement" by the British, which the Zionists had expected, was not readily forthcoming, causing much Zionist anxiety. The Government was deeply involved in other compelling matters — and greatly concerned by the rising opposition to Zionism's demands. The Zionists had not been idle — and had won over more British leaders through the belief of their apparent influence in America. The War Cabinet, before taking any action, decided to poll various leaders in an effort to get a summary of Jewish opinion to serve as justification — and perhaps vindication — for their contemplated act. Accordingly an enquiry was sent to eight interested and prominent Jews. They were — Leonard L. Cohen, Claude Montefiore, Sir Stuart Samuel (brother of Lord Samuel), Sir Philip Magnus, Lord Rothschild, N. Sokolow, Dr. Weizmann and the chief Rabbi, Dr. Hertz. Three of these (Cohen, Montefiore and Magnus) "replied strongly opposing the proposed statement." Sir Stuart Samuel was neither strongly hostile nor enthusiastic. The most compelling and favorable answer came from the chief Rabbi whose ecclesiastical authority had weight with the War Cabinet. He assured the members that "the proposed declaration would be hailed with enthusiasm by the vast majority of the Jewish people in the British Empire." Apparently no effort was made to get sentiment of the non-Jewish population of the British people.

119

ZIONISTS PAID WITH
BALFOUR DECLARATION

This was the strange final rite or ceremony that preceded the birth of the fantastic Balfour Declaration — a document that within forty years was destined to be the major cause of Middle East discord, warfare and peoples' dislocation. It set this area up as a probable time-bomb for another world war. Ironically, it marked the beginning of the end for Britain in the Middle East.

"The original draft of the (Balfour) Declaration," says Mr. Malcolm, "was prepared by Dr. Weizmann and his friends in London in the summer of 1917 at the instance of Sir Mark Sykes, and read (after various amendments at the instance of the anti-Zionists) as follows:

"His Majesty's Government views with favor the establishment in Palestine of a National Home for the Jewish Race, and will use its best endeavors to facilitate the achievement of this object; it being clearly understood that nothing shall be done which may prejudice the civil and religious rights of the existing non-Jewish communities in Palestine, or the rights and political status enjoyed in any other country by such Jews who are fully contented with their existing nationality and citizenship."

This draft, explains Mr. Malcolm, "was cabled by Sir Ronald Graham to Brandeis in Washington for submission to President Wilson and to secure his concurrence. Baron Edmond de Rothschild also agreed to it and it was then submitted to the War Cabinet and to Mr. Balfour who would have to sign it as Foreign Secretary." So we see that the "Balfour Declaration" was not Balfour's declaration at all — except that it was submitted to him for signature. So goes the world.

Mr. Malcolm, in his filed report, explains that after the document was sent to Justice Brandeis and his Jewish colleagues in America, it underwent further amendments. The word "people," for instance, was substituted for the word "race" and the last sentence was changed to omit the "fully contented" phrasing.

As indicated in Chapter IX, a book called "The Great Betrayal" by Rabbi Stephen S. Wise and Jacob de Haas contains a paragraph which reads —

"The final draft of what became known as the Balfour Declaration was amended by the authors of this book. After consultation with Justice Brandeis it was submitted to Colonel House who transmitted this version to President Wilson upon whose agreement and express authority the final text was issued by the British War Cabinet."

ALL WAS NOT GOLD THAT GLITTERED

Consequently the Balfour Declaration, as finally signed and published with much acclaim, read as follows:

Foreign Office,
November 2nd, 1917.

Dear Lord Rothschild,

I have much pleasure in conveying to you, on behalf of His Majesty's Government, the following declaration of sympathy with Jewish Zionist aspirations which has been submitted to, and approved by, the Cabinet

'His Majesty's Government view with favour the establishment in Palestine of a national home for the Jewish people, and will use their best endeavours to facilitate the achievement of this object, it being clearly understood that nothing shall be done which may prejudice the civil and religious rights of existing non-Jewish communities in Palestine, or the rights and political status enjoyed by Jews in any other country"

I should be grateful if you would bring this declaration to the knowledge of the Zionist Federation.

The closing paragraph must appear somewhat ludicrous in view of the fact that the top Jewish-Zionist leaders knew all about this — in fact had been at work for a long time trying to get it — and finally they actually wrote it.

*   *   *

It was toward the end of October, 1917, that Sir Mark Sykes reported to Mr. Malcolm that the War Cabinet, in view of military progress, was about to give consideration to the "Declaration" as to approval. The day that was to happen Sir Mark asked Malcolm to wait for him in the vestibule of the War Cabinet and arranged a code word to let him know the result. As Sykes came out of the conference he called to Malcolm "It's a boy," which indicated approval. "I knew then," writes Mr. Malcolm, "that at last, after many anxious weeks and months, my seed had borne fruit and that the Government had become an ally of Zionism." He adds that it was strictly correct for Professor Temperley, official historian of the Paris Peace Conference, to describe the Balfour Declaration as "a definite contract between Great Britain and Jewry." (The word "Jewry" is objectionable to some Jews when it is used by the Zionists as all-inclusive.)

The work of achieving the Balfour Declaration by the Zionists was described by Mr. Malcolm. "Our method of operation from the outset," says Malcolm, "had been the following. Once the Government had decided to adopt the pattern of pro-Zionist policy, it became necessary to pick up the various strands to be woven in to the pattern. Of these the most important was the work of enlightenment regarding Zionist aims, on which Dr. Weizmann had been concentrating since the outbreak of the War. Through the good offices of the late C. P. Scott, Editor of the "Manchester Guardian," and the late Professor Samuel Alexander of Manchester University, Dr. Weizmann had, over a period of years, interested in the movement Mr. Lloyd George, Mr. Balfour . . ." Here follows a list of several other important people.

"Books, pamphlets and articles were written and published by a small group of Dr. Weizmann's disciples and friends . . ." and here again Malcolm lists a number of names, among whom he mentions especially the late Herbert Sidebotham, military correspondent of the Manchester Guardian and The Times, and also a correspondent for the London Observer under the name of "Scrutator." Then there

122

was the weekly publication "Palestine," published by the "British Palestine Committee" established in Manchester at the suggestion of Dr. Weizmann. Mr. Malcolm gave further details of the extensive and feverish program of propaganda and activity by the Zionists and the pro-Zionists to accomplish what has been recorded in this chapter.

He closed his written account by saying — "When I look back on that strenuous struggle I feel happy indeed that a kind Providence gave me the opportunity to place all my personal and official connections freely and fully at the disposal of my Zionist friends. Thus I was able to be of some service to the Jewish people at a great historic moment. In so doing I knew I was acting in the best interest of Britain and for the good of the world.

"Although in a letter to me Dr. Weizmann has recognized my initiative in this work, I think it only fair to state that without his dynamic and persuasive personality, and without his quick and courageous decisions behind the scenes and the important secret and hazardous missions he successfully undertook, we might not have succeeded at all." Malcolm adds more to his eulogy of Weizmann whom he seemed to idolize as some sort of a Messiah.

There were millions of Americans who never knew of these machinations to get the United States and its resources into a war that gave birth to Bolshevik Communism — and set in motion world revolutionary activity that has steadily developed to produce a cascade of successive crises throughout all the world. The full significance of this particular chapter may be better understood when other chapters are read and weighed along with it — particularly the chapter that follows, which examines and documents the machinations which culminated in the Zionist coveted Balfour Declaration.

9. BALFOUR DECLARATION — OPENS THE FATEFUL GATE

The so-called Balfour Declaration was undoubtedly the most important cornerstone in the Zionist design to convert Palestine into a Jewish State. A book published in New York in 1918, titled "Great Britain, Palestine and the Jews," containing laudatory "Resolutions, Statements and Messages by Zionist Organizations," also carried a subhead referring to those pro-Zionist expressions of congratulations on the issuance of the Balfour Declaration as "Jewry's Celebration of Its National Charter." These celebrants also called it "The Charter of Zionism."

The Zionists, by the record, built their whole program of immigration-conquest upon getting some such "legal commitment" (to serve as an immigration visa) as was finally obtained in the form of the Balfour Declaration. It is so important as a unique historical landmark of international political finesse as to demand close inspection — not just to satisfy the interest of the present reader but especially to satisfy the call for historical truth to benefit scholars and statesmen of the future.

The Balfour Declaration did not represent any great emotive outpouring of British enthusiasm or benevolence for a cause. It was born out of the wedlock of scheme and pressure-struggle. By the tradition of British statesmen, it was hardly a document that even Balfour would have signed out of the fullness of his heart — but rather something considered as a commodity of exchange in a national need. It was the pay-off in a process of which he had lost control. Perhaps he may even have recalled the biting rejoinder of Disraeli who countered the great Gladstone with words to the effect that he

124

didn't object to his distinguished opponent playing cards from his sleeve, but he did protest the implication that God put them there.

The record and documentation dealing with the Balfour "covenant" as here presented comes from indisputable source records and from personal examination of the British government file on the document after its release from fifty years under wraps.

The document, as reproduced in the preceding chapter, was strangely issued in the form of a letter to an individual — a prominent member of the international Rothschild banking family, who had been won over as an ardent pro-Zionist. After the "declaration" had been conceived and tediously worked-over by the Zionist strategists and then put before the reluctant British government (something akin to a pill hard to swallow), there apparently was no official world-Jewry organization to whom it could be addressed. The Zionist generalissimo, Chaim Weizmann, suggested it be formalized to the wealthy Rothschild who, for some reason, had been honored with a Lordship. This routing doubtless had its strategic value.

A LOOK AT THE WORDING

Before examining the background of this strange and yet historical document, it may be educationally helpful to take a close look at its peculiar wording. (See copy in preceding Chapter 8.) First is the somewhat ambiguous viewing "with favor the establishment in Palestine of a national home for the Jewish people." This is what a former distinguished Englishmen, Charles Dickens, might have called an "artful dodger" promise. The term "a national home for the Jewish people" is clearly equivocal in that it did not give to the world, and especially to the Arabs, the meaning of such a "home" as the Zionists had in mind and which the British statesmen knew they had in mind.

Then there is that qualifying statement that "nothing shall be done which may prejudice the civil and religious rights of existing non-Jewish communities in Palestine," which, when equated with the later refugee-camp status of some million former Palestinian Arabs, would seem to repudiate and nullify the whole of the Balfour document. The pious "Declaration" is, of course, now at this date, purely academic as just so much political water over the dam. It has served its Zionist purpose and now reposes in the make-believe museum of historical diplomacy as more or less a discredited antiquity.

Also in relation to the phrase "a national home for the Jewish people," some pertinent questions arise. Outside of the meaning that the Zionists read into this (and successfully implemented), one may ask — what specific interpretation did Mr. Balfour and Lloyd George place upon it? Did they expect it to become a "national home" for the vast number of Jews who live in England and the United States who were putting up the great sums of money required to finance this giant Zionist movement? If so, was any consideration given to the danger that a "national home" in Palestine might eventually engender a dual loyalty for Jews in Britain, America and other lands? And what about the great number of Jews who at the time, were not in favor of Mr. Balfour and a minority group calling themselves Zionists, arrogating to themselves the authority to pick out a certain already populated land and anoint it as a "national home" for "the Jewish people"? Does this, as some people have declared, take on the character of fraudulency? Why, some people are still asking, were the euphonious words "a national home" used when it was well known by the Zionist authors and the Balfour-Lloyd George group that this was nothing more or less than a deceptive threshold step to a "Jewish State"?

Lastly, as to the wording, it is not, we believe, improper or uncharitable to draw attention to the last paragraph of Mr. Balfour's "Declaration" where he asks Rothschild if he "would bring the Declaration to the knowledge of the Zionist Federation." The naive or clever implication is that the members of the Federation would be surprised to hear about it. The truth was that all leading Zionists had known for a long time that the Zionist apparatus was turning heaven and earth to get a Zionist-Palestine commitment from the British — who actually had no authority to give it.

It has since been made clear, and certainly should have been plainly understood then, that the reason the Zionists were exerting such unrestrained pressure to get this "official" Declaration was to use it as "legal" entree for mass immigration of European Jews (particularly from Eastern Europe) into Palestine. And the purpose of this, which should have been equally clear to any official with eyes and ears, was to turn Palestine into a Jewish State.

We have read a statement in the official War Cabinet records as of October, 1917 (one month before the Declaration was issued), which made it clear for all to understand that the purpose of "a national home for the Jewish people" was a covering phrase for an intended "reassembled" nation. Can there be any doubt about the real meaning of this? To turn Palestine into a Jewish State has been the central objective of political Zionism from Herzl on. It is the way in which all of this was done that makes it such fascinating history. The purpose here is not to pass judgment, but to put facts into the record for inquiring minds of the future.

A SHOCKING REVELATION

Many people in America were grievously surprised when they by chance learned that the late Supreme Court Justice, Louis D. Brandeis, was the leader of the Zionist movement in the United States — and that he had played a major role in writing and polishing the so-called Balfour Declaration as it was being readied for Balfour's approval. Likewise they did not know of his dual political interest in the sovereignty of another country — Palestine.

The Brandeis relationship with Zionism, Palestine and the Balfour design was not publicized to any extent in the United States. Because of public sentiment and the close working contacts he had developed with President Wilson, the Brandeis leadership of political Zionism was of the hush-hush order. There was much anti-Zionist feeling in America in those days by both Jews and non-Jews. The elder Morgenthau, for instance, was one of many of America's distinguished Jews who opposed the Zionist political ideology.

Tremendous pressure was being exerted from French and British, as well as American Zionist sources, to persuade President Wilson into approval of the Zionist-Balfour plans for Palestine. The records indicate that Brandeis and Edward Mandell House constituted the liaison to the President. If the sub rosa activities of these pro-Zionist leaders had been aired in the press at the time, it would most certainly have created a great public furor. The political climate in such matters in this country has, however, been radically changed since those days — but the "pressure bloc" in America is another story.

The importance of Justice Brandeis as a Zionist figure is evidenced by the fact that the British draft of what was eventually to become the Balfour Declaration was sent to him by the Weizmann-led British Zionists for his corrections and approval before submitting it to Foreign Secretary Balfour. This information comes from the book "The Great Betrayal" (Brentano, 1930), co-authored by Rabbi Stephen Wise and Jacob de Haas, wherein they say — "The final draft of what became known as the Balfour Declaration was amended by the authors of this book." The document, they tell us, had been sent to Justice Brandeis for consultation and approval. After "very important" changes had been made and approved by Brandeis, it was then given to Colonel House (Wilson's alter ego) who transmitted it to the President — "upon whose agreement and express authority the final text was issued by the British War Cabinet." That "final text," however, was trimmed materially by the worried British statesmen.

Later, however, the Brandeis role was documented by his biographer, Jacob de Haas, who says that Brandeis became chairman of the Provisional Executive Committee of General Zionist Affairs in August, 1914 — which meant that he became the leader of Zionism in America — or of what Rabbi Wise presumptuously called "American Israel." Brandeis was an able and clever lawyer and a prominent figure in Jewish affairs which, as a voting bloc, was developing greater consideration in American politics. Brandeis' status in the general Jewish community brought him to the attention of President Wilson who, in 1916, appointed him to the bench of the U.S. Supreme Court.

In 1917, Lord Balfour visited Washington and met Justice

Brandeis. According to Mrs. Dugdale, Balfour's niece and biographer, who quotes the British statesman as — "assured by his conversations with Justice Brandeis and by what he learned from him of the President's attitude, that there would be active sympathy (for Zionism) there." This was a short time before the Balfour Declaration was issued and the signing of that Declaration was undoubtedly influenced by some of the things Balfour learned in Washington on that visit. This could have included such material matters as extended war cooperation as well as financial and other kinds of aid; for after all, Balfour was a trained and experienced British diplomat and these gentlemen have a way of being highly practical.

DOCUMENT THAT ROCKED
THE MIDDLE EAST

Because of the tremendously important political role this document played in international affairs, some greater detail should be given to the Zionist maneuvering that secured it. Authors Wise and de Haas, in their forthright book accusing the British of a "Great Betrayal," explain that in July of 1917 Lord Rothschild "submitted a draft text which became the base of the Declaration."

Up to that time — and all during World War I — Weizmann and his Zionist colleagues had been playing their cards to get a concession from the British for immigration of Jews into Palestine. Finally, after much clever maneuvering and favor of fortune in British cabinet changes, hopes brightened for getting the British to sign some such agreement. We learn that the first draft of what the Zionists wanted was struck off by Lord Rothschild. This was revised and reworked with finesse from every angle and then sent to the "Brandeis regime" in the United States for further study, amending and approval. President Wilson was then persuaded by Justice Brandeis and Colonel House to give the text his assent after which it was returned to the Weizmann group in Britain, who presented it to Balfour for his and hopefully for the Cabinet's approval.

From then on for the next several weeks until November 2, 1917, when the document was finally signed, there was much nervous anticipation and trepidation on the part of the

Zionist leaders. In his autobiography, Weizmann states: "On August 17, I was able to write Felix Frankfurter, in the United States: 'The draft has been submitted to the Foreign Office and is approved by them, and I heard yesterday, it also meets the approval of the Prime Minister (Lloyd George)'." About a month later (September 18), Weizmann says he learned that "our declaration" had been discussed at a Cabinet meeting where "the sharp intervention of Edwin Montagu had caused a withdrawal of the item from the agenda." Edwin Montagu, a distinguished member of the Government, was Weizmann's chief anti-Zionist bete noire.

All of this was wearing heavily upon the nervous Zionists. Weizmann writes: "I did not feel as desperate as Lord Rothschild, but the situation was unpleasant. We saw Balfour separately, I on the nineteenth, Lord Rothschild on the twenty-first." Balfour reassured Weizmann and insisted that Montagu's attitude had not changed his sympathy. Weizmann then sent the following cable to Brandeis in America:

"Following text declaration has been approved Foreign Office and Prime Minister and submitted War Cabinet: 1. His Majesty's Government accepts the principle that Palestine should be reconstituted as the National Home of the Jewish people. 2. His Majesty's Government will use its best endeavours to secure the achievement of this object and will discuss the necessary methods with the Zionist Organization."

By examining the Declaration as it was finally issued, it may be noted that the word "re-constituted" was jettisoned. This the Zionists had dearly hoped to include to establish historical connections with ancient tradition. Also the terse and vague document finally approved by the War Cabinet was a far cry from the encompassing conditions suggested by the Zionists.

The tenseness of the situation impelled Weizmann, on October 9, to cable Justice Brandeis, which included this urgent appeal:

". . . It is essential to have not only President's (Wilson's) approval of text, but his recommendation to grant the declaration without delay. Further your support and enthusiastic message to us from American Zionists and also prominent non-Zionists most desirable to us. Your support urgently needed."

Weizmann states that Brandeis tried hard to "obtain from President Wilson a public statement of sympathy" but failed to get it. Colonel House, however, on October 16, acting as the President's right-hand man, cabled the British Government asurances of America's support of the substance of the document. Balfour asked Weizmann to whom the letter-declaration should be addressed, and Weizmann suggested Lord Rothschild.

ANXIOUS WAITING

On the day the Cabinet was in session to give its answer, Weizmann says he was waiting outside — within call. Sir Mark Sykes brought the document out to Weizmann, exclaiming "It's a boy," as he also did when he passed Malcolm who was waiting in the rotunda for the news. Weizmann writes that he did not "like the boy at first" as it was not what he had hoped for, but it was the best that could be done. If the British statesmen believed they were containing the nationalistic ambitions of the Zionist leader by limiting the declaration to sterile and vague verbiage, they simply did not understand the people with whom they were dealing.

PROTEST THAT WAS TOO LATE

Two pages back, reference is made to Mr. Edwin Montagu's oppositon to Zionism at the time the Weizmann cabal was pushing England for a commitment to the Zionists on Palestine. Mr. Montagu, as Minister of State for India, was the only Jew in the British cabinet at the time and his belated opposition was worrying Weizmann greatly. Just before Balfour signed the trouble-laden "Declaration," Mr. Montagu issued a lengthy statement of protest — revealing that the dealings between the Zionists and Balfour were new to him and that he suspected there had been considerable prior confidential bargaining. His protest, he explained, was the result of his having received copy of a letter from Lord Rothschild, dated July 18, 1917, and that Balfour was expected to answer it in August. (Actually, the Declaration was not issued until November 2, 1917.)

Mr. Montagu expressed fear that, under the circumstances, his protest would be too late, but he warned that — "the policy of His Majesty's Government is anti-Semitic in result" and would stimulate anti-Semitism throughout the world. He could

131

have well added that it would foreshadow the end of British influence in the strategic Middle East. The Protest is much too lengthy to be reproduced here, but from it is taken the following short excerpt:

> "Zionism has always seemed to me to be a mischievous political creed, untenable by any patriotic citizen of the United Kingdom. If a Jewish Englishman sets his eyes on the Mount of Olives and longs for the day when he will shake British soil from his shoes and go back to agricultural pursuits in Palestine, he has always seemed to me to have acknowledged aims inconsistent with British citizenship and to have admitted that he is unfit for a share in public life in Great Britain, or to be treated as an Englishman."

*   *   *

As already mentioned, the early draft of the Balfour Declaration stipulated a "national home" for the "Jewish race" which was later changed to read "for the Jewish people." The British Government files (long held as secret) contain many highly interesting papers and communications. One of these is a hand-written letter dated October 12, 1917, and signed "Rothschild," which requested that a change in the draft be made from "Jewish Race" to "Jewish people" — "to obviate much unnecessary controversy."

10. ARABS AGREE TO FIGHT TURKS — BRITAIN PROMISES INDEPENDENCE FOR ARABS — COMPLICATIONS FOLLOW

At the time the Zionists were pushing Britain (and, incidentally, the United States) into the Balfour commitment — with the implied threat that it was needed to insure the mobilization of world-wide Jewish influence for the Allied cause in World War I — it appears that Britain was in an awkward spot with two previous commitments which would stand as complete contradictions to what was demanded by the Zionists and what was finally given in the so-called Balfour Declaration.

One of these was the Sykes-Picot agreement negotiated in May, 1916 by Sir Mark Sykes (British) and M. Picot (French) which provided that after the Turks had been defeated, the Mid-East territories they had controlled would be divided into Zones of influence (covering Iraq, Syria and Palestine) to be supervised by Great Britain and France in agreed upon zones. Russia was to get certain territory in and around Constantinople. It is not necessary at this late date to describe all of the divisions proposed in that agreement since it died in a clash with the later Zionist-Balfour Declaration deal.

Another complicating commitment, made by the British prior to the Sykes-Picot treaty, was an agreement with the Arabs inducing them to revolt against the Turks to aid the British in driving the Turkish forces from the Middle East. This agreement was arranged through contractual correspondence between Sir Henry McMahon, representing the British, and Hussein ibn Ali, the recognized Arab leader at that time. This particular agreement will be discussed here in some detail because of its clashing conflict with the later Zionist Balfour Declaration.

In Appendix "A" there appears a brief history of the Arab people, but for the purpose here, both as to the agreement between Great Britain and "the Arabs" and also in relation to the early stages of the Arab-Zionist conflict, the Arab record begins with the first World War — in the 1914-15 era. At that time, the Sherif Hussein, through a Mohammed-Islamic hereditary line, ruled the Arabian Hejaz — a coastal area bordering the Red Sea which contained the two Islamic Holy cities, Mecca and Medina.

Because of this his prestige was extensive in the Arab world, and with his known opposition to Turkish suzerainty over the Arabs, more and more Moslems who were longing for independence came to regard Sherif Hussein as titular spokesman for the Arab people. He was the man whom the British recognized as the Arab leader to deal with when they needed Arab help in the first World War. When Turkey joined Germany as an ally, the British began negotiating with the Arabs for two special purposes. One was to block Jehad (Holy war) from spreading through the Arab world as was being urged by the Sultan. The other was to enlist the Arabs in a revolt against the Turks to help oust them from the Middle East.

Some spade work in such negotiations had been begun by Lord Kitchener of Khartoum. In January, 1915, Sir Henry McMahon became the British High Commissioner for Egypt and the Sudan (replacing Kitchener) and he inherited the task of serious negotiations with the Arabs. Letters were exchanged between McMahon and Hussein which led gradually to an agreement of terms involving post-war independence for the Arab lands if the Arabs would join in an all-out successful war to drive the Turks from their homelands. This exchange of negotiations covered a period from July 14, 1915 to January 30, 1916. From an examination of territorial descriptions, there seems no doubt but that Palestine was included. Certainly the Arabs felt that they had spelled it out to cover all areas predominantly inhabited by Arabs.

The communications are printed in full in "The Arab Awakening" (1938) by the late highly respected journalist, George Antonius. Hussein's first letter of July 14, 1915, laid down the terms by which the British would have the collaboration of the Arabs. McMahon's reply, lukewarm and cautious, brought a sharp rejoinder from Hussein requesting McMahon to be more positive and authoritative.

BRITISH ACCEPT HUSSEIN'S TERMS

McMahon's next letter, October 24, 1915, seemed to be a clear acceptance of Hussein's specific terms. In it Great Britain made a slight modification in Hussein's territorial demands of independence, and to this added: "Subject to the modifications stated above, Great Britain is prepared to recognize and uphold the independence of the Arabs in all the regions lying within the frontiers proposed by the Sherif of Mecca."

It is true that the word "Palestine" was not mentioned specifically in the McMahon-Hussein correspondence. On the one hand, Sherif Hussein (as was general among the Arabs) regarded Palestine only as a section of Syria, which understanding had long been common to the history of the Middle East. On the other hand, the British negotiator, schooled in diplomatic practice, could hardly be expected to be any more precise than necessary. So there it rested until later when the matter became a political "hot potato." For political convenience McMahon could later intimate he did not believe it was intended that Palestine should be included in the promise to Hussein for post-war independence to the whole of the Arab lands. If there had been purpose not to include Palestine in the agreement, then it would seem strange that it had not been so stated, since it was clear that Hussein was deeply interested in all the Arab populated lands.

There is a further important matter of record in this sticky controversy. In June of 1918 when the Arabs first learned with alarm of the Balfour Declaration — several months before the war ended — a Memorial of Inquiry was submitted to the British Foreign Office by a delegation of Seven Arabs (all important in Arab status) who were then domiciled in Egypt, asking for a clear-cut statement of British intentions.

On June 16, 1918, the Foreign Office issued a Declaration to the Seven, which George Antonius includes in "The Arab Awakening" and describes it as "by far the most important statement of policy made by Great Britain in connexion with the Arab Revolt . . . and, more valuable still, provides authoritative enunciation of the principles on which those pledges rested . . . In so far as it referred to Syria, Palestine and Iraq, the Declaration to the Seven contained two assurances of fundamental importance. One was that Great Britain had been working and would continue to work not only for the liberation of these countries from Turkish rule but also for their freedom and independence." The other was that she pledged herself to ensure that no regime would be set up in any of them that was not acceptable to their population.

Hussein, not being familiar as yet with Western diplomacy, accepted the McMahon correspondence as an honorable agreement, not perhaps realizing the importance of exactness of contracts — which later he was to learn. He apparently did not have any notion that within two years — after the Arabs had gone all out in desperate battling to help the British drive the Turks from the Middle East (including Palestine) — the British Foreign Office would make a commitment to the Zionist leaders which, as was well known to the principals, gave the Zionists the spurious "right" to impregnate a Jewish State into the heartland of the Arab states — and without even telling the Arabs it was being done.

GERMANS SURRENDER—WAR ENDS

One year after the Zionists succeeded in securing the Balfour Declaration, the great World War ended — with the German surrender-armistice on November 11, 1918. During the year the Zionists had not been able to get much benefit from the Balfour grant — except to lay plans for post-war activity, since Palestine was still under the control of the Turks until their Middle East control began to crumble with the surrender of the city of Jerusalem to British General (Sir Edmund) Allenby on December 9, 1917. The General entered the historic city two days later through the Jaffa gate and had a proclamation read from the top of the Citadel steps in English, French, Italian, Arabic and Hebrew, from which the following excerpt is quoted:

136

"Furthermore, since your city is regarded with affection by the adherents of three of the great religions of mankind, and its soil has been consecrated by the prayers and pilgrimages of multitudes of devout people of these three religions for many centuries, therefore do I make known to you that every sacred building, monument, holy spot, shrine, traditional site, endowment, pious bequest, or customary place of prayer, of whatever form of the three religions, will be maintained and protected according to the existing customs and beliefs of those to whose faiths they are sacred."

There was nothing in General Allenby's proclamation to indicate that the spilling of British and Arab blood to drive the Turks from Palestine was also for implementing the Zionist interpretation of the Balfour letter to Lord Rothschild. The driving of the Turks from the Middle East was no inconsequential task. To do this the British needed the help of the Arabs. Their aid was sought and — after tedious negotiations between Sir Henry McMahon (Britain's High Commissioner in Egypt) and King Hussein of the Hejaz (Sherif of Mecca) — Arab cooperation was obtained. This was based upon very specific promises that the Arabs would have independent possession of their Middle East homelands after the Turks were driven out. When the exchange of correspondence is read carefully, there seems little doubt but that this agreement covered Palestine. The fighting between the revolting Arabs and the Turks was savage and deadly. From the reporting of the British journalist, J. M. N. Jeffries, we read:

"Allenby landed in Egypt on the very day, the 6th of July, that the Arabs under Lawrence captured Akaba by skilful manoeuvre. They had taken two months to reach their objective. The six-hundred-mile route 'was so long and difficult that we could take neither guns nor machine-gun stores nor regular soldiers,' (wrote Lawrence). They started out from Wejh (Saudi Arabia), a mere reconnaissance-group on camels, and raised their force by degrees from the Arab tribes through or near whose districts they passed . . . They picked their way over lava and through desert scrub, in solar heat and often enveloped by sandstorms. 'Some even of the rough tribesmen broke down under the cruelty of the sun, and crawled or had to be thrown under rocks to recover in their shade.' But they ran about and showed themselves at all points to give an impression that they were more numerous than their real numbers.

" 'The hill-sides were steep and exhausted our breath, and the grasses twined like little hands round our ankles as we ran . . . The limestone tore our feet, . . . Our rifles grew so hot with sun and shooting that they seared our hands. The rocks on which we flung ourselves for aim were burning, so that they scorched our breasts and arms, from which later the skin drew off in ragged sheets. The smart made us thirst, but even water was rare with us.'

137

"The Turks fired vainly on them with mountain-guns. The Arabs on their camels charged Turkish infantry formations and broke them. They captured one strong outpost of Akaba by favour of an eclipse of the moon. By their methods of fighting the Arabs shattered the Turks' morale, and they had already deceived them upon their objective, so that when they came down finally upon their goal the garrison, and the men of the outposts driven in to it, hesitated, parleyed and surrendered. The five hundred Arabs took prisoner seven hundred Turkish men and forty-two officers."

Concerning this remarkable military achievement by the Arabs at Akaba (at the tip of a Red Sea finger) which opened the way to the capture of Damascus and other Turkish strongholds, the noted British military strategist, Liddell Hart, said: "Strategically, the capture of Akaba removed all danger of a Turkish raid through Sinai against the Suez Canal or the communications of the British Army in Palestine . . . it ensured the Arab ulcer continuing to spread in the Turkish flanks, draining their strength and playing upon their nerves."

NOTE: As to what happened as the Arab States began to settle and adjust in the post-World War I period, this book is mainly concerned with Palestine. This little country was quite definitely a part of the Arab lands that were to have post-war independence. But the difference between Palestine and the other Arab lands is that the Zionists had strategic designs on it as a Jewish "Homeland" or "State." They advanced their purpose publicly by obtaining the so-called Balfour Declaration (of doubtful legal or moral validity) and the favor of the Lloyd George Government. What happened to promises of Arab independence as related to Palestine is documented in Chapters XIV to XX.

---

11. ZIONISTS WANT BRITAIN TO HAVE MANDATE OVER PALESTINE — EXPECTING THIS TO INSURE ENFORCEMENT OF BALFOUR DEAL

The Balfour Declaration for the Zionists was a stepping stone to further British collaboration which was planned to come later (at the Paris Peace Conference) in the form of a British trusteeship over Palestine. The first obvious purpose of the Balfour document for the Zionists was to clear the way for mass immigration into Palestine, but this could turn out to be wasted struggle and strategy unless out of the Peace settlement would come an authority over that country which would be amenable to the Zionist purpose.

After touching the British for the Balfour indulgence it was, some believe, fairly reasonable for the Zionists to conclude that their program would fare well under a British trusteeship in Palestine. Consequently, the next Zionist task was to help secure this mandate-authority for Great Britain. Taking no chances with fate, however, the Zionists at the same time began their propaganda to let the British know what was expected.

In December of 1918, while Rabbi Stephen Wise (the great thundering voice of Zionist leadership) was "in London and in consultation with Zionist officials" (The Great Betrayal, pp. 51-2), an American Jewish Congress, meeting in Philadelphia, adopted a resolution calling for the establishment in Palestine of the right political administrative and economic conditions as would assure "under the trusteeship of Great Britain, acting on behalf of the League of Nations as may be formed, the development of Palestine into a Jewish Commonwealth . . ." (Esco Foundation report, p. 153).

Here we find the Zionists projecting a "League of Nations" and "a British trusteeship in Palestine" long before either agency had been discussed officially as a possibility. Here also, the Zionists boldly project the design to develop "Palestine into a Jewish Commonwealth." No advance signal could be plainer than this. We are also told (The Great Betrayal, p. 52) that Rabbi Wise cabled his colleagues in New York an "interpretation of Jewish National Home into Jewish Commonwealth . . . at the suggestion of British Officials." The officials are not named.

HAS THIS BEEN THE "SOLUTION"?

From this same book (same page), the authors (Wise and de Haas) inform us that in January of 1919 "with government aid," there was prepared in London a "Memorandum of the Zionist Organization Relating to the Reconstitution of Palestine as the Jewish National Home." The book's authors say the inclusion of the word "Reconstitution" was not an accident. They also quote from the mentioned document wherein it said that the Balfour Declaration "sought to reach the root of the Jewish problem in the only way it can be reached — by *providing the Jewish people with a country* and a home."

This document, continuing along the same line, was formally dated February 3, 1919 and was a "statement of the Zionist Organization" which was discussed and revised at the Hotel Meurice in Paris by Zionist leaders Weizmann, Sokolow, Flexner and de Haas. The statement by de Haas in "The Great Betrayal" that this document was prepared with "government aid" seems to stem from the fact that the ardent Zionist, Sir Herbert Samuel, "acting unofficially for the British government" sat in with the other Zionists at the Hotel Meurice conclave. It may be worth adding that when the Palestine trusteeship was handed to Britain (by the newly created League of Nations), Sir Herbert Samuel was made the first High Commissioner in Palestine under the British trusteeship. This, presumably, was in further deference to the Weizmann-Zionist organization by the British Foreign Office idealists.

Mr. J. M. N. Jeffries, in his book "Palestine: The Reality" (Longman's, Green & Co., London, 1939), reported the Paris

140

Peace Conference in great detail. He explained that as the Conference proceeded to create the League of Nations and the insertion of the Mandatory system into its constitution, the "key men were the Zionists' men." "Most of the original plan for these institutions," Mr. Jeffries stated, "was drafted by General Smuts, and in lesser degree by Lord Cecil." After Balfour, writes Jeffries, "there were no more ardent and no blinder propagandists than those two."

Mr. Charles Thompson in "The Peace Conference Day by Day," tells how, after talks with such pro-Zionist leaders as Balfour, Colonel House and Tardieu, Rabbi Wise "wrote out a statement that a very definite plan was under way." This plan provided, among other things, that Great Britain should be given a mandate over Palestine. He quotes Rabbi Wise as follows:

> "Great Britain should be given and I believe will be given the Mandatory of Trusteeship over Palestine. I have reason for saying, Great Britain will not accept save by the common consent of such *disinterested* (italics ours) people as our own. Great Britain's trusteeship over a Jewish Palestine will be . . . for the sake of the Jewish people and the Jewish Commonwealth which they are in time to realize."

Rabbi Wise, says Mr. Jeffries, was writing with aplomb about the British Mandate for Palestine more than three weeks before the Mandate was authorized. Reporters who covered the Peace conference have well documented the activities of a highly organized pro-Zionist mechanism operating throughout the Conference to help shape the Zionist future of Palestine.

Without further exploration into the origin of the British Mandate for Palestine, it would seem that sufficient documentation has been presented to show: (1) that the Zionists seemed more interested in getting the Mandate for the British than the British themselves were; (2) that the Zionists were making every possible effort to impress the British with an understanding that when they did get the Mandate, they were expected to implement the Zionist plan to turn Palestine into a Jewish State; (3) that while the Zionists were not publicizing it, the implication was clear that the British trusteeship was to be a temporary matter — lasting only until the conversion of Zionism to political Statehood had been accomplished.

ENTANGLING ALLIANCES BEAR THEIR FRUIT

Further, the documentation presented here, as well as that for which there has not been sufficient room, shows that while the Zionists were able cleverly to get certain statesmen "over the barrel," so to speak, where they could no longer dodge some kind of commitment to them, the British leaders were, at the same time, trying desperately to avoid going on record with the kind of forthright concession that they knew the Zionists were driving for.

To what extent Balfour and Lloyd George were convincingly converted to the worthiness of the Zionist cause will, of course, never be known. In international diplomacy, statesmen have a way of straddling a troublesome issue and hedging in an effort to "be all things to all men." It is only fair to them to say that Great Britain, caught in the vortex of a world cataclysm, was at the time of the Balfour Declaration, in desperate need of American help. The Zionists understood their strategic posture well. Yielding to their pressure may have been largely a British experiment in questionable expediency. The long, tortuous road of statesmanship down through the ages is well paved with diplomatic blunders. "The moving finger writes; and having writ, moves on."

BRITISH MILITARY OCCUPIES JERUSALEM—ZIONISTS WANT ACTION

When General Allenby captured Jerusalem from the Turks, the vacuum of government had to be filled; and this was done with the establishment of a British military occupation administration. Under this order of things, time moved on while the interminable minutiae of arrangements for a peace meeting moved slowly forward. The Paris Peace Conference finally met in Versailles Palace beginning in January, 1919. The story of this long drawn out affair cannot be told here with all the haggling, intrigue, manipulation and diplomatic fencing that went on spicing its veneer of statesmanship-like dignity.

Before any attempt to discuss the germane incidents of

142

the Conference, some reference should be made to the disposition of the Zionists during the time that Palestine had been under British post-war occupation government. The efforts of the Zionists to capitalize the so-called Balfour Declaration and advance their immigration plans had not received much favorable attention from the British military forces which were otherwise busily engaged trying to bring order out of the chaos which would naturally follow a violent and sudden change of rulership. Zionist leaders, however, as indicated by Weizmann in his autobiography (and otherwise), had become greatly irked, impatient and discouraged at the turn of events.

In America, Justice Louis D. Brandeis, who had strongly exerted his Jewish prominence and greatly influenced President Wilson on behalf of the Zionist cause in Palestine, became alarmed at the reports he had been receiving about the slowness with which the Balfour design had been advancing. He decided to make a personal on-the-spot inspection trip to see what was happening.

BRANDEIS DOES SOME CHECKING

When the U.S. Supreme Court adjourned for the summer of 1919, Justice Brandeis, with his devoted biographer, Jacob de Haas, took off for London, Paris and the Middle East to see whether or not the Balfour letter was being properly respected in its role to help build a Jewish State in Palestine. Although the United States had no authorized responsibility whatever in the Palestine scheme, Justice Brandeis apparently felt that he did.

For what happened on his Zionist political junket, we have the reporting of his traveling companion, Jacob de Haas, in his Brandeis biography. During the early summer of 1919, Brandeis and de Haas sailed for London on their way to Palestine. Stopping there for conferences with Chaim Weizmann and other Zionist leaders, he was briefed on the general Zionist outlook. Leaving London, the two travelers reached Paris on June 28 — the very day that the Versailles Peace Treaty was signed.

In Paris they spent a few crowded days calling on President Wilson (who was there for the Peace Conference), Colonel House (Wilson's strange alter ego from whom he later became alienated), Lord Balfour, Baron Edmund de Rothschild and others, including several members of the French Cabinet. From Paris, Brandeis and his companion went to Egypt, where they met and talked with General Allenby at his headquarters in Cairo. The visitors did not find much warmth for their interests from the great General who had driven the Turks from Jerusalem. He was not a politician like Balfour, but was interested only in the orderly administration of Palestine, without fear or favor concerning either the Jews or the Arabs.

NOTE: Colonel Edward Mandell House, mentioned above, was the incognito author of an odd fantasy-plan for a socialistic-dictatorship for the U.S., titled "Philip Dru, Administrator." His World War I "peace" work as a U.S. emissary in Europe brought estrangement between House and the President.

What Brandeis had learned in Paris, and the steadfastness he found in General Allenby's impartial devotion to administrative duty, concerned him deeply. He sensed the ascendency of British military thoroughness over Foreign Office political diplomacy in Middle East policies. It seemed clear to him that the British Commander-in-Chief, along with his military and civil aides, regarded the Balfour Declaration as an inconsequential gesture of political expediency during the war. It appeared to Brandeis that the British were concerned too much with strengthening their own posture in Palestine and that they also took a partial attitude by regarding the Arabs as Palestinian natives.

Brandeis left General Allenby's headquarters in Cairo and headed for Jerusalem via the Sinai overland route. On arriving there, he went straight to the army occupation on the Mount of Olives and, according to his chronicler, "expressed some definite opinions on the matter to General Money." Brandeis told the Chief Administrator of the Jerusalem occupation forces that "ordinances of the military authorities should be submitted to the Zionist Commission." This commanding advice from a stranger who was no more than an American judge must have struck General Money as officious rudeness. At any rate, Brandeis was bluntly told that as a lawyer he should know that "for a Government to do that would be to derogate its positon."

THE BRANDEIS MODUS OPERANDI

Neither abashed nor impressed, Brandeis retorted that "It must be understood that the British Government is committed to the support of the Zionist cause" and, he continued, "Unless this is accepted as a guiding principle I shall have to report it to the Foreign Office."

The British writer, Mr. J. M. N. Jeffries, reports in his book "Palestine, the Reality" that Brandeis, dining later with a senior officer of the Administration, repeated to him the strong opinions he had on this subject; and then using a trick of cajolery, praised the Zionist purpose and suggested to the Official —raising his glass —"if you will give us a word of adherence — I drink to the future Governor of Palestine. What I say to Wilson goes." His presumptuous reference was to President Wilson.

Receiving very little satisfaction from the military administration of Palestine, the persistent American jurist reached London as soon as possible and "unburdened himself" to the British Foreign Office. It was to Mr. Balfour he talked. After his "unburdening," according to the trip report, action followed fast:

"A few hours later the British Foreign Office through the British War Office was reminding the military authorities in Egypt and Palestine not only of the verbal contents of the Balfour Declaration, but also that it was chose jugee (a matter decided) . . . The Brandeisian direct-action diplomacy had achieved results."

Mr. Jeffries reports that some British officers who did not "like Balfour, see eye to eye with the Zionists, began to lose their posts. They were either forced into resignation or removed." He also explains that Lord Sydenham, during a Lords' debate a few months later, directly accused the Government of taking action against British officials, under Zionist influence.

12. PARIS PEACE CONFERENCE ZIONISTS OUTNUMBER AND OUTPLAY ARAB DELEGATION

After World War I ended in 1918, the next order of business was to have a "peace conference" where, as so often has happened before, the seeds for other wars could be sown. The place selected for this great meeting of the Allied Powers' statesmen was the historic Hall of Mirrors in the Palace of Versailles, just outside Paris. Here the ghosts of other tragedies in this Palace were to watch with envy a new generation at work.

The rich splendor of the Palace that had cushioned intrigue at the court of Louis XIV had lost none of its seductive influence for savoir-faire, as this new breed of statesmen and lobbyists gathered to reappoint the world order. Everywhere political and diplomatic finesse was in its best form, over tall glasses and in sideroom conferences, where the art of arm-pulling and nimble-witted cajolery was often but little less than thinly veiled intrigue.

The four great statesmen were there with their able entourages — and never far from them were the numerous members of the Zionist delegations from New York, London and other parts. With the latter, as evidence disclosed, were plans for the future — probably more carefully prepared than those of any statesmen, unless it was President Wilson's famous fourteen points.

Also present was a lonely man from Arabia who, with quiet dignity and perplexed uncertainty, found himself in a diplomatic environment unlike anything in his previous experience. This man was Amir (Prince) Feisal, son and delegated representative of King Hussein, with whom the British had entered into promises for Arab help to drive the Turks from the Middle East. His father had sent him to the peace conference with instructions to see that the promises made to the fighting Arabs were kept in the making of the new order of things. Feisal was soon to learn that the cards had already been stacked against him.

The first plenary session of the Peace Conference was held on the 18th of January, 1919, in this famous and grandiose Hall of Mirrors, made available to the Allies by France, in one sense as a grand gesture of retaliation in commemoration of an event in 1871, when the newly united German-Prussian kingdom, after defeating France in war, imposed upon that nation a peace settlement carried out with great pomp and ceremony in this same Hall of Mirrors.

THE BIG FOUR

The chief representatives at the 1919 Conference to settle with the defeated Turks and Germans were Clemenceau and Pichon of France, Lloyd George and Lord Balfour for Great Britain, Orlando and Sonnino for Italy, with President Wilson and Lansing for the United States. These, known as the "big four," constituted the Supreme Council of the Allied Powers. There were also thirty-two States which, in one way or another, had opposed the Central Powers, who had representatives present.

Mr. J. M. N. Jeffries in his splendid report "Palestine, the Reality" (1939) stated that the great thing at this Conference was to be "admitted to the privacy of the principals." "The Zionists," he continued, "had all the necessary admissions, as inner Peace Conference history attests . . . In movements easeful and triumphant as high summer's, like bees visiting and fecundating flowers, Messrs. Weizmann and Sokolow and (Rabbi) Wise flew from the President to House and from House to Balfour and Balfour to Lansing and from Lansing to Tardieu, and from Tardieu to Lloyd George through long honey-making days." "Yet," wrote Mr. Jeffries, "the Zionist group was the sole group in Paris which almost could have dispensed with these intimate visits." The reason for that, he explained, was that half of the principals there were already "vowed to the Zionist dogma."

147

Of the many Zionist delegates that hovered over the Peace Conference, Jeffries considered the chief ones to be Lloyd George and Balfour. "Acetone and accessory," he added as a biting reference to the naive way in which Lloyd George had praised Weizmann's chemical formula for making acetone as an alibi or reason for giving the Zionists the Balfour commitment for a "Jewish homeland" in Palestine. Acetone was helpful at the time in making explosives. The official delegation, next in importance as "vowed" Zionist allies at the Conference, was rated by Mr. Jeffries as being the group from the United States. It appeared that the spadework in these two countries had been well handled.

* * *

ARABS BADLY DISADVANTAGED

The Arabs came to the Peace Conference with no great advantage of political activists. And there were no Arab votes nor Arabs of moneyed influence living in either England or America upon whom they could depend. Their representative came to the Conference with no hidden design — as did others. The Arabs had been promised ——and they had trusted. They had fought and many had died. Now they were asking for only what had been pledged — and earned.

The individual whom the British had selected as the top Arab leader with whom to deal for an "Arab revolt" against the Turks was Hussein, Sherif of Mecca — ruler of the Hejaz. Hussein had four sons. Two of them played major roles in the war against the Turks. One of these was Feisal, who had served as an officer under the Turkish government in Syria, and therefore had gained considerable native diplomatic experience. In lieu of going to the Peace Conference himself, the aging Hussein sent his son Feisal — with strict instructions to avoid diplomatic traps and stand steadfast for the Arab rights upon which he and the British had agreed.

NOTE: The other Hussein son of historical importance was the Amir Abdulla. In 1921, through the influence of the British, the new State of Trans-Jordan was formed and Abdulla was made ruler and later given the title of King. Prior to this, the area of Trans-Jordan had gone for a year, during adjustment of the British and French Mandates, without any central government.

When Feisal arrived in Paris for the Peace Conference (January, 1919), he found himself face to face with three major influences that would make his task difficult. These, according to Antonius in "The Arab Awakening," were "the British imperialist interest in Iraq and Palestine; the French imperialist interest in Syria; and in league with the first, the Zionist nationalistic interest in Palestine."

"FEISAL IN JUNGLE-LAND" OF INTERNATIONALISM

Mr. Antonius describes Feisal's first visit to Europe as "an adventure in bewilderment." He first visited France where he was met by two French officers of high rank, who informed him that while the Government welcomed him as a visitor and would extend all courtesies, it could not recognize him as a representative in any official capacity. In London, official effort was made, according to Mr. Antonius, to get his assent to the objectives that had already been established. "They were particularly insistent on the subject of Palestine, and instructed Lawrence to use his influence — which was then considerable — with Feisal to induce him to give formal recognition, on behalf of the Arabs he represented, to Zionist aspirations in Palestine."

The Zionists were equally active in their efforts to get Feisal to sign a document called a "Treaty of Friendship" to be concluded between him, acting on behalf of Hussein, King of the Hejaz, and Dr. Weizmann, acting for the Zionist Organization. This was a cleverly worded statement about the future of friendly and amicable Jewish and Arab relationships in Palestine. It contained ten concluding clauses which would have bound the Arabs to acquiesence of the whole Zionist design. As a plan to get Feisal's signature, this "Treaty of Friendship" with its sugar-coated binding obligations was described by a student of diplomacy as being typical of the clever line of strategy that designed and created the State of Israel.

Feisal, coming from the ways of the Old World into the feverish political activity of the Western world where he was a stranger, was much confused by being pulled and pushed to do this and that, much of which he did not understand

149

and which he regarded as extraneous to the purpose of his mission. He communicated some of these matters to his father, King Hussein in Arabia, who insisted that he do nothing and accept nothing less than fulfilment of the pledges made by Great Britain as to Arab independence for Arab help in driving the Turks from the Middle East.

After much pressure, Feisal, distraught by issues and events, according to authentic reporting, consented to sign the agreement with Weizmann which had been so forcefully urged upon him — but in doing so, he wrote in along with his signature a stipulation that the agreement was valid only if the Arabs obtained their independence as demanded in his Memorandum to the British Foreign Office dated January 4, 1919 — and that if the slightest modification was made — "I shall not then be bound by a single word of the present agreement which shall be deemed void and of no account or validity, and I shall not be answerable in any way whatsoever."

This document and the scheme it quite obviously carried, dated January 3, 1919 (just after Feisal's arrival in Europe) was rendered completely impotent and useless for the Zionists by Feisal's foresightedness. Documentation appears to prove, however, that the plan to get Feisal committed to some compromising statement favoring the Zionists — which, it has been claimed, could be used by experts in distortion of meaning — was not abandoned.

THAT FRANKFURTER LETTER

Within two months after Feisal had been besieged to sign a so-called "Treaty of Friendship," he was interviewed in Paris by some of the Brandeis group of American Zionists; and soon after, a letter addressed to "Dear Mr. Frankfurter" and signed "Feisal" was publicized by the Zionists. Felix Frankfurter (who later helped President Roosevelt establish the "New Deal") was at that time a Harvard law professor and Zionist delegate to the Peace meeting and, according to Mr. de Haas, had been summoned to Europe to "aid in advancing the American idea of mass-action speedily accomplished."

The "Dear Mr. Frankfurter" letter read in part as follows:

"I want to take this opportunity of my first contact with American Zionists to tell you what I have often been able to say to Dr. Weizmann in Arabia and Europe. We feel that the Arabs and Jews are cousins in race, having suffered similar oppressions at the hands of powers stronger than themselves, and by a happy coincidence have been able to take the first step towards the attainment of their national ideals together.

"We Arabs, especially the educated among us, look with the deepest sympathy on the Zionist movement. Our deputation here in Paris is fully acquainted with the proposals submitted yesterday by the Zionist Organization to the Peace Conference and we regard them as moderate and proper. We will do our best, in so far as we are concerned, to help them through. We will wish the Jews a most welcome home."

The letter continued with three more paragraphs following the Zionist line of the "Treaty of Friendship" which Feisal had been persuaded to sign but which he rendered worthless with a handwritten stipulation.

The letter then closed as follows:

"I look forward, and my people with me look forward, to a future in which we will help you and you will help us, so that the countries in which we are mutually interested may once again take their places in the community of civilized people of the world."

Mr. J. M. N. Jeffries, who printed the letter in full in his book, commented that it was difficult to imagine what the Arabic version of this "mawkish" letter could have been — "if ever there was an Arabic version." "Nothing," he continued, "was ever found in Feisal's papers to confirm it." Since Feisal used only French and Arabic, Jeffries believed that either would have been difficult to translate into such typical American-English idiom. Jeffries also contends that the views put forward in this letter as "those of the Arabs" are "so grossly unreal, that it was raw and childish to get Feisal to put his name to them" — but — "he was being pestered to death at the time to sign this and that."

What was Feisal's opinion of the Frankfurter letter? Some ten years later a British Commission of Inquiry was conducting hearings in Jerusalem concerning certain Jewish-Arab disturbances when a Zionist witness introduced into the record this "Feisal to Frankfurter" letter. A Mr. Auni Bey Abdel-Hadi, chief of Arab counsel, cabled Feisal (then King of Iraq at Baghdad), explaining introduction of the letter to show that Feisal had acquiesced to Zionist policy in Palestine. A reply came back from Rustum Bey Haidar, private secretary to King Feisal, saying — "His Majesty does not remember having written anything of the kind with his knowledge." At this late date the letter has no value other than as testimony of what went on at the Peace Conference.

NOTE: The above reference to the late Felix Frankfurter is a reminder of his long record of liberalism and political activity. As far back as December 19, 1917, a former President (Theodore Roosevelt) wrote Frankfurter, criticizing his liberal-extremism and calling it helpful to the Bolsheviks. Frankfurter attached himself to the President Wilson administration — presumably through his Brandeis friendship — and later took an active part in promoting Franklin D. Roosevelt to become President and in helping to create the so-called "New Deal." During this time, he was closely affiliated with the Brandeis-Zionist group, and because of these and other attainments he was appointed to the Supreme Court by Franklin D. Roosevelt to succeed Justice Brandeis.

MORE ARAB PROBLEMS AT PEACE CONFERENCE

Feisal was at the Peace Conference to represent the Arab cause and to plead for a post-war settlement that would recognize the aims of independence for which the Arabs had joined Britain to overthrow Turkish control of the Middle East. He did not ask for a centralized Arab government but suggested that Arab traditions and geographical as well as economical conditions, long established, would call for separate entities in some form of federation; and that it would be advisable for the whole to be placed under some form of European mandatory supervision which would help in building roads and other improvements and developments, until such time as post-war adjustment would allow a full measure of the independence they had been promised.

One great handicap for Feisal was that when he appeared before the great ones of the Peace Conference he spoke in Arabic. None of the Conference leaders could understand this language and there was no official interpreter or translator. Lawrence of Arabia was present at times and did some interpreting, but not officially. How much of Feisal's pleading of the Arab cause was understood by the big four at the Conference table, who were to make the crucial judgments on the future destiny of the Arab countries, could not be determined, nor, perhaps, did it make too much difference. The die had been largely cast before the meeting. The age-old "persecution plea" — with heavy political overtones (the Balfour deal with the Zionists and the Sykes-Picot agreement concerning British and French interests) — had long before set the stage for the Peace meeting.

The two strong men at the Conference upon whom the Zionists had placed their bets were President Wilson, leader of the "New Freedom" political philosophy in America, and Prime Minister Lloyd George, great humanitarian and leader of the British Liberal Party — which, under his guidance, started a humiliating drop in national importance. This was the springtime emergence of minority power in international politics.

At the Peace Conference the Arabs were hindered also by their own "new status" in the field of world diplomacy. They also lacked national unity among themselves, for one reason because they had, for hundreds of years, been under the yoke of their Turkish overlords. Because of this, their economic status was low, which prejudiced their image in competing with the affluent and cosmopolitan Zionist leaders. It would seem that favor should go to the underdog, but in the world of politics it is money and influence that count.

HIGHLIGHTS OF PEACE CONFERENCE

Down through the ages post-war Peace Conferences have come and gone — and as yet there is no Peace. Peace settlements have usually left an aftermath of bitterness and hatreds that ignited other conflagrations or deepened enmity among groups and nations. Certainly the Paris Peace Conference spawned its share of martial after-effects. In Europe its determinations were one cause of the Hitler uprising with its World War II — while in the Middle East its deals and decisions brought the Jewish-Arab conflict and the 1948 war between these two Semitic peoples.

The only landmarks of the Conference we need bother with here are: (1) It created the League of Nations; and (2) Out of this came a new experiment in handling countries liberated by war — a type of trusteeship called "mandates." Both of these political inventions have fallen and are now forgotten. They are mentioned here as highlights only because they contributed materially to the Zionist-Arab conflict with which this book is concerned.

One further reference to the mandates may be made — especially to the mandate for Palestine, which became a nightmare for the British mandatory authorities when the ill-fated partnership that worked to secure this trusteeship was turned into a "war of liberation" by the Zionists, so that their hands might be free of British restraints that were blocking the great Zionist design. In retrospect, there is little doubt that each partner had his own reasons for wanting Britain to have this mandate authority.

The Zionist purpose should have been quite clear. They already had obtained the Balfour Declaration and had plainly stated their own interpretation of its meaning to them. This purpose was further disclosed when they succeeded in getting the gist of the Balfour commitment incorporated into the Mandate document, which had the purpose first of putting upon it the sanction-seal of the League of Nations; and secondly, it emphasized for the British the preferential status of the Zionist-Jews and that they must be so regarded by the mandatory authority.

The British Foreign Office, it is quite probable, had in mind not so much an interest in having this mandate responsibility for any special benefit of its own as it did in the danger of the trusteeship going to some other power. It was well known, of course, that the British had a keen interest at that time in protecting the waterway through the Suez canal, the Red Sea and on into the Indian Ocean. After all of the professions of friendship and assurances of future cooperation the Zionists had expressed in their drive to obtain the British (Balfour) commitment, it was doubtless reasonable for trusting souls like Balfour and Lloyd George to believe in the Zionists' promise to serve as a "bulwark" ally in this strategic area.

MONDAY MORNING HEADACHE

One thoughtful Britisher, in looking back, framed his reflections into a question by asking what had come from all the honeymooning with the Zionist leaders of that period.

What, he meditated, is our status and our image in the Middle East today, after all this flirting with a mirage? Mr. Jeffries, in "Palestine, the Reality," asks — "What was the result of all the wild bidding for Zionist international help? . . . Resolutions in Zionist coteries in Berlin and Petrograd did not go far to give us victory . . . What did world-Jewry accomplish? No doubt world-Jewry did something. But what did it do on a great scale; what did it do that can be traced and expounded?"

According to the Malcolm story (Chapter VIII), the Zionists were first courted with the idea they could be powerful in swinging America into the war on the Allied side. The Zionists clearly were aware of this new assumption of influence but there is no record, and they have never dared boast of any such accomplishment. What happened was that their leaders, being shrewd men, sensing their opportunity, devoted themselves to using this assumption of Washington influence, toward the shaping of the great Zionist design.

In the opinion of one political sage who is wise in the ways of the world, the Zionist leaders must be credited with the almost perfect follow-through execution (from conception to completion) of one of the most deliberate and brilliant political and diplomatic coups of history. One finesse of strategy is for the practitioner to have things happen without appearing to have made them happen.

Mr. Jacob de Haas, biographer and intimate of the late Justice Brandeis, privy to all that was going on in the Zionist movement, wrote — "The Jews had no official status at the Peace Conference," and follows this with an explanation that U.S. Secretary of State, Robert Lansing, handled the Zionist hearing details.

Writer de Haas used the word "Jews" as though it was synonomous with "Zionists," and behind this interplay of meaning there has apparently been concerted propaganda effort, for today the public impression is wide-spread that "Zionism" is essentially identical with "Judaism" and therefore so religiously intertwined as to be regarded as inseparable. This, naturally, gives "political" Zionism the protection from criticism that is properly enjoyed by "religious" Judaism. This confusion must be cleared, say a considerable number of highly respected Jews who do not wish to have their religion tainted with either politics or nationalism.

The political Zionist leader, Chaim Weizmann, explains that in his first meeting with Balfour — "I dwelt on the spiritual side of Zionism. I pointed out that nothing but a deep religious conviction expressed in modern political terms could keep the movement alive, and that this conviction had to be based on Palestine and on Palestine alone." The persuasive Weizmann, through long and tedious effort, apparently sold Balfour on the idea that there was a close affinity between religious Judaism and political Zionism.

It is not unlikely that Weizmann was well aware of Mr. Balfour's religious background of devout orthodoxy involving Old Testament tradition. With such foregained knowledge, it would have been easily possible for him to concentrate his persuasive powers at the most vulnerable and responsive point of emotional impact. The whole story of the Zionist conquest reveals the close entwining use of religious appeal and political action wherever this interplay offered possibilities.

*   *   *

So far as the subject matter of this is concerned, it seems hardly necessary to burden the reader with greater details of the Paris Peace Conference. Our interest here is only in the maneuvering and decisions relating to Palestine. Feisal had discovered, at the Peace Conference, a world new to him — a world of affairs in statesmanship where fast-moving diplomacy with its devious hypocrisy of double talk and the question of motives and forces were too complicated and too entrenched for him. The odds were insurmountable. He left Paris a sadder and wiser man.

The Paris Peace Conference not only set the stage for Hitler and the Second World War — it also created the conditions that made tragedy and war in the Middle East a certainty. "Peace, peace; when there is no peace," echoes all down the corridors of history.

13. MASSIVE JEWISH IMMIGRATION BRINGS CONFRONTATION THAT LED TO CONFLICT

It seems impossible to present all of the numerous facets of the Jewish-Arab conflict in Palestine without repeated emphasis upon the basic and well known cause of forced alien immigration into a small country already well populated. When it became clear to the existing Arab population that this was really the intrusion of an extraneous State pregnancy aimed at Palestine conquest, not much imagination is required to foresee that trespass and confrontation would soon lead to trouble.

The Zionist plan for a State "homeland" had, by the time of the second World War, become so conspicuously evident that everyone but the most credulous understood it well. The "hidden" objective was no longer top-secret.

The population chart, reproduced in Chapter II, shows how the Jewish population in Palestine was pushed from 83,790 in 1922 to 463,535 in 1940. If a similar immigration percentage had been forced upon England or the United States, or any other already organized community, it is not difficult to speculate on what would happen. The problems of coping with immigration are all too well known to those mentioned countries — and they should have known what they were helping to spawn.

NOTE: Going sequentially ahead of our story for a single reference, it may properly be noted that what did happen in the case of Palestine was that the Jewish immigration population had advanced from 83,790 in 1922 to 2,167,000 in 1965, and the "take over" was far on its way. The world well knows today (1968) what has happened, but since the purpose of this book is to help people understand "how it happened," it will be necessary to give some of the details of the modus operandi involved.

TRACING THE PROCESS

Going back to the earlier days, the gradual immigration encroachment stimulated irritation and soon alarmed the old time Arab inhabitants as they began to sense that immigration was increasing to flood tide. Resentment against the Mandatory power (British) rose as it appeared to the Arab population that the blame for this threatening condition lay with the powers in control — the British Mandatory. They had been told that the Balfour Declaration was no threat because it read, in part: "nothing shall be done which may prejudice the civil and religious rights of existing non-Jewish communities in Palestine." Month my month they grew more skeptical of these fine words.

The native resentment against what appeared to be an unlimited plan of Jewish immigration brought unrest and riots. Serious disturbances began particularly in 1929 — then more in 1933 — and really serious trouble in 1936 when the Palestinian Arabs declared a general strike, which was proclaimed to continue until the Jewish immigration was stopped. During this strike period there was considerable violence with rather heavy casualties to Jews, Arabs and the British peace-keeping forces. Arab bands, provoked by rumors caused by the Jewish influx and fear of what would happen to their families and communities, roved the country, widely intensifying the violence. It was the Arabs, however, who in the nature of the circumstances, felt that they were on the defensive. It was all leading to the inevitable combustion which Lloyd George, Balfour, President Wilson and other statesmen, in their great wisdom, were unable to foresee.

The British Government sent a Royal Commission to investigate the turbulence in Palestine, and its causes. This Commission, headed by Lord Peel, arrived in Palestine November 11, 1936, and in July of 1937 filed its Report of findings and recommendations. It forthrightly stressed the great mistake that had been made — and the promises to the Arabs on the one hand and to the Zionist Jews on the other were irreconcilable, thus making the Mandate, in its present form, unworkable. It recommended radical surgery in a suggestion to partition Palestine into two separate States — one for the

Jews and the other for the Arabs. This was the origin of the Partition idea which was to go through much discussion and controversy before the United Nations resolution No. 181(11) authorizing partition was passed November 29, 1947.

PARTITION PLAN AS SOLUTION MET RESISTANCE

The proposal of partition was unpopular and immediately rejected by the Palestinian Arabs and the surrounding Arab States. Some Zionists at first seemed to favor the idea on the basis that it was a chance to get greater official recognition of their "national" status. When the Commission first met, it invited each side (Arabs and Jews) to present a statement (Memorandum) giving its views. For the Zionists, the Memorandum was presented by the Jewish Agency which, as the alter ego of the World Zionist Organization, was the early official maypole of the "Jewish State" movement.

According to the ESCO Foundation report, the Zionist Memorandum emphasized three terms of reference that had been thoughtfully inserted into the Preamble of the Palestine Mandate when it was issued to Britain at the San Ramo Conference (by the Supreme Council of the Peace Conference) in 1920. This Mandate was finally approved by the League of Nations in 1922 — the League itself being the child of the Peace Conference, sired by President Wilson's 14th of his famous Fourteen Points. The three terms mentioned by the Zionist (Jewish Agency) Memorandum were "Jewish people" — "historical connection" — and "reconstitution," which were explained as follows:

"The Mandate is concerned with the Jews, not as individuals, but as a people. What is contemplated is not merely a scheme of colonization for the benefit of the individual Jews, but the provision of a home — a national home — for the Jewish people as a whole. The reference to the 'historical connection' of the Jewish people with Palestine and the use of the expression 'reconstituting' are clearly intended to indicate that in establishing their national home in Palestine the Jews are to be regarded, not as an alien element imported into Palestine and dwelling there on sufferance, but as a people returning to the soil from which it sprang, there to rebuild the fabric of its national life."

Ben Gurion, later to become head of the "Jewish State," added his ambiguous disclaimers as to the Zionist goal of state-

159

hood but included a reminder that the first Zionist program announced at Basle in 1897 had defined the Zionist objective as a "Heimstatte" in Palestine. After considerable discussion, the Zionists also rejected the Peel Commission suggestion for "partition," on the basis that such action would infringe upon the rights of "the Jewish people" as guaranteed by the Balfour Declaration. The question·never seemed to arise as to where Mr. Balfour (speaking for the British Government at the time) got his authority to guarantee "rights" to strangers in a land not possessed, nor even then ruled militarily, by Britain.

The Peel Commission report, with its suggestion of Partition, satisfied no one. The British then sent a second "fact finding" group to Palestine, known as the Woodhead Commission, which reached the conclusion that Partition was impracticable but submitted a three-point proposal — the details of which have no significance at this late date. The British Government then issued what was known as the White Paper of 1938. This contained some of the Woodhead Commission report, but also called for a meeting of Palestine leaders, hoping that some miraculous solution of the Palestine conflict might come from it.

That meeting, known as the London Conference, met from February 7 to March 17, 1939. The leading Zionist spokesmen were Dr. Chaim Weizmann, Rabbi Stephen Wise who was there to represent American Zionists, and several other leaders. Palestinian Arab leaders had been carefully selected as the most responsible representatives that could be found. These two groups were adamant in their opposition to each other. Their viewpoints were basically different — the Zionists being largely alien invaders while the Palestinian Arabs and their ancesters had been indigenous there for some 1,300 years. No truly constructive results came from the London Conference.

BRITISH STRUGGLE WITH ENIGMAS

Following this meeting, the British Government issued a statement of Government policy, known as the White Paper of 1939. This restated the obligations of the Mandatory power (Britain), mentioning particularly (1) securing a "national home" for the "Jewish people" in Palestine; (2) safeguarding the religious and civil rights of all inhabitants of Palestine; (3) placing that country under such political administration and economic conditions as would secure the developing of self-governing institutions.

The British Government admitted there had been many previous ambiguities, such as the much-mouthed phrase "a national home for the Jewish people," and that now, with the confusion and turmoil that had developed, the idea of Partition seemed to hold promise. The Government then made a declaration of intentions as to the future of Palestine.

It proposed that within ten years an independent Palestine State would be established, with treaty arrangements with Great Britain. Both Arabs and Jews were to share responsibilities of governing this new state, so that the essential interests of each community could be safeguarded. It was proposed that 10,000 Jewish immigrants were to be allowed to enter Palestine each year for the next five years, and after that immigration would stop, unless the Arabs of Palestine were willing for it to go on. The statement said that 25,000 Nazi refugees would be admitted as soon as provisions for their maintenance could be arranged. One important stipulation was that the British High Commissioner would have the power to regulate land transfers.

Those who prepared this Statement must have known that it could not be implemented — but a showing of effort had to be made. They were confronted with a dilemma and the fact that it was of their own making did not now matter. They (the British) were the Mandatory power over Palestine, and having "a tiger by the tail" always calls for nimble footwork — just to stay alive.

Many have expressed amazement that the Lloyd George-Balfour Government did not divine the purpose of those who demanded a document covering immigration rights (the Balfour Declaration) and the clash that this would inevitably bring. Equally guilty of political stupidity was President Woodrow Wilson, who likewise was an easy victim of what has been referred to as "master-minding."

By the time the inescapable trouble began to erupt, the noble statesmen who had laid the groundwork for it had passed from office and responsibility. Others had inherited the potential volcano. It seems to be the nature of politics that those who make colossal blunders are rarely blamed for them. Memories are too short — and yesterday's events are blotted out by those of today. One gets the idea that professional politicians seem to understand this strange immunity.

ZIONISTS TURN AGAINST BRITISH

The White Paper of 1939, by which the British somewhat revised their Palestine policy under their mandatory power, died aborning. The plans for Palestine immigration controls were acceptable to neither the Zionists nor the Palestinian Arabs. The Zionists were violent in their denunciation of the plan and of the British who proposed it. Demonstrations were held through Zionist communities in Palestine and "an oath was read in synagogues and public meetings denouncing the White Paper as a treacherous document which never could be accepted by the Jews" (ESCO Report, p. 909).

Ben Gurion, chairman of the Executive of the Zionists' central organization (Jewish Agency), sounded the typical battle cry. "The Jewish demonstrations of yesterday," he cried, "marked the beginning of Jewish resistance to the disastrous policy now proposed by His Majesty's government. The Jews will not be intimidated into surrender if their blood be shed" (Ibid. p. 910). From here on, Zionist resistance to British administration in Palestine — under its Mandate — became more inflamed and militant.

As Zionist resentment increased over the British White Paper, limiting Jewish immigration and land purchases in Palestine, the words of the Zionist leaders began to clarify their basic militant intentions, which time has disclosed. Instead of the milder term "homeland," the word "commonwealth" was heard more and more. Soon the bolder word "State" was being mentioned by Ben Gurion and other leaders.

Referring to the British White Paper program, Ben Gurion said — "The Jews will fight rather than submit to Arab rule . . . It is in the darkest hour of Jewish history," he con-

162

tinued, "that the British Government proposes to deprive the Jews of their last hope and to close the road back to their Homeland. This blow will not subdue the Jewish people. The historic bond between the people and the land of Israel cannot be broken" (Ibid p. 911). It was and is typical of the Zionist leaders to represent themselves as speaking for "the Jewish people" — which presumption is vigorously opposed by anti-Zionist Jews. (The 1967 pro-Zionist demonstrations, however, show who is in now the saddle.)

BRITISH MANDATE BECOMES A PROBLEM

The Zionists now demanded that the British abandon their Mandate authority over immigration into Palestine and turn this operation over completely to the Jewish Agency, which is another name for the World Zionist Organization. The Zionists had worked untiringly to get the Mandate put into Britain's hands originally — assuming, undoubtedly, that since it had been easy to extract the Balfour Declaration from them as a starter, British leadership would continue to be amenable to Zionist demands under the Mandate.

The British Government had been lenient in the matter of immigration — but the excessive flow of immigrants into Palestine was clearly heading for some kind of disaster. One of the Commissions of inquiry sent to Palestine by the British to investigate this situation reported that the great increase in Jewish immigration "opened up the intolerable prospect of a Jewish State — of Palestinian Arabs being ruled by Jews" (ESCO Foundation report, p. 662).

This same (ESCO) report quotes Ben Gurion in angry condemnation of the British restriction on Zionist action as follows: "The White Paper has created a vacuum which must be filled by the Jews themselves. The Jews should act as though they were the State in Palestine and should so act until there would be a Jewish State there," cried this Zionist leader, who continued: "In those matters in which there were infringements by the (British) Government, the Jews should act as though they were the State."

Another top Zionist leader, Nahum Goldmann, is quoted in "Two Studies in Virtue," by Christopher Sykes, as saying

— "The object of the Jewish State has been the preservation of the Jewish people, which was imperiled by emancipation and assimilation." This statement brings forward many questions — but it and other statements seem to make clear that there has never been any question among Zionist leaders as to the eventual purpose of mass Jewish immigration into Palestine.

The Zionist-Arab conflict increased in violence. The Mandate which the Zionists had helped the British obtain in a mutual compact had now, it appeared, reached the end of its service and advantages for the Zionists — and certainly had become an intolerable burden for the British — or was fast becoming so. The British, however, kept on trying to carry out their Mandate job.

MILITARY INTENTIONS DEVELOP

One problem for the British in trying to deal with Zionist resistance and intransigence — and in suppressing warlike belligerence between the Jews and the Arabs — was that the Jews had the nucleus of a latent "military" force, known as the Haganah (Defense). This had started as a group of guardsmen when the early Jewish settlements decided they needed protection. It was "disbanded" at the beginning of the British Mandate, but as tensions all around increased, it was revived and trained as a secret force responsible to the Jewish Agency regime and the Jewish labor organization, called Histadrut. (See Chapter XIV that details the "underground" story.)

All of this was taking place as a side-problem for the British Government as that nation, together with France, was negotiating urgently with Russia in an attempt to check the growing threat of Hitler's power in Europe, which had escalated tremendously. His stormy threats had the world in jitters as the clouds of another world war seemed to be gathering fast. As it later became known, a British-French mission had left England on August 8, 1939, and arrived in Moscow on August 11, in an effort to negotiate a pact with a Russian delegation headed by Marshall Voroshilov who, with the usual Communist cunning, stalled the proceedings for a few days until Germany's Count Ribbentrop arrived to meet Stalin on August 23, when the famous non-aggression pact between Germany and Russia was signed. This pact was the green light for the start of World War II when, in a few days, Hitler and Stalin attacked and divided Poland. Britain and France had made defense commitments to Poland — consequently they were involved — and World War II was on. (The later involvement of the United States is too extensive to be given in this volume.)

Now that Britain was at war with Germany, it put a somewhat different coloration on the split between the Zionists and the British authority in Palestine over the White Paper to which the Zionists had taken great umbrage.

Hitler's anti-Jewish policies had embittered the Jews all over the world toward him and German Nazism. This new turn of events changed the attitude of the Jews in Palestine toward Britain considerably — for the time — as Jews began joining in the fight against Hitler's Nazi Germany. The Jewish Agency wanted to organize a special Jewish military force, which would be primarily to defend Palestine, but the British Government, with their understanding of conditions in Palestine, rejected this plan. The Zionists still had their friends in Britain and this Jewish demand for a separate force brought many debates in Parliament.

Finally in September, 1944, the British gave in to the Zionists, as they had done so many times before, and agreed to the formation of a Jewish Brigade with its own flag. This brigade was organized and trained in time to get some action during the final days of the war. Prior to its organization, several thousand Jews had volunteered and served with the British army. It was equally true of the Palestinian Arabs that thousands of them had also joined the British army in the fight against Nazism. In fact, according to General Glubb, the Arab State of Trans-Jordan had actually declared war on Germany in 1940 after the fall of France. The Trans-Jordan Arab army fought on the side of the Western Allies from 1940 to 1945.

From 1939 — outbreak of World War II — to 1942, there was comparative quiet on the Zionist front, as both Jews and Arabs were directing considerable effort towards

165

helping in the war against the Nazis. By 1942, however, the Zionists decided it was time to reinforce their position in Palestine, to realign it with their interpretation of statehood under the Balfour Declaraton. It may be purely coincidental that they were to make demands during the pressure of World War II, as they had done during World War I when they obtained the Balfour commitment. Now they had the added and appealling argument of needing Palestine as a Jewish nation for the resettlement of Jews escaping from Hitlerism.

ZIONISTS PRESSURE RENEWED
AT STRATEGIC TIME

In May of 1942, the Zionists called a meeting of Jews at the Biltmore hotel in New York — the most heavily Jewish populated city in the world as well as the major center of wealthy and politically influential Jewish leaders. At this meeting the Zionist plans for Palestine were reformulated — and set forth in no uncertain terms. The results of the meeting became known as the Biltmore Program. The Zionist-dominated conference demanded fulfilment of the Balfour Declaration and the Mandate privileges according to their own interpretation — which meant complete freedom for Jewish immigration and unrestrained progress toward turning Palestine into a Jewish State.

The British White Paper, which gave a 1939 statement of British policy, interpreting the Balfour Declaration according to its text, was rejected forthwith by the New York Zionist meeting. The demand for a Jewish military force under its own flag in Palestine was reiterated and supported. Moreover, unlimited immigration of Jewish "refugees," with sole responsibility being in the Jewish Agency (actually the World Zionist Organization), was demanded — and also that the Jewish Agency have authority to reorganize and develop the country. The meeting in New York City insisted that Palestine should be converted into a Jewish Commonwealth — in other words a Jewish nation. Power, it has been said, grows as it feeds upon itself. At any rate, it can hardly be denied that the Zionist movement had expanded tremendously from the days when Weizmann moved to England with essentially

166

no organization and no political contacts of any consequence whatever.

These demands were summarized most succinctly by Dr. Erich W. Bethmann, Director of Research for American Friends of the Middle East, in a Study already mentioned. "In summary," he reported, "the Biltmore Program called for a completely independent Jewish state, having its own army, own flag, and administration, unfettered by the policy of the Mandatory power. In fact, it implied that the Mandatory power should surrender vast stretches of unoccupied land not yet purchased by the Jewish settlers in Palestine. Not a word was said about a bi-national, bi-lingual state of Palestine where Arabs and Jews would live side by side as two ethnic groups, developing the same country."

"The Biltmore Program," continued Dr. Bethmann, "became the generally accepted program of World Zionism. Although dissenting voices were raised at the time, they were drowned in the generally favorable clamor. One of the dissenters was Dr. Judah L. Magnes, the first president of the Hebrew University in Jerusalem. Dr. Magnes belonged to the Ihud Party, which called for a bi-national state . . . with the Arabs of Palestine. Another group of Americans of Jewish faith, who never had subscribed to the idea of Jewish nationalism or a Jewish national state, organized itself after the Biltmore Conference. This was the American Council for Judaism, which affirms that Judaism is a religious faith and not a national entity, and that Jews in their spiritual affiliations should be loyal citizens of their respective countries, which are their homelands. Their adherence to Judaism should be a religious affiliation like that of Catholics to Catholicism, or that of Protestants to their respective denominations." (More about the American Council for Judaism's position on Zionism in Chapter VII.)

Dr. Bethmann states that after the Biltmore Conference, and as a result of it, Zionist propaganda "became increasingly active in the United States." The power of Zionism upon people in high places in the United States was shown when Resolutions were introduced in both houses of Congress (1943 and 1944) urging the fulfilment of the Biltmore Program, and that the British withdraw the White Paper of 1939 (already described).

PALESTINE ARABS ALARMED

It is not difficult to imagine the alarm among Palestinian Arabs when they learned about the Biltmore meeting and program. The Palestinian Arabs were neither highly organized nor well articulated, as were the Zionists — nor did they have the vast financial backing or highly professional propagandists back of their cause, as did the Zionists. The Palestinian Arabs, being poor people in the main, had to depend upon the sympathetic support of their Arab co-religionists in the surrounding Arab countries. In 1944, the then Amir Abdulla of adjoining Trans-Jordan (who became King Abdulla on March 22, 1946) cabled a protest to President Roosevelt concerning the new aggressive Zionist program as a result of it emanating from the United States. President Roosevelt replied that it was the view of the United States Government that no decisions altering the situation in Palestine should be taken without consultation with both Arabs and Jews.

It became plain to the Arab world, of which Palestine had long been an integral part, that Zionist aggression in this country had to be met with some kind of over-all Arab protection, and as a consequence the League of Arab States came into being in March, 1945, to serve as a unifying Arab agency and to coordinate defense and protection for the Arab world.

The Palestine problem, already overwrought because of Zionist agitation prior to World War II, was now multi-plagued with the new development where Jews were scurrying from northern and eastern Europe to escape Nazism. The Zionists, seeming to sense this as an advantage to their purpose, dramatized the issue as having one urgent remedy — all of these refugees must be jammed into the little country of Palestine, which was already populated with more people (Arab inhabitants and Jewish immigrants) than its limited production potential could sustain without outside help. There were many unpopulated areas in the world where refugees could have been settled, with great farming and production possibilities — but the Zionists, according to knowledgeable informants, were set on a policy of making Palestine a Jewish State. It was not overlooked by the Arabs that aside from the terrible plight of these refugees from Hitler there was also the quite obvious fact that if these masses immigrated to little Palestine, the over-balance of population would put the Zionists in the driver's seat for that country.

Concerning this, George E. Kirk, eminent British scholar, in "A Short History of the Middle East" (Praeger, Inc.), reported: "While these parleys with Zionists and Arabs were going on, the British authorities in Palestine had to deal with the rising flood of unauthorized Jewish immigration by sea from Central and Eastern Europe, where the desperate Jewish survivors of the Hitler terror had, since the collapse of Germany, been encouraged by a concerted barrage of Zionist propaganda to expect and demand immediate admission to Palestine."

Mr. Kirk refers to the immigration impasse by saying, "The Arabs had rejected any further immigration, and the Zionists refused to admit the principle that the Arabs should have any say in determining Jewish immigration." On the same page, Mr. Kirk refers to a committee the United Nations Organization had sent to investigate conditions in Palestine, saying that "Jewish terrorist activity which had ceased while the Anglo-American Committee of 1946 was in the Middle East, went on during the presence of the U.N. Committee," and he added, "Nor did the Haganah allow the Committee to leave without witnessing the arrival of the largest single contingent of illegal immigrants ever to reach Palestine, numbering 4,500 in all."

TERRORISM AS A WEAPON

The Haganah (Zionist defense army, mentioned earlier) continued to grow from the beginning, and during the days of hectic conflict between Zionists and the British mandatory forces, as well as between Zionists and the Arabs, two other "military forces" were operating on the Zionist side. One of these was the Irgun Zvai Leumi, sponsored by the Revisionist party and headed by Menachem Begin, a Polish refugee.

Begin, according to his book and from some opinions, was a heedless, swashbuckling bombastic fellow. "The fact that the mighty British Government," he wrote, "not only failed to put an end to our struggle but, on the contrary, continued to be subjected to blows of ever increasing severity, exercised a very healthy influence upon the Arabs. Their imagination did the rest." He apparently was referring to "psychological warfare." While the Zionists claim that the Palestinian Arabs fled the country and became homeless refugees because their own leaders advised them to leave, with assurances they could soon return, the Arabs (particularly the Refugees) say they left to save their families from terrorism — such as the ruthless massacre of the village residents of Deir Yaseen. In the book just quoted, "The Revolt Story of the Irgun," its leader, Menachem Begin, also wrote: ". . . Arabs throughout the country, induced to believe wild tales of Irgun butchery, were seized with limitless panic and started to flee for their lives. The mass flight soon developed into a maddened uncontrollable stampede." Terrorism, especially where women and children are endangered, is a frightful weapon. (See "Story of the Underground," Chapter XIV.)

The other auxiliary "military force" aiding the Zionists was the Stern Gang, headed by one Abraham Stern who finally was shot and killed by police. The Stern group also specialized in terrorism. George E. Kirk, in "A Short History of the Middle East," has this pungent comment of these two terroristic groups: "The Irgun Zvai Leumi made an unsuccessful attempt to kidnap the (British) High Commissioner; and the Stern Group went one better by murdering in Cairo the British Minister-Resident, Lord Moyne, who, they believed, has as Colonial Secretary obstructed the admission into Palestine of Jewish refugees from the Axis terror."

This, with Chapter XIV, constitutes a very brief examination of the forces and processes — the provocations and terrorism — that irritated and frightened the Palestinian Arabs and discouraged the British authorities trying to direct an orderly procedure of civil government in that little country, which brought the British decision to turn the whole complicated and seemingly insoluble problem over to the United Nations. (See Chapter XV.)

* * *

This 1961 "Open Letter" pamphlet is by U.S.N.R. Commander Elmo H. Hutchison who is also author of "Violent Truce" (Devin Adair) which book gives his observations while serving (1951-2) as Military Observer in Palestine for the U.N. Truce Supervision Organization — then as head of the Israel-Jordan Mixed Armistice Commission (1952-5). First paragraph of the "Open Letter" reads:

"Regardless of Zionist strength and methods of exerting political pressure, it would be impossible now to obtain sufficient backing among members of the United Nations to bring about Partition of Palestine. The present 104 member nations of U.N. are not laboring under the same lack of true information and the mass of Zionist inspired misinformation that led to the victimization of the Palestine Arabs 14 years ago."

171

14. TERRORISTIC "UNDERGROUND" CRUSADE TO DRIVE BRITAIN FROM PALESTINE

In the previous chapter (XIII), it was noted how the Zionists turned violently against Britain because of the 1939 British White Paper, which limited Jewish immigration into Palestine, in an effort to curb the growing conflict between the immigrant Jews and the resident Arabs. Their hostile outrage against Great Britain seemed in utter disregard of all the favors and Balfour concessions with which Britain had appeased the hard-dealing Zionists.

Suddenly something happened in 1939, soon after the White Paper had been issued, that quieted somewhat the Zionist rage that exploded in vehement verbal assaults against the British for imposing restraints upon the Zionist design for Palestine. World War II erupted causing the Zionist leaders to divert their attention, for the time, to the rising Hitler threat directed at the Jews of Germany and Eastern Europe.

The Zionist storm that had flared up over the White Paper curbs quieted somewhat, while activities were directed toward getting America into the war against Hitler. Because of American public opinion against another big war involvement, with its huge cost in money and lives, time and strategy were required to overcome this, but it was accomplished in December of 1941 by President Roosevelt, after the much questioned Pearl Harbor affair took place.

As the war moved along, the Zionists began to make use of the "Hitler terror" as reason why the immigration gates to Palestine should be immediately opened wide to accommodate the Jews fleeing from Eastern Europe. This, naturally, put a tremendous emotional thrust behind the Zionist goals for increasing Jewish population in Palestine.

In May of 1942, the Zionists called a meeting at the Biltmore hotel in New York (described in the preceding chapter) where the "Biltmore Program" was formulated on Palestine, in which "the Palestine Executive of the Jewish Agency played a guiding role," according to the two-volume report of the Esco Foundation. This program demanded that Palestine be opened for full immigration; that the Jewish Agency be vested with control over this immigration, and that "a Jewish Commonwealth" (Jewish Nation) be constituted there.

The program adopted by the Zionist-Jews at the Biltmore meeting served the purpose of "throwing down the gauntlet" in a challenge to Great Britain either to give in to the Zionists or give up the Palestine Mandate and get out of the country. For the British to abandon responsibility would, of course, have meant giving a free hand to the rapidly arrogating assumptions of the Zionist bandwagon and a betrayal of the Arabs who had long constituted the dominant population. Despite all the growing pressure of Zionism and pro-Zionist needling by United States officials, the British continued in a courageous effort to maintain order and administer the country fairly, as between Jew and Arab.

The Zionist drive to get the British out of the way soon took on the nature of an "underground" guerrilla-type assault by terroristic organizations known as the Irgun and the Stern Gang — operating clandestinely, but with cautious cooperation from the Zionist Establishment. Writing about this so-called "war of liberation" (to get rid of British hindrance), General Sir John Bagot Glubb, in his book "A Soldier With the Arabs," has this to say:

"When Germany appeared to be winning," writes General Glubb, "and while the issue still hung in doubt, both Arabs and Jews in Palestine remained inactive, watching, as it were fascinated, the battle of the giants. As soon, however, as it became obvious that the final result was no longer in question, violence and bloodshed recommenced. But whereas, from 1920 to 1939, it had been the Arabs who had been in revolt against the mandatory government, henceforward it was Jewish terrorism which went over to the attack. It was directed solely against Britain, the Arabs being neglected as though they did not exist. The principal Jewish underground organization was the Irgun Zvai Leumi under Menachem Begin, a Polish Jew who arrived in Palestine only in 1942.

"The Irgun devoted itself to attacks on British forces. Not only were British soldiers and police murdered, but some were kidnapped, flogged, ill-

173

treated and hanged. Mass murders were carried out, such as the blowing up of the King David Hotel, which was in use as the secretariat of the Palestine government. British, Arab and Jewish officials alike were buried in the ruins."

For a report "direct from the horse's mouth" on how the underground "war of liberation" was conducted, it will be helpful to consult "The Revolt" — a book by Menachem Begin (Hadar: Tel Aviv, 1964) who, as just noted by General Glubb, was a recently arrived Polish agitator who at once assumed the task of organizing and commanding the secret Irgun Zvai Leumi, which had the purpose of harassing, terrorizing and hampering the British in their administration of Palestine. It may be mentioned that the book was written by Begin with no under-estimation of his own valor and genius. It sparkles with the hit-and-run, cloak and dagger melodrama so common to the earlier stories of Russian nihilism.

Just as Begin came from the Polish-Russian area, so did Zionism itself and most of the people who crowded into Arab Palestine during the days of mass immigration. So rests the whole picture of Zionist "Israel" as of today. This was one of the problems from the beginning — and apparently it will so continue to be. Only minimal numbers of Jews have migrated to Israel from other countries — mainly a few from some Christian nations and greater numbers from Yemen and other "Oriental" areas.

The book is now so difficult to get — even in Tel Aviv where it was published — that some believe the Israel regnancy would be well pleased if the book could be forgotten so that the deeds it portrays will not haunt the Zionists and Israel in history. Begin has a chapter in his book titled "Army of the Underground" in which he says "They called us terrorists to the end." He explains that "the underground fighters of the Irgun arose to overthrow and replace a regime" — meaning the British regime who had been given a mandatory over Palestine by the League of Nations. His artful dodging in semantics to explain away the label of "terrorists" leads one to think "he doth protest too much." His explanation of the Irgun was that "it was in very truth a People's Army," which seems a poor phrase in view of its popular usage by the Communists.

174

Before dealing with the King David Hotel tragedy and other "terroristic" events, a brief explanation of Menachem Begin's "revolt" against the British authority in Palestine will help the reader to understand why and how the 1947-8 Zionist-Arab conflict shifted in the main and for a time to be a war of "revolt" against the British forces in Palestine by the Zionist-Jewish immigrants who had moved into that country, using the Balfour Declaration as a "legal" visa. The Zionists, in their growing conflict with the Palestinian Arabs, had already developed a military force known as the Haganah. The Palestinian Arabs had nothing of the kind.

When Begin reached Palestine, after a round-about journey from Poland and Russia, filled to overflowing with throbbing zeal and passion for the Zionist plan to turn Palestine into a glorified Jewish "ghetto" state, he and some associates who met at various places in "never ending" conversations (p. 63) laid "the foundations of our revolutionary struggle." These plans for an underground force to carry the war against the British Palestine forces were based upon the apparent assumption that the existing Haganah military had neither the right purpose nor the "special touch" that the formative Irgun was being created to give.

An early link of the Irgun to the United States (principally New York) is revealed by Begin when he says that "Arieh Ben-Eliezer passed the first years of World War II in the United States as a representative of the Irgun." (About this time there was a wide-spread underground movement among pro-Zionists in the United States, not only to collect money for the Zionist-Palestine underground — but also to obtain and ship war materials clandestinely to the Zionists in Palestine.) Begin explains that Ben-Eliezer reached Palestine in 1943 on behalf of the Hebrew Committee of National Liberation which had been set up by Hillel Kook and Samuel Merlin. The term "Liberation" meant "liberating" the Zionists from British authority. Some who knew their history likened this to the old Roman-Zealot problem in the same area, with the same characteristic insubordination.

NOTE: The Hillel Kook referred to above was reportedly a nephew of Chief Rabbi Kook of Jerusalem, well known in America under the name of Peter Bergson. Further evidence of the Irgun underground having strong roots in

175

New York is the big reception (endorsed by hundreds of notables) given to Menachem Begin at the Waldorf Astoria in New York, November 29, 1948 — as noted elsewhere in the "Refugee" chapter.

In the almost full-page advertisement of the Begin "Reception" (New York Times, 11-23-48) the announcement began: "A man who has become a legend in his own lifetime, Menachem Beigin, the former Commander-in-Chief of the Irgun Zvai Leumi, who at one time carried a price of ten thousand pounds on his head, will arrive at 2:30 p.m. today at La Guardia Field."

After other extravagant editorial accolades, the ad-writer further elevated Mr. Beigin by saying: "It was because of the valiant fight waged by the heroic underground that the whole structure of the British regime in Palestine collapsed, making possible the declaration of Hebrew sovereignty and the establishment of the State of Israel." The New Yorkers who brought Menachem Beigin to this country for a $50 a plate dinner spared no adjectives in polishing the posture of the man to whom they gave credit for driving the British out of their mandated authority in Palestine, so the Zionists could become a "nationality" instead of a religious grouping.

An explanation should perhaps be made of the different spellings of the underground leader's name. On the title-page of his book his name is spelled "Menachem Begin." All through the New York Times advertisement announcing the reception for him, his name was spelled "Menachem Beigin." When he was in a Russian prison in Wilno (Vilnyus, Lithuania) and was being questioned, he says (in his book) the questioner addressed him as "Menachem Wolfovitch" and that "for the hundreth time" he proclaimed his name as "Menahem ("c" omitted) Wolfovitch Begin." So much for the record.

It is interesting to turn the pages of Mr. Begin's book "The Revolt" and note how he describes the stealthy operations for which his New York devotees gave him such royal acclaim as the little David who defeated the giant Goliath. Certain British army men have expressed the opinion that his exploits (as publicized) were greatly magnified in importance but when added to other factors they were sufficiently terroristic to have a really damaging nuisance effect. The British forces, they say, could, with a free hand, readily have handled the Zionist underground and above-ground also — but reduced, as Britain was after fighting two world wars and with heavy dependency upon the United States for financial aid, a whole new set of problems had arisen. Consequently, the British leadership that had ultimately inherited the Palestine Frankenstein spawned by Balfour and Lloyd George realized the hopelessness of fighting both the Zionists in Palestine and the U.S.A. Establishment which was sponsoring the so-called "Resistance Movement."

This, to the British, was a nasty problem which they were trying to solve and were getting no help from the outside, except critical interjections from the U.S.A. and the U.S.S.R. Menachem Begin writes:

"The Eretz Israel Communist newspaper Kol Ha'am and the pro-Soviet Mishmar were completely nonplussed when the Soviet Union, in spite of the past, took its stand among the supporters of an independent Jewish State." He explains that the writers of "these Jewish Communist papers" found difficulty in adjusting to this "momentous declaration of the Soviet Union . . . But only to such short-sighted observers did Soviet policy appear to have changed overnight. The historic truth," he goes on to say, "is that the change had slowly been evolving during the long nights of the revolt.

"On the heels of the revolt came also the United States' demand for an immediate solution to the Eretz Israel question. It is noteworthy that the American, Warren Austin, in supporting the demand for the replacement of British rule in Eretz Israel by a new regime, used language almost identical with that of the Russian, Gromyko." (p. 58.)

Struggling against such odds was draining the British financially and otherwise. In 1947 they decided that Palestine had become a hopeless problem — a dream that had turned into a nightmare. They announced May 15, 1948 as their day of leaving. As the British pulled out the Zionist-Jews quickly moved into the vacuum which they anticipated. It all amounted to an epoch in history to be long remembered.

*　　*　　*

It is not possible to define a precise moment or action which marks the generally accepted or acknowledged beginning of what Begin calls "The Revolt" — otherwise described as the "Resistance Movement" or the "War of Liberation," all of which means the concentration of Zionist purpose to get the British authority out of Palestine — and out of their way. It seems, however, to have polarized around the arrival and activities of Menachem Begin in Palestine. If he had lived in Palestine in the days of Roman suzerainty, his fierce zeal for Zionism could be likened to the Zealots who fought Roman authority, and strangely enough there was a Zealot leader in those days of Vespasian and Titus named Menahem.

Begin was a dedicated apostle of Vladimir Jabotinsky, an earlier Russian Zionist activist, whose passion in Palestine was for more militant action against the British mandatory authority. In the early 1920's, his militancy against the British authority brought him a prison sentence — later remanded.

In reading Begin's book, one gets the idea that when he was released as a Russian prisoner he made his way quickly to Palestine to carry the flaming torch which his hero, Jabotinsky, had dropped at his death in 1940. According to the Standard Jewish Encyclopedia, Jabotinsky was "the spiritual father and nominal head of the Irgun." He was one of the first to call for a Jewish Army and vigorous action to establish the dominancy of Zionism in Palestine.

The roots of the Irgun Zvai Leumi (meaning National Military Organization), as well as the Stern Gang, run back to an extremist wing of Zionist revisionism in Poland and a Youth movement started in Latvia in 1923 called "Betar" — now known as the Herut party in Israel. The distinctions of these two groups is noted in the two-volume "Study of Jewish, Arab, and British Policies in Palestine" (Yale University Press) which says:

"The Irgun Zvai Leumi directed its activities against the institutions and machinery of Government, and set out to destroy police stations, post offices and other Government buildings . . . The members of the Irgun protested against being called terrorists; they regarded themselves as a Jewish military underground operating against 'the enemy,' i.e. Great Britain.

"The Stern Gang was an out-and-out secret terrorist society. Its members hid in the large cities under aliases and their parents were generally unaware of their activities. It is thought they were organized in groups of ten and that no member knew any of the terrorists outside of his own group . . . the majority were young Polish born Jews. Their purpose was to drive the British out of Palestine and they believed that assassination of the higher Government officers was an indispensable step toward this end . . . The group took its name from Abraham Stern, a Polish born Jewish intellectual with a messianic complex."

Menachem Begin, leader of the Irgun, in his book tells of many "underground" raids and attacks against the British forces in Palestine. One of the early ones was a raid for guns and ammunition on the R.A.F. air field at Akir, near Tel Aviv. The underground's Chief of Operations was a young man named Gideon. He planned this raid because there were "tremendous stores of arms and ammunitions there," things that were badly needed by the Zionist military. Gideon organized his raiding party — fitting it out with uniforms, caps and arms to look "absolutely like a British unit." They were provided with both passes and credential papers for each member as the disguise uniforms might not be sufficient.

The party arrived at Akir looking much like an ordinary truck load of British soldiers. At the airfield gates their papers were examined and approved and the truck passed normally inside. One of the party had a trained Scottish twang. In the ammunition store were some soldiers and Arab workers. The soldiers saluted the tall underground leader who promptly pulled his revolver and quietly ordered "Hands up, please." The British soldiers, stunned, exclaimed — "What's this?" "Hands up, quick," came the command. "I'm not a bloody British soldier. I am a terrorist of the Irgun Zvai Leumi." All hands went up quickly, Begin reported.

Members of the raiding party (with the aid of the coerced British soldiers) went to work quickly loading the truck with machine guns, sub-machine guns and ammunition — then quickly roared away. But the roads were muddy and before they could reach their destination the overloaded truck mired and stalled. They quickly transferred as much of their loot to a jeep as it would hold and scurried away, dodging British searching parties and sorrowfully leaving behind considerable of their pirated booty. This early raiding exploit was, according to Begin's book, followed by many more successful incursions as the "revolt" stretched into months and then into years of harassing the British authorities.

In the course of his narrative, Begin lists many names of the more prominent of the underground members among whom were Gideon, Amitzur, Avraham, Yoel, Reuven, Yitshak, Schmuel and others who played their various leadership roles. He also relates how he himself kept out of the hands of the British police by moving from place to place, living under different names. His first disguised residence was at the small orthodox Savoy hotel, 5 Geulah Street, Tel Aviv, one block back from the sea shore, where he lived as Mr. Ben-Zeev. After some four months he moved to a more isolated quarter under the assumed name of Israel Halperin.

Later he moved from this Hasidoff Quarter back to a little house on Joshua Ben-Nun Street in Tel Aviv and changed his name to Israel Sassover. He was playing quite a dramatic cloak-and-dagger role while slowly organizing the "underground." His role and purpose had not yet been accepted by

179

the Zionist Jewish Agency control. It was while living at this address, Begin writes, that the hounding of his Irgun group by his "fellow-Jews reached its climax." Some of his followers were betrayed to the British by certain of his "fellow Jews" who apparently feared his rise to power. But it was during this period also, he says, that the "hounding came to an end." A growing appreciation of "underground" possibilities brought about a better unity of the Jewish factions and the united "Resistance Movement was founded."

During that "unity" period, Begin relates that there were many "operations" including the storming of the British Government and Military headquarters in the King David Hotel. This spectacular and tragic demonstration of terrorism apparently broke up the "unity" between the "underground" and the constituted Zionist authorities, at least for the time, because of world publicity of the episode.

The next move by Begin was to Yosef Eliahu Street where he took on the name of Dr. Yonah Koenigshoffer and shaved the beard he had worn as Israel Sassover. A certain Israel Epstein, who had become a close friend and co-worker, was sent by Begin to Europe in 1946 "to engage in the training of a large reserve force we were building up abroad." Soon after Epstein's arrival in Rome the British Embassy there was blown up. A number of Irgun members known to be in Rome were arrested — Epstein included. As a result newspaper rumors heralded an imminent terrorist invasion of the British Isles — which report Begin writes "was very useful." Epstein tried to escape jail and was shot fatally in his attempt.

KING DAVID HOTEL BOMBED—MANY KILLED

There is space here only to mention briefly the various "operations" of the underground. One of the most spectacular of these was the blowing up of the King David Hotel located in the new Jerusalem of Israel as the divisions existed prior to the Israel expansionism of 1967. It presents a dramatic example of the harassment-strategy against the British authority in Palestine by the Zionist "underground."

One wing of this quite elegant hotel had been taken over to house such major British institutions as the Military G.H.Q.

and the Secretariat of the civil Government of Palestine. In a building close by the British Military Police and the Special Investigation Bureau had their headquarters. In an adjoining open space a substantial military unit was stationed. Because of the known danger to these important British administration units, careful watch and strong guard were constantly maintained.

Despite all of this, the "underground Resistance Movement" (chiefly the Irgun) decided to blow up this wing of the hotel. Begin tells how his men stealthily reconnoitered and made their plans. In the Spring of 1946, he says, they submitted their plan to the Command of the Resistance Movement. He informed Sneh and Galili "that we" (the Irgun) would undertake to penetrate the Government wing of the hotel in an "extensive sabotage operation — and that explosives would be used with a new device, invented by Giddy (Gideon)." (Moshe Sneh and Israel Galili, just mentioned, were top-brass in the regular Zionist Haganah-Security set-up.) The bomb when planted was to have time-detonation, presumably giving a chance to alert the hotel guests so they could escape.

The Haganah Command, writes Begin, "did not at once approve our plan" as they regarded it too daring and ambitious. "They were not against the principle," he explains, "but it was their opinion the time was not yet ripe. However," comments Begin, "we did not give up our plan." He kept communicating with the Haganah chiefs by code and conversation. The code name for the King David Hotel was first "Malonchik" but later was changed to just "Chick."

In the meantime another "underground" group called the F.F.I. (Freedom Fighters for Independence) but popularly known as the "Stern Gang" had prepared a plan to attack another government building. The Stern group, headed by a militant activist named Abraham Stern, had split off from the Irgun over some trivial differences of policy. Abraham Stern was later killed in a tilt with Police, and the group was then commanded by Yitshak (Isaac) Ysernitzky.

According to Begin, both the F.F.I. plan and that of the Irgun to deal with the King David Hotel were approved by the Zionist Haganah Command and Begin reprints in his book a letter of approval as of July 1, 1946, for the hotel "operation." Preparations for this "Operation Chick" were started at once, but for several arising circumstances there was considerable delay of execution. The modus operandi of the attack when it finally came is well worth noting — as detailed here.

HOW HOTEL WAS BLOWN UP

The Assault Unit with the commander wearing the dress of a hotel worker delivered some innocent looking milk cans to the cafe entrance of the hotel. The delivery workers then divided into two groups. The first group doing the "break through" carried the cans into the basement by way of the Regence Cafe. They subdued the Cafe employes and locked them in a side-room. The terrorists were surprised by the entrance of two British soldiers who had become suspicious. A short skirmish ensued which caused the "break-through" group hurriedly to place the "milk cans" — set the timer for thirty minutes and get out. A cracker-bomb was exploded outside to confuse and frighten people away and at the same time provide a cloud of smoke to cover the exit of the terrorists.

Some ten minutes later the terrorist chief reached the "telephonist" who was ordered to alert the hotel and notify two other nearby buildings. That apparently left only about twenty minutes as a warning to all these endangered people. At the exact thirty minute timing, the whole area shook with a tremendous explosion. The milk cans with their mixture of T.N.T. and gelignite had done their work. One whole wing of the big hotel had been "cut off as with a knife." More than two hundred people were either killed or injured. The "alert" to the hotel had failed — as could hardly have been otherwise — regardless of the rhetorical tears that Begin sheds in defending their intentions to warn the people "in time."

World opinion was aroused at this terrorist act. The Zionist Command was staggered by the outcry. Begin reports that one Haganah officer "made a series of wildly conflicting statements." First, he advised the Jewish Press not to denounce the "operation," "broadly hinting that the Haga-nah had prior knowledge of the attack."

Later in the day of the bombing when the larger number of casualties became known, this same spokesman for the Jewish Agency-Haganah establishment advised the press, according to Begin, to make no comment at all — and then later, as world revulsion began to frighten the Zionist establishment, this spokesman suggested that the blame be laid at the door of the "dissidents" — meaning the Irgun and the Stern group. If what Begin reports here is factual, it plainly shows the character of the drive against the British. It is Begin's plaint through much of his book that while there was general over-all approval of the "underground" tactics of the two terrorist groups, the Zionist-establishment wanted to stay "righteous" in the eyes of the world; and while reaping the benefits of the "underground operations," did not want to share any of the blame.

ARTFUL DODGING AMONG FRIENDS

An example of this elusive strategy is exposed by Begin when he reports that while the King David bombing was being planned, the Haganah leaders demanded that he should not "publish the identity of the attacking body," but immediately after the explosion (and the furor it started) he received a note from the leader Galili (on July 22, 1946) "asking us to announce that it was the Irgun" that was responsible. Begin states that his group complied by drafting and publishing "a full factual statement," omitting only one thing — that on July 1st the Haganah had asked the Irgun to carry out this precise operation.

Begin says that when he was asked to publish the admission of guilt, the officer told him the Haganah would publish no statement at all, but the very next day (July 23) the Haganah radio issued a release that "The Hebrew Resistance Movement denounces the heavy toll of lives caused in the dissidents' operation at the King David Hotel." Here, it seems, we get a peek at the rules of the game of war as it was being played in Palestine with the financial support of the American Diaspora, while from Washington pressured critical harassment was being dished out to the British.

After the Zionist underground-guerrilla warfare against the British mandatory in Palestine became menacingly intolerable — such as the blowing up of official offices in the King David Hotel with heavy loss of life, destructive attacks on airfields, the harassing of all kinds of British administrative activity — a statement to his soldiers was issued by the British commander, General Barker, in which he said:

"I am determined that they (the terrorists) should be punished and made aware of our feelings of contempt and disgust at their behavior. We must not let ourselves be misled by hypocritical sympathy expressed by their leaders and representative bodies and by the protestation that they are not responsible and cannot curb the terrorists. I repeat that if the Jewish community really wanted to put an end to the crimes, it could do so by cooperating with us." The announcement then proceeded with an order that all social contacts between the officers and soldiers with Jews was to end — and specific directions to that effect were included. The purpose was to protect intelligence and avoid the danger of officer kidnapping.

Begin, in his book, resented this act by the British commander and referred to the "hateful contents" of the message. Further on, he also says: "We regarded Barker, who tried to crush our people, as our enemy. We sentenced him to death, but were foiled in our efforts to execute the sentence. Several times we almost broke through the elaborate precautions he took for his personal safety, but on each occasion good luck favored him."

*   *   *

Begin writes that as a result of all the furor and public resentment about the King David Hotel bombing, the impression became quite widespread that the Zionist-Haganah authority had divorced itself from the "underground" (which apparently was the impression intended) but, he says: "It seems to me their relations with us were probably never more close than in the period following 'Operation Chick'." In August of that same year, continues Begin, "we put forward an operational plan for sinking one of the British deportation ships anchored in Haifa harbor." This plan was called "Operation Launch." A bit later, the Haganah officer wrote Begin that the "Launch" matter was "receiving serious attention." Begin seems anxious here to confirm their "togetherness."

"It was not the King David Hotel attack," writes Begin, "that brought about a severance of relations between the Haganah and the Irgun." This affair served only, he says, to "reveal the true character of those relations which were actually severed several months later." It is the way of history in our complex and swirling world that this tragic terrorist act and its purpose have long been forgotten. The severance that he mentions as of a later date is explained with such foggy verbiage as to be quite unclear except, perhaps, for those who are "in the know."

ZIONIST AUTHORITY IN PRE-ISRAEL PALESTINE

From 1920 (roughly) until 1948, there were actually two separate "governments" in Palestine. One was the Zionist apparatus and the other was the constituted authority of the British mandatory government created by the League of Nations.

The Jews in Palestine, while being subject to the official British Mandate authority, were more loyal and submissive to a sort of amorphous and clandestine "government" known as the World Zionist Organization (W.Z.O.) and its alter ego — the Jewish Agency. The first principle activity of this double-named organization was promotion of "immigration" — that is, the bringing to Palestine a large inflow of European (particularly Eastern European) Jews. Many of them in the late thirties were pitiful refugees from the plagues of Hitler-Nazism. As one of the accidents of fate, this tragedy fitted well into the "Jewish homeland" immigration plans of the Zionist leaders, adding a tremendous emotional surcharge to the grand Zionist design. Much furor was made over the Jewish refugees — and the world was rightly sympathetic. The Zionist Palestine solution, however, only created another mass refugee problem about which world sympathy has been grossly negligent.

Beyond getting the incoming Jews settled somehow in Palestine, the W.Z.O. structure soon found, as a result of inevitable clashes between the resident Arabs and the mass-immigrating Jews, that a "security system" was needed and this led to the gradual formation (as documented elsewhere) of the Palmach "spearhead" and the Haganah — described by Glubb Pasha as an "embryo Jewish army." Then leeching on to this "security system," with added plan of ousting the British authority from Palestine, came the "underground" Irgun Zvai Leumi and its offspring — the Stern Gang.

All of this — and more, of course, was tied in with and dependent financially upon, the Zionist Organization "authority." The one unit that tried to be arrogantly independent and autonomous was the "underground" which grew up under the leadership of Menachem Begin out of a group of young militant Zionists he gradually got together.

DUAL ROLE OF W.Z.O. AND JEWISH AGENCY

It may be helpful at this particular point briefly to redefine the Zionist structure. The World Zionist Organization was established by Herzl and his Zionist delegates at the first Zionist Congress in Basle in 1897, as a world body to advance Zionist goals. The Jewish Agency was created as a sort of counterpart of the W.Z.O. in a subtle manipulation of Zionist influence when the words "Jewish agency" were written into the Mandate over Palestine, given to Great Britain by the League of Nations in 1922. This put the "camel's foot" inside the Palestine tent. The language was as follows: (Article IV)

"An appropriate Jewish agency shall be recognized as a public body for the purpose of advising and cooperating with the Administration of Palestine in such economic, social and other matters as may effect the establishment of the Jewish national home and the interests of the Jewish population in Palestine, and subject always to the control of the Administration, to assist and take part in the development of the country.

"The Zionist organization so long as its organization and constitution are in the opinion of the Mandatory appropriate, shall be recognized as such agency. It shall take steps in consultation with His Britannic Majesty's Government to secure the cooperation of all Jews who are willing to assist in the establishment of the Jewish national home."

It appears quite clear that the reference to "a Jewish agency" was regarded by the Mandate authors as an unimportant and subordinated concession to the Zionist wranglers. But soon, so to speak, it took on the role of "a tail wagging the dog." The Zionists knew that they could not get the World Zionist Organization mentioned in the Mandate but they did know "a Jewish agency" could be made to serve the same purpose. This inclusion meant a cleverly manipulated "League of Nations' sanction" for wording that was to become a pregnancy for what, at the proper time, was to produce the birth of a Jewish State. Both the Balfour and the Mandate documents were charmingly clothed with innocuous verbiage and while concealed within this legerdemain was the fundamental objective of the Zionists, it also carried for the Lloyd George-Balfour Government a nightmarish snare into which they had walked, intoxicated with both gullibility and political adventurism.

NOTE: While most people in retrospect may evaluate Balfour and Lloyd George as sentimentally stupid in their understanding of the Zionist question, no one would charge them with being conspiratorial, even though they were warned as to what the outcome might be. They apparently gambled with conscience instead of reason — and England lost. It may be noted here that there was no time limit placed on the mandatory authority over Palestine given to Britain by the League of Nations. This, of course, would be a real obstacle in the path of Zionist aims and may be a major explanation as to why the Zionist elements combined in a so-called "war of liberation" to oust the British from Palestine. They may have decided there was no other way to gain control.

---

*　　*　　*

GROWTH OF POWER AND ACTION

In considering the Zionist "underground," the Zionist Haganah "security" and the general build-up of the Zionist drive to "liberate" Palestine from the British Mandate, the question must arise for the thoughtful person as to where all of the money came from to carry out this program. Altogether it was an expensive operation. From time to time herein, reference has been made to the "Zionist establishment" which may briefly be described as a combination of the World Zionist Organization — the Jewish Agency — the considerable number of "helper" organizations devoted to money-raising — and of course, the emotional arousement of a new "nationalistic-religious" movement that cemented Jewish solidarity in most of their world communities.

As already noted, the Mandate over Palestine (after World War I) included reference to a "Jewish agency" to be organized to consult with the British mandatory authority where interests of the Palestinian resident-Jews were concerned. Soon after the Mandate had been officially granted, the title of Jewish Agency was established by the Zionists as a kind of Siamese-twin to the World Zionist Organization; and that arrangement needs some clarification, if possible.

From what followed over the years, it is clear that the Zionists gave a much more widely stretched interpretation to the functional purpose of the "Jewish Agency" than did the British as custodians of Palestine. The Jewish Agency soon became an extending-organization with the J.A. Executive spreading its authority and activities by incorporating an Immigration Department and moving steadily into other Zionist-oriented proliferation. The president of the World Zionist Organization also served as president of the Jewish Agency. This gave the twin bodies a single head.

The Jewish Agency also took over from the Zionist Organization the Palestine Foundation Fund (Keren Ha-Yesod) which had been the early financial arm of the Zionist Movement, with a chief purpose to utilize the Balfour Declaration for the fullest implementation of the Zionist goals in Palestine.

The transfer of this Fund in 1929 to the enlarged Jewish Agency made this combination-arrangement an efficient transmission belt for money from the Jewish communities in the United States and elsewhere to Palestine to meet the needs of the rapidly developing Zionist functional apparatus. According to the Jewish Standard Encyclopedia, the Keren Ha-Yesod (meaning "foundation fund") financed all of the Jewish Agency's activities (including "security" forces) until establishment of the new State of Israel in 1948.

After that took place, many of the numerous functions of the Jewish Agency (which had been serving more or less as a Zionist "government" organism for years) passed to the new Israeli government. In 1951, Keren Ha-Yesod was reaffirmed as the sole fund of the World Zionist Organization, apparently better to serve the public image. K-H was given the additional name of United Israel Appeal, by which it is known in the United States.

The United Israel Appeal (for fund raising in the United States) was originally founded as the United Palestine Appeal. The Standard Jewish Encyclopedia explains that this organization and the American Jewish Joint Distribution Committee merged their fund-raising work and established the United Jewish Appeal. According to the records, these various agencies have been able to raise astronomical amounts for Zionist activities.

ZIONIST FECUNDITY IN THE U.S.A.

Another proliferation of the evolving Jewish Agency was to organize, in 1939, the American Zionist Emergency Council to coordinate four divisions of Zionism in the United States. These were: the Zionist Organization of America (U.S. branch of the World Zionist Organization) — Hadassah (the Women's Zionist Organization, now organized with chapters in all States) — the Poale Zion and associated Labor Zionist groups — and the Mizrahi (orthodox Zionist group). It may be noted here, also, that the Zionist leader, Dr. Chaim Weizmann, on behalf of the Jewish Agency, appointed a number of Zionist leaders to the American Emergency Council. The full Council included also Hashomer Ha-tzair, known as "The Young Guard" (Zionist Youth Organization, Marxist-oriented, according to Standard Jewish Encyclopedia.)

NOTE: Poale Zion is in fact a Zionist Socialist party movement. Its greatest leaders were Nachman Syrkin and Ber Borochov (both Russian socialists). Syrkin claimed — "There can be no Zionism except Socialist Zionism." Borochov, according to A. L. Patkin, Russian authority on Jewish socialism, regarded Karl Marx as his "highly revered teacher and guide."

The American Zionist Emergency Council, mentioned above, was reorganized in 1949 as the American Zionist Council, with a public relations program to "impart to Americans a knowledge of Israel's problems." It, in turn, sponsored the Student Zionist Organization and the Zionist Youth Council.

Much of what is being reported here will be news to Americans generally. Many of those who have known something of Zionist activities have long objected to the United States being used as a base for a network of agencies and activists whose international designs have been detrimental to America's friends and former allies — and which, at the same time, lead in the direction of international complications that could be disastrous to America's own best interests and even survival. But these founding-stock American pro-testors find they have not so much influence with the "new society" politicians as do these closely-knit, internationally-minded newcomers whose purposes and loyalties are not always easily discernable.

With the ever increasing growth-ramifications of the Zionist movement, the needs for money have naturally grown heavier. This has led into a vast complex of interrelated Zionist-Israel fund raising agencies and organizations creating an interlocking structure, too complicated to be fully explained here. It would be folly to make such an attempt when Senator Fulbright, in an official Senate investigation of the interlacing Zionist and Jewish money raising organizations in the United States, admitted publicly he could not understand the intricacies of it all.

NOTE: For more details about this investigation concerning the Jewish Welfare Funds and Jewish Agency-Israeli money gathering and distributing procedures, see Chapter XXIII.

ZIONIST ATTENTION SWITCHES FROM BRITAIN TO U.S.A.

The tremendous proliferation of Zionist activity in America shows how Zionist leaders changed their strategy during the period following the first World War. As shown in other chapters, the first concentration of Weizmann-Zionist attention was directed at Great Britain because Weizmann astutely saw in this war a great opportunity to capitalize British problems into concessions that could build a Zionist bridgeway into Palestine.

NOTE: Weizmann's strategy worked well. His concentration of tactics on Britain during World War I did produce the Balfour Declaration which the Zionists could use as a "legal" right of immigration to create a "Jewish homeland" in Palestine — on the presumption that the British Mandate over that country would be useful as a friendly extension of the Balfour immigration concession. Under the British Mandate military authority, however, there developed a stern regard for law and order that placed limitations on mass Zionist immigration which soon brought Zionist hostility toward the whole Mandate idea — and resentment of British military authority. Gradually this indignation developed into a wide-spread intolerance and militant desire to be rid of British restraint. History was repeating itself. This gradually led to "revolt" and the so-called "war of liberation" — liberation to be free to create the Jewish State about which Herzl had originally written in his "Der Judenstaat."

It was during this period of growing disillusionment with the British that Zionist leadership began concentrating more and more attention on the rich and fertile United States where, with the beginning of the Roosevelt "New Deal," the social and political climate became highly favorable. The two-volume Esco Foundation report (Yale University Press) states that the Zionist policies on immigration into Palestine "found expression both in Palestine and the United States, now the two main centers of Jewish life."

The dependence of Zionist-Israel upon the United States for financial support — for political strength — and for emergency military aid for its survival becomes clearer as the record of the years is examined. The pronouncements of the Jewish members of Congress — the American Jewish press predominantly — and all of the numerous Zionist organizations and Israeli spokesmen make that abundantly clear.

*　　*　　*

MONEY FROM U.S.A.
VITAL TO ZIONIST NEEDS

The United Jewish Appeal (U.J.A.) appears to be the agency with the widest over-all spread in the United States for raising contribution money for Zionist-Israel causes. An advertisement for U.J.A., including the Combined Jewish Appeal (the latter operating in and for the Chicago community), appearing in the Chicago SENTINEL (3-24-66), announced the 1966 campaign drive for $73,420,000. The 1966 appeal for contributions said: "You can help U.J.A. bring many more thousands to Israel, the U.S.A., Canada, and other free lands."

The New York Times (12-9-66) carried a story headed "Dinner With $10,000 Minimum Opens U.J.A. Drive," which announced the opening of the U.J.A. 1967 money campaign. The article stated that the 1967 goal was $73,000,000 and that 60 percent of the money raised by U.J.A. is for "relief and settlement work in Israel. The rest," it continued, "is used to help Jewish immigrants in America and other countries." The chief speaker was Governor Romney of Michigan. The notices were sent to a highly selected list — and read:

191

"Minimum Contribution $10,000. Black tie. R.S.V.P." More
than 600 attended.

NOTE: Added to the above 1967 drive, the New York Times (1-16-67)
carried a story headed: "ISRAELI BOND GOAL PUT AT 115-MILLION."
The kick-off was at a Waldorf-Astoria dinner in New York. Israeli's Finance
Minister came to give starting impetus to the bond sales (larger than in
1966) which the Israel official said is important to support a sagging economy. "Since the first Israel bond campaign in this country in 1951," the
Times story said, "more than $923,000,000 in Israel bonds have been sold,
with the greater amounts in this country."

There is also a U.J.A. sub-division called the "United
Jewish Appeal of Greater New York" which sponsored a
full page advertisement in the New York Times calling for
money for an "Israel Emergency Fund," which said in big
headlines: "THE EMERGENCY CONTINUES SO THE
EMERGENCY FUND MUST CONTINUE . . . to meet
greater humanitarian needs in Israel."

U.J.A.'s Vice President, Rabbi Herbert A. Friedmann,
was quoted in the Times as saying — "Once a man identifies
himself with our work, it lasts for a lifetime." The Jewish
people must certainly be credited with a "group loyalty,"
rarely, if ever, matched in history. The Zionist organizations
have added greatly to this solidarity. The power potentials
of political Zionism among Jewish people — as well as its
impact upon non-Jewish institutions — appear to be unparal-
leled as a political phenomenon.

It is not the purpose here, however, to make reference
to any matters, Jewish or otherwise, that do not in some
way correlate with Middle East history, past and present, to
which this book is devoted. So far as money-gathering is
concerned in the United States for Zionist causes, there are
many special gifts and collections that go to buildings and
programs too numerous to mention here. The larger amounts
that go to Zionist-Israel aid are obtained through: (1) sale
of Israel Bonds; (2) contributions to the United Jewish Appeal and its auxiliaries; (3) contributions to some 200 Jewish
Welfare Foundations (discussed in Chapter XXIII). The
total runs into the high millions annually.

JEWISH AGENCY GROWS AND GROWS

Among the very few Americans who know anything

about the structure or activities of the Jewish Agency are some who have raised questions about its money-raising programs in the United States. The Jewish Agency of Israel (integral part of the Israel Government) has organized the Jewish Agency, Inc., a twin affiliate to function in the United States. The American Examiner (7-25-63) carried a story headed — "Jewish Agency Authorizes 12 Israel Campaigns in U.S." The twelve campaigns authorized were:

American Committee for the Weizmann Institute of Science
American Friends of the Hebrew University
American-Israel Cultural Foundation, Inc.
American Red Mogan David for Israel, Inc.
American Technion Society
Federated Council of Israel Institutions, Inc.
Hadassah, the Women's Zionist Organization of America
Jewish National Fund
Mizrachi Women's Organization of America
National Committee for Labor Israel (Histadrut Campaign)
Pioneer Women (Women's Labor Zionist Organization of America, Inc.)
Women's League for Israel (New York area only)

The Examiner story said — "The list has been made public by the Jewish Agency's committee on control and authorization of campaigns, which serves as a clearing house for fund-raising activities for Israel in the United States. It was set up under the auspices of the Jewish Agency and includes representatives of the National United Jewish Appeal, New York U.J.A., and the Council of Jewish Federations and Welfare Funds."

The ingenious arrangement of combining a network of organizations for the gathering and distributing of American money for Israel has the result, if not the purpose, of making the whole process so complicated as to put it beyond the understanding of the average human mind. The only official investigation, so far attempted, caused the Senate committee Chairman (Senator Fulbright) to admit frankly it was all too complex for him.

The activity of raising millions in America and funneling a large part of it on to be used by the Zionist organization in Israel (during the years before and after the Zionists proclaimed their "Jewish State") had begun to get some attention — probably due to the publicity given it by the anti-Zionist American Council for Judaism.

193

This apparently made the Zionist high-command somewhat nervous and apprehensive that their magical power in Washington might not always protect the flagrancy of the procedure. Consequently, a somewhat changed arrangement for handling these funds was initiated which, for the average individual, only made the process more obscure. The Jewish Agency (already a dual-entity with the World Zionist Organization) took on a Siamese-twin act when it was arranged for the Jewish Agency (in Israel) to do teamwork with a "Jewish Agency for Israel" (incorporated and officed in New York) in some kind of a money-transfer arrangement the purpose of which has been quite puzzling. One suggested explanation is that it may have been so arranged with the U. S. Foreign Agents registration act in mind.

A news article in the (American) "Jewish Voice" (April 15, 1960) told how the national chairman of the United Jewish Appeal and the chairman of the Jewish Agency in Israel (Dr. Nahum Goldmann, who is also chairman of the powerful World Zionist Organization — and in truth the big-voice of the world Zionist movement) devised a new method "of allocating American Jewish philanthropic funds for the work of the Jewish Agency in Israel." These two Zionist leaders, the story said, "outlined the details of the reorganization under which the Jewish Agency for Israel (in Israel) and the Jewish Agency for Israel, Inc., in New York" would work together to use the money collected in the United States — and that the Jewish Agency for Israel "will be the sole agent for the implementation of the projects supported by the American corporation." To this should be mentioned again, for emphasis, that the Jewish Agency in Israel is a constitutional part of the State of Israel itself.

NOTE: The references here concerning American money going to Zionist uses are but part of the story. A more detailed examination of the Zionist money-collecting system in the United States is documented in Chapter XXIII.

15. BRITISH RELINQUISH MANDATE AUTHORITY TO UNITED NATIONS; U.N. IN DESPERATION ORDERED PARTITION OF PALESTINE

The conditions in Palestine (political and martial) had by late 1947 become so intractable, encouraged by forces outside Palestine over which the British Mandate authorities had no control, that the British Government decided to withdraw from the scene completely and put the problem in the hands of the United Nations.

It should be pointed out that a heavy burden of blame for conditions rested on the political shoulders of the United States — first, because of the President Wilson-Brandeis contribution to the Balfour delusion, and later because of the Presidents Roosevelt and Truman policy of kowtowing to voting-bloc influence of the Zionist brand in needling the British trusteeship, which was trying to maintain order between Jews and Arabs. During 1946-47, when the Zionist pressure was on in Palestine, General Glubb, who was close to the scene of action, wrote in his book, "A Soldier With the Arabs," that "no voice in America was raised to support the Arabs."

Many knowledgeable Americans knew well, and often so expressed themselves, as to how both Presidents Wilson and Truman, especially after 1933, had become prisoners of a political pressure-bloc system, inside and outside Government, which began its real rise to strategic power under President Wilson and his entangling alliance with what was known as the Brandeis group.

BRITISH CLOSE THE LEDGER

On September 26, 1947, the British Colonial Secretary gave clear indication that because of the chaotic and apparently insoluble situation in Palestine, the British Government might soon find it necessary to withdraw. It was not long, accordingly, until Great Britain served notice on the United Nations that it should prepare to assume responsibility in Palestine by May 15, 1948, which date was named as the time when Britain would relinquish her Mandatory authority, also withdrawing her troops and administrative personnel. Consequently, the British command at once began the extensive and hazardous removal task in order that it could be completed by the date set — May 15.

This sudden turn of events brought the inchoate and inexperienced (two years old) United Nations face to face with a dynamite-loaded problem. Here was a group of politically appointed men or varying experience, of whom but few knew any more about the Palestine situation than what they had read from news reports —often garbled and frequently slanted. These novitiate administrators of a new political instrumentality (formed under shadows and questions) were, in obvious unpreparedness, catipulted into the responsibility of coping with one of the most complicated and volatile political conflicts existing anywhere in a troubled world.

They simply had no answer for this baffling enigma other than to resurrect the previously repudiated suggestion of the Peel Commission, which was to "partition" Palestine into two separate "States" — one for Jews and the other for Arabs. They were faced with a quick and pressing imperative to do something — and it was perfectly clear that they were grabbing in the dark — with possibly some outside pushing.

U.N. NOVICES ORDER PARTITION

Since there appeared to be no alternative at hand, a United Nations decision to partition Palestine was issued as U.N. Resolution 181, on November 29, 1947. It provided that Palestine was to be divided into a Jewish State — an Arab State — and an International Zone of Jerusalem.

The Partition plan gave roughly fifty-six percent — or 3,815,417 acres — of the total land area — including the fertile coastal plains and the rich citrus belt — to the largely immigrant Jews from Eastern Europe. Jewish philanthropists had, over the years, purchased settlement land for Jews who might wish to go there, but at the time of the Partition, according to the tediously prepared Hadawi study, less than ten percent of Palestine land was Jewish owned.

With the Zionist-Jews being apportioned the larger acreage, it left only forty-four percent (2,857,467 acres) of the land for the native Palestinian Arabs, and a so-called International Zone — a proposed sort of enclave to include the Old City of Jerusalem. This was never implemented. To this point, the U.N. partitioning process did not give the beleaguered Arabs much hope of protection or fairness from this international agency.

The United Nations Partition Resolution provided that a Palestine Commission be "set up, consisting of one member of each of the Member States" to be elected by the U.N. General Assembly and that this Commission was to take over the Palestine "trusteeship" as the British relinquished it, and to administer the areas as evacuated until such time as the Arab and Jewish States (and International Zone) could be organized, which was to be completed within two months after British relinquishment.

JEWS SEE CHANCE—MOVE QUICKLY

The Zionists had neither patience nor apparent intention to wait out the two months. They jumped the gun by being all ready to memorialize an *arc de triumph* of the great Zionist design by a self-declaration of their Jewish State of Israel, one minute after the British-announced withdrawal time. The young United Nations, apparently awed by Zionist aggressive power, made no effort to oppose this brazen disregard of its stated plan for orderly transfer of authority in Palestine. Not only that — but the perplexed U.N. allowed the Jews to seize and hold as their own a considerable part of the land the U.N. had reserved for itself as the "International Zone." It was the possession of this area that enabled the Zionist-Jews to build their new Israeli capital (which they call Jerusalem) right up to the borders of the venerated Old City.

It is important to note that while some of the U.N. stipulated "International Zone" was taken over by the Zionists without anybody apparently objecting, a purpose to grab it all seemed imminent. Zionist underground units had quietly infiltrated the Old City section of the proposed "International Zone" immediately on the heels of the British forces as they moved out, and had secured themselves in the key buildings and defense spots.

Jordan's Arab Legion (commanded by General Glubb) had been requested by the British not to engage in action until the British had left, which was an advantage for the infiltrating Zionist-Jews. By the time the Legion was able to respond to the cries for help from Jerusalem Arabs — and the increasing threat to Jordan's frontier — it was almost too late to save the Old City from the Zionist plot to take it. The valiant fighting by which it was saved is described in Chapter XVII.

U.N. RIGHT TO PARTITION CHALLENGED

When the British announced their decision to withdraw from Palestine and leave the trusteeship in the hands of the United Nations, and the U.N. in turn announced its plan would be to "partition" the country, the Arabs rejected the decision with vehemence and boycotted the U.N. hearings on the proposal, believing that if they participated it might be considered an acknowledgement of the United Nations' right to divide the country. They claimed the Arab rights to Palestine were firmly based on four distinct foundations:

(1) The natural right of the people to remain in possession of the land of its birthright should be valid; (2) Palestinian-Arabs have lived predominantly in Palestine for over 1300 years; (3) At the time partition was announced by the U.N., the Arabs were the rightful owners of most of the homes and fields which partition (and seizure) gave to the Zionist Jews; (4) In addition to these valid claims, the Arabs charged that partition by U.N. would be illegal, improper and unnecessary.

NOTE: Anti-separation sentiment was widespread throughout the world but the crisis had become so acute that no other remedy was forthcoming. One noted Irishman put the truth on the line when he said,— "The U.N. has no more authority to partition Palestine than it would have to separate Ireland into two States — one for the northern faction and one for the southern."

The Arabs might, however, have been better off if they had appeared at the U.N. "partition hearings" to protest the Jewish claims rather than letting them go through by default. It is conceivable that with a hard fight they might have been given the Negev. They were, however, putting their faith in the power of world opinion, and like many others they learned that Justice is often blind, fickle and indifferent where political pressure is at play.

WERE ZIONISTS BACK OF "PARTITION"?

The United Nations' decision to partition Palestine may not have been altogether without outside influence. It is interesting to note an observation by the Zionist leader, Chaim Weizmann, in his Autobiography wherein he reveals his own interest in the matter of partition. He states that the idea of partitioning Palestine was first broached to him "by the Peel Commission *in camera*" on January 8, 1937 — ten years before the U.N. decision. At that time he pleaded "no opinion" until he could talk with his Zionist colleagues. When the Peel plan was abandoned by the British Woodhead Commission as unworkable, that does not mean it was also abandoned by Dr. Weizmann. According to him it started Zionist thinking along a new line.

NOTE: Weizmann"s recorded observations after the Peel Commission suggested "partition" to him clearly show that he was intrigued with the idea and its political possibilities. "I felt," he wrote, "that the suggestion held great possibilities and hopes. Something new had been born into the Zionist movement." But this "something," he mused, "had to be handled with great care and tenderness . . ."

Weizmann devotes several pages to his contemplations, analysis and reasoning as to the plan's advantages. One can readily assume that a man with his political sharpness would not overlook the advantages of having the great United Nations put its seal of "authority" on the apportionment of a large section of Palestine as a "Jewish State." This would be a tremendous step forward in the Zionist design over the fence-straddling Balfour Declaration — which by now had served its purpose and was more or less a dead issue. The main value of the Balfour document was when the Zionists succeeded in getting its more salient points incorporated into the Mandate document and this Mandate by tenuous assumption was inherited by the 1945 United Nations.

Prior to the partitioning decision by the United Nations — during the period of the strange "biting the hand" liberation-war to get rid of the British — Weizmann had discussed this idea of partition with his Zionist colleagues. Some were for it and some against it. But when the U.N. announced its plan for separation (which would give official sanction to "a Jewish State" as a de facto entity), the Zionist-internationale was widely enthusiastic.

HOW PARTITION OF PALESTINE WAS PUSHED THROUGH

As indicated, the partitioning of Palestine was welcomed by the Zionists who, according to the record, at once mounted a frenzied drive to mobilize the necessary votes to assure adoption of the proposed plan in a somewhat unpredictable Assembly.

It would seem important here to make record of some of the evidence pointing up the pressure influence that was used in the desperate action to insure the passage of the U.N. Resolution for partition.

The late James Forrestal, former Secretary of the U.S. Navy and the first U.S. Secretary of Defense, is regarded as one of the most patriotic and dedicated public officials to grace the Washington administration during the 1944-1949 period. During his terms in the two high offices he held, he kept a personal diary which was later published in serial form by the New York Herald-Tribune and still later was published in book form. The following excerpts from the Forrestal Diaries are pertinent to the Palestine situation — especially while the pressure was on to push the partition-deal through:

14 July, 1946: "The Middle East: America has lost very greatly in the Arab world by our attitude on Palestine. The British say they cannot do all they would like to for the Arabs because of the pressure that we were able to exert in connection with the British loan."

November 26, 1947: "Lunch today with Senator McGrath. Prior to it I had read the secret report on Palestine prepared by CIA. I said to McGrath that I thought the Palestine question was one of the most important in our American foreign policy, and that if we were talking about lifting foreign affairs out of domestic policies, there was nothing more important to lift out than Palestine, with all its domestic ramifications. I said the Palestine-Jewish question was similar to the Eire-Irish question of forty years ago and that neither should be permitted to have any substantial influence on American policy . . ." (The editor of the Diaries adds that Forrestal understood from McGrath that Jewish sources had made substantial contributions to the Democratic National Committee "with a distinct idea on the part of the givers" that their opinions on the present Palestine question would be seriously considered.)

December 1, 1947: "Lovett (Under Secretary of State) reported on the result of the United Nations action on Palestine over the week end. He said he had never in his life been subject to as much pressure as he had been in the three days beginning Thursday morning and ending Saturday night. Swope, Robert Nathan, were among those who had importuned him . . . The Firestone Tire and Rubber Company, which has a concession in Liberia, reported that it had been telephoned to and asked to transmit a message to their representative in Liberia directing him to bring pressure on the Liberian government to vote in favor of partition. The zeal and activity of the Jews had almost resulted in defeating the objectives they were after.

"I remarked that many thoughtful people of the Jewish faith had deep misgivings about the wisdom of the Zionists' pressures for a Jewish state in Palestine, and I also remarked that the New York Times editorial of Sunday morning pointed up those misgivings when it said, 'Many of us have long had doubts . . . concerning the wisdom of erecting a political

200

state on the basis of religious faith.' I said I thought the decision was fraught with great danger for the future security of this country."

December 3, 1947: "Lunch today with Jimmy Byrnes. We talked Palestine. Byrnes recalled the fact that he had disassociated himself from his decision of a year ago to turn down the Grady report which recommended a federated state for Palestine or a single Arabian state. He said the decision on the part of the President to reject this recommendation and to criticize the British for their conduct of Palestinian affairs had placed Bevin and Attlee in a most difficult position. He said that Niles (David K. Niles, administrative assistant to the President) and Sam Rosenman were chiefly responsible for the President's decision; that both had told the President that Dewey was about to come out with a statement favoring the Zionist position on Palestine, and that they had insisted that unless the President anticipated this movement New York State would be lost to the Democrats . . .

"I asked Byrnes what he thought of the possibility of getting Republican leaders to agree with the Democrats to have the Palestine question placed on a nonpolitical basis. He wasn't particularly optimistic about the success of this effort because of the fact that Rabbi Silver was one of Taft's close associates and because Taft followed Silver on the Palestine-Haifa question. I said I thought it was a most disastrous and regrettable fact that the foreign policy of this country was determined by the contributions a particular bloc of special interests might make to the party funds." (It was no secret that heavy contributions to the Democratic Party from Jewish sources were considered as playing a role in pressure action.)

February 3, 1948: "Visit today from Franklin D. Roosevelt, Jr., who came in with a strong advocacy of the Jewish State in Palestine, that we should support the United Nations 'decision,' and in general a broad, across-the-board statement of the Zionist position. I pointed out that the United Nations had as yet taken no 'decision,' . . . and that I thought the methods that had been used by people outside of the Executive branch of the government to bring coercion and duress on other nations in the General Assembly bordered closely onto scandal."

NOTE: The David K. Niles, mentioned by Mr. Forrestal, was given a chair in the White House during the Roosevelt "New Deal" as a sort of ambassador-extraordinary for "minority causes" — a remarkable assignment considering his background. This was something new but reflected the emerging "new order" in Washington politics. Niles (Neyheus) made a strange career of anonymity in his highly influential liaison role as set forth in a 1949 Saturday Evening Post article — and otherwise. . . . The Samuel Rosenman mentioned was a New York lawyer — one of the original New Deal "brain trusters" who became the confidant, speech writer and adviser to President Franklin D. Roosevelt. This was a turning point in American politics . . . The Forrestal Diaries (edited by Walter Millis for the Viking Press) is a great tribute to a great statesman — an honest man — and a monument to his political martyrdom.

The late Sumner Welles, former Secretary of State and holder of several other U.S. diplomatic posts, said:

"By direct order of the White House every form of pressure, direct and indirect, was brought to bear by American officials upon those countries outside the Moslem world that were known to be either uncertain or opposed to partition. Representatives of intermediaries were employed by the White House to make sure that the necessary majority would at least be secured."

President Truman has been quoted as saying in his Memoirs (Life Magazine, January, 1956):

"I do not think I ever had as much pressure and propaganda aimed at the White House as I had in this instance. The persistence of a few of the extreme Zionist leaders — actuated by political motives and engaging in political threats — disturbed me and annoyed me. Individuals and groups asked me, usually in rather quarrelsome and emotional ways to stop the Arabs, to keep the British from supporting the Arabs, to furnish American soldiers to do this, to do that, and the other."

Someone may ask, "Why, if President Truman felt that way about the pressure, did he meekly submit as indicated by the statement by Mr. Welles?" A realistic answer probably would be that he was preparing to run soon (in 1948) for re-election and was a captive of our American unbalanced presidential electoral voting system where bloc-colonization in six or seven "key" states — especially New York with its large electoral vote — can materially affect a national election. It is well known that this condition does hamper the freedom of action of every presidential candidate, because he is a prisoner of the sensitive political machinery upon which he must depend. (Parenthetically, there seems to be an easy answer to this. It is to change the counting of electoral votes to districts within a state, instead of by state-majority count. It is not easy, however, because of the power blocs that benefit from the pressure system.)

MORE PRESSURE REPORTED

On the subject of Zionist pressure to get Palestine partitioned (so their status in Palestine could be "legalized"), Alfred Lilienthal, in his most excellent book "What Price Israel?", reports that United Nations' action favorable to the Jews was urged by the Chief Rabbis of Palestine acting jointly, while among those in the United States pushing the matter were the American Jewish Committee, the American Jewish Conference, the American Christian Committee for Palestine (a sort of political front), the Jewish National Council, and others. One of these was the New Deal's leftish labor-arm, the C.I.O. Mobilized into action were also several left-wing publications and organizations, too numerous to

202

mention. It was an impressive and effective mobilization.

As to the brazen pro-Zionist position of our Truman Government at the time, here is the opinion of Dr. Millar Burrows, distinguished former professor of Biblical Theology at Yale, author of books including two of the best on the Dead Sea Scrolls, and famous archaeologist. In his book "Palestine Is Our Business" he writes:

> "The vote for partition in the United Nations Assembly on November 29, 1947, was forced through by our Government with a shameless resort to the time-worn methods of power politics."

The United Nations, left to itself without all the promptings and pressures brought upon it, would most probably not have passed the "Partition" resolution in any such form as it did — possibly would not have passed it at all. Here, it seems, is an eloquent example of polished use of minority pressure — a widely accepted part of the weaponry of rugged diplomacy; but surely there is a line of demarcation between pressure and persuasion.

*　　*　　*

For a quick look at what did actually happen when the U.N. Assembly got down to the business of voting on the plan to partition Palestine, the following quotation is reprinted from "A Soldier With the Arabs," by General John B. Glubb, formerly Commander-in-Chief of the Arab Legion, in his highly objective report on turbulence in the Holy Land:

> "The first visible results of Britain's resignation of the Mandate was the arrival (in Palestine) of yet another committee. This one was called UNSCOP — United Nations Special Committee on Palestine. It did the usual tour, it heard the same old evidence, and it disappeared again. On August 31st, 1947, UNSCOP submitted its report. It was not unanimous. Seven members recommended partition. Three voted for a Federal State with Jewish and Arab cantons. One member wished the Committee to report the facts to the General Assembly without recommendations.
>
> "The General Assembly," continues the General, "appointed an ad hoc committee to study the report. By 25 votes to 18, with 11 abstentions, the committee rejected an Arab proposal that the Balfour Declaration be submitted to the International Court of Justice. By only 21 votes to 20, the committee dismissed the question of the competency of UNO to enforce partition without the consent of the majority of the inhabitants of Palestine. A resolution on the subject of the absorption of Jewish displaced persons in countries other than Palestine was defeated by 18 votes to 15.
>
> "Eventually a proposal to adopt the UNSCOP report in favor of partition was adopted by 25 votes to 13, with 17 abstentions. In other words, in a committee of 55 members, only 25 voted for the proposal. The statement

made by the Canadian representative was typical of the feelings of most of the members. 'We support the plan,' he said, 'with heavy hearts and many misgivings'."

Quoting further — "The Pakistani Foreign Minister, Sir Muhamad Zafrullah, uttered a prophetic warning to the Western Powers when he said: 'Remember that you may need allies in the Middle East. I beg of you not to ruin and blast your credit in these lands'."

The final vote on the Partition Resolution was set for November 26, 1947 but was temporarily postponed — apparently to give the pro-Zionist backers a little more time to be sure they had the votes to assure passage. It would hardly have been done to accommodate the Arabs as their articulate numbers and political influence at the time were inconsequential in the world of polished international diplomacy. The Resolution was finally brought up for vote on November 29, 1947, and the result is here quoted from the 1948 World Almanac:

"Nov. 29 — By a vote of 33 to 13, with 10 abstentions, the U.N. General Assembly at Flushing Meadow, New York City, approved the plan for the partition of Palestine into sovereign Jewish and Arab States, effective Oct. 1, 1948. The United States and the Soviet Union were among those voting for partition, while Britain, the mandatory power, abstained. Spokesman for the five Arab nations denounced the vote as a violation of the U.N. Charter and served notice they would take no part in carrying out the plan or share in the responsibility for the dire consequences which, they warned, would follow. Adoption of the partition plan was received with rejoicing by Jews in America and in Palestine. Assembly President Aranha of Brazil appointed a commission composed of representatives of Bolivia, Czechoslovakia, Denmark, Panama and the Philippines to supervise the orderly transfer of authority from Britain to the two new states."

WHAT OF THE FUTURE

Only time can give the answer as to what will come from the maneuvering and partitioning in Palestine, which introduced into that land of ceaseless trouble and conflict a "Jewish State" greatly resented by a surrounding Arab world, made hostile by the very tactics of intrusion.

The Zionists made the Palestine adventure with what is widely considered as two particular aces in the sleeve. One is that the Arab States are too disunited to mount a substantial attack upon Israel as an intruder; and the other is a feeling of assurance and dependence upon the high concentration of Jewish wealth and influence in the United States to protect Israel's existence — regardless of by what means it was established.

Frequent headline slips like — "Israel Would Fall If It Were Not For Help of America" and — "Lebanon Alarmed at Word 6th Fleet Will Protect Israel" seem to hint at Israel's dependence upon America. The reference to the 6th Fleet was the headline of a Los Angeles Times' story (April 18, 1967), based upon a reputed allusion by Israel's Premier implying Israel's confidence in the protective, peace - keeping ability of the U.S. Sixth Fleet, stationed in the Mediterranean. Such dependence, at its best, would not seem to be too comforting for a long-range view with the rapidly changing world conditions — and with America's strength being strained by heavy involvement in other parts of the globe.

Look to history — the glory that was Greece and the grandeur that was Rome. Turn the pages of Volney's "Ruins of Empires" (1872), and reflect. Only yesterday, in the span of time, the navy of Great Britain ruled the seas and her sterling bloc was master of world trade. All history calls out to warn that those who spread too far may not retain their strength too long. The federal debt in America is astronomical and continues the upward spiral year by year. Being a so-called "leader" is to travel the path of peril.

NOTE: Since this chapter was written, there have been material changes through the blitz-advances of Israel in the further acquisition of Arab lands (1967), which at time of publication are in a confused and uncertain state of final settlement. (See Chapter XXI.)

---

16. BRITISH DEPART FROM PALESTINE ZIONISTS STAGE COUP—PROCLAIM "JEWISH STATE"

On the morning of May 14, 1948, the street canyons that plough through the skyscrapers of New York city echoed and re-echoed the çacophony of sidewalk news venders barking out the big black newspaper headlines which announced with great dramatic flare the birth of the new "Israel" to this Zionist conscious city.

The New York Post covered its front page with a copy of Israel's "Declaration of Independence" in the center, boxed in with a story datelined Tel Aviv on one side, announcing the new self-proclaimed Jewish State — and on the other was a story datelined Damascus, announcing that: "The Arab League's General Secretariat proclaimed last night that a state of war exists between the Arab countries and Palestine Jewry."

What all of this added up to was that at the stroke of twelve (midnight) May 14, 1948, as the British relinquished their Mandate authority over Palestine to the United Nations, the Zionist-Jews executed a fast coup d'etat, and without consulting the United Nations or having any authority other than their own force majeure, announced to the world that they had taken over the better part of Palestine and made of it "a Jewish State . . . to be called Israel."

As justification for the coup, the Zionists issued a "Declaration of Independence" which rang loudly with high-sounding rhetoric — some of which has been questioned as to accuracy. The first sentence, for instance, reads: "The land of Israel was the birthplace of the Jewish people."

NOTE: Palestine, according to the Hebrew Bible (Old Testament) was certainly not the "birthplace" of Abraham, who is credited as being the chief progenitor of "the Jewish people." He was born in far away Ur of the Chaldees and did not, during his nomadic life, reach Palestine until he was over 75. Even then he hurried on through Canaan for a considerable sojourn in Egypt, until ejected by the Pharaoh. The Israelites who conquered Canaan by the sword were all born in Egypt and along the 40-year trek from that country to Canaan. The Israelite leader Moses, the most central figure in Judaism, was born in Egypt — not Palestine. Yet the Zionists opened their Declaration for their new "nation," claiming the land as "the birthplace of the Jewish people." (See Chapter VII for more discussion about "the Jewish people" phrase.) The "Declaration" claiming Palestine next says — "Here they wrote and gave the Bible to the world." They refer, of course, to the Hebrew Bible, but the obscure records of who were the writers seem to indicate that much of it may have been written in Babylon where the Babylonian Talmud was written.

Most Jewish scholars are frank in admitting that they do not know precisely where or by whom the Old Testament was written. The Zionist "Declaration" goes on to base the "legality" of their right to "reestablish" an ancient nation, upon the 1947 United Nations' Resolution ordering the partition of Palestine to include "a Jewish State" and "an Arab State." There is much doubt that the United Nations had any authority to divide a country — and the circumstances surrounding the "partition" and the later "self-proclamation" of a "Jewish State," as examined in this volume, can be nothing less than enlightening to present and future students of history.

A CLAIM NOT SUPPORTED BY THE RECORD

The Zionist "Declaration" says further that "Jews strove throughout the centuries to go back to their fathers and regain statehood." The record on this is documented in other parts of this book. Until political Zionism was organized and inflamed an awakened political vision of the great strategic value of the Palestine "gateway" to world commerce and prestige, there was very little to indicate any great urge on the part of Jews in general to return to the moneyless deserts of the Middle East.

For 1,800 years after the Romans dispersed the Jews from the small area called Judea, Jews migrated throughout the world and prospered beyond anything imaginable that could have happened to them in Palestine. There does not appear to be any mad rush of the millions of Jews in America — even those crowded into New York tenements — to go back to the new Israel.

The Zionist "Declaration" for the new Jewish State says further that "the right of the Jewish people to a national revival in their own country . . . was acknowledged by the Balfour Declaration and affirmed by the mandate of the League of Nations." A well informed observer gave the following analysis of that claim: (1) The so-called "Balfour" letter to Lord Rothschild (called a Declaration) was prepared by the Zionists themselves to fit their own plans, and after final approval by the "Brandeis group" was handed to Balfour for signature; (2) The facts about the Mandate for Palestine are that again it was the Zionists who planned and worked to put this scheme through, expecting, it seems clear, to continue their influence over Britain.

RABBI WISE FRANKLY GIVES MANDATE MEANING

A revealing item on this Mandate matter was recorded in the authoritative releases of Mr. Charles Thompson, called "Peace Conference Day by Day" and included in the thoroughly documented 800-page book "Palestine: The Reality" by the late British journalist J. M. N. Jeffries. This was during the early days of the Paris Peace Conference in 1920 where statesmen and professional politicians had gathered to "make the world safe for democracy" at the end of the first World War. The telltale item states: "Following his talk with Balfour and Colonel House and later with Tardieu, Dr. Wise wrote out a statement which disclosed that a very definite plan was under way. This statement included three propositions: (1) that a Mandate be given Great Britain as the trustee over Palestine; (2) that a Mandate be given to France as the trustee over Syria; (3) that a Mandate be given the United States as the trustee over Armenia." Then from the statement by America's leading Zionist, Rabbi Stephen Wise, the following forthright words are quoted:

"Great Britain should be given, and I believe will be given, the Mandatory of Trusteeship over Palestine, which trusteeship, I have reason for saying, Great Britain will not accept save by the common consent of such disinterested peoples as our own. Great Britain's trusteeship over a Jewish Palestine will be because of the summons or mandate of the League of Nations, and for the sake of the Jewish people and the Jewish Commonwealth which they are in time to realize."

This seems to make crystal clear that the Mandate (Trusteeship) was long planned and that its purpose of an eventual Zionist Commonwealth (Jewish State) was well understood.

Mr. Lloyd George seemed eager to have the mandate — and if anyone doubts that there was "horse trading" in this newly invented "mandate" business, he may weigh the plain words of Lloyd George as chronicled by Lord Lagard and others when, in an unguarded moment, he said: "France would be compensated for the oil wells of Iraq by the Mandate for Syria" — which mandate was predicted by Rabbi Wise in his statement just quoted.

In retrospect — with the "Jewish Commonwealth" now realized as predicted by Rabbi Wise who, with Felix Frankfurter, was at the Peace Conference to join the other Zionist leaders to protect Zionist interests — not much beyond the adding up of facts and statements is needed for clarity as to the nature and purpose of the Mandate over Palestine. As between the Lloyd George-Balfour government and the Zionist leaders it seems clearly to have been a matter of "you scratch my back and I'll scratch yours." The British, however, got clawed well in the scratching when Zionism turned into a booby trap for them in Palestine.

Something further concerning the Balfour Declaration and the Mandate for Palestine should be noted — they both were perfidiously contradictory. They both promised a "homeland" for "the Jewish people" (which the Zionists interpreted to mean "a Jewish nation" — while at the same time promising the Arab inhabitants that their rights and freedoms would be protected. These assurances were dishonest political experiences — as subsequent events have disclosed. (See Chapter XVII for reference to the King-Crane Report on danger of encouraging a Zionist-Arab conflict.)

*　　*　　*

Referring again to the Zionist "Declaration" through which the State of Israel was proclaimed, it is important to note the tactics which completely ignored the authority of the United Nations which has assumed Trusteeship over Palestine when the British relinquished it. And to the authors of the "Declaration" must go the highest kudos for a masterful tapestry of words with its convincing coloration for the uninformed. It reflected fully the artful genius to which Zionism owes its amazing development and success.

209

This remarkable "Declaration" of the new State passes on from a reference to the long dead League of Nations to the present United Nations, linking them by inference, then making mention of the Partition Resolution passed by the U.N. in November (1947) — insinuating that this Resolution authorized the "re-establishment" of an independent Jewish State in Palestine. The call was made for all concerned to take such steps as necessary to establish this new Israel. The assumption seems clear that the Zionists were now in full possession of their own destiny upon the authority of the U.N. Resolution and that from there on the Zionist movement was responsible to no one — including the United Nations.

A PRODUCT OF PRESSURE

Since the Balfour Declaration had served the Zionist purpose and died of pernicious anemia — and the British Mandate had been destroyed by a Zionist "war of liberation" — and all claims of statehood-existence were now being arrogated to the U.N. Partition resolution, it is worth taking a look at just how that Resolution was obtained. The facts are that it was accomplished only through strenuous Zionist pressure plus the invaluable votes of the Soviet bloc — and only then passed by a narrow margin. It was driven through in the heat of a political battle that has rarely been exceeded for its wire-pulling and intimidation.

Alfred Lilienthal, in his excellent book "What Price Israel?" (Henry Regnery Co.), has described the pro-Zionist pressure as a shocking example of ruthless pressure exploitation — naming individuals and organizations. He quotes the late Robert Lovett (then Under-Secretary of State) as saying: "Never in his life had he been subjected to as much pressure as he had in three days" while the Resolution was being considered. The Palestinian Arabs, who had been the predominant inhabitants of Palestine for centuries, charge that the United Nations had no more moral or legal right to divide their country than it would to divide England or the United States.

The Zionist Declaration alleges that "recognition by the United Nations of the right of the Jewish people to reestablish their independent state may not be revoked." This, of course, is mere self-pleading. Legislative acts at all levels have a continuous record of revocation throughout the world. This brief examination of the Declaration has covered only the high points. To it should be added one other question.

All through this proclamation of the Zionist State, argumentation of national status or national sovereignty has been presented in the name of "the Jewish people," which many Jews consider a non sequitur. Non-Zionist Jews claim that such use of "the Jewish people" is false arrogation. Out of this seems to come the question — has political Zionism succeeded Judaism as the dominant and accepted image of "the Jewish people?" That is a question — not just for Jews — but for others as well.

* * *

Throughout the Jewish world, of those who by belief or propaganda were of Zionist persuasion, there was wide rejoicing and shaloming as the news went forth that a new "Jewish State" was aborning. Few, of course, knew much about its real meaning or its purpose; how it had been brought about; how its economy could be sustained; or of how much world trouble it would be the harbinger. All that mattered at the moment was that it sounded like something big for the glory of "the Jewish people."

The Zionist leaders, however, knew well what was happening. They had been feverishly busy for weeks prior to the announced date of British retirement (May 15, 1948), setting the stage for the new statehood proclamation. Things were moving well. The British retirement was the goal the Zionist "underground" had sought for many months.

Top leader Weizmann and some of his close lieutenants, including Moshe Shertok, were at United Nations headquarters (Lake Success, New York), keeping close watch on critical happenings there as the Zero hour approached when the British would turn Palestine authority over to the United Nations. Weizmann also had other interests to take care of in the United States. He was well aware of the strategic influence of voting blocs in New York and other big-city states on the presidential candidate in the upcoming election.

ZIONIST ACTION IN U.S.A.

In his autobiography, Weizmann states: "In the early part of May . . . I strengthened our contacts with our friends in Washington, and affirmed my intention of going ahead with a bid for recognition of the Jewish State as soon as it was proclaimed." On May 13 (two days before the proclamation of the new State, Weizmann wrote a letter to "Dear Mr. President:

> "The unhappy events of the last few months will not, I hope, obscure the very great contributions which you, Mr. President, have made towards a definitive and just settlement of the long and troublesome Palestine question. The leadership which the American Government took under your inspiration made possible the establishment of a Jewish State . . . It is for these reasons that I deeply hope that the United States, which under your leadership has done so much to find a just solution will promptly recognize the Provisional Government of the new Jewish State. The world, I think, will regard it as especially appropriate that the greatest living democracy should be the first to welcome the newest into the family of nations.
>
> Respectfully yours,
> Chaim Weizmann"

Confronted with this brilliant display of diplomatic charm and technique, it may be easier to understand why great politicians like Arthur James Balfour and David Lloyd George were so readily amenable to the artistry of the great Zionist leader from Russia. Opposite the reprint in his book of the letter to the President, Weizmann, with a show of audacious technique, reproduces a photograph of himself presenting President Truman with a beautifully decorated Scroll of "The Law" — indicating a subtle and seemingly intentional suggestion that there was a compelling relationship between the Judaic religion and the political formation of the new federal Jewish State.

The interesting climax to this illustrious performance was the inglorious demonstration of the sad state of "political democracy" in the United States when Mr. Truman (the incumbent presidential candidate for that year) with dramatic haste arranged "to be the first" to recognize the new Israel. This histrionic affair is so excellently described by Alfred Lilienthal in "What Price Israel?" that short quotation is truly priceless history. The scene was the White House. The time was May 14, 1948, a few hours before the momentous

212

Zionist act of self-proclamation. White House tension was feverishly high.

"A serious revolt threatened the President within his own Party," states Mr. Lilienthal. "On May 14 the President was closeted with his intimate advisers. One of the few callers he received that day was Frank Goldman, President of B'nai B'rith, an organization whose membership prominantly included Mr. Truman's intimate friend and old Kansas City partner, Eddie Jacobson. Congressman Sol Bloom of New York, Chairman of the House Foreign Affairs Committee, had wired the President that the U.S. had better take the lead in recognizing the new Jewish State in order to help keep Palestine and the Near East from Soviet domination' . . . Around eleven-thirty that morning, Elisha Epstein (later, as Eliahu Elath, the first Israeli Ambassador to the U.S.) was called to the White House. Epstein, then representative of the Jewish Agency in Washington, was told that the U.S. would like to accord de facto recognition immediately upon the declaration of Israel's independence." (For greater detail on this historic event, Mr. Lilienthal's book is recommended.)

One matter that has been troubling more and more American citizens is the growing tendency of U.S. officialdom, especially in Middle Eastern policies, to submit to the articulate and demanding insistence of minority political blocs. Some people are outspoken in saying that this is a growing threat — not only to America's world posture — but of even greater importance as it tends to destroy some of the nation's greatest traditions.

To close this report on the culmination of the Zionist design into "the Jewish State," first blueprinted in Herzl's "Der Judenstaat," it is interesting to turn to the writing of the Zionist "underground" leader, Menachem Begin, in the final pages of his book "The Revolt — Story of the Irgun."

"A regime resting on a hundred thousand bayonets had collapsed," he writes, referring to the British mandatory authority over Palestine. "In its place and on its ruins a new regime was about to arise; a nation was coming to life; a very old nation . . . There is no doubt that the revival of Hebrew national independence in our generation has no precedent in human history."

Begin then explains how on May 15 (day of Israel proclamation) he went to the secret radio station of the underground Irgun Zvai Leumi in the heart of Tel Aviv and made a speech to the people in every town and village who had listened to the call of the underground for years. "The Hebrew revolt of 1944-48," Begin told his listeners, "has been blessed with success — the first Hebrew revolt since the Hasmonean insurrection that has ended in victory . . . The State of Israel has arisen in bloody battle. The highway for the mass return to Zion has been cast up . . . The State of Israel has arisen, but we must remember that our country is not yet liberated. The battle continues, and you see now that the words of your Irgun fighters were not vain words: it is Hebrew arms which decide the boundaries of the Hebrew State. So it is now in this battle; so it will be in the future."

213

Menachem Begin did not fade from the Israel picture when the "underground" war was won, making it possible to set up the Jewish State. His underground movement (the Irgun Zvai Leumi) was converted into — or added to — a Political Party (the Herut) and Begin is now a prominent member of the Knesset (Israel Parliament).

Eight years after the new Israel had been instituted, the Jerusalem Post (October 2, 1956) reported a speech by Menachem Begin, head of the Herut Party, where, speaking at its convention in Tel Aviv before some 1,400 people, he reportedly said, "The day is fast approaching when the pupils of Jabotinsky (early founder of the militant Revisionist Party, sponsoring the underground Irgun) would present themselves to the President of the (Israel) State to form a new government in cooperation with other groups to replace the Mapai (Ben-Gurion's socialist) regime . . . If the disciples of Jabotinsky came to power," Begin continued, "they would assert Israel's right to its entire territory, not on the basis of the land now occupied, as Mr. Ben-Gurion did, but on the basis of its historic boundaries (both sides of the Jordan) . . ."

Israel also has the distinction of having, as a former member of the Knesset, the head of the major branch of the Communist Party in Israel, Mr. Moshe Sneh. During the years of the "underground" activity against the British, Sneh was one of the leaders of the Jewish Agency's military arm (the Haganah) and, according to Menachem Begin's book, was the contact who conferred with Begin concerning certain activities of the "underground" Irgun.

*　　*　　*

This chapter has regrettably, but necessarily, been but a brief review of a tremendously eventful period-development in the Zionist drive of conquest in Palestine. It may, however, serve as a launching pad for those inquiring minds who are seeking the truth of what has happened to create the dislocations and miseries that are so clearly evident as one visits the Palestinian refugee camps today.

214

17. PALESTINE ARABS CALL FOR HELP. NEIGHBOR ARAB STATES RESPOND — BUT INADEQUATELY. 1948 WAR STARTS BETWEEN ZIONIST-JEWS AND ARABS

The confrontation between Zionist-Jews and Palestinian Arabs continued to grow more acrimonious and difficult as the mass inflow of Zionist Jews crowded into that small and already well occupied country. It is not difficult to imagine the aggravations that would arise from such aggressive encroachment.

When the Zionists, already well equipped with an underground military arm, on the 15th of May, 1948, proclaimed a "Jewish State" in the midst of the Palestine Arab community, the resident Arabs were convinced that this meant the end for them unless they had quick defensive help. A hurried call consequently went forth to officials of the Arab League of States for urgent aid.

The crisis had arrived. Press and radio shouted the news. The front page story of one New York newspaper (date lined Damascus, Syria, May 14, 1948) read in part: "The Arab League's General Secretariat proclaimed last night that a state of war exists between the Arab countries and Palestinian Jewry."

Certain of these Arab countries, notably Egypt, then ruled by King Farouk, Syria, Iraq and Lebanon sent token forces, with Jordan's Arab Legion permitted to join only after the British soldiers had left the Jerusalem area. The Arab Legion concentrated on defense of the Old City of Jerusalem and the Latrun area of the road to Tel Aviv. The response of the other Arab States was a hurried matter which

215

lacked unity and coordination as well as sufficient forces for the job to be done. The problem had been, perhaps, too lightly regarded. Some of the details of the war, as it developed during the next few weeks, will be herein related.

COOKING THE DEVIL'S BROTH

The main purpose of this chapter is to examine the war of 1948 between the Zionists and the Arabs, toward which the road was paved by the incredulous Balfour Declaration. Both this document and the Mandate over Palestine, conceived and co-authored by the Weizmann-Zionists, were perfidiously, and perhaps purposely, contradictory. They both promised a "homeland" for "the Jewish people," which the Zionists promptly and dogmatically interpreted as a "covenant" for a "Jewish Nation." These documents, at the same time, promised the Palestinian Arabs (then greatly preponderant as unarmed inhabitants) that their rights and freedoms would not be disturbed. A promise of protection — by whom?

Any realist should have known the futility of this — in the nature of the forces and conditions with which they were dealing. When the British Palestine authorities did try to protect the Arabs from the mass immigration design, a drive to get rid of the British was started by Zionist underground harassment — combined with needling criticism from high United States officials — all of which gave little comfort to the British caught in their own diplomatic pitfall.

WILSON'S INVESTIGATION IGNORED

Many believe that Britain could have been saved from some of her Middle East ignominies if she had paid more attention to the findings of the special investigation of Syrian-Palestinian sentiment ordered by President Wilson in 1919. An appeal for such an investigation was made by the Arab leader Feisal at the Paris Peace Conference when he became aware of the well laid Zionist immigration plans.

The proposed investigation was first approved by the Big Four power-bloc but was abandoned later largely because of France's opposition, based upon her self-interest apprehensions. President Wilson, sensing that ill-boding machinations

216

were in motion that would disregard the rights of the pre-ponderant Arab inhabitants, appointed the King-Crane Commission (headed by two eminent Americans) to make an independent survey of prevalent opinion in the area concerning the Zionist-Balfour integration plans. It is not necessary at this late date to take space for details of the Commission's findings, other than to say they dealt largely with the proposed Mandate system over Syria-Palestine and Iraq and recommended strongly that limitation be placed on Zionist aspirations.

The Commission had become convinced, after listening to Jewish representatives, that Zionist plans meant the eventual conquest of Palestine, and what would happen would be a gross violation of the rights of the dominant Arab inhabitants — as well as an ignoble end to the peace principles proclaimed by the Allies and emphasized in Wilson's famous Fourteen Points. The President failed to secure Senate approval of membership in the League of Nations, a newly spawned mechanism conceived by the master minds who were formulating the ill contrived peace plans that laid the groundwork for "nothing but trouble."

The United States was thus barred from further peace-settlement involvement and the final participating powers (Britain, France and Italy) completely ignored the recommendations of the U.S. King-Crane Commission. What followed is now a matter of living record.

MASS INVASION FOMENTED WAR

Tracing the consequences of the ill-fated Peace Conference, we find that by May 15, 1948, the mass Zionist invasion into Palestine had led to the proclamation of the conquest that had been anticipated by the King-Crane Commission. This naturally led to war. The Zionists (referred to after the above date as Israelis) claim that this 1948 war between Arabs and Israelis was set off by outside Arab States sending armed forces to help the unarmed Palestinian Arabs defend themselves.

The Arab answer to this is that the war was the inevitable culmination of Zionist-Israeli aggression, intended to oust the

217

Arabs and turn Palestine into a Jewish State. They say it was the final acts of Israeli terrorism, as the British prepared to leave the country, that caused the Palestinians to flee for safety and call for help.

They point out that before the British left and before any soldiers from other Arab States appeared in Palestine, the Zionists had aggressively occupied some territory reserved (in the partition plan) for the "Arab State" and the "International Zone of Jerusalem," besides the territory proposed for the "Jewish State," taking over the homes and properties of some 300,000 Arabs who had fled to safety across the neighboring borders. It was this situation, declare the Arabs, that caused the Palestinians to call for help from their neighbors and religious brothers.

While it is true that certain Arab States responded to the call for help from the besieged Palestinian Arabs, it is also true that the response was poorly organized, and because of that was completely inadequate. The Arab States simply were not, at that time, prepared for such an eventuality. It is for this reason, plus planes and arms supplied the Israelis by the Soviet bloc, that the new State of Israel was able to hold its anchorage and survive. The Israelis must be given credit for a determined, well planned and directed military operation — otherwise, even with the Arab inadequacy in numbers and coordination, they would have been defeated.

COMPARISON OF STRENGTH

The frequently repeated mathematical myth that 650,000 Israelis were pitted against 40,000,000 Arabs can make sense only to the uninformed. No Arab State was highly militarized. There had never been much unity among them — for one reason because of ancient feuds, both personal and political from earlier years, that still persisted. Each of them, for political reasons and competitive prestige, boasted of greater military strength than they had. King Farouk's Egypt was supposed to have army strength of 50,000 men, but had great difficulty in mustering 10,000 when it was decided to go to the aid of the Palestinians.

Syria, which had become independent only two years before (in 1946), had an army of only about 7,000 in 1948 when the Palestinians called for help. Lebanon, which had also become independent only two years before this call for help, had only about 3,500 in her armed strength. Iraq, the Arab country farthest away from Palestine, had about 21,000 armed and this included the police or gendarmery. Saudi Arabia, the vast desert state, had no trained army. Trans-Jordan, the country that bordered the river Jordan on its east side, had by far the best trained army although small (about 6,000) and was undoubtedly the most effective holding and stabilizing force in the Arab-Jew war of 1947-1948. This was the one national army in the Arab states that had been subsidized by Great Britain, mobilized and trained by a former British officer, its Commander-in-Chief, General John Bagot Glubb — widely known as Glubb Pasha. The Jordanian forces were not, however, allowed to participate until the British had evacuated.

The Arab states had for several hundred years been in serfdom under the Turks, followed after World War I by being mandated under the French and British. They were new in learning the ways of independence and pulling themselves out of economic inadequacy. They could not afford great military expenditures as they had no rich sponsors in America to help them. Their first and urgent call was to look after their difficult economy and the welfare of their needy populations. The reference of comparative strength to 40,-000,000 Arabs in a military sense at that time was meaningless.

The Israelis, on the contrary, were being equipped with money and military supplies by the combined effort of great numbers of co-religionists throughout the world — and every able-bodied Jewish man or woman who had immigrated into Palestine was being trained and put into some form of defense service. They had the advantage of being concentrated, while the Arab states, coming to aid the Palestinians, had to invade at such points as seemed strategic along a rather lengthy and difficult border line.

219

Among the surrounding Arab countries the position and role of Trans-Jordan was somewhat unique. This story, as well as a full and vivid narrative of the 1948 Palestine war, is well detailed and documented in the book "A Soldier With the Arabs" by General Sir John Bagot Glubb, whose part in this war was extraordinarily important — especially as it related to the Old City of Jerusalem.

"We in Trans-Jordan," he wrote, "produced our own solution. We favored partition, but we considered it essential to retain British garrisons in Jerusalem and Haifa. If such a plan had been adopted, fighting would have been avoided. Any necessary exchanges of population could have been carried out without unnecessary hardship and there would have been no destitute refugees. Such parts of Palestine as were allotted to the Arabs would have been incorporated in the neighboring Arab states. Galilee would have joined Lebanon; Samaria and Judea would have been united to Trans-Jordan; and the Gaza-Beersheba district to Egypt. Lord Moyne, British Minister of State in the Middle East, to whom I explained the idea, professed himself to be keenly interested. But before he could take up the scheme, he was assassinated in Cairo by Jewish terrorists sent down from Palestine for the purpose.

"When the Arab Legion originally planned to enter Palestine on the termination of the Mandate, no war with the Jews had been visualized. It was proposed only to occupy the central and largest area of Palestine allotted to the Arabs by the 1947 partition. The Jews were most likely aware of this proposal and did not appear to object to it, although they were probably anxious to secure Jerusalem for themselves. But two factors subsequently transformed all these plans: Firstly, the fighting in Jerusalem during the Mandate, the arrival of the Liberation Army and the Arab attempt to cut the road to Jerusalem, and eventually the outbreak of Jewish-Arab fighting over the whole area — while the British Army was still in the country and the mandatory government in charge. The second factor was the insistence of Egypt and the other Arab governments on invading. These two factors

220

made the execution of the UNO partition plan impossible, even before the Mandate ended.

"Had they" (the Arab governments), continues General Glubb, "restrained the Palestinians and used their considerable influence in UNO to secure modification of the partition plan, the result for the Palestinian Arabs would have been far better.

"On the other hand," he observes, "Jewish forces were already well into Arab territory west of Jerusalem. The commander of the Jewish forces in Jerusalem had proposed the evacuation of Jewish colonies in Arab territory, but the Jewish Agency had refused and had told him to defend them at all costs. It is doubtful, moreover, if the Jews would have been satisfied with an international Jerusalem. And, finally, even if the Israeli government had decided to abide by the UNO plan, the Irgun and Stern would have certainly made trouble. If the Israeli forces had moved forward on May 15th and the Arab Legion had not crossed into Palestine, the Jews in a very short time would have conquered all Palestine up to the Jordan."

The Arab Legion had a number of reasons for moving across the Jordan river and up to the Old City of Jerusalem. First was in answer to the anguished cry of unprotected and frightened humanity. For days before the British forces were to leave, the people in Jerusalem had been flooding King Abdulla of Jordan with prayer and supplication for protection. They knew what had happened to nearby Deir Yaseen where men, women and children were slaughtered by the terrorist gang. They were begging for protection by the Arab Legion so that a similar fate might not be theirs.

Another reason was that the capture of Jerusalem by an enemy could mean the greatest possible threat to the survival of Jordan. Another reason — King Abdulla's father was buried in Jerusalem. He and all Jordan loved the Holy City which is sacred to Moslems as it is to Jews and Christians.

*   *   *

Great effort on the part of the United Nations and other agencies reflecting Zionist pressure was made to prevent the

Arab Legion from going to the aid of the frightened people in Jerusalem. The Jordan forces moved slowly but definitely. There was no precipitous action. General Glubb did not relish the idea of having his men, trained for desert action, become mixed in Jerusalem street fighting and in house to house encounters "at which the Jews were expert." His men were not familiar with the narrow winding streets of Jerusalem and confusion there could bring disaster.

FACING THE MOMENT OF TRUTH

There was, however, no way of evading the test. The British High Command and the last of the British troops left Jerusalem on the morning of May 14, 1948. They had not been gone more than half an hour until fighting flared in the streets of Jerusalem. The British army had held several large buildings in the center of the city which dominated the area. The Jewish Haganah had slipped into these buildings and taken up battle positions even before the British were all out. It had clearly been carefully planned. Quickly the whole city was heavily engaged in fighting. "Officers of the Haganah (Jewish army), in specially prepared vans with loud speakers," reported General Glubb, "drove through the streets calling out in Arabic 'The Jericho road is still open. Fly from Jerusalem before you are all killed'."

The Arab Legion, which had been careful to abide by the rules not to enter Jerusalem before the British left, was at this time east and beyond the river Jordan. In Jerusalem, defending against the Jewish invaders, were only Arab irregulars. They were not organized and had no leader. They were fighting almost as individuals. But they were fighting desperately to save the sacred city.

It may be a little difficult for the person who has never been to Jerusalem to understand what happened the day following the British evacuation but this paragraph from General Glubb's book "A Soldier With the Arabs" will at least show how desperate the situation was becoming.

"Early on May 15, the Haganah advanced in three columns to clear the Arab part of the city. In the south, they occupied the railway station, the German colony and Allenby

Barracks. On the north, they cleared the Shaikh Jarrah quarter and established contact with the Jewish garrison of the Hadassah Hospital and the Hebrew University on Mount Scopus. The remaining Arab irregulars took refuge in the Old City and closed the gates. The Haganah loud speakers continued to blare out in Arabic — 'Take pity on your wives and children and get out of the blood bath.' 'Surrender to us with your arms. No harm will come to you'."

*　　*　　*

General Glubb's book explains that the four regiments of the Arab Legion (remembering that the whole of the Jordan army then consisted of only some 6,000 men) which were to cross from Jordan to Palestine on May 15th had been camped in the Jordan desert some ten kilometers north of Amman and about 75 kilometers from Jerusalem. On the 14th they were to move to Amman and then down the twisting road to the Jordan valley, four thousand feet below, and cross the river Jordan on the Allenby bridge (near Jericho) at dawn on May 15th (Jerusalem time). The British mandate over Palestine was to end officially at midnight, May 14-15 — although the British actually left Jerusalem on the morning of May 14th. The flat-roofed stone houses along the way were crowded with cheering women and children as the Jordan troops passed by. For two months the Arab people in and around Jerusalem had been hoping — begging — praying — for the Arab Legion to go into action to protect them.

It was a long, hot trek for the Jordan soldiers on the way to Jerusalem where Jewish troops and terrorists had already invaded the city trying to frighten the people into surrender. Fighting between Jewish invaders and defending irregulars was becoming violent. Entrance into the fray by the four Jordan regiments in defense of Jerusalem was being delayed by urgent restraint on the part of the "truce group" in Jerusalem made up of the Counsels General of France, Belgium and the United States, who were trying desperately to prevent war by attempting to get the two sides to agree on something. It was all in futility as war was already on. This effort to delay the Jordan troops was only working to the advantage of the Jewish invaders. Jordan's General Glubb did not want to put his limited troops, which might be badly needed by the Arabs at other points in defense of Jordan, into this street-fighting brawl — but the Holy City of Jerusalem was in danger.

POOR ARAB COORDINATION

General Glubb had only general intelligence as to what other Arab countries were planning as an answer to the call by the Palestinians for help. He understood that Egypt was sending some troops into southern Palestine along the Mediterranean route through Gaza; that some Lebanese and Syrian troops would enter Palestine from the north; and that Iraq was to send in one armored car regiment and one battalion. Beyond that he was not informed. It was a great weakness of the Arab countries that they had no organized or coordinated plan — and a dangerous lack of unity.

It was this lack of Arab unity and coordination plus their inability to put large numbers of trained men into the Palestine defense that gave the Israelis final victory in that contest. The Arab governments — new in the world of independent nations — struggling for organized stability yet largely in the hands of politicians inexperienced with war — lacking in men trained or experienced for military leadership — were handicapped in confrontation with an already well equipped military machine, directed by seasoned and experienced leaders from other wars and countries. "In 1948," writes General Glubb, "the number of armed Israelis in the field was always much greater than that of the combined Arab armies attacking them."

May 16 passed as the situation in Jerusalem became more critical. King Abdulla of Jordan and General Glubb of Jordan's Arab Legion were waiting with anxious patience while the truce group kept trying for a "cease fire" between the Jews and Arabs who were fighting for control of the city. In Amman, capital of Jordan, there was a bristling tenseness. "Every little while the telephone from Jerusalem would ring. 'The Jews are attacking the city. They have scaled the walls on Mount Zion. They are up to the New Gate.' The police were holding the Citadel. Hour after hour the news came through. 'Save us! Our ammunition is finished! We can hold no longer! Where is the Arab Legion? For God's sake! Save us'!"

In late 1966, we talked with a person who has lived in Jerusalem more than fifty years and who survived the 1948 tragedy when the Jews tried to take the Holy City which had just recently been declared an "international zone" by the United Nations. "Why," we asked, "did all of this happen? Why did the Jews want to get possession of Jerusalem?"

Our friend, who was American born and not an Arab, replied: "This, of course, is not for me to answer. I do not know the purpose. The Jewish-Israeli leaders have said that it is futile to talk of the Arabs being returned to their previous homes in Palestine because, for one thing, those homes are not there. I suppose they mean they have been torn down for other construction. These same Jewish-Israelis seem to think that by some token Jerusalem is theirs because some 2,000 years ago the early Hebrews, for a few years, had a capital here with a wall around it — a temple and some other buildings. But, by the same standard they now apply to the Arab refugees — those buildings and that wall — and everything that represented that city at that time, is gone. Nothing remains — but a small segment of a wall (the so-called Wailing Wall) which is said to date back to Herod temple construction, but no one actually knows just what it was."

"You must also remember," our friend continued, "Jerusalem was a Jebusite (Canaanite) village before David captured it from them and made it his capital. It was called Jebus and had a history long before the Hebrews invaded Palestine." The Old Testament confirms this (II Samuel: 5). This chapter as well as II Samuel 11 - Judges 19 — and others give an interesting picture of the times.

* * *

NIGHTMARE FOR PEOPLE OF JERUSALEM

The battle of 1948 for Jerusalem was a terrible ordeal for all those living there. The call for help was as yet unanswered and the valiant unorganized defenders were waging an uphill battle to hold the line. It was clear they could not continue to do so.

"The Jews were reported to have broken into the Old City by the Zion Gate and to have made contact with the Jewish quarter inside the walls," reported General Glubb later, who at that time was holding four regiments of the Arab Legion in readiness for orders. "This operation," he continued, referring to the Jewish invasion, "had been carried out by the Palmach, the spearhead of the Israeli army. The Jews were now everywhere using mortars and armoured cars as well as small arms. A major battle had developed in Jerusalem. There seemed to be little hope now of saving the Jerusalem truce.

"The whole responsibility seemed to rest on me . . . I had opposed both the King and the government for forty-eight hours, in the hope of obtaining a truce. If, by any chance, the Old City should suddenly fall, all would be lost. Something must be done to prevent that. It was early morning. I decided to use one of the infantry companies then on the Mount of Olives."

The next paragraph from General Glubb's book is too majestic to omit. "The morning was still bright and cool when the 1st Infantry Company filed down the lanes from the top of the Mount of Olives and past Gethsemane, the same gardens through which our Lord was led away by the soldiers to His Passion. They crossed the little valley of Kidron, past the tomb of the Virgin Mary, then up the slope where Saint Stephen was stoned outside the walls. Passing through the gate, they entered the walled city. An hour later they were manning the walls from whose site, nearly nineteen hundred years ago, the Jews themselves had cast their darts at the advancing legions of Titus."

General Glubb calculated that the presence of 100 men of the Arab Legion would give the defenders added courage and would check the Jewish attack on the walls for a few hours at least. The Palmach were driven out and the Zion Gate which they had blown out to get inside was blocked again — with rubble and coils of wire. "But 100 men of the Arab Legion could not control the situation in a city which contained 100,000 Jews. Moreover the Old City was an island in the center of Greater Jerusalem. The Jews were in occupation of Shaikh Jarrah (a strategic road control suburb); soon they would attack the Mount of Olives, and then the Old City would be cut off from the east and surrounded. There seemed to be no alternative but to break into Jerusalem from the north, clear the Shaikh Jarrah and establish contact with the Old City. Then a continuous line of defense could be built up across the city and the Jewish offensive halted."

The Arab Legion's 4th Regiment was already engaged with the enemy at Latrun along the road from Jerusalem to Tel Aviv. The 1st and 3rd Regiments were needed to hold Samaria, some 35 miles north of Jerusalem. The 1st Regiment was at that time engaging a Jewish force at Qalqiliya in Samaria — at the Jewish line a little north of Tel Aviv. Again stressing that the Legion's full strength was around 6,000 men, it is easy to picture the enigma that faced its commander.

CRISIS—AND DECISION

In the evening of the 18th (May, 1948) General Glubb took a drive down a dusty earth track toward Jericho and suddenly made up his mind. There was no reason to wait longer, hoping for a truce. His decision was to intervene in force in Jerusalem. He gave orders to division headquarters to attack Shaikh Jarrah at dawn the next morning (the 19th) and break through that suburb settlement to make contact with the Old City. The 8th Infantry Company on the Mount of Olives was to move across the Kidron valley as the 1st Infantry had done the day before — and join them in defense of the Old City. The die had been cast. The Arab Legion had been forced by necessity to take chances in spreading its limited forces thin, as it would never have done under ordinary circumstances or in recognized military action. It was a gamble that had to be taken. One British General later described it as "lunacy," but it was a gamble that saved Old Jerusalem in 1948. "Thank God!" chorused the citizens of the Holy City.

As to the battle that ensued, General Glubb states: "The Jews had for weeks been erecting concrete defenses in their quarter of the city. Streets had been closed by concrete walls and roadblocks, and concrete pill boxes and machine gun emplacements, trenches and barbed wire covered every approach. On the Arab side, of course, nothing had been done — there were no leaders, no plan and no organization."

In the battle of May 18th for Jerusalem the Arab Legion, now entering that fight in force, quickly completed its occupation of Shaikh Jarrah and took possession of that road center. Road blocks and obstacles were dealt with in experienced military fashion. Several dangerous operations brought the armored car squadron which headed the Legion column to the Damascus Gate of the Old City. It is not possible here to go into the details of the battle for Jerusalem as described in General Glubb's book "A Soldier With the Arabs." It is a fascinating and revealing documentary. In speaking of his 3rd Regiment consisting of men enlisted from the nomadic tribesmen of the desert, General Glubb proudly quotes from the early Christian Father and historian, Origen: "They dwelt in the desert where the air was more pure, the Heaven more open and God more familiar."

DEADLY HAND-TO-HAND FIGHTING

A few highlights of the battle can be mentioned. A central section of Jerusalem just north of the walls of the Old City was called Musrara. It was largely dominated by a block of large buildings, massively built, of which the most important was the Monastery of Notre Dame de France. In this war it now represented a vast fortress. Since the end of the Mandate it had been held by the irregulars, but before the Arab Legion entered the city it was captured and manned by the Jews. The Legion undertook to recapture this strategic building.

The attack began at noon on May 23. The narrow streets made approach and attack difficult. The infantry made slow progress and was too close below the walls of the monastery to allow for any shelling by mortars or artillery to assist them. In spite of this they managed to stay within the monastery garden, finally getting ten men inside the building who, finding themselves almost surrounded, had to retreat and fight their way back to the others in the garden. The Legion soldiers had been under fire not only from the Notre Dame

Monastery but also from the nearby Italian Hospital and also the nearby French Hospital — all of which were occupied by Jewish fighting forces.

Casualties were numerous and alarming by late May 24. Of the 200 men who had set out on the 23rd to capture Notre Dame from the Jews, nearly half were either killed or were stretcher cases. "Throughout three days of battle, the officers and men of the 3rd Regiment had fought with unflagging bravery . . . Always thirsty, dirty, and even hungry, they fought on . . . 'No troops would have done better and most not as well,' wrote their commanding officer, Bill Newman — and he was an Australian and knew something about fighting men."

The performance of Arab soldiers in Jerusalem under the most trying conditions gives the lie to any and all statements that the Arabs cannot fight. When they are properly trained and commanded they are the equal of any fighting men in the world. One prominent American general has indicated to us that if the Arab countries had been far enough advanced in their new independence at the time to have had soldiers trained as were those of the Arab Legion, and organized for coordination, that the outcome in all of Palestine would likely have been along the lines of what happened in Jerusalem where the small but highly efficient Arab Legion defended that city.

DEATH STRUGGLE IN THE HOLY CITY

And it was in that city's desperate fight for freedom immediately after the British army had left (1948) that the two Arab Legion companies, with thinning numbers, were fighting to dislodge the Jewish fighters who had invaded and still held Notre Dame and other important buildings. The Legion fighters lined the city walls on the west, from the Zion Gate on through the Citadel (built on the site of Herod the Great's towers) and around opposite Notre Dame to the Damascus Gate.

General Glubb says: "There was something strangely moving to me in seeing my own soldiers on these historic walls, their rifles thrust through mediaeval loopholes, shaped long ago to the measurement of crossbows . . . By turning their

229

heads, they could see the Dome of the Rock and the Aqsa Mosque from which the Prophet Muhamad had ascended to Heaven. If the soldier were a Christian, the dome of the Holy Sepulchre lay only a few hundred yards behind him, while over the city roofs he could see the gardens on the Mount of Olives, where his Lord had suffered in anguish before His Passion. These men had no doubts. They were fighting and dying — fi sabeel Illah — in the path of God."

It was this kind of fighting that ended the "Jewish drive to seize the whole of Jerusalem" in 1948, a drive that was slowly checked with the loss of many lives. Finally the Jews were driven from the Old City but remained on Mount Zion outside the city walls. At the time of Christ, Zion was inside the city walls. Tradition places in Zion the house of Caiaphas, the Sadducee, and High Priest de facto in Jerusalem (son-in-law and successor to Annas) where Jesus was taken the night of his tragic arrest, there, according to the New Testament, to be accused and mercilessly brow-beaten. Here in Zion is also where Peter heard the cock crow and nearby is the reputed site of the Upper Room, place of the Last Supper.

General Glubb gives a graphic description of the Old City and especially the Jewish quarter where the Jews withstood the Legion's efforts for ten days: "The whole of the Old City was built in mediaeval style, houses crowding on top of one another, and cellars and courtyards sinking down into the earth. The only thoroughfares were narrow streets, often paved in steps. In many places the narrow bazaars were roofed over, while the cobbled alley-ways were spanned by bridges of flying buttresses connecting houses on opposite sides of the street. Sometimes these bridges carried whole buildings, so that the narrow lanes passed through tunnels under blocks of houses. Old Jerusalem, moreover, is built on several small hills divided by little valleys, with the result that the narrow paved streets often enough climb up and down in steps, or in steep irregular slopes between overhanging houses.

"Of all the narrow, tortuous and overcrowded quarters of Old Jerusalem, the Jewish quarter was perhaps the most crowded and ramshackle. A pedestrian threading his way through the narrow alleys caught glimpses through half open doors of tiny inner courtyards, crowded with women and children, and staircases going up to rooms above, and steps going down to subterranean dwellings below. The whole of the teeming rabbit-warren lay on top of the spoil and rubble of centuries — perhaps rather millennia — of poor human dwellings. Throughout most of Palestine, the Jews were not Jews only — they were also (some predominantly) Germans, Russians, Poles or Americans . . . But the Jewish quarter of the Old City was essentially Jewish and nothing else — the ancient Judaism of the Law and the Prophets, the Middle Ages and the Ghetto."

*   *   *

JERUSALEM SAVED— PRISONERS WELL TREATED

Finally after ten days of resistance to the Arab Legion, the Jews in the Old City (on May 28) raised white flags. There were about 1,500 Jewish prisoners captured in the Old City, including women and children. About 300 of these were Jewish soldiers — not residents of this quarter. They had been sent there to fight, some before the end of the Mandate, and some after May 15th, but before the arrival of the Arab Legion.

"Two days later," states General Glubb, "the Hagana prisoners and young Jews of military age were transferred to a prisoner-of-war camp east of the Jordan. The old men, women and children were sent across the lines to the Jewish side, under the supervision of the Red Cross. As the little caravan struggled through the narrow alley-ways of Old Jerusalem, Arab Legion soldiers were seen to be helping along the sick and the old women, and carrying their bundles of possessions."

A European press correspondent watching the convoy exclaimed: "That is what I call chivalry." General Glubb said simply, "It was our answer to Deir Yaseen." He was referring to the raid and ruthless massacre of the inhabitants of that village by Zionist terrorists.

In the story of this battle for Jerusalem, the suburb of Shaikh Jarrah has been mentioned. In the edge of this section is the American Colony — a California-type hotel consisting of three stone buildings surrounding a patio with flowers, fountain and shrubs. It is owned and operated by Mrs. Bertha Spafford Vester who was taken to Jerusalem by her parents in 1881. Her father was a Chicago lawyer who took his family to visit the Holy Land and with a small group of other American friends decided to remain. The Group took a stone house (all houses in Jerusalem are stone) on a high spot inside the walled city, between the Damascus Gate and Herod's Gate. This building is today (with certain additions through the help of the Ford Foundation) the Spafford Memorial Children's Hospital under the direction of a very fine surgeon, Dr. M. T. Dajani. Mrs. Spafford has mothered the hospital where babies are relieved of deformities and other infirmity problems so they may grow up to be healthy and normal. We have been through this hospital and on top of it where the view of all Jerusalem is a great and inspiring sight. "The American Colony has spent seventy-three years in Jerusalem administering to the needs of the poor and sick without discrimination of race or creed." It has served a worthy and important need.

The American Colony Hotel, which is some distance from the hospital, is a lovely and hospitable place. The hotel was transformed into a temporary hospital with a clinic across the street during the Jewish-Arab war for Jerusalem in 1948. They treated nearly 50,000 patients. "The Red Cross flag flew over our American Colony," writes Mrs. Vester in her delightfully interesting book "Our Jerusalem" (foreword by Lowell Thomas) "but bullets and trench mortars hit it."

MRS. VESTER TELLS
OF BATTLE FOR JERUSALEM

"The surgeon of our casualty clearing station was Mrs. MacInnes, wife of the Ven. Archdeacon MacInnes of St. George's Cathedral. He was accompanying his wife to the station when he was shot at our gate. His leg was broken and hemorrhage followed. On our one and only stretcher a dead man had been taken away . . . it was twenty hours before we could get a doctor . . . Next day, my brother-in-

232

law, Mr. Whiting, was shot by a Jewish bullet . . . Doctors were scarce and over-worked. No one would come to Shaikh Jarrah, where the American Colony is situated. One of our men risked his life to get the penicillin which helped Mr. Whiting . . . Three of our helpers and one of our nurses were wounded . . . It was estimated by an American resident that many thousands of Arab houses had been sacked and destroyed in Jerusalem."

On May 26, 1948, Mrs. Vester wrote in her diary: "A fierce battle started last night just before midnight. The fiercest battle so far is being fought right at our doors. Many windows broken pierced by bullets. Twenty-five Arab Legion soldiers at the Nuseibi house, across the street from the American Colony, beat off an attack by the Stern Gang. We were roused at 4 a.m. to attend to many wounded who were brought in to our casualty clearing station. One died almost at once. Shot through the head . . . Hand grenades were thrown right at the American Colony."

Again on May 28th she wrote: "I went to the Children's Hospital. All the west windows have been broken by bullets. We moved all the babies to the lower story. Later, the Friends' Mission allowed us to take the fifty babies rescued from Deir Yaseen massacre to a dormitory in their Boys' School at Ramallah."

The purpose here is not to give great detail concerning the Jewish-Arab war in Palestine — but merely to give highlights that will present a generalized picture of what happened and how it happened.

ZIONIST-ARAB WAR IN PALESTINE— OUTSIDE JERUSALEM

After the Jewish advance in the effort to capture Jerusalem had been halted by Jordan's Arab Legion, the main fighting of the Palestinian war centered around Latrun, which is about fifteen miles out of New Jerusalem (Israel) on the road to Tel Aviv. The Arab Legion's 4th Regiment was holding the end of a mountain spur where it comes down to the coastal plain. This closed the road to trucks carrying supplies from Tel Aviv and other points to the Jewish colony in New Jerusalem. Opening of the road therefore became a main objective of the Israeli forces. A strong attack opened on the Arab Legion's men by the Israelis during the night of May 25th. It was now ten days since the British forces had departed from Palestine leaving the impotent United Nations in charge — with open warfare raging between Arabs and Zionist Jews. The Israelis attacked at Latrun with a brigade of infantry supported by a heavy three-inch mortar bombardment and high velocity guns of about seventeen pounder calibre. They had been well equipped from some source. The fighting lasted for several hours before the Israelis withdrew.

The Arab Legion which had withstood the attack "counted six hundred dead Jews where the Israelis had fought. Many weapons (including 200 rifles and a quantity of Bren guns) were left behind by the Israelis. The Israelis employed great numbers of mortars at Latrun, and each attack was preceeded by a considerable bombardment. The mortars and bombs were manufactured in Israel. They made a deafening noise on detonation, but it gradually became apparent that they inflicted few casualties." The repeated heavy attacks continued until June 11th, when the first truce took effect. It was during this period that Israel armament began to strengthen from a heavy flow of planes and other war materials from the Soviets.

"Throughout all the fighting," says General Glubb, "the Arab Legion proved itself the master of the battlefield. Never on any occasion did it lose a position. Never was it obliged to retire. In attack, the only failure was that of the attempt to seize the Convent of Notre Dame in Jerusalem. I myself forbade further efforts, in order to avoid casualties. But if the Arab Legion was undefeated in the field, in the air it did not exist. We did not possess a single aircraft." The Israelis did not at that time have bombers or fighters but they had reconnaissance planes to fly above and determine Arab positions.

After all of its valiant fighting in Jerusalem and other strategic fronts the Arab Legion received, on May 30, 1948, its worst blow — not from the Israelis — but from its ally, the British Government. The Arab Legion, from its early days, had been largely subsidized by the British Government.

One reason was that at the San Remo Conference in 1920 the British had been given a mandate over the lands east of the river Jordan known as Trans-Jordan. Another reason, of course, was that Trans-Jordan's economic status could not alone support an army. Most of the second command of the Arab Legion were British officers.

On May 30th the British Government ordered that all of these officers were to leave their commands and withdraw from battle. This order is stemmed from a U.N. Security Council meeting on May 29 calling for a four weeks' truce in Palestine. The resolution did not mention the recall of nations of other countries who were fighting in this war as, for instance, a U.S. army colonel, named David Marcus, who was commanding the Israeli forces attacking Latrun. The Arabs concluded that this order to cripple them was the influence of New York pressure to which the British government bowed.

A military treaty of alliance was in effect between Britain and Jordan but it did contain a clause that nothing in it should prevent either government from fulfilling its obligations to the United Nations. The United Nations had already shown its impotency in dealing with Palestine (its solution conference had been ignored by the Jews when they arbitrarily set up the Jewish State) but here was a case where the U.N. was using its super-power to cripple the Arab battle line while leaving the Israeli side unmolested. The Jordanians, surprised and dismayed by this action, voiced the question — "What is the use of a treaty if either side can abandon its ally in a crisis, on the grounds that the United Nations wishes her to do so?".

What made this order to pull the British officers out of the Arab Legion particularly harmful was that the most senior Jordanian officers in the Legion had only eight years of military training. The Legion had operated from 1926 to 1939 as a gendarmerie — or police force with much of its work devoted to stopping lawless raids among the desert Bedouins. In 1940 it was expanded into a Jordanian military force. The British regular officers who took charge of training and organizing the various branches were more or less

UN 1947
PARTITION PLAN

JEWISH
ARAB

OCCUPIED
PALESTINE

LEBANON

HAIFA
TIBERIAS
SYRIA
NAZARETH

NABLUS

TEL AVIV
AMMAN
JERICHO
JERUSALEM
BETHLEHEM
DEAD
SEA

GAZA

EL ARISH
BEERSHEBA

EL AUJA
TRANS-
JORDAN

E G Y P T

ABA

1947

The black areas on this upper
map show the domain allotted
by the 1947 U.N. Partition Resolution to "a Jewish State." War
between Jews and Arabs ensued.
At close of that 1948 war the
Israeli sphere was considerably
expanded through armistice arrangements. The circle around
Jerusalem was set aside by U.N.
as an International Zone because
of the Holy places and shrines.
This area has been occupied and
is being settled by the Israelis.

The three areas shaded
with lines in this lower
map show 1967 expan-
sionism of the Israelis
with their June air-blitz
occupation of Sinai,
Old Jerusalem and Jor-
dan west of the river —
and a section of Syria,
thereby adding greatly
to the Refugee dilem-
ma.

(These maps are re-
printed by courtesy of
the ARAB Magazine,
London.)

MEDITERRANEAN
LEBANON
DAMASCUS
Haifa
Koneytra
OCCUPIED
PALESTINE
SYRIA
Tel Aviv
JORDAN
RIVER
AMMAN
Port
Said
Gaza
JERUSALEM
El-Arish
Dead
Sea
Suez
Canal
GAZA
STRIP
NEGEV
Suez
JORDAN
SINAI
Elath
Aqaba
E G Y P T
Gulf of
Aqaba
Gulf of Suez
SAUDI
ARABIA
Sharm
Sheikh
Strait
of Tiran
0   50
MILES
RED SEA
1967

the keystone of its operating success. This kowtowing to hidden hand influences by Britain was not only a blow to the Jordan army but also to British prestige in the Middle East.

The Arab Legion at that moment was engaged in wide range battling to put a holding line on the foraging Israelis and at first this loss of the British officers seemed a more terrible disaster than it turned out to be. The Arab Legion's senior Jordanian officers rallied to their new responsibilities and with indomitable spirit carried on at all points with bravery and success. A few British officers remained, including Chief of Staff General Glubb. These were individuals who had resigned from the British Army in order to serve the Jordan Government. Those who were obliged to leave were still members of the British Army and had only been lent to Jordan.

While the Arab Legion had been holding lines and winning battles, other Arab countries had started dispatching troops to Palestine. Egyptian units had advanced along the Mediterranean coast as far as Ashdod — about half way between Gaza and Tel Aviv — and had halted there. On May 22 an Egyptian army column had come overland via Beersheba and reached Hebron and Bethlehem. Some Iraq army units had crossed the river Jordan into Palestine some distance south of the Sea of Galilee and had relieved the Jordanian forces in Samaria. Some Iraqi forces advanced across Palestine to within a few miles of the sea, some ten miles north of Tel Aviv. The Syrians had begun on May 16 by capturing the town of Samakh, on the Syrian border at the south end of the Sea of Galilee. The Lebanese had entered Palestine where their borders meet in the north. These operations lacked the coordination and spirit of unity necessary for success. Because of this their main objectives were doomed to failure at the start.

LIBERATION ARMY — ADMIRABLE BUT FUTILE

There was another Arab force fighting inside Palestine known as the Liberation Army. In December of 1947 (soon after the Partition proposal had been introduced and when it

237

was clear that the British would be moving out to leave the Arabs and Jews to fight it out), the Arab League approved the organizing of armed irregulars to go to the aid of the frightened and beleaguered Palestinian Arabs. A call was made for volunteers and recruiting centers were set up in Beirut, Baghdad, Damascus and one or two other places. Several Syrian regular army officers were relieved of their posts to help train the recruits. When the Liberation Army was finally launched, it was commanded by a soldier of fortune-type fellow — a Lebanese Moslem named Fawzie Kaukji. Recruits responded well and when the detachments of this Liberation army began to infiltrate Palestine in January of 1948, the "army" had a full strength of some 5,000 men. It was split into four commands and distributed mainly in central and northern Palestine. It was these units that did most of the Arab fighting — outside the Jerusalem area — in the early part of the Palestine war.

In retrospect it is easier to see the futility of this action than it probably was at the time. Those who ordered this move were politicians — not soldiers. It was an example of early Arab misconceptions: (1) Anyone knowing anything about military matters would have realized how utterly impossible it would be to take green recruits and convert them into a well trained and disciplined army in three or four weeks. (2) It demonstrated that the Arab League countries, at that stage, had no realization of how well the Jews had organized and trained their population for fighting. Arab authorities apparently believed that this rag-tag force of irregulars could turn the tide and that there would be no need for their regular armies to participate.

"The Arab-Israeli War — 1948," a book by Edgar O'Ballance, gives a great deal of documentation on the battles conducted by the Liberation Army and it must be said that these men, regardless of all the bad features, were entitled to credit for effort and bravery — particularly in fighting to get possesion of the police fortresses scattered through Palestine, as well as forts, camps and even airfields, as they were abandoned by the British. In grabbing these strategic places, the Israelis had the advantage of inside information due to their highly organized intelligence service coupled with a well developed central planning program.

It may be that the Arab authorities who approved the organization of the Liberation Army had in mind that some of the rough elements that had been recruited would be an answer to the Jewish terrorist gangs. A little consideration would have shown that this could not work. The purpose of the Jewish terrorists was in the nature of psychological warfare — to frighten and cause the Arab populations to abandon their homes and towns — clearing the way for the Zionist nationalist plans.

There are two or three ways in which the Liberation Army of quickly organized irregulars may have aided the Zionists instead of hurting them much: (1) The Haganah (Jewish army) was being brought out of cover and enlarged with new recruits — and therefore needed the kind of fighting experience the Liberation Army provided. It toned them for later meeting with Arab regulars; (2) Some of the Liberation leaders had the mistaken policy of urging Palestinian Arab inhabitants temporarily to get out of the fighting zones so the Liberation forces could better operate. These were incidental cases and are not to be confused with the Jewish allegation that "an order" was isued by some high command of the Arab States requesting general evacuation. These incidents may, however, have given them the idea for the story.

WHY DID ARAB FAMILIES FLEE?

The departure movement of Arab families from their homes was, according to the best information available, initiated by fear growing out of psychological warfare methods which movements, after the terrible Deir Yaseen massacre, quickly developed into an uncontrollable stampede — thereby leaving homes, farms, businesses and land open for Jewish occupancy; (3) The Liberation Army often used Arab villages from which to operate, thereby bringing reprisal attacks from the Jews — and this in turn brought to the frightened population the urge to get out of the area. Psychological warfare (terrorism and fear) was a one-way street. The Arabs could and did run from it. The Jews allowed no movement among their own people. No exit permits were allowed.

There was no place to go. They had to stay where they were.

The Liberation Army carried on its operations in Palestine for nine months, by which time there was only a remnant left holding a few villages in the extreme north of Palestine. By the end of October, 1948, this final remnant was driven over the border into Lebanon and that was the last of it.

*   *   *

HISTORY OF HAGANAH

The Jewish Haganah (army) in Palestine had roots running back to a nucleus of early Settlement police. As Zionist immigration into Palestine grew after World War I under the Balfour Declaration, there was evidence that this police force was expanding into something more. This was particularly true during the turbulent years from 1936-39 when increased immigration brought frequent clashes between the new Jewish immigrants and the native Arab citizens.

Then came World War II with the Nazi nightmare and that drew, not just Haganah members, but Jews from other countries to join the British and American forces fighting Germany. After World War II was over in 1945, many of these who had been militarily trained and experienced were welcomed into the Jewish army expansion in Palestine. In this and other ways (some Jews had had some training in the Polish Army — and perhaps also in the Roumanian forces — and at various times in the French army) the Jewish fighting forces in Palestine (the Haganah with its Palmach, the Irgun and the Stern groups) had developed considerable military strength by the time the outside Arab countries decided to send some military units into Palestine to aid their badly harassed Palestinian co-religionists.

Edgar O'Ballance, in describing the various units of the Jewish fighting forces and the equipment they had about the time the British mandate ended, estimated 60,000 plus as the probable organized fighting Jewish man-power strength; but at the time, due to slowness and difficulties of getting equipment through, only about one-fourth of these were armed for fighting. He states that although mobilization notices had gone out to practically the whole Jewish male population,

240

these men could be taken into active service only as arms and equipment became available.

It is not necessary, nor would it be interesting to the average reader at this late date, to go into the history of the fighting forces of the various Arab States, nor even as to their divisonal compositions at the time of the war for Palestine in 1948. A description of armies and military competency for either the Arabs or the Israelis of 1948 would be meaningless today. They both have moved so far forward that any comparision would be like contrasting airplanes of 1948 with those of today. Tremendous strides have been made in science and progress all along the line.

*   *   *

The outside Arab forces had entered the Palestine conflict May 15, 1948 when the British abandoned their mandatory authority. The most dramatic fighting was by the Jordan Arab Legion to save the city of Old Jerusalem. A first truce in the war for one month was arranged for June 11, 1948. It ended July 9th with the beginning of an intensive Israeli offensive. Another truce (the "shooting truce") was arranged for July 18th. It did not have too much effect on the fighting. Count Bernadotte, the United Nations' Mediator, had been striving diligently for a basis of settlement to bring peace for Palestine. He had submitted a report calling for a partition that was most displeasing to the Israelis. It brought action from the terrorists. Bernadotte was assassinated on September 17, 1948 (as noted elsewhere).

ZIONIST INFLUENCE IN U.S. POLITICS

The Bernadotte plan, however, was a source of much heat and controversy. Concerning this argument, or as a result of it, General Glubb, in "A Soldier With the Arabs," reports on an article in the London Spectator in early October of 1948 which — "stated that the British and American viewpoints were moving farther apart. Britain, the paper continued, steadily supported the Bernadotte plan, but the United States was more concerned not to offend the Jews than anything else. The fact that the United States Presidential elections were to take place a month later may have influenced the policy of that country.'

"The question drifted on in the United Nations. Any decision seemed to be dependent on Anglo-American agreement. I find a rather bitter note in my diary: 'All our troubles seem to be due to politicians — American as much as Arab — for the Presidential election seems to be spoiling all hopes of a firm settlement by UNO'."

*   *   *

As already mentioned, the Egyptian army (of ten or twelve thousand) entered the fighting with a two-pronged advance, one along the coastal route which progressed without too much opposition until it reached within twenty miles of Tel Aviv on May 29. The other prong traveled inland via Beersheba and on to Hebron and Bethlehem, which sector it took over, relieving the Arab Legion on May 22nd.

In the northeast sector where the Syrian army had entered and gone into combat with the Israeli forces, there was fighting back and forth, points would be taken and then lost. It was something of a see-saw action with no spectacular results.

The Arab contingent (of roughly 10,000) from Iraq was not too successful at its point of invasion. It may have been that their troops were not well enough trained as yet for the commanders to take chances with them. It is probable their attacks and enthusiasm were dulled because they ran into much stiffer opposition from the Israelis than they had expected. The Egyptians and the Iraqis who were the farthest away from Palestine had apparently misjudged the strength and fighting spirit of the Jewish army and did not come properly prepared for the task.

Within a few days after the British left Palestine, the Israelis made a rapid advance in the northern section around Haifa, capturing an important police post and occupying, without much trouble, the coastal area extending practically to the Lebanese border. The Israelis also had but little trouble in taking over the villages in the central area around Tel Aviv. It is true that the Arabs had been attacking with courage and vigor and had also taken control of many of the Arab communities but they were not driving "the Jews into the sea" as many people had thought would be the case.

During the first six weeks or so of fighting there had been no battles or victories of a decisive nature.

One thing had become apparent — the Arabs had shown no evidence of a "master plan" such as had been charged by the Zionists. Syria, Iraq and Egypt all had some aircraft but they were not being purposefully used. The Egyptians did considerable air-raiding with Spitfires at Tel Aviv and lost one plane as the Israelis began to get anti-aircraft guns from abroad. Because of this the air-raiding tapered off.

When the first truce in the fighting was arranged by the U.N. for June 11, 1948, the most significant result of the conflict so far was that the Israelis had survived the Arab attacks which some had predicted would be annihilating. There is no question but that the Israelis were glad to have this truce for some much needed reorganizing, both as to military and civil programs. Many Arabs still think this truce gave a big advantage to the Zionist-Israelis and without it the Israelis would have been soon defeated. Another reason some Arabs did not like the truce was that up to that point the Israelis were more or less a self-constituted, self anointed but unofficial entity. Once they were acknowledged by a truce agreement through the United Nations, it blessed the Israelis with a certain national status.

There were, however, responsible Arab leaders who, too, welcomed the truce. It had advantages for them also. The commanders of some of the Arab armies that were getting their first combat experience against a substantial enemy had discovered many problems and shortcomings in their own ranks and operations. Outside of the Arab Legion the Arab armies had shown need of considerable overhauling. One of the greatest faults of the whole Arab offensive was lack of unity and coordination. With the right kind of pre-planning and maneuvering coordination their dream of dispersing the Zionists might have become an early reality.

UNITY—A UNIVERSAL PROBLEM

Admittedly one of the hindrances to the unity that would have brought better coordination and cooperation were some long time political jealousies that were still heated by feeling. Perhaps the most outstanding was an old time conflict between the late King Hussein of the Hejaz (a section of Arabia) and Ibn Saud who was a Prince in control of another section of Arabia called Nejd. It was King Hussein with whom the British had dealt in getting the Arabs to revolt and help drive the Turks from the Middle East. The rivalries between Hussein and Ibn Saud culminated finally in Ibn Saud driving the Old King from his throne in the Hejaz. Hussein was father of the Hashemite family of four prominent sons — the ones most involved here were Feisal who later became King of Iraq and Abdulla who became King of Trans-Jordan and who was still living and reigning at the time of this war.

Rumors are always rife in the Middle East as they are in other parts of the world and there were fictions spread that Abdulla, during his reign of Trans-Jordan from 1921 to 1949 — first as Amir and then as King, had ambitions to be the voice of the Arab world; and there were indications that King Farouk of Egypt aspired to be the dominant figure as the dream of unity blossomed.

Suspicions were natural under conditions that prevailed as several new countries, tied together by language, culture and religion, were seeking to evolve from recent subjection into a cooperating civilization under great difficulties that had been imposed upon them by centuries of subjection and privation.

ARAB LEAGUE FORMED FOR UNITY

For several years before the British Government decided to abandon its Palestine Mandate, it had realized the problem of working with the separate Arab governments on Palestine problems and had urged the formation of a cooperative organizational structure that would make it easier to deal with their common needs as well as other urgent issues. Such an organization called the Arab League of States was actually formed on March 22, 1945. Its purpose was to coordinate interests and action in all fields of common concern.

One of the first serious problems to confront the League was the Zionist invasion of Palestine which was in fact a gathering storm at the time the League was founded. On February 9, 1948, representatives of the new organization met in Cairo and reached a determination to do all they could to prevent the rise of a Jewish State in their midst. When it was learned that Great Britain could no longer carry the burden of the Palestinian discordance and had announced that British forces would be withdrawn, in May of 1948 the Arab League met again, this time in Beirut, and reached a decision to send troops to aid their hard pressed Arab brothers in Palestine at such time as the British should depart and leave the Palestinian Arabs at the mercy of the "Zionist terrorists" and the impotent United Nations.

In the resulting battle struggle between the Zionists and the allied-Arabs, the United Nations had arranged what was known as the "first truce" — and as had already been stated this truce ended on July 9, 1948 with the Israelis mounting a high-powered offensive, principally in the central area and in Galilee on the Syrian front.

In the Israeli drive on the towns of Lydda and Ramle (about twelve or fifteen miles inland from Tel Aviv), Edgar O'Ballance, in his book on the Arab-Israeli War, states that. the majority of the 60,000 unarmed Arabs in those towns fled for safety. "Israeli vans with loud speakers," he wrote, "drove through the streets ordering all inhabitants to evacuate immediately and such as were reluctant to leave were forcibly ejected from their homes by the triumphant Israelis whose policy was now openly one of clearing all Arab civil population before them . . . As the bulk of them withdrew over the open country on a blazing hot day, some Israeli mortars opened up to help them on their way and it is reported that several women and children died of heat and exhaustion during the exodus."

(Note: This would seem to be a somewhat moderated retake of the picture as presented in Joshua VI:21 when the Hebrews of old ransacked and slaughtered the people of Jericho in the conquest of Palestine.)

*   *   *

Not too far away from the two towns just mentioned was Latrun, a vital point on the road from Jerusalem to Tel

Aviv, which was being held and garrisoned by Jordan's Arab Legion. O'Ballance tells how the Israeli Palmach (spearhead of the Israeli Haganah Army) began encircling tactics around Latrun, supporting the action with five tanks which riddled the police post there. The Arab Legion had only one gun on the roof of the police post. All the crew of this gun were killed but were immediately replaced with volunteers who rushed to take their places. Gradually the five Israeli tanks were disabled one by one but the gun on the police post manned by Arab Legion soldiers continued in action. The Israeli commander, Colonel Alon, was forced to adopt other tactics, but before these became effective a second truce was declared on July 18, 1948. Later we drove down the winding road through Latrun and saw many destroyed Israeli tanks rusting at roadside.

Just what would have happened in this test between the brilliant fighting Arab Legion and the more heavily armed Israeli force at Latrun is now merely for conjecture. It is understood that Glubb Pasha was sending additional men from the Jerusalem sector, which probably means he intended to make the test rather than withdraw the small force he had defending Latrun. Colonel Alon, who was one of the ablest military leaders the Israelis had, about this time was called upon to check the Egyptians who were encroaching from their Bethlehem position toward the vital supply road from New Jerusalem to Tel Aviv. It was one of his brigades that had just driven the Arab population from Lydda and Ramle.

The second truce was achieved quite suddenly through the indefatigable efforts of Mediator Count Bernadotte. It was merely a cease-fire and known as the "shooting truce" because there were raids, encroachments, occasional shellings and a generally nervous and uneasy attitude on the part of both sides. It was not a negotiated truce — but was ordered as an attempted show of power by the U.N. It was not very effective. Regardless of confusion and disorder, mediator Bernadotte pushed tirelessly on trying to map out demarcation lines in an effort to control Israeli-Arab incidents.

THE BERNADOTTE ILL-FATED PLAN

To keep the picture clear it may be worth restating that the Bernadotte plan to bring peace to Palestine was to leave the Negev (southern Palestine) to the Arabs and the Jews were to return Lydda and Ramle (which they had recently taken, pushing the Arabs out) to Trans-Jordan; the whole of Samaria was to go to the Jews; Jerusalem was to become a corpus separatum under the United nations. Haifa was to become a free port and Lydda was to be a free airport. All Arab refugees were to be allowed to return to their homes or to be compensated. Jewish infuriation over this proposal was explosive.

The proposal ended aborning when Count Bernadotte and his colleague, French Colonel Serot, were assassinated by members of the Stern gang while driving in a Jerusalem sector. Edgar O'Ballance, in his book "The Arab-Israeli War — 1948," reports that Israeli authorities did nothing about this affair for twenty-four hours — then as it developed into an international incident Ben Gurion ordered a roundup of the Stern fighters. Some 400 were arrested, including Fried-mann-Yellin, their leader. There was no outcry nor sympathy expressed in Israel, says O'Ballance, and the general feeling was that just another enemy of Israel had fallen. The murderers were never brought to justice, he reports, and no determined effort was made to find them. Sweden protested strongly but in vain. Many of the friends of Israel were seriously disturbed over this lawless incident. (Count Bernadotte was succeeded as U.N. official by Dr. Ralph Bunche.)

NOTE: General Glubb, in his book "A Soldier With the Arabs," gives a detailed account of the terrorist attack on Count Bernadotte of which the following is a brief. The Count had flown in from Damascus, landing at Kulindia airfield near Ramallah. He drove to Jerusalem — attended a luncheon at the Y.M.C.A. — after which with a convoy of three cars he drove to the Government House, former official residence of the British High Commissioner for Palestine.

After inspecting the building proposed as U.N. headquarters, he returned to Jerusalem. As they drove through the Katamon district (Arab section) they came suddenly upon a jeep standing in the middle of the road, seeming to have trouble getting turned. Four men in Israeli uniform were in the jeep. "Three of the occupants of the jeep," writes General Glubb, "jumped out and walked towards the U.N. convoy. Count Bernadotte was in the third or rear car. One of the Israelis walked down one side of the cars and two walked down the other side. They went straight to the third car. The driver remained seated in the jeep.

"The single man went up to the window of Count Bernadotte's car. The passengers thought he was a Jewish soldier about to ask for their passes and began to pull them from their pockets. Suddenly the man thrust the mouth of an automatic pistol through the window and fired a burst of shots at point blank range at the Count and at the French Colonel Serot, who was sitting beside him. At the same instant, the other two Israelis pulled out automatic pistols and fired at the wheels and radiators of the convoy cars — presumably to prevent pursuit. The men then jumped into the jeep, which disappeared at full speed. A truck full of Israeli soldiers was seen to be halted some forty yards away.

"It subsequently transpired that the murderers in their jeep had been waiting on the road for at least an hour before the convoy arrived. Count Bernadotte had received six bullet wounds, one of which, through the heart, must have caused death instantly. Colonel Serot received seventeen bullets.

"Next day, the murderers, who belonged to the Stern Gang Jewish terrorists, sent the following letter to the press:

'Although in our opinion all United Nations observers are members of foreign occupation forces, which have no right to be on our territory, the murder of the French Colonel Serot was due to a fatal mistake: our men thought that the officer sitting beside Count Bernadotte was the British agent and anti-Semite, General Lundstrom'." (Here is an example of confusion. General Glubb points out that General Lundstrom was in fact Count Bernadotte's chief of staff and an officer in the Swedish army.)

*　　*　　*

During the truce that began July 18th, the Israelis had been trying to get supplies through to their villages and roving military units in the Negev. The Egyptians, headquartered at Gaza and in control of the roads in that area, were able to block all convoys. The Israelis decided to ignore the truce in an effort to break through this blocade and open a convoy route to the Negev which was vital to their future plans. The strategy used by Colonel Alon who was in charge of the action (called the operation of the "Ten Plagues") was in every sense militarily skilful. The Israelis fought desperately and so did the Egyptians who were handicapped by having their line stretched out along an extensive shallow front. The mobility of the Israelis plus other advantages including an ingeniously discovered ancient road that could be cleared for use, eventually gave them victory in break through — and victory as to possession of the Negev.

While the Egyptians were suffering their reverses in the Negev, says war historian Edgar O'Ballance, the other states of the Arab League impassively sat back and watched. With the exception of Glubb Pasha's move into the Hebron district, none made any move to help. It was this lack of co-ordination, stressed often by General Glubb, that was a major factor towards the final outcome of the Jewish-Arab war for Palestine. That, of course, is water over the dam. The situations and the managements in all of those countries have changed materially since then.

FINIS OF THE 1948 PALESTINE WAR

The first major move toward bringing about a "permanent" truce in the Palestine War of 1948 was a mediation move between Israel and Trans-Jordan. On November 30, 1948, a cease-fire was agreed to in the Jerusalem area allowing the Israelis to establish a regular convoy service to their position on Mount Scopus. As far back as July 7, 1948, an agreement had been reached by the Arab and Israeli commanders of the area, at the instance of King Abdulla upon whom considerable American pressure had been exercised, whereby the buildings of the Hebrew University and the Hadassah Hospital, isolated on Mount Scopus, would not be attacked by the Arab Legion nor defended by Israeli soldiers, but would be placed under U.N. control for protection. The agreement further permitted the Israelis to maintain a civilian police guard there to watch the property. This arrangement for an Israeli convoy of supplies to Mount Scopus from New Jerusalem on the then Israeli side — passing through the Mandelbaum gate and through the Old Jerusalem section of Jordan — soon became quite a "changing of the guard" performance, with certain dubious overtones which are reflected in the following note.

NOTE: The Israelis were permitted (by U.N. approval) to take a convoy of vehicles from Israel through the Mandelbaum gate and through the old Jerusalem section of Jordan, to Mount Scopus — ostensibly to provide supplies for the "police guard" of the abandoned university and hospital buildings there, and regularly to change the guard personnel. This arrangement was obtained through Zionist pressure emanating from America, allegedly to guard the buildings from deterioration. Although an Arab-guard vehicle accompanied the Israeli convoy procession, no examination of the contents of the convoy vehicles was allowed by the Israelis.

The Arabs, familiar with the "barrel incident" related by the late Commander E. H. Hutchison (official U.N. military observer) in his book "Violent Truce," and other incidents, demanded that the United Nations inspect and report on the convoy's cargo into those buildings. The request was based upon the strategic position of Mount Scopus, which could be a military danger to Jerusalem and Jordan if military strength could be mounted there. The buildings were large and could be turned into an effective military redoubt.

U.N. inspection officials did attempt to make such a search, but were not allowed by the Israelis to see inside certain rooms. The original permission granted the Israelis the right to maintain only civil guards on Mount Scopus. At first the men wore police uniforms. Later Jordan heard they were really infantry and used the police uniforms for the occasion. Under the armistice agreements, Mount Scopus was supposed to be demilitarized and placed under U.N. control. But the Israelis were able easily to take essential control for themselves from the impotent U.N.

In 1963, we saw, in a children's hospital near the wall in Old Jerusalem, the hole made by a bullet that had recently passed through a sterilizer and buried itself in the wall of the operating room — coming in through a window in direct line with Mount Scopus, indicating there could be long-range firearms there. If Israeli arms were illegally stored there, as many Jordanians believed, they could possibly have played a role in the 1967 takeover of the Old City.

* * *

JERUSALEM ARABS ASK FOR JORDAN ANNEXATION

In the war that followed the setting up of the new Jewish State, Jerusalem escaped conquest by the Jews only because of Jordan's fighting Arab Legion. This close call so frightened what was left of the Palestinian Arabs that their leaders met with the Jordanians at Jericho (December 1, 1948) and sought annexation by Trans-Jordan. This was then legally accomplished, with King Abdulla of Trans-Jordan being proclaimed also King of Arab-Palestine. Later in the month (December 13), the Trans-Jordan Parliament put its stamp of approval on this merger of States and decreed that thereafter and henceforth these combined territories would be officially the Hashemite Kingdom of Jordan. The Palestinian Arabs wanted this — in fact needed it — to give them a stable government and a protective military force. Israeli expanionism was to them a hovering spectre — and what was left of Arab Palestine looked to the Arab Legion as its "last best hope on earth." Out of this union, however, arose a temporary incident of conflicting Arab designs as Egypt had already established the Palestine Arab Government with headquarters in Gaza. The weight of circumstances and proximity resolved this conflict of purposes in favor of the Trans-Jordan-Arab Palestine union.

NOTE: After the foregoing was written, Israel military (in 1967) seized Old Jerusalem and the Palestinian area that had been incorporated into Jordan, and began a hurried job of "making the Old City over." As this book is published, no facts are available as to the fate of property ownerships — and no predictions as to the further plans for Israel expansion.

CLOSING DAYS OF ISRAELI-ARAB WAR

Returning now for a final glance at the 1948 field of battle — the Egyptian situation had deteriorated badly under the irrepressible Israeli attacks and with King Farouk's Egyptian army reeling under heavy blows, the British entered the picture with strong political pressure and demanded that Israel withdraw her troops from Egyptian territory into which they had advanced. Egypt had a military treaty with Britain which was one reason for this, but another was that Israeli troops were within Sinai territory of which Britain did not approve. Consequently Israel, with great reluctance, did withdraw her troops in order to avoid direct intervention by Britain.

The Israelis then turned their attention to Egypt-controlled Rafah, in the lower Gaza strip. Egypt, realizing the hopelessness of her isolated position there, quietly stopped the fighting, and since it had essentially ceased in other quarters, this was more or less the end of the 1948 Israeli-Arab war.

With no further opposition from Egypt, there was nothing to hinder the Israelis from completing their occupation of the entire Negev, which U.N. Mediator Bernadotte had earmarked for the Arabs. It took the Israelis from January to March (1949) to complete the occupation of that rugged, arid desert section all the way to its southern tip at the Gulf of Aqaba, which is a leg of the Red Sea. It is at this point that the Negev (now absorbed by Israel) and the State of Jordan come together, separated only by the huge and desolate Wadi Arabah. On the Israeli-Negev side at this point is the village port of Elath — the presumed ancient Biblical site of King Solomon's copper mining operations. On the Jordan side is the village-port of Aqaba — the only outlet that Jordan now has to the ocean highways since the Zionist capture of Palestine has cut her off from her former use of the port at Haifa. When the Jewish occupation forces reached Elath it was natural that Jordan should be concerned as to what might happen. King Abdulla called upon Great Britain for protective aid by invoking an existing Anglo-Trans-Jordan treaty. British troops were immediately sent to Aqaba. Under these circumstances no complications or action resulted and each country has since respected the territory of the other — in this area.

TWO IMPORTANT NEGEV QUESTIONS

A noted British military authority has called our attention to two quite important facts relating to the Zionist-Israeli capture and development of the Negev rugged desert country. The first is that this acquisition has no traditional or cultural relationship with the "Zionist dream" of reconstituting the ancient nation of Israel. Neither the early Hebrews nor any of their blood-line descendants ever inhabited the Negev other than the possibility that the Israelites may have crossed it on their legendary trek from Egypt to Canaan via Jericho. Beersheba was the farthest point south for the Hebrews. Solomon may have had a small copper mining operation near Elath but it was not in Hebrew territory.

The other item of importance is that the Israelis, in extending their territory through the Negev to Elath, cut off the Arabs of Asia from those of Africa. "This," our British authority reminds us, "has a major strategic objective." The Arab States of the two continents are now separated by a land area controlled by the Zionist Israelis. The effect of this is unpredictable. Our authority mentions also that the Crusaders did this same thing with the same objective 800 years ago — and the Crusaders are now only a part of history.

*   *   *

As to the 1948 "War for Palestine," the Zionist-Jewish forces that had immigrated into Palestine and consolidated themselves there, had withstood such attacks as the Arab states had made and, in fact, had found it possible to take the offensive and vastly expand the territory they held at

252

the time the war started. This conquest expansion included the fertile coastal plains with their established groves and farms. Nearly a million Arabs had abandoned these properties in terror, fleeing to refugee camps on foreign soil. After the Egyptian debacle and armistice approval and with essentially no action of consequence on any front and none in the making, it seemed to Dr. Ralph Bunche, U.N. Mediator, that armistice arrangements could be accomplished.

WAR ENDS WITH ARMISTICE PACTS

He was able to schedule meetings for the consideration of armistice discussions at Rhodes during February, March and April of 1949. These resulted in armistice settlements being agreed upon — first, between Israel and Egypt. This agreement was signed on February 24. The next armistice pact was signed by Israel and Lebanon on March 23; and the settlement agreement between Israel and Jordan was closed on April 3 with Jordan representing Iraq also for a concluding compact. Iraq would not negotiate with Israel nor have any personal dealings with the new Zionist State. No arrangements were made with Syria at the time — for one reason because Syria at the moment was enjoying an internal revolution. Another reason was that Syria refused to withdraw troops from some Palestine villages they had occupied.

SUMMARY OF THE WAR

A short summation of the 1948 Jewish-Arab war over Palestine would show that the Jews (otherwise referred to as Zionists — and later as Israelis) came out with substantial victories. The Zionists, with the ending of the British mandate, had declared themselves a State or Nation. Outside Arab nations responded to the call for aid from the Arab inhabitants of Palestine. The response was, in the light of history, poorly organized and appeared to be something of a half-hearted token effort by some of the Arab states.

It soon became clear that the Arab League states possessed but little understanding of how well the Jews were organized; or of the religionistic zeal that cemented them in their determined goal; or of the unlimited Jewish world backing they had; or of the weakness of their own (Arab) military plans in facing a tightly knit, centralized foe. The Jordan government was the only Arab group that seemed to realize the size and extent of the problems. During the first month of the fighting the Arabs held the upper hand.

The Zionist Jews were hard put but held on, fighting desperately. After that the situation began gradually to change. The Jews began to get more equipment and armament from their extensive sources. Lack of proper coordination by the Arabs also began to show. As the tide of battle began to turn, momentum increased. By the time the Arabs began to realize their mistake, it was too late to revamp. Many authorities felt that if an over-all strategy command had been established with capable military direction at the time of decision for concerted Arab action, the outcome would have been radically different.

NOTE: The war just discussed was in 1948 — the second step in the conquest of Palestine — the first having been mass immigration. The hostilities caused by these methods of take-over which made homeless refugees of close to a million Palestinian Arabs did not end with the 1948 war. Hate was kindled among Arabs far and wide — and they are a fast growing population. The Zionists seemed, however, to feel that the Arabs should now forget the whole matter and make the best of their vile refugee camps. The Arabs did not forget and will probably be a long time forgetting.

The question arises — can people who have been driven from their homes look back at them across a military demarcation line and not seek to return? Natural irritations and provocations have continued and war erupted again in June of 1967 when a quick Israeli air blitz drove more thousands of Palestinian Arabs into refugee camps — with the Israeli-Jews expanding their conquest to essentially the whole of Palestine and a major part of Sinai.

One pro-Zionist, speaking over American television in March of 1968, said — "Palestine no longer exists — it is now Israel." The Holy City that was carefully preserved in character with all its shrines of all three religions by the Arabs for more than a thousand years is now being radically reconverted through Zionist control. Opinion is widespread that the conflict is far from over. A million destitute refugees, living on world charity in hovels, will not just "fade away." Their very existence points a constant finger of shame toward the people who engineered this displacement — and the nations that helped.

---

18. TRAGIC STORY OF THE PALESTINIAN REFUGEES

The Arab community in Palestine began when the great Arab-Islamic crusade swept out of the Arabian deserts and reached Syria (including Palestine) during the first half of the seventh century. The Caliph Omar conquered Jerusalem in 638 A.D. There was incidental penetration by the Crusaders in the eleventh century but this did not seriously interfere with the growing Arab population. Most of the Middle East, including Syria and Palestine, came under the rule of the conquering Turks in 1516 who, with the exception of ten years (1831-41), ruled the country and the preponderant Arab population until driven out by the British and their Arab allies during World War I.

It is the record of history, therefore, that the Arabs as a people constituted the dominant population of what is known as Palestine for some thirteen hundred years. During that time they developed towns and farms throughout the country, planted and cultivated olive groves and developed a substantial citrus fruit industry. They lived quietly according to their naturally limited resources, never asking for outside help. As the centuries passed, the generations that were born on the land became, by all standards of civilization, the legitimate "children of Palestine."

Dating especially from 1947-8 events, radical and violent changes have taken place in Palestine. By that time mass Zionist-Jewish immigration, mainly from Eastern Europe, had pushed into this Arab-populated country so heavily as to produce inevitable clashes and the 1948 Zionist-Arab war. Essentially all of the native Arab residents have been displaced from their homes and homeland and are today destitute refugees living in disreputable, bare-subsistence camps, unable to return to their former homes. The United Nations General Assembly, on December 11, 1948, passed Resolution No. 194, calling upon Israel to repatriate or compensate the Palestinian refugees — according to their individual wishes. That Resolution has been reiterated by the General Assembly each year since that date. It has been consistently dodged by the Israelis and no other organized body has taken any action. This is unquestionably a major cause of why Arabs, in their hopelessness, have been turning to the Soviets for aid. This mounting situation, according to certain substantial opinions, is building into a time-bomb that sooner or later will explode with world-shaking reverberations.

FLIGHT—IN TERROR

In the heat of the 1948 conflict between the invading immigrants and the old time residents, Zionist terrorists (by the record) invaded the village of Deir Yaseen (April 9, 1948 — a strategic date) resulting in the slaughter of 250 men, women and children. This was widely considered as an act to create panic during the few days before the Zionists planned to establish the "State of Israel," which they did on May 14, 1948 (Palestine time) immediately upon evacuation of the British forces. As the news of this frightening tragedy spread, so indeed did panic race through the unarmed and unprotected villages. Families fled headlong to get across the borders, believing, according to much refugee testimony, that a genocidal fate was planned for all of them.

The mass flight into neighboring Arab states of nearly a million people created an immediate emergency problem for which the only answer was to herd these unfortunate victims of terror into quickly established makeshift and ill-provisioned camps, scattered around the perimeter of Palestine from Gaza on the south to Jericho and Lebanon on the north.

The Zionists have publicized the claim that the Arabs fled at the call or on orders from the Arab leaders who promised that they would be able to return home soon — when the Zionists had been driven out. There are a great many matters of known fact that challenge this claim, but to leave no stone unturned the matter has been carefully checked. We journeyed to Oxford, England, to see Dr. Walid Khalidi who has made an extensive and tedious inquiry concerning these charges. He has examined the files of all newspapers and publications that might have known of such orders — or would likely have printed them. He checked with telegraph agencies and read all available communications of that particular period and nowhere, he says, could he find any evidence of such "call" or "order" being issued by any Arab authority.

TERRORIST LEADER TESTIFIES

The most revealing indication of what happened (and why) is on record in the words of Menachem Begin, Polish leader of the Irgun Zvai Leumi (known as the main "terrorist" organization of the early operating Zionist-Israeli armed forces) in his book "The Revolt." The Deir Yaseen massacre (spelled "Dir Yassin" by Begin) created such world revulsion that the Zionist-establishment made a hurried apology and excused it as an irresponsible "underground" act. In his book, Begin, in self defense, throws the lie at this alibi and states pointedly, "Dir Yassin was captured with the knowledge of the Haganah and with the approval of its commander." (Haganah was the name at the time of the early Zionist armed force.) Begin also quotes a letter from the Haganah regional commander to the Irgun regional commander indicating that the planned attack on this village was understood and approved.

NOTE: After the 1948 so-called "war of liberation" was over with two major achievements: (1) British driven from their Palestine authority, and (2) most of the Palestinian Arabs lodged in refugee camps outside the country, it is interesting to note that Mr. Begin, underground leader and author of "The Revolt", become a member of the Knesset (Israel Parliament).

The Irgun leader indicates repeatedly that when something would go sour, the Jewish Agency-establishment would use the "underground" Irgun as a scapegoat for public-image effect, while at the same time leaving to it the jobs that might require public apology. In the "Dir Yassin" case he says that because of the bad world reaction, propaganda was used "to besmirch our name." But, he says, the "Dir

Yassin" affair helped. "Panic overwhelmed the Arabs of Eretz Israel" (land of Israel), he writes.

Begin explains how the attack on "Dir Yassin" and other villages such as Kolonia, Beit-Iksa, Kastel — all helped to create "panic" among the Arabs. "The legend of Dir Yassin," he says, "helped us in particular in the saving of Tiberias and the conquest of Haifa." He explains that the Israelis knew the date that the British were to evacuate Haifa and prepared to be ready to take advantage of it. As the British moved out he said Jewish forces "advanced through Haifa like a knife through butter." In recounting the capture of Haifa, the Irgun "underground" leader reveals in one short sentence how the Dir Yassin massacre paid off. He writes, "The Arabs began fleeing in panic, shouting 'Dir Yassin'." These few words seem to tell the underlying story of the Palestinian refugee problem that hangs like the sword of Damocles over the Middle East today.

Menachem Begin tells in his book how he was in hiding during that period — using several different names — moving from hiding place to hiding place in Tel Aviv to keep the British from finding him.

Although he repeatedly claims that the Jewish Agency and Haganah officials of the Palestine-Zionist establishment used him and his group as both convenient "underground" storm-troopers and likewise as "whipping boys" when expedient, the record shows clearly that Mr. Menachem Wolfovitch Begin(or Beigin) was a highly important man in the Zionist move to take over Palestine for a "Jewish State," and that his work was well known to American Zionists as the following paragraph will show.

The New York Times (November 23, 1948) carried an almost full page "ad" announcing a big $50 a plate "Welcome" and money raising dinner at New York's plush Waldorf-Astoria hotel for November 29, 1948, which "ad" was headlined, "The Man Who Defied an Empire and Gained Glory for Israel," with a sub-head which read, "Menachem Beigin, former Irgun Commander-in-Chief Arrives on Good Will Mission Today!" The reference about defying "an

Empire" was honoring Beigin for his "underground" crusade to drive the British Mandatory out of Palestine. The "Good Will Mission" reference was explained as the cementing of close relations between the United States and the new self-declared State of Israel. The $50-a-plate admission was to go to the "Rehabilitation Fund for Veterans of the Hebrew Resistance."

NOTE: The Times "ad" was a masterpiece of political ingenuity and show of Zionist influence. It touted the "underground" leader in the "war of liberation" against Britain as — "A man who has become a legend in his own lifetime . . . considered by many to be the logical and natural candidate for Prime Minister in the coming election in Israel . . ." The "ad" was decorated with the names of hundreds of prominent U.S. personalities. Included were 11 Senators — 71 Representatives — 11 Governors — 9 Mayors — 17 Judges — 99 Rabbis with a few Christian clergy — 69 listed as "Educators" — 58 listed under "Arts and Letters" — and a long list of "Other Classifications." Names are not listed here for lack of space — and other reasons that could be well understood by some of them. In this amazing display of dignification, they represented a memorial "worthy of a dead deity," to quote Ingersoll at Napoleon's tomb.

SEASONED NEWSPAPER MAN
DESCRIBES REFUGEES

In preparing this chapter on the Arab Refugees, hundreds of newspaper and magazine clippings (including Jewish and Arab publications), dealing with all phases of the subject over the years, have been checked. In late 1965, the Chicago Tribune ran a series of seven articles by Chesly Manly (one of the most capable and reliable newspaper men in the United States), giving a detailed, first-hand report on the condition of the camps and the lives of the refugees. These reports were so closely akin to our own personal investigation of the camps and the people that considerable reference here will be made to his findings.

The Chicago Tribune, in editorial reference to the Manly articles, said:

"We are not pro-this or anti-that but this is a problem which should trouble the conscience of the world. If a million and a quarter Chicagoans were forced to vacate their homes and live as squatters in the forest preserves, keeping body and soul together on the meanest subsistence level, it would cause horror and revulsion . . .

"The refugees contend they were driven from their homes and lands at the time of the Arab-Israel war in 1948. The Israelis said they decamped in response to orders of Arab leaders. There is no disposition in Israel to readmit any substantial number of the exiles or to hand them back their property . . . the refugee population lives out its days in squalor and misery on a United Nations allowance of 10 cents per day for each person, covering food, shelter, education and health services. There is no work for most of the people and the future is hopeless.

"The U.N.," continued the Tribune editorial, "which voted in 1947 to partition the refugees' homeland, has a sorry record of non-performance in coming to grips with the refugee problem . . . while boasting of its 'achievements', it has stalled for years and looked the other way."

The Chicago Tribune, in mentioning the 1947 United Nations partitioning of Palestine, puts its finger on the main secondary cause of this refugee tragedy where a million or so Palestinian Arabs (many of them Christians) seem doomed to a "future that is hopeless." The primary cause was the Balfour Declaration and the mass-immigration of foreigners it stimulated.

Mr. Manly, in his first Tribune article, explained how one and a quarter million Palestinian Arabs, seventeen years after they fled their homeland, "are still living in exile and appalling poverty, many of them under conditions that would not be suitable for hogs on a good Illinois farm." Their food ration is only four and a half cents a day each.

"Their plight," continues Mr. Manly, "is one of the most pathetic human tragedies of our time." He refers to a previous reporting trip he made to the refugee camps in 1958 when he wrote: "So long as the refugee problem remains unsolved there can be no peace in the middle east."

After visiting and talking with many officials and representative spokesmen in the Arab countries (including the refugee camps), also visiting and inquiring in that part of Palestine now called Israel, in 1963 and again in 1966, our findings agree with those of Mr. Manly. The feeling of the Arabs concerning the immigration-infiltration of the Zionists, followed by what they regard as aggressive usurpation, is just as strong and active as it was in 1948.

GLOOMY OUTLOOK

The current of emotion over this grievous coup d'etat continues to run so poignantly that any Arab leader who should even suggest a settlement that would not include the return of the Palestinian Arabs to their former homes would almost certainly be committing political suicide. Admittedly the "return" into a land that has been repopulated with two million people brought from other countries — with patterns of living everywhere altered to meet these changed conditions — would present a most complicated and knotty poser, but the Arabs do not consider this as their problem. The blame for it all is placed first on the "illegal" Zionist invasion — but there is a feeling that responsibility hangs heavily over the two countries that contributed to it — Great Britain and the United States. If there was ever a living monument to political blundering, this seems to be it.

The Israeli-Zionists, on the other hand, are not surcharged with similar emotional concern about the matter since they are now in possession of the land and appear to regard themselves as securely entrenched with their wide-spread co-religionist support and its powerfully strategic influence on world action. Some observers believe that in this temporary situation — since the world is ever changing — a time bomb may be developing since it is so well known that Soviet Communism is always on the prowl, watching for openings. It may be, they say, that Zionist alienation of the West from the Arabs could be playing dangerously by driving the Arabs to the Communist bloc for defensive help — thereby paving the way for confrontation between powers that could mean global war.

The warm feeling the Arabs once had for the United States has been cooling during the last few years because of pro-Israel acts and statements by some American vote-conscious public officials (examples later in this chapter), which are widely publicized by certain group papers to give the Arabs the impression that the United States is playing favorites. This endangers good will for America in the Middle East.

The temperament of the Arab people (especially the refugees) is highlighted by Mr. Manly's talk with Ibrahim abu Rish, then leader of the sprawling Aqabat Jaber camp in Jordan, who told him: "Our people are more determined than ever to go back but they no longer believe in promises. They have had so many promises from the U.N., U.N.R.W.A. and others that they don't believe anybody. They believe they must rely upon their own efforts."

NOTE: U.N.R.W.A. is the letter-abbreviation for the United Nations Relief and Welfare Agency for Palestine Refugees in the Middle East. It was established by the U.N. General Asembly (Resolution 302 — December 8, 1949) to collaborate with local governments in direct relief work programs for the Palestinian Arabs now in refugee camps. This organization solicits funds from the various U.N. member governments and then uses its budget to give the extremely limited necessities that house, feed and train the refugees. More than half (up to 70 percent) of this fund is provided by the United States.

"Life in some of the camps," wrote Mr. Manly, "is unimaginably miserable. The winters are cold and wet and there is no heat. Many of the camps are ankle deep in mud. The summers are hot and dry and dust swirls through the dirty alleys. There are no sewers and the improvised drainage systems — mostly shallow ditches — are repugnant to the senses of sight and smell. In the Burj el Barajneh camp, south of Beirut, for instance, the stench is intolerable to one not inured to it.

"Old people live out their wretched lives and children by the thousands are born and grow up in dehumanizing poverty and hopelessness. Among the saddest of the U.N.R.W.A. wards are intelligent young men and women who have finished secondary school and can neither continue their education nor find a job.

"Because of the U.N.R.W.A.'s excellent medical service the refugee death rate is less than 2 percent a year. With an annual birth rate of 4.5 percent, the annual increase is about 2.5 percent. The net increase from June 30, 1964 to June 30, 1965 was 34,238. The number of Arabs who fled from their homes in Palestine in 1948, is not known, but the best estimate is 750,000 . . . "

The number of Palestinian Arab refugees (including both Islamic and Christian) is now estimated at more than 1,250,000. It is becoming increasingly difficult for U.N.R.W.A. to provide the ever mounting costs of maintaining this growing mass of helpless humanity even at the present low level of bare subsistence, which grows as a shocking spectacle when contrasted with the millions of dollars that are raised annually in America (and perhaps a few other countries) as necessary transfusion to sustain Israel's economy.

It seems therefore clear that the Palestine-Zionist-Arab problem is not decreasing with the passing of time (as some have hopefully wished it would) but is increasing with explosive potential danger to world peace while also standing out as blatant mockery of the much touted hypocrisy called "brotherhood of man."

Chicago Tribune reporter Manly quotes Dr. Laurence Michelmore, Commissioner General of U.N.R.W.A., as saying the refugees "feel 'that they have been betrayed, and their resentment is directed against those whom they regard as the chief authors of their exile but also against the international community at large, whom they hold responsible for the partition and loss of their homeland which they regard as an offense against natural justice."

The Tribune reporter reinforces this by explaining that he had heard hundreds of refugees express the same sentiment and this writer has had essentially the same experience. Mr. Manly says, "They (the refugees) look upon Israel as their arch-enemy, but they blame the U.N. and particularly the United States for the adoption of the Palestine Partition resolution in November, 1947." The role of the United States in helping to create this Palestine debacle is documented in chapter IX dealing with the Balfour Declaration.

NOTE: The "Partition resolution" mentioned by Mr. Manly, although described in chapter XV will, for reading clarity, be briefly mentioned here. This scheme to "partition" Palestine between the long-time Arab citizens and the newcomer immigrant Zionists was a final and desperate attempt by the impotent United Nations to deal with a crisis that had been invited and encouraged by the Zionist-manipulated Balfour Declaration. After the first World War, the League of Nations (predecessor of U.N.), warmed by Zionist zeal, gave to Great Britain a Mandate (mandatory authority) over Palestine — a newly devised artifice for the convenience of international politics. After Zionist immigration into Palestine (made possible by the Balfour Declaration) became massive, the Zionists grew ambitious to be rid of the British "mandatory" which was restraining their goal in Palestine. To the momentum of this Palestine objective was added the propelling impetus of World War II — with Jews fleeing from Hitler's persecution — all of which combined to turn Zionist aggression and Arab resistance into a conflict made worse by "influenced" but non-authoritative meddling by the United States. The concatenation of all circumstances made Britain's mandatory position so difficult that finally the British government announced it was withdrawing from the scene as of May 15, 1948, at which time the Palestine problem would be in the lap of the United Nations.

After this announcement, the U.N. took steps to handle the "hot potato" crisis that had already been created — starting with the Balfour Declaration. The only solution it could come up with (the conflict having advanced so far) was a plan to partition Palestine into a "Jewish State" and an "Arab State." This scheme was immediately rejected by the Arabs — first, because they argued, the U.N. had no "jurisdiction to partition countries" — and asked for an opinion by the International Court of Justice. Secondly — they objected to a "Jewish State" where less than ten percent of the land was owned by the invading Zionist Jews.

PARTITION PLAN ADOPTED BY U.N.

The Palestine "partition" resolution No. 181 was adopted by the U.N. General Assembly on November 29, 1947. The records indicate that the Zionists stepped up a campaign to control as much Palestine territory as possible before the British moved out and before the "partitioning" could take place. This reaching-out campaign brought such strife and turmoil between Zionists and Arabs that an alarmed U.N. called an early meeting (March, 1948) and began discussing Palestine as a U.N. Trusteeship. On April 4, 1948, a terroristic attack was made by Zionist "underground groups" (Irgun and Stern crew) upon the small village of Deir Yasseen.

This evil deed that then "shocked the world" — but now seems forgotten — so frightened the Arabs in their unprotected villages that panic quickly ensued with Arab families fleeing the country in all directions — leaving most of their possessions behind — hurrying to safety across the borders. The brief reference here to the partition plan is to place emphasis on it as the starting point of the "refugee problem." After the 1948 Israel-Arab war, the lines were redrawn as a result of Armistice agreements between Israel and several surrounding Arab countries — with increased Israel territory. In 1967 came the six-day Israel "blitz" whereby the Zionists expanded their land-holdings to cover most of old Palestine.

* * *

As explained by Mr. Manly, the refugees "feel they have been betrayed" and one of the reasons, as he points out, has been the inability of the U.N. to enforce its Resolution No.

264

194 of December 1948 which resolved that the refugees should be allowed to return to their homeland, if they so desired, or otherwise to receive compensation for their abandoned properties now in the hands of the Zionist-Israelis.

The official United Nations act known as the "Conciliation Resolution" was based upon recommendations made by Swedish Count Folke Bernadotte, then U.N. Mediator who, striving desperately for a solution to the Palestine crisis, said: "The right of innocent people, uprooted from their homes by the present terror and ravages of war, to return to their homes should be affirmed and made effective with assurance of adequate compensation for the property of those who may choose not to return." He also said: "The liability of the provisional government of Israel to restore private property to its Arabs owners and to indemnify those owners for property wantonly destroyed is clear."

BERNADOTTE ASSASSINATED

In his report the U.N. Mediator (Count Bernadotte) had also said — "The Jewish State was not born in peace as was hoped for in the (partition) resolution . . ." The Bernadotte recommendations were received with great hostility by the Zionists.

*　　*　　*

Concerning terrorism as a weapon in the early Middle East conflict the newspaper files are replete with that unhappy record. We take note of a Chicago Tribune story (1-14-46) headlined — "ZIONIST SCHOOL FOR 'TERRORISM' OPENED IN NEW YORK." This news item described an activity where 98 already enrolled teen-agers were being drilled and trained for service in the anti-British "underground" movement of Palestine. Prior to that — in November of 1944 — two youths of the Stern gang (aged 22 and 17) were sent to Cairo where they assassinated Lord Moyne (British Minister of State in the Middle East) in the underground-resistance drive against the British Palestine mandatory. Members recruited in the Palestine terrorist gangs were, in the main, youthful. Youth is more amenable to the stirring of passion and action (as we see in the world today) and

265

readily submissive to radical leadership. Professional adult revolutionary leaders seem able to mobilize substantial numbers of ebullient youth to do for them the boisterous and violent work that they, themselves, are afraid to do.

Another Chicago Tribune story (6-15-46) carried a story titled — "PALESTINE JEWS TOLD TO LAUNCH GENERAL REVOLT."

> "The secret radio of Irgun Zvai Leumi, illegal Jewish underground," the Tribune said, "tonight summoned all Jews of Palestine to a general revolt against the British and called for formation of an underground Zionist government and army. The broadcast urged that Irgun and two similar resistance movements — Haganah and the Stern gang — combine as the nucleus of the army" and requested all Palestine Jews to volunteer. "We must exert our every strength in a constant war against two enemies — the British and time," the broadcast said.

VISITING WITH THE REFUGEES

The Chicago Tribune reporter, Chesly Manly, visited the ancient Philistine town of Gaza where was located one of the larger refugee camps. Gaza is on the Mediterranean coast in the narrow "Gaza strip" — an enclave remnant of old Palestine but left, after the 1948 Israel-Arab war, under control of Egypt. Israel, in its 1967 "blitz", occupied this area and now dominates it and its rich citrus fields, built up by the Arabs.

NOTE: For those interested in history, it will be worth noting that Gaza was a key town for nearby civilizations during the latter several hundred years B.C. The old trade routes from Egypt, Arabia and Petra — and those of Syria and Mesopotamia met there. Its fortress withstood Alexander the Great for five months (332 B.C.). From the Old Testament we have the story of the strong man, Samson, who came visiting a harlot in Gaza. When the Philistines learned of it and sought to catch him, he reportedly tore off the city gates and carried them near to Hebron.

Gaza's first mention in history is in the famous Tell-el-Amarna clay tablets (letters between an Egyptian Pharaoh and his governors in Palestine) — the finding of which has been a great boon for archaeologists, as they date from the early thirteenth century B.C. The town was captured by Napoleon during his ill-fated 18th century venture into Egypt (and Palestine).

It was in modern Gaza in late 1965 that Mr. Manly watched women refugees filing through the ration distribution center where they were receiving a fifteen-day allotment of flour, rice, lentils, sugar and vegetable oil. A woman noting that he carried pencil and note paper, and perhaps mistaking him for a U.N. official, addressed him through his interpreter. "Why don't you stop giving us these miserable rations," she exclaimed, "and help us get back to our homes? We have been here 17 years. Isn't that long enough? We would rather go back home and eat grass, if we had to, than stay here and eat this stuff."

Manly learned that she had come to the camp in 1948 when she was fifteen. There she married another refugee and they have five children. One was born after the ration cut-off date (a limitation adjustment that U.N.R.W.A. had found necessary) so the family of seven was now drawing rations for only six. Another woman held a cup of 300 grams of dried lentils (a 15-day ration) and complained through the interpreter — "Do other people think we are chickens? Look at this stuff. Do you believe it is enough for a person to live on? If our husbands can't find jobs, how can we live?"

Before the Zionist-Arab trouble in Palestine, the Gaza Strip had prosperous farmers who owned land over a considerable area which was highly productive — with citrus, wheat and barley farming that gave work to many Palestinian Arabs. After the 1948 Israeli-Arab war most of the rich Palestine coastal plains were in the hands of the Israeli Zionists — except for the Gaza strip which remained in the control of Egypt. It was during this latter period, as Mr. Manly points out, that the Arabs living in the Strip had developed a flourishing citrus industry, mainly because it was within the last fifteen years that the world citrus price had increased to open a wide export market.

"Last season," reports Mr. Manly (writing in 1965), "the strip exported 1,250,000 crates of oranges and enough young trees are growing to increase the total to 2,000,000 boxes in two or three years. This," he says, "is proportionately a much greater production than Israel's 14,000,000 boxes a year. The Arabs, too," he writes, "can make the desert bloom if they have the money to level the sand dunes, mix in a little manure with the sand and clay, and dig wells." In 1967 the axe fell on the Gaza Strip. The Israeli-blitz took it and the orange groves over for the Zionists. Such news as seeps out of the Strip (1968) does not augur well for the long predominant Gaza Arabs.

OUTSIDE MONEY SUPPORTS ISRAEL

Much propaganda has been put out about Palestine being a wasteland until the Israelis took over. This is, of course, largely bunkum, as the Arabs have done well with what they had to do with. They want the world to know that the Jewish immigrants came heavily financed with a constant flow of millions of dollars sent them by New York and other Jewish communities — as well as millions of foreign aid from the United States government — and still more millions in German reparations. Prior to the success of the Weizmann leadership in promoting Zionism for Palestine, most of the Jews who lived there (mainly in Jerusalem) were dependent upon a dole from Jews in other countries.

Available records indicate that the Jews who lived in Palestine around the turn of the century were no more progressive — and generally not so much so — as the resident Arabs when all were restricted to the same natural resources. The Arabs never had an organized outside charity-supported system. The Jews did — through world-wide collected halukkah. One knowledgeable official who has been close to the Palestine problem put into a few words what has been expressed by many in different ways when he said: "It is outside money that has made any difference in showing and that has caused most of the trouble — outside money inspired by world-prestige objectives."

The Palestine-refugees inflame with anger when they hear boasts of Zionist achievements. "The olive groves and the oranges and farms are there to show that we were industrious," one refugee near Jericho exclaimed with vehemence. "We did more in developing Palestine under the handicap of Turkish and other overlords than the Jews did when the Israelites had a free hand at it. We populated the land and

268

built villages and towns where we were happy until we were invaded. We didn't have rich relatives in New York and other cities to send us millions of dollars. But is it right," he asked, "that people with rich backers can take over a country — any country — and oust the native-born population who, following their forefathers, have lived there for hundreds of years? If so then who will say that we have advanced from the days of the Assyrians, Babylonians and Israelites when it was common policy to grab and hold by force — anything coveted?"

In the lobby of the King's Palace hotel in Athens we engaged in brief conversation with a small group that had just come in from the Middle East — as we had. Reference was made to the refugee problem. One talkative lady who had visited briefly one of the camps observed that the refugees looked to her like a lot of lazy people just loafing around. "Why don't they get out and get jobs?" she asked. She was probably equating the desert country to an American city like New York where she lived. The incident is mentioned here because it is typical of great numbers who look but do not see — who read but do not comprehend — who utter thoughtless opinions without any basic understanding of this refugee problem and how it came to exist.

REFUGEES NOT LAZY — PLEADING FOR JOBS

Perhaps, however, the lady should have an answer. Large numbers of the refugees have found places for their native skills in the limited economy of the Arab countries. All opportunities are quickly filled as they develop. For instance there is Moussa who as driver for a Taxi-Travel Service has long serviced the Damascus-Amman-Jerusalem area. He is a careful driver — a fine gentleman — quiet, non-obtrusive and non-agitational. He has driven us many times. He is a 1948 refugee. Once, in driving us from Jerusalem to Bethlehem, he took us near the troubled border (which prior to 1967 divided Israel and Jordan) and pointed in the distance to what had formerly been his home — to which he could not return.

In Damascus we once had a guide — a quiet, courteous young man, disinclined to talk about himself but from whom we drew something of his experience. In the fury of conflict that panicked the refugees from their homes and villages in 1948, his father was killed. His mother, he said, leading her two boys (one 5 and this young man then 8) was trying to reach safety when she too was slain. The boys were raised as orphans and now as young men, striving to be independent, are eking out a living as part time guides. In Beirut we found a highly intelligent refugee working as a clerk in our hotel. These people, as we found them, have excellent innate ability and are extremely ambitious, with high ideals generally. America and other countries might do well to have more of them.

One more case — that of a young man serving as a guide inside the old walled city of Jerusalem. We selected him to help us find some special places with which we were not familiar. During our conversations we mentioned our friendly acquaintance with a famous doctor there (also a refugee) who gives a large part of his time to the surgical mending of little bodies that have been born deformed or otherwise afflicted. When we finished with the guide and offered him his pay, he refused to take it and we could not persuade him to accept. When pressed for the reason he said very simply — "You are a friend of Dr. Dajani and it is a pleasure to serve you." We have found the Arabs to have high ethical and moral standards — friendly — deeply religious — ambitious and industrious — and not constantly grasping in matters of money.

WHAT ANSWER DOES THE FUTURE HOLD?

There seems to be no early solution of the "Palestine problem" in sight. It is not the spirit of the Arabs to accept their fate as exiles from the country they consider to be their natural homeland as native born citizens — measured by the standards of modern civilized nations. Their spirit of patriotism is akin, they think, to that of Francis Scott Key when he wrote the "Star Spangled Banner" or Sir Winston Churchill when he gave his speech on "blood, toil, tears and sweat."

Depressed as they are in these desolate camps, the refugees are keeping patriotism and hope alive. Mr. Manly, in one of his Chicago Tribune articles, explained the formula by which this was being done through drill and exercise in the boys' schools. This may by now have been changed. Strict controls are reported in the camp areas (Gaza, Jericho, etc.) that were seized by Israel in the 1967 blitz. Certain reports appearing in the London Observer, Manchester Guardian, and other sources, indicate that the Arabs in these newly conquered Jordanian areas are being rigidly and severely treated.

Marching to classes — patriotism — order — discipline — these were routine in all the Arabic schools (both boys and girls) where we have visited them. There is an alertness — an eagerness to learn — a dedication to purpose among the students that could well be copied by some of our western nations where softness has deteriorated into sloppiness. The Arabs, so far as our contacts can determine, are dedicated to the ideal that — after centuries of servitude — their future depends upon better education and they are improving their schools everywhere from the lowest grades to colleges and universities. They are working hard to improve their economic conditions as they know they must make their own way. They know this all will take time but they believe time is on their side — and as they grow stronger they are on the march to a better day. The refugees, now helpless, are, too, entitled to education and opportunity.

WHAT ABOUT "RESETTLEMENT"?

From leading representative spokesmen one gathers it would be highly satisfying to the Zionist-Israelis if the "refugee problem" would be solved by some nation or nations (other than the people who created the displacement) by finding homes and jobs for these tragically uprooted and deserted people. That would get an ugly skeleton out of the Zionist closet — and leave them to enjoy their gains with perhaps a freer conscience. What are the possibilities? The very people who were exerting every possible pressure, during the Hitler terror, to have the U.S. Congress pass special "refugee legislation" in 1953 to admit 240,000 European "displaced persons" are now the ones who turn a deaf ear to the Palestinian

271

refugee disaster. This unanswered question has been asked: Does any part of the millions collected in the United States for the Zionists in Israel go to help the Palestinian refugees?

Is it unreasonable to ask whether the refugees themselves have any voice — any choice — about what happens to them? Are they to be mere pawns in a chess game of international politics? A responsible spokesman for the refugee cause says that they (the refugees) do not wish to become a burdensome problem saddled upon some other nation — especially when they have basic rights to their own homeland and their own once self-sustaining properties. These they want as their own again so they can solve their own problems.

This spokesman gave three main reasons why the Palestinian refugees do not wish or expect to be resettled in the Arab states: (1) It would mean the equivalent of abandoning their basic moral and legal "rights" in Palestine; (2) It would destroy all hopes of recovering their civilization in its strategic location where they were once happy citizens; (3) The economic status of the Arab states makes accommodation of the refugees there utterly impossible.

There are people today, this spokesman said, who are completely unfamiliar with economic conditions in the Middle East, who have doubtless taken their cue from Zionist publicity and have concluded it is the responsibility of the other Arab states to take care of the ousted Palestinians. It is difficult to follow the logic of such reasoning. There are more than a million and a quarter refugees in the scattered and sprawling camps. Each Arab State has its own urgent problems in taking care of its own normal population growth. That is not all — the refugee problem is not one that the Arabs created.

The Arab States have had their national freedom from foreign overlords for only a comparatively few years. Their countries are made up largely of desert wastes with limited water supply. The most fertile lands held by the Arabs were the rich coastal plains of Palestine. And in the final analysis of the question, the Arabs contend it was not they who created the refugee problem but the Zionists who did it by their "conquest through immigration" in an illegal coup fostered by international political chicanery.

"Look," one irate Arab refugee who had obtained a temporary job in a Damascus bazaar exclaimed when interviewed, "Look — who are these people who are in possession of our former homeland? Go check their records and see for yourself where the big wheels and the little ones who are running our country today came from. You will find that but few of them, if any, were born anywhere near Palestine. They are there and we are here — and that is what burns me."

"YES" AND "NO" OF REFUGEE PROBLEM

The core of the Arab refugee problem is the question of their being allowed to return, if they so wish, to their native homes and places of business in Palestine. The Israeli position on this (regardless of the United Nations' resolution supporting that right) is that their return to their homeland cannot be allowed. Their contention is that, after what has happened, the refugees could not be trusted to be friendly neighbors and obedient citizens of the Zionist-Israeli government that has supplanted them in what was their own homeland.

When the matter of compensating the Arab refugees for their lands and properties is brought up, the present Israeli officials express willingness to discuss the question of settlement if a negotiating conference can be arranged, but the one basic proposition is the ancient one of conquest upheaval. "What is there to discuss?" ask the Arab refugees. "Palestine was our natural and national homeland. Now our places are being enjoyed by some two million foreigners brought from afar, largely from Eastern Europe, while we have been pushed out into these miserable camps." No one can truly understand this unless he is one of the refugees.

The Arab refugees refuse to become entangled in any "negotiations" that would not start with recognition of this basic "right of return." The Arabs do not believe that the Zionist-Jews have any "rights" of rulership over Palestine other than the fait accompli of occupancy by force, which they refuse to recognize as legally or morally valid in our modern

273

world. Here the matter stands as a political impasse — and a potential time bomb.

LET'S SETTLE THIS THING — OUR WAY

There is no dearth of willing hands on the Israeli side to present formulae for settlement. Herewith is an example of many recommended plans — this one submitted by U.S. Congressman Leonard Farbstein (New York) as reported in the Jewish Post and Opinion. The major ten points of the Farbstein proposal are as follows:

1. UNRWA should discontinue issuance of new ration cards.
2. Rolls of refugees should be rectified as a conditioning process.
3. Responsibility for refugees and refugee camps should be turned over to the host countries.
4. Financial arrangements for relief (etc.) should be made with the host countries through UNRWA during the phasing out period.
5. There should be a gradual transition of UNRWA to an agency for vocational training and placement.
6. Young people should be urged, but not compelled, to seek employment and give up their refugee status.
7. Ration cards should be taken up from refugees who are self-supporting or have obtained employment.
8. Refugee rolls should be reduced annually allowing a period of 5 to 10 years for the dissolution of the problem.
9. The United States should serve notice of the date on which it will terminate its support of UNRWA.
10. This point covered four requirements which should be asked of Israel: (a) to allow aged refugees to return to relatives on conditions set by Israel; (b) reasonable compensation for properties; (c) formation of bilateral agreements if possible; (d) these should first be made with countries having the least number of refugees.

The Arab refugees do not want any part of such plan. To them it would completely ignore their rights as lifetime inhabitants and owners of Palestinian land and properties. This would place their destinies — as the dominant inhabitants of Palestine for centuries — at the dictation of their usurpers. The Arabs regard this as a base scheme to force over a million destitute people upon "host nations" who, out of mercy gave temporary asylum to neighbors fleeing for their lives — and it would also have the flagrant purpose of "phasing out" United Nations world relief for these unfortunate victims of

20th century politics — leaving them it would seem to starve.

One weakness that seems to be indigenous to these proposed plans is a fault based either on intention to confuse or ignorance of the Middle East as a region. In this case, for instance, this New York gentleman recommends that the young refugees should "seek employment" and "give up refugee status." The answer: (1) Anyone with any understanding of the refugee situation knows that every able-bodied Palestinian Arab who can find work within his possible reach has avidly grasped it. (2) The author of this plan seems to be confusing the desert lands with New York and Washington (where he spends most of his time) as a place where one can answer want-ads or walk up and down miles of city streets, knocking on doors to "seek employment." (3) Most of the camps are surrounded by vast desert country where jobs are a rarity. Proposals such as the Farbstein plan may have political value in New York, but they provide no help whatever in solving the tragic and highly complicated refugee problem in the Middle East. Those who created the refugee situation here seem completely indifferent toward accepting any responsibility for it. There are those who look at this problem with great apprehension as to what may come out of it.

AUTHORITATIVE VOICES
SPEAK OF REFUGEES

Mr. John Reddaway, Deputy Commissioner-General of U.N.R.W.A. in Beirut, on December 3, 1967, addressed the Sunday Forum of the University Christian Center, American University, on the question of the Palestinian Arab refugees — a problem with which he was officially concerned. He made it clear he was not necessarily reflecting the official policy of U.N.R.W.A. or the United Nations.

"In my view," he said, "there is very little truth in those ideas about the Palestine refugees which are unfortunately widespread and all too readily accepted in Western countries and which depict the refugees as idle, good-for-nothing people, content to live on international charity, stagnating in idleness in the refugee camps, a perpetual burden on their fellow men, pawns in the game against Israel heartlessly

275

manipulated by Arab governments which have made no effort to solve the problem" — a problem which, incidentally, they did not create. (Quote from "The Middle East Newsletter," March, 1968.)

In his talk, Mr. Reddaway gave a number of illustrations of wrong impressions about the refugees, including reference to a recently published paperback titled "The Six Day War" by two scions of a late British statesman. The book had referred to the 1948 Palestinian refugees as having for nineteen years been "rotting in idleness." If the statement had been fully representative, it could have said "enforced idleness," because the world forces that turned them into refugees made no organized effort to rehabilitate them. The responsibility was plainly upon the organized governments and other forces that helped create the conditions that frightened these people into flight for safety — and then conveniently forgot them.

In this book we have made no effort to quote other U.N. officials who have dealt directly with the Israeli-Arab conflict — such, for instance, as the late Commander E. N. Hutchison, Military Observer and Commander of the United Nations Truce Supervision Organization (1951-1954). His book "Violent Truce" (Devin Adair) is a revealing story. Notable also is the book "Between Arab and Israel" by Lt. General E. L. M. Burns, formerly Chief of Staff of the U.N. Truce Supervision Organization (1954-1956), and then Commander of the U.N. Emergency Force (1956 to 1959). To go into these records would require a second volume.

*　　*　　*

A powerful full page editorial titled "Tears That Cry to Heaven" appeared in The Sign (National Catholic Magazine) for April, 1957, in which the editor pleaded the tragic cause of the Palestinian Arab refugees. In this editorial, Father Ralph Gorman, C.P., said: "Statesmen can talk as much as they like about the Gaza Strip and Aqaba, about the Aswan Dam and the Suez Canal and oil and strategy. It will all be to no avail unless we do something really effective to right the awful wrong, to make reparation for this crime that is almost genocide. This must be the first step toward peace in the Near East."

About these unhappy refugees, he also wrote — "The spirit seems gone out of them except when you mention their homes, or lands, or vineyards, or shops, and then they look over the hills to where they once lived, and their eyes burn with hatred . . ." From long experience in the Holy Land, Father Gorman knows the country and the people well.

NOTE: This report on the Palestinian Arab refugees deals mainly with the refugees resulting from the 1948 Jewish-Arab conflict. This was written prior to the 1967 Israeli blitz — which made more Arab refugees. The hate-building refugee problem continues to worsen. As this book goes to press, a news dispatch appearing in the Los Angeles Times (February 22, 1968) says an official U.N.R.W.A. communique describes a "mass exodus" of new Palestinian refugees from camps and towns of the Jordan River valley, estimated at well over 70,000, who have fled into Jordan where they have been given temporary shelter in mosques and tents. According to U.N.R.W.A., more than 200,000 Arabs have fled the territory occupied by the Israelis in the June blitz.

19. INTERESTING FACTS ABOUT SOVIETISM, SOCIALISM AND ZIONISM IN THE MIDDLE EAST

The impression has been widely and actively spread that Russian influence is infiltrating and extending its political controls throughout the Arab States (particularly Egypt) through financial and military aid. Certain people who find it greatly to their prestige advantage to spread this image among Americans who know little about the Middle East, but who do dislike Sovietism, have made great headway with "guilt by association" propaganda. The pro-Zionists who may find it profitable to stir public opinion with an ugly Arab picture have an amenable and extensive communication industry at their command.

This issue of status-manipulation is adumbrated with so much confusion, misinformation and propaganda, all of which is loaded with emotional dynamite, that the whole subject of who is pure and spotless should be carefully examined. Most controversial matters are heavily weighted with touchy passion, but this Middle East situation has been built into an explosive mass that may easily set half the world afire. It is time, before that happens, for sober minds to know the facts more clearly and evaluate them more cautiously.

Communists are always prowling where trouble brews and trouble began brewing here with the confrontation and friction that reached the boiling stage after Communist Russia and capitalistic United States combined their weight in the "partition" vote to create a "Jewish State" in the heartland of the Arab world.

SOVIETS WERE EARLY ZIONIST PALS

Many, perhaps, paid little attention or have already forgotten, but the whole world had a chance to see some crafty political card shuffling in November of 1947 when (as reported elsewhere) the Zionists were making frenzied effort to have Palestine "partitioned" as a means of getting United Nation's recognition as a "Jewish State." In that critical struggle the Russian Soviets, for reasons which lately, at least, have been partially disclosed, joined the vote-conscious United States Truman government in vying for first place in voting and otherwise helping the Palestine "partition" Resolution through a reluctant U.N. General Assembly.

With that accomplished, Soviet Russia then raced the United States for priority in "recognizing" the new Jewish State when it was self-proclaimed at midnight, May 14, 1948. President Truman, hard pressed and badly in need of the New York Zionist voting bloc in the oncoming Presidential election, won in that race for first place; but Communist Russia, not to be outdone by the Truman Administration, extended *de jure* recognition to the new Jewish State on May 17, and became the first country to recognize the new Israel fully and officially.

* * *

MORE EARLY BACKGROUND

It would seem important to those who are now pointing an accusatorial finger at the Arabs for accepting arms from Russia to keep in mind that the first major Soviet penetration into the Middle East conflict was to help set the stage for creation of the "Jewish State"; to help establish the Zionists as a political entity (nation); and to supply that nation with Soviet-bloc weaponry.

There are those who believed then — and now — that Russia's political romance with the Zionists was typical Communist penetration strategy to stir up trouble and through it destroy what the Russians regarded (as put by one writer) a "preserve of Western power." With so many of the Zionist leaders, as the records will show, active in socialistic and revolutionary movements, it was perhaps not unnatural for the Soviets to regard them as people with whom they could work advantageously, in a somewhat common cause.

They knew that it was out of the Social Democratic (socialist) movement that Lenin, with the help of many

279

Russian Jews, had carved Bolshevik communism — and that it was out of the "Left Wing" of the Foreign Federations of the Socialist Party in the United States that agents of the Moscow Comintern had formed the U.S. branch of the Communist Party; and knowing well the dominant make-up of the U.S. Communist apparatus, they probably looked upon the Middle East Zionist development as soil ready for cultivation.

Whatever the motivation, the partnership did not long survive. It has been said that the Zionists and the Communists were too much alike in their urge to build their own empires and run their own shows. However, that did not deter the first Prime Minister of the new Israel from expressing deep thanks to the Soviets for their help in getting Israel off the launching pad. David Ben Gurion, of long time socialist persuasion, was the first Prime Minister, and here is the expression of gratitude as carried in the Israel (Government printed) Year Book for 1952:

> "Israel does not forget," stated Israel's Prime Minister, "the stand taken by the Soviet Union in the Assembly of the United Nations on the historic 29th day of November, 1947, nor does it forget the like stand of the United States of America. It remembers as vividly the aid it received from Czechoslovakia during the War of Independence, and the attitude of Poland toward Jewish immigration to Israel, manifestations which without doubt bespoke sincere sympathy with Israel's enterprise."

It was David Ben Gurion, recognized and honored by his followers as the architect of the new Israel, who set the pattern for the present Zionist State. Ben Gurion's political classification was stated by the late Rabbi G. George Fox in his January 14, 1954 "Column" in the Jewish SENTINEL (Chicago) under the heading — "Old Socialist Pioneer Ben Gurion Lives Up To His Ideals." In the story Rabbi Fox said:

> "Ben Gurion and his fellow builders of the Israel of a few years ago dreamed of a socialistically economical state, based upon prophetic ideals. They were idealists and most of them socialists."

SOCIALISTIC INGREDIENTS

David Ben Gurion (the Ben meaning "son of") tells of his early political life in a book titled "Ben Gurion Looks Back," edited by his friend, Moshe Pearlman (Simon & Schuster, 1965). He was born in a Polish town near Warsaw in 1886, and raised under active Zionist influences. He states that orthodox religion influenced him when he was about seven years old — but not after that. By the time he had finished high school, he was completely enveloped in the Labor Zionist Movement which, according to the New Jewish Encyclopedia, was known as Poale Zion and was "founded by Eastern European Jews after the first Zionist Congress in 1897."

Poale Zion's ideals, the description continues, were Zionism and Socialism — and its main objective was the formation of a Jewish Commonwealth (a Jewish State) in far away Palestine. According also to the Encyclopedia, Poale Zion's purpose "emphasized that such commonwealth be based upon socialistic principles." Following World War I (after Weizmann had secured the Balfour Declaration), the center of Poale Zion was moved to Palestine, where it became one of the leading Zionist political parties.

It was Ben Gurion, who had long been an active leader of Poale Zion, who was likewise active in putting this socialist organization in first place as a political movement in Palestine during the days of the British trusteeship. He and his Zionist-socialist following, in 1920, formed the Histadrut (General Federation of Hebrew Workers in Israel) with Ben Gurion as its General Secretary and leader. This powerful movement in Israel was and is constituted mainly of labor groups, co-operatives and similar collectives. It is doubtless the most powerful force in political Israel.

In 1930-31, Ben Gurion's Poale Zion merged with the Tzeire Zion (Zionist Socialist Youth movement) to form the Mapai (Israel's Workers Party), and continues as the major political party in Israel, although it is now (1968) the political base of Prime Minister Levi Eshkol. (See Chapter XXIV regarding Israel's political machinery.) The Mapai, according to the Standard Jewish Encyclopedia, after it was formed in 1931, "entered the Second International."

NOTE: Some readers with inquiring minds may ask, "What was the Second International?". There have been several so-called "Internationals" —all far to the Left. William Z. Foster, long time figurehead of the Communist Party (U.S.A.), in his book "History of the Three Internationals," says the group which established the Second International met for that purpose in Paris, July 14, 1889 — the meeting being "called by the German and organized by the French Marxists". Across the meeting hall was a large banner proclaiming the event as in honor of the 1848 and the 1871 European revolutions and that greetings were extended to "the Socialistic Workers of both Worlds." Foster declared that, "The Paris congress demonstrated that Marxism had become dominant in the world labor movement, particularly in its political wing."

Without going into detail concerning the platform and purpose of the Second International, it will be sufficient to say that it was a Socialist movement to help coordinate Socialists in their effort to organize all countries into a Socialist world network. It is not to be confused with the more extreme Third (or Communist International set up by the Moscow Bolsheviks in 1919). The Second International, after being suspended during the first World War, was revived again as the Labor and Socialist International and later suspended — finally passing out of any effective existence.

SHIP OF STATE LISTS LEFTWARD

"Socialists Strong in Israel Regime" was the headline on a news story in the New York Times on September 12, 1948, four months after the new Jewish State was proclaimed. The Times correspondent said that "if judged by the current party distribution among the doctrine-minded citizens, it is apparent that state socialism," something like the Socialist Labor Party of Great Britian, would be favored in the upcoming elections and "thereafter a socialist system will indubitably develop." He referred to the central federation of leftish and labor groups put together as Histadrut, and said: "In point of fact this became a socialist empire in miniature." Histadrut was a basic organization in the formation of the Jewish State and continues as such.

Along this same line, an article appeared in the strongly Communist-oriented paper "National Guardian" (March 17, 1956) about the Kibbutzim in Israel, titled "Settlements Are Hard Core for Socialism." At that time the author said there were 220 of these collective communes or settlements in Israel "associated with the three main Left parties of Israel: Mapam (United Workers' Party), Achdut Avoda (Unity of Labor Party), and Mapai (Israel Labor Party), the last being (at that time) the largest in the country."

*   *   *

RUSSIAN ARMS FOR ISRAEL

When the first Prime Minister of the new Israel expressed the gratitude of Israel to Soviet Russia for the help it had given in making the "Jewish State" possible, he included also reference to the Soviet puppet state of Czechoslovakia. This citation was to the weaponry supplied by the Soviet-bloc to Israel during her 1948 war with the Arabs.

The story of the arms-flow from this Communist source (the Skoda Works of Czechoslovakia) has never been sufficiently understood by the American or British people. During the first eventful year of its life, Israel was the only country in the Middle East to receive military material from the Soviet-Communist bloc. There is not room here for the full story, but the following documentation is sufficient to establish the reality of that aid.

The 1948 war between the Zionists and the Arabs began immediately after May 15 when the Palestinian Arabs, frightened at the Zionists' proclamation of a Jewish State in their midst, called upon other Arabs for defensive help. This war was waged fiercely until June 11 when the U.N. Security Council succeeded in getting both sides to agree to a four weeks' truce. At that time, certain military observers thought the Arabs had an advantage. The Security Council called upon all U.N. members to abstain from supplying war materials to combatants; but General Glubb, writing in "A Soldier With the Arabs," states that during the truce — "aircraft and weapons were continually arriving in Israel by air."

General Glubb, then Commander-in-Chief of the Jordan Arab Legion, further explains:

"During the truce the Israeli forces had been regrouped; time had been available for planning, and, above all, a regular flow of weapons and ammunition had been obtained from Communist Czechoslovakia . . . By the end of the truce an Israeli air-force was already in being . . . Meanwhile, however, although the fact that Israel was receiving arms and ammunition from Czecho-Slovakia was well known, the U.N.O. blockade was still in force, and the British Government refused to supply us" (meaning Jordan). "The least she (Britain) could have done," he writes, "could have been to denounce Czecho-Slovakia (and Russia) and to state that, unless Russia and her satellites ceased to aid Israel, Britain would abandon the blockade of Jordan." (NOTE: In brief Britain was observing the truce — at the expense of her ally Jordan — while Russia and Israel were violating the truce which helped Israel win the 1948 war.)

On November 13, 1948, the London Daily Telegraph reported from Hof, Bavaria, as follows:

"Czecho-Slovakia has supplied the Israeli Air Force with at least 100 Messerschmitt fighter planes, a Jewish informant declared here today. He asked that his identity be withheld for fear of reprisals. Airfields at Zatec, Chemutor, Rekycany, and Pisek were used to despatch the planes, he said. Pilots flying supplies to Palestine included former United States Air Force officers and Hungarians. As many as four transports a day had left Zatec."

FURTHER EVIDENCE

A New York Times dispatch from Vienna (December 20, 1948) revealed that a group of displaced persons, possibly financed from the United States and supported by Russians in Austria, had been buying arms in Czechoslovakia and shipping them to Israel.

Dr. Fayez A. Sayegh, noted Arabic scholar, in a well documented little book, "Communism in Israel," quotes from a February 18, 1956 Saturday Evening Post article by the well known American correspondent, Don Cook, as follows:

"By May (1948) shipments of Czechoslovakian rifles and automatic weapons began arriving (in Israel) in quantities . . . The story of the Jewish efforts to beat the United Nations arms blockade in itself is full of fantastic episodes." (To understand the importance of this is to recall that the Zionist-Arab war began in May of 1948.)

American Secretary of State, John Foster Dulles, appearing before the Senate Foreign Relations Committee, February 24, 1956, answered Senator John Sparkman's question by saying —"Israel itself has in the past gotten substantial amounts of arms from the Soviet bloc." Arms aid was also flowing to the Zionists in Palestine from some non-Communist countries without government approval. The American press gave frequent notice about "gun runners" who were collecting and smuggling arms out of the United States during the 1947-48 Zionist-Arab struggle. This present discussion, however, concerns the collaboration of the Soviets with the Zionists during the critical period that produced the birth and the early days of the Jewish State (Israel).

SUMMARY OF VITAL SOVIET-ZIONIST COLLABORATION

(1) In 1947, Soviet political aid turned the tide in favor of the Zionists by supplying the necessary votes to pass the U.N. Resolution to "partition" Palestine and thereby give "official" recognition to the plan for a "Jewish State"; (2) In 1948, the Soviets gave the Zionists diplomatic support by "recognizing" the new Jewish State; (3) In 1948, when war

developed as a result of the Arabs' attempt to resist the intrusion of a "Jewish State," the Soviets supplied the Israelis with substantial war equipment to help turn the tide of battle.

SOVIET-ISRAEL LOVE AFFAIR ENDS
WITH BROKEN ROMANCE

Whether the Soviets helped to put the new "Jewish State" in business, expecting to use it as a transmission belt into the Middle East — or whether the purpose was to start trouble that would lead to conflict and chaos from which she could pick up the pieces — has long been a matter of conjecture by observers of "the moving finger" in that area.

After the Soviets had helped put through the "Jewish State" partition of Palestine, and helped the Zionist-Israelis win the 1948 war against the Arabs, trouble soon began to brew between the new Israel and Russia. A news story in the New York Times (February 15, 1953) date-lined Tel Aviv, carried a headline that read: "Break With Russians Adds to Israel's Woes." The story told how the Zionists, for more than four years before and after Israel was "created," had striven to avoid offending the Russians in order "to stave off the day that came this week . . . when the Soviet Union broke off diplomatic relations with the Jewish State."

The article reaffirms pointedly that "the birth of the (Jewish) state was made possible very largely by a temporary agreement between the United States and the Soviet Union. The Soviet Union," it continues, "was motivated by tactical considerations. The Soviet Union saw the Zionist movement as a weapon against the British in the Middle East and hoped that Communists could infiltrate the new state and make it an outpost of the Communist world in the Middle East."

*　　*　　*

THE END OF "AN AFFAIR"

Be all of that as it may, the Russian Communists and the Zionists, both adept in underground tactics (as the records reveal) soon found their relationships becoming sticky. The Russians began to show their displeasure by such acts as suppressing the last Yiddish paper in their domain and they also closed the Jewish Anti-Fascist Committee which had been allowed to function during World War II when Russia was highly dependent upon American "Lend-Lease" aid — ELEVEN BILLIONS of it. Another Zionist-needling act was to close a Russian Jewish theater — and in October of 1953 two Israeli Jews, arrested for alleged espionage crimes in Czechoslovakia, were sentenced.

An item in the Chicago Tribune (November 3, 1953) said that one of them, "Mordecai Oren, leader of the leftist Israeli Mapam party, was arrested in Prague in December, 1951, while on his way back from a conference of the Communist-led World Federation of Trade Unions in Rome." He was accused of subversion against the Czech state and received a 19-year prison sentence.

There was also the widely publicized case where a number of Jewish doctors in Russia were arrested and charged with plotting to murder certain Russian officials. And there were other acts, apparently intended to impress upon the Israelis what was expected of them for the political midwife help they had received in 1948.

All this time, Ben Gurion and other Zionist leaders persisted in pleading friendship for the Soviets in an effort to keep the Russian association. It eventually became apparent, however, that the Soviets were through with their Israel experiment, and, as one observer opined — "It may have been a case where each was playing the other for advantages — with each being equally tricky about it."

RUSSIA SWITCHES FOREIGN POLICY IN MIDDLE EAST

Some two years after the Russian-Israel romancing had ended, there came the announcement (in 1955) that the Soviet bloc (largely through Czechoslovakia) would supply armament to Egypt. Before examining this new "foreign policy" switch, it seems important, in the interest of continuity, to start with the 1952 Egyptian revolution and evaluate the ensuing events with their possible meanings.

STEPS THAT LED TO RUSSIAN AID FOR EGYPT

The defeat of the Arabs in the 1948 war with the Israelis may, to some considerable extent, have been due to the immense outside aid the Israelis received (making possible a vital overpowering air force), but it also revealed a woeful lack of unity, strategy and military sufficiency on the part of the Moslem countries. It appeared that they had been fooling themselves while trying to impress their neighbor states as to their own military status. This doubtless reflected a sort of competitive pride in the new era that had come to them after they had helped oust their overlord Turks in the first world war. The 1948 war with the Israelis, however, awakened the Arabs to the reality of a world of tooth and claw — and made them understand that self-preparedness is essential to present day security.

EGYPT MOVES IN NEW DIRECTIONS

Out of the unrest that was stirring and building in Egypt, partly as a result of defeat by Israel (although King Farouk's Egypt was at great disadvantage in the 1948 war, with a thin line of soldiers to cover a wide line of Sinai front), there gradually arose among the younger officers a revolutionary group that wished to substitute a Republic for the old Monarchy. One of the leaders of this group that in July, 1952, obtained the abdication of King Farouk, was a dynamic young army colonel named Jemal Abdul Nasser.

Another prominent personality was an old line army officer with a distinguished record — General Mohammed Neguib — who, because of his prestige, was made chairman of the revolutionary Committee of Twelve. When the King abdicated (on demand), Neguib became Prime Minister and Commander-in-Chief during the reorganization interim. When the change of government to a Republic was completed, Neguib became President and Premier with Nasser as Vice President and Minister of Interior.

Trouble gradually developed between these two top leaders over policies, and after it became manifest that the popular backing of Nasser was the greater, General Neguib "stepped down" to an honorary position and Colonel Nasser became the "strong man" President. Whether Egypt's leaders had dreams of empire to rehabilitate and unify the Arab world, as some critics have claimed, is not documentable and therefore not germane to this story. The record shows that the Nasser regime began immediately to institute building programs (like the High Dam and industrial plants) to provide the necessities for a rapidly growing population. These we have seen.

Reorganization of Egypt's social, political and economic life was no mean task itself, all problems considered, and because of its geographical position its national destiny demanded greater attention and interest in world affairs. One of the early moves in international directions that led to Nasser's considerable recognition as a public figure, was his attendance at the Conference of Asian and African Nations at Bandung, Indo China (April, 1955). There, naturally, Nasser met many leaders among the official delegates from some 28 countries attending. It was at this meeting that the Bandung Pact was fathered.

RUSSIAN AID COMES TO EGYPT

Five months after the Bandung meeting (September, 1955), an announcement was released that Russia (through Czechoslovakia) would supply armament to Egypt. This came as a surprise to some — to others it was not particularly unexpected.

First, let this be reasoned from Egypt's side. The country was not only loaded heavily with internal reconstruction program expenses, but was also facing an aggressive Israel with its constantly growing war-machine. Egypt, there is reason to believe, had fear of this and also felt her heavy responsibility of a leader-state in the Arab world where the general hostility toward encroaching Israel was great. Egyptian leaders, like those of the other Arab states, could not well act other than in response to the suffering and anguish of more than a million Palestinian Arab refugees who had been deprived of their homes, properties — everything.

The best available information is that Egyptian leaders became highly sensitive to the adverse criticism that continuously flowed from pro-Zionist sources which, some believe, had two purposes: (1) to provoke diplomatically unwise utterances from Arab leaders which were in turn promptly used for further "public opinion" purposes; and (2) to reduce the image of the historic country which the Israelis feared more than any other Arab state. Information seems to confirm that it was such a combination of provocation, apprehension and feeling of need that pushed the Egyptian leaders to accept the arms-aid from Russia. Those who are acquainted with the Arab lands know that there is very little ideological affinity among either the Moslems or the Christian Arabs for Communism.

It appears that relations between Egypt and the West were not helped any by the unfortunate timing of a financing incident that disappointed and angered Egyptian officials. Here is the incident briefly stated:

Soon after Colonel Nasser became President of Egypt, plans were initiated toward getting greater hydro-electric power and irrigation facilities from the Nile River — the life-stream of Egypt for 4,000 or more years. Engineering firms from different countries prepared designs and estimates that were presented to Egypt in 1954. Soon afterwards Egypt approached the International Bank for Reconstruction and Development concerning help in financing the proposed High Dam at Aswan. This was a monumental project and vitally needed for Egypt's reconstruction. Although Egypt had a standing offer of financial and technical aid from Russia, the Nasser Government preferred to work with the United States and Britain through the World Bank. In December, 1955, the World Bank announced it had agreed to loan Egypt $200 million of which $150 million was to be provided by the United States and $14 million by Britain, with the balance coming from other sources. Suddenly on July 19, 1956, the U.S. State Department withdrew its promised participation — and that killed the World Bank agreement. No particular reason was given but our research learned from high authority that Washington was at variance with some of Egypt's spending policies. The Egyptians reacted to this as an open affront and blamed it upon Zionist influences in American politics. They believed it had some relevance to the armament deal between Egypt and Russia, concluded the year before — in 1955.

The Arab countries, largely dry and unfertile desert, held in subjection by the Turks for a long period — having no rich diaspora upon which to lean — have been desperately in need of help and "hedged in" by world finance, and are, in wide opinion, being driven to sources that could be disastrous for the West — and the whole of the Middle East.

One outspoken opinion on the Arab-Zionist controversy, from the center of things, was that the Zionists, after pushing themselves into Palestine with the result of causing around a million Palestinian Arabs to flee their homes and become refugees, settled down on the Palestinians' properties with the attitude of expecting the surrounding Arab states to be acquiescent and friendly neighbors. But when the surrounding Arabs showed displeasure and hostility at this intrusion, they, the Arabs, were blamed and taunted for their lack of hospitality. But, this commentator asked, where in the world would you find people who would react differently?

*   *   *

As to Russia's motives in making the arms deal with Egypt, there could, some believe, have been other reasons than the profits from sales. As already documented, Russia first flirted with the Zionists. This experiment ran into trouble and was cancelled by Russia to the expressed disappointment of Israel. Concerning this courtship, the New York Times (February 15, 1953) had this to say:

"The Soviet Union was motivated by tactical considerations. The Soviet Union saw the Zionist movement as a weapon against the British in the Middle East and hoped that Communists could infiltrate the new state and make it an outpost of the Communist world in the Middle East. For that reason, even though Zionism remained illegal in the U.S.S.R., the Soviet Union permitted Czechoslovakia to deliver arms to the Israelis and allowed a considerable movement of emigrants from satellite nations to Israel."

The story goes on to say that after the 1948 Arab-Israeli war had ended, Russia was disturbed about the improvement of Israel-British relations, apparently having helped the Israelis in the belief they could completely rid the Middle East of the British and their influence. Another aggravation affecting Russian-Zionist relations was the "impertinence" of Jewish organizations in using this Russian-Israeli "friendship" as a basis for offering advice as to how the Russians should treat the more than 2,000,000 Jews still in the Soviet Union.

*   *   *

RUSSIAN INTEREST IN THE MIDDLE EAST

In switching its aid to Egypt, Russia has been accused by some as viewing Egypt's extreme difficulties as another opportunity to penetrate the Middle East — and a much better one than through the tiny land-based Israel.

It is well known to political and military international experts that Russia, for the last two centuries at least, has had hungry eyes on the Middle East — and particularly on Egypt. This would naturally include control of the Mediterranean as a vital naval base — and also domination of the Suez and Red Sea warm waterway to the Indian Ocean. This outlet, however, is not nearly so important to Russia for her own international commerce as it could be in serving as a squeeze-play blockage point to make the Middle East, as well as the whole of Europe, submissive to Russia's purposes and caprices. This could, under extreme pressures, leave America without much in the way of allies in a crisis.

General Sir John Bagot Glubb (Glubb Pasha), the internationally known military strategist, in a series of addresses in America during October, 1967, pointed out that world geo-political authorities, ·with Napoleon Bonaparte's advice as an example, have widely regarded control of Egypt as strategically important in the three-continent world to which it is the central gateway. He also points out that all of the "great Empires" of the past, from Assyria and Babylonia down to and including the British, have made it a point to have control of Egypt as a "keystone" to the Middle East.

A well known authority on Russia, when asked for an opinion on Soviet strategy in the Middle East, pointed out that the astute Communist leaders are not noted for altruism or philanthropy. When they give, he said, they carefully appraise every move on its value to their objectives. They are hard-headed realists — and never mushy sentimentalists. Their record is one of quiet, artful action for conquest. After the June 6-day war, the Soviets quietly but boldly moved their fleet into Mediterranean waters — a highly strategic Soviet gain. His closing observation was "Caveat emptor!"

20. THE PROBLEM OF RATIONALIZING SOVIET COMMUNISM AND CERTAIN ZIONIST PHENOMENA

Here is subject matter that may understandably be distasteful to some and for this the authors have the greatest sympathy. The facts, however, are definitely pertinent to the history being recorded and reflect the over-all play of the forces and processes involved.

The early status of Jews in Russia under the Czars was largely the spawning provocation that gave birth to political Zionism. It was out of these same general Czaristic conditions that Soviet-communism was born. The Bolshevik leader, known as "Lenin," was the alert and intelligent son of a newly awakened Social-Democratic school teacher. Lenin was not Jewish, but many of his top co-leaders were. Unrest was being aroused in the Russian industrial centers. Take note that strikes and "demonstrations" were growing — getting more and more out of hand — fomenting revolutionary action. The natural pattern of revolution was unfolding.

Lenin, in exile, staying safely away from Russia, was directing the organization of revolution from Paris and Switzerland. In Zurich in 1905 (the year of the first revolutionary attempt in Russia), Lenin issued his famous address on "The Jewish Question" in which he said:

"The hatred of Tsarism was directed particularly against the Jews . . . the Jews provided a particularly high percentage of leaders in the revolutionary movement." In his Bolshevik appeal to the Jews, he warned against the evil of "nationalism," which was the very heartbeat of the then budding Zionism which he feared as a competitive Russian revolutionary movement. "The slogan of 'national culture'," he said, "is a bourgeois fraud. Our slogan is the international culture of democracy and the working class movement."

Lenin was by no means the first to give attention to what, from the 19th century, was frequently alluded to as the Jewish Question. The earliest attention drawn to this subject was the Old Testament itself, which was devoted largely to the early problems of the Hebrews and the Israelites as forerunners of the present day Jews. One of the most forthright and yet friendly of the early 20th century discussions on this immensely historical question is the now difficult to find book titled "The Jews" (Houghton Mifflin Company, 1922), by the distinguished Catholic writer, Hilaire Belloc.

The frame of reference here, however, is to present some interesting and appropriate documentation to show that both Zionism and Communism (in that order) have ridden this question down to our present era where, out of both clash and cooperation, they must still be regarded as basic and dynamic forces in an exploding world — and particularly in the Middle East.

*   *   *

A very large proportion of the more than 2,000,000 presumed Jews who have moved into Palestine after 1917, using as a "right" the meaningless Balfour Declaration, came from Russia and the Iron Curtain bloc. Many of the "leaders" referred to by Lenin as part of the 1917 Bolshevik Revolution are named in the reports of President Wilson's Special Representative (Edgar Sisson) who was in Russia during that Revolution. A list of names for the record is also in the book "The Mystical Body of Christ in the Modern World," by the Reverend Denis Fahey, Professor Philosophy and Church History, Holy Ghost Missionary College, Kimmage, Dublin.

MASS IMMIGRATION
"A COMPELLING FORCE"

The purpose of mass immigration into Palestine was clearly, from Herzl on, to change an Arab state into a Jewish state. Changes of this kind are not always apparent when they come gradually. Mass immigration into America, for illustration, since the turn of the century, has had an increasing impact upon social and political trends — with far-reaching influence in mixing America into the Middle East fracas. Recent years have seen the rise of Zionism — as well as Communism — as startling political forces in the United States.

Zionism is, by its very nature, a nationalistic movement inside Jewry — but it also has an immeasurably farther-reaching impact — and that is a major reason for this examination. Communism has inevitably wormed its way into this whole intermixture and the meaning of it all is moving more and more into high level political complications. The confusion and misapprehension that emerges from these entangling complications spawn ever greater suspicion and anxiety as people become curious and seek the underlying causes. As the roots are traced, they inevitably go back to two basic and tragic events of 1917: (1) the Balfour Declaration; and (2) the Bolshevik Revolution.

These two events were widely acclaimed in 1917 by Jewry throughout the world. They rejoiced because they believed that both of these developments meant a new day for the Jews who had been plagued by Czarism on the one hand, and Hitlerism on the other.

Assessing the situation today — 50 years later — the answer to the switch from Czarism to Sovietism by the Jews themselves now seems to be questionable, judging by their present denunciation of "anti-Semitism" in Russia. It is noteworthy, however, that this criticism was not heard during 1947-48 while the Soviets were giving invaluable aid to the Zionists, but has gained momentum since Russia switched its aid from Israel to the Arabs.

Such criticism has been appearing mostly in Jewish papers and in the Congressional Record, but to show its purpose of creating public opinion, a full page advertisement appeared in the New York Times (December 10, 1967), sponsored by 25 national Jewish organizations, containing significantly the names of some 350 Congressmen who joined the Jewish organizations in criticising Russia's "suppression of Jewish spiritual and cultural life in the USSR."

THE PROBLEM OF CONSISTENCY

In checking the record on the running positions of the Jewish press on the question of Soviet Russia, there appears to have been variable attitudes. For instance, one of its most powerful papers and a leader in the present spate of criticism on Russia's "anti-Semitism" is the Chicago Sentinel. In that paper's issue of May 11, 1944, there appeared a full page editorial titled "Soviet Jewry Speaks," in which Solomon Mikhoels, addressing a Jewish Anti-Fascist Committee in the U.S.S.R. in Moscow, was quoted as follows:

> "Sons and Daughters of the Jewish nation, brothers and sisters! . . . We are gathered here at a time of glory and grandeur for our motherland, the Sovietland, at a time of brilliant victories of the heroic Red Army, at a time of triumph for Stalin's strategy . . . We are fighting arms in hand. Our Soviet country has given us this right, has accorded us this honor. We appeal to the Jews all over the world to follow the example of the Soviet peoples, to follow the example of Soviet Jews."
>
> The same Sentinel (on December 21, 1944) began a full page editorial as follows: "No more significant utterance has been issued on the subject of Jew-baiting, politely known as anti-Semitism, during this war epoch, than comes in the Information Bulletin of the Soviet Embassy . . . For in that measured statement, the resources of one of the three most powerful governments in the world are pledged to stamping out this most corrosive evil of our age."

The interesting point about these examples of praise for Soviet Russia (and there were similar expressions over the years in other papers) is that the Jewish problem in Russia was essentially then what it has been ever since — or it was even worse from 1939 to 1941 when Russia was embracing Nazism with a friendship pact. The important propaganda purpose of this Soviet Embassy Bulletin, which the Sentinel quoted gratefully, was to butter American Jews to get their help in promoting the many Communist-front organizations that have flourished in America. Also, when the Sentinel was praising the Soviets, it apparently had overlooked the brazen Stalinist "trials" of 1936 when the Jewish leaders who helped Lenin and Trotsky organize the 1917 Revolution were tried and executed.

During the war years, in addition to the Communist-directed "front" activities in the United States, there was also a traitor clique that stole and passed America's atomic secrets to the Soviets; and there was the planting of Communist cells in the U.S. Government departments under the direction of Soviet agents, identified as Jacob Golos, Isador Boorstein and others. That would have been a good time for every dedicated American to denounce the evils of Soviet Russia.

The charges that have been building up through American pro-Zionist sources about "anti-Semitism" in Russia, especially since Russia switched its military aid from Israel to the Arabs, appears to be directed solely against "restraint on Jewish culture and religious activity," which is good — so far as it goes. Many of the Jewish papers refer to this as "anti-Semitism," but the big man in Zionism, Dr. Nahum Goldmann, was quoted in the Chicago Sentinel (October 11, 1956) with the cautious statement that while 3,000,000 Jews in Russia "do not suffer anti-Semitism, they do not have the opportunity to live a Jewish life." Is this Soviet Russia's only evil?

Dr. Goldmann, who heads two powerful international movements (World Jewish Congress and the World Zionist Organization which, interrelated with a large number of other organizations, appear to constitute a kind of world-Jewry protectorate condominium), seems to draw a distinction between the widely-popularized all-coverage "anti-Semitism" and his own definition. Many charges have been made as to the causes of "anti-Semitism" — including the rise of Christianity — but the subject is not relevant here other than in the Zionist frame of reference — which is highlighted by the present pro-Zionist crusade against Soviet Russia's "anti-Semitism."

There would seem to be two particular reasons why this is of interest and concern to the American people: (1) the danger of more trouble than we now have with Russia if a drive of this kind against the Soviets and their internal affairs is given momentum in the United States, with public officials being used to give it the appearance of national policy; (2) the matter of confusion it raises by bringing into the open the considerable extent of pro-Communist feeling and activity that solid documentation shows to be alive in the American Jewish community.

The questions involved in this have many Americans confused and concerned — especially when they are being solicited to join in a crusade as, for instance, were the 350 Congressmen whose names were included in the New York Times ad, sponsored by the 25 Jewish organizations. The

Chicago Sentinel (November 2, 1967) carried an editorial titled "What Is the Solution?" which refers to a move by the Zionist Organization of Chicago to arouse public opinion against Soviet anti-Semitism, and in the same article refers to "world wide revulsion against our actions in Viet Nam." Then followed a significant statement that "discrimination" against Soviet Jews, "like many other problems, could be settled if we could find a way to end the Cold War." It is difficult to see how mobilizing American action against alleged anti-Semitism in Russia will help "end the Cold War" any more than can an American drive against Russian anti-Christianity.

WHAT ARE THE FACTS?

What appears especially interesting about the above is that in the very next issue of the Sentinel (November 9, 1967) there appeared two stories which discount the severity of the charge of Soviet discrimination against Russian Jews. One story was titled "Young Soviets Throng Streets for Simchat Torah," and the other was headed "20,000 Moscow Jews Dance, March with Scrolls on Simchat Torah." The stories described a gala affair with orchestra, singing and dancing. Since Simchat (Simhat) Torah is an important Jewish religious festival, these stories do not indicate that the Soviet Jews are too much restrained in their cultural and religious activities. What can one believe in contradictions of this kind?

To confound and perplex the average American more about all this strange activity that is stirring around him, there is the added clash between two groupings of Jews — one of which is sounding the cry of "anti-Semitism" in Russia, while the other is vigorously denying the charge and claiming that Soviet Jews are being well treated.

HERE ARE SOME EXAMPLES: The substantial Jewish magazine COMMENTARY in July, 1956, presented a complaint that Russia was restraining its Soviet Jews. This was promptly answered by the Communist Daily Worker, which quoted from the New York (Yiddish) "party-line" Morning Freiheit, which claimed that at least 74 Jewish writers were "producing work in the Soviet Union." The magazine Jewish Currents is a Communist party-line ardent defender of Soviet policy — including Russia's treatment of its Jews.

The Communist press, operating in the United States (made up of newspapers, magazines, radio records and great numbers of books and booklets

297

which are available in their own big city bookstores, is heavily weighted with Jewish officials and writers. To illustrate: among the scores of booklets that may be purchased at these stores (addresses printed frequently in the WORKER), such propaganda products as "The Fraud of Soviet Anti-Semitism," by Herbert Aptheker; "Soviet Anti-Semitism — a Cold War Myth," by Hyman Lumer; "Soviet Anti-Semitism — the Big Lie," by Moses Miller, and published by Jewish Currents Magazine; "Jews in the U.S.S.R.," by Solomon Rabinovitch (published in Moscow — 1965), and others.

This list and this subject could be greatly expanded, but it is not the desire here to do other than document the subject sufficiently to point it up as one of the confusing anomalies that appear to be indigenous to a growing problem. Many fear that this has been transplanted to the shores of America to become troublesome to the United States, as it did to Great Britain in the Palestine debacle — and even act as a time bomb to involve this nation in a devastating confrontation in the Middle East. It would seem that every American has something at stake in this puzzling potential.

21. HIGHLIGHTS OF 1967 "SIX DAY" ISRAEL EXPANSION WAR. MYSTERY OF ISRAEL ATTACK ON U.S.S. "LIBERTY"

As an aftermath of the June (1967) blitzkrieg carried out by Israel against certain Arab states, there has been advanced by substantial authorities the opinion that this confrontation was engineered by Russian manipulation wherein Egypt and Syria were activated to a state of defensive mobilization by Russian "tips" that the Israelis were preparing to attack Syria as the first step to further invasions. This "on the ready" mobilization is presumed, by these same authorities, to have led Israel to believe that these Arab countries were preparing for an early attack on Israel, and that Israel's only hope was to hit first — hard and with surprise — which it did. Others say that the Egyptian mobilization gave Israel the excuse of surprise attack for which it had been waiting.

It has also been charged that the direction of Israel's air-practice maneuvers for some time before the 6-day June war indicated that an attack on Syria was being planned, perhaps, to throw Egypt off guard. It has been said that the alleged Soviet "tip" of Israeli intentions was based upon the war-training maneuvers just mentioned. Out of it all came high arousement of emotions as the news spread that an impending Israeli attack could be the prelude to the greatly feared Israeli program of expansionism which had already cleared the Arabs out of most of their former Palestine homeland. This ugly fact of a million or more former Palestinian Arabs now rotting away in desolute refugee camps seems to be completely overlooked by the Israelis and many Americans when the problem of settling "the Palestine issue" is being brought up.

VICTORY BASED ON INTELLIGENCE SYSTEM

The effectiveness with which the 1967 blitz was carried out indicated clearly that the Israel Intelligence had exacting knowledge concerning Egypt's 26 air bases and other military concentrations. This led to the charge that Israel had help in obtaining this information. If this were a fact, it could have come from spies who in some way worked inside Egypt — as that is a common practice — well perfected since the Bolshevik revolution of 1917.

The status of the world today is such, with its unleashed suspicion, hate, intrigue, and turmoil, that each nation must, as a precaution for survival, develop a system of Intelligence, as highly perfected as possible, as a vital branch of its military coordination. After the June blitz, a rather wide opinion was expressed that the Arabs were unnecessarily weak in their military Intelligence facilities, or otherwise they would not have been so easily trapped. In all forms of personal defense, such as boxing, wrestling, karate, et cetera, it is fundamental never to take eyes off one's opponent and each antagonist must be prepared at all times to defend himself.

Among theories advanced for the quick victory by Israel over Egypt, Syria and Jordan, one was that mysterious and highly secret techniques and devices of magnetic, electronic, and even gaseous natures were used to paralyze Egypt's field communication system, such as telephones, radar and radio. There appears to have been no substantial verification of this charge, and any conjecture involving highly mysterious conceptions has to be regarded cautiously until supporting facts are shown.

BUT WHAT ABOUT THE U.S.S. "LIBERTY"?

There have also been numerous theories circulated concerning the U.S. information ship "Liberty" which was located in the Mediterranean about twelve miles off the Sinai coast. This ship, under the C.I.A. control, was fully fitted out with extensive electronic gear and was obviously serving U.S. Intelligence. Some of the early rumors claimed that the Israelis may have obtained information from this source. Later reflections and obvious facts would appear to contradict this theory — unless Israeli agents had managed to infiltrate the Liberty's staff in highly strategic capacity. While this would appear unlikely, its possibilities should not be too quickly dismissed.

On the fourth day of the 6-day Israel-Egypt war, the U.S.S. Liberty was riding her position in waters off the Sinai coast when suddenly three Israeli fighter planes dropped out of "a clear sky" and sweeping across the ship's starboard bow raked the boat with machine guns and cannon fire "on at least six strafing runs." Life magazine (June 23, 1967) carried the story and pictures of the riddled ship being towed to the Island of Malta — also pictures of wounded and dead being transferred to the U.S. carrier America. 34 Americans were killed and 75 wounded. The Liberty's flag was wantonly shot away — but quickly replaced by Commander William McGonagle.

Following the blitz from the air, three Israeli torpedo boats moved into position on the Liberty, blasting it with machine guns while two of them loosed their torpedoes. The ship managed to stay afloat and fortunately its records were preserved. Whether these records will ever be made public will depend, not on public officials, but upon the insistent demand of the American public. (For those interested in greater detail of this horrific incident, go to your local library and you will find the frightening story on pages H 12170 to H 12176 in the Congressional Record, September 19, 1967.)

In the face of a storm of public revulsion at this seemingly wanton attack, the Israelis released a simple apology, saying the ship had been mistaken for an Egyptian boat. In America only the extreme pro-Zionists believed that such a mistake could happen in bright daylight when the U.S. flag was floating high above the ship. But politically weak-kneed American officials, it has been charged, accepted the apology instead of regarding the attack as an act of war as well as a gesture of contempt and open scorn. When our ships were so attacked at Pearl Harbor, President Roosevelt called it an "act of infamy" and asked Congress for a declaration of war. There was a similarity in the attack on the Liberty, as it was a vital intelligence vessel attached to the American Sixth Fleet in the Mediterranean.

WHAT WAS THE MOTIVE—AND PURPOSE?

The question naturally arises — Why was this attempt to destroy the U.S.S. Liberty made by the Israelis? Many conjectures have been offered as to the possible reasons for this almost unthinkable insulting affront. One is that the Israelis, knowing that the Liberty was an Intelligence ship and that it doubtless had recorded the activities and monitored the communications showing how the blitz was started and carried out, may have decided that this affair was none of the United States' business — and that the records should never become publicly known.

But obviously this was a matter of concern to the United States because: (1) the money that made Israel what it is came largely from sources inside the United States and what happened as a result thereof could seriously affect U.S. world prestige; and (2) it could foreshadow a costly and even disastrous American involvement in an easily triggered Middle East conflagration.

Typical of the Jewish press reactions in the United States was a short item in the Chicago (Jewish) Sentinel, July 5, 1967, headed "Claim U.S.S. Liberty Used Egyptian Signals." In part, the item said:

"Reports received in Washington from Israel quoted highly-placed sources as asserting that the Liberty answered an identification challenge with the same signals used by Egyptian destroyers during the 1956 war . . . When the Israelis received the Egyptian routine in reply (A-A, meaning identify yourself first), the attack was ordered."

This raises the question, first, where did the Israelis get authority, outside their own waters, to make an "identification challenge" to an American ship flying the Stars and Stripes? Even without the U.S. Flag as identification, the ship had the distinctive hull and superstructure that showed clearly it was a converted U.S. Victory ship of World War II. Secondly, was not this brazen attack an open flaunt of the well known Johnson-American policy where in Haiphong Harbor American bombing was restrained for fear of hitting non-combatant ships. U.S. News & World Report (5-13-'68 — p. 12) says the Liberty was the victim of a 'shoot first and ask questions later' Israeli-blitz policy.

NOTE: As this book goes to press (June 1968) it is reported that Israel has made financial settlement with the families of the 34 American sailors killed in Israel's attack on the U.S.S. Liberty and is considering the cases of the 75 who were injured. The tragedy is in the happening.

AFTERMATH OF THE 1967 ISRAEL BLITZ

This book is now overlength and several of the chapters have had to be abridged. It is therefore impossible to undertake any detailed account of the effects and the suffering that resulted from the further military expansionism by Israel in June, 1967. Essentially the whole of Palestine has now been seized and appropriated by Israel; and thousands of fleeing Arabs have been forced to join the desolate refugee camps outside the country in which they lived, where they had their homes and properties.

If there were space here, a heart-rending, passion-stirring story could be put together from the first-hand reports our research has produced direct from the common people of the areas invaded by Israel, which reflect suffering and hardship of the severest nature. The quotations that follow have been selected from what seems one of the most rational and substantial accounts dealing with Jordan, which is perhaps the most critical and strategic area involved. Possession of Jerusalem was, according to the record, from the very first, the Zionists' most coveted goal. "Next year in Jerusalem" had been the ringing cry of Jewish Zionism since the days of Theodor Herzl. Now that they have it, the ultimate purpose of Zionism may be expected to proliferate from here.

DOCUMENTATION ON POST-BLITZ JERUSALEM

What was it like in Jerusalem after the Old City was taken over by the Israelis during the June, 1967 air blitz? A rather vivid picture of conditions was given in a widely circulated "Open Letter," dated June 25, 1967, written by Mrs. Nancy Nolan Abu Haydar. Mrs. Haydar is an American, born in Grosse Isle, Michigan, graduate of Wellesley College. She is the wife of Dr. N. Abu Haydar, member of the Faculty of International Medicine of the famous American University of Beirut, Lebanon.

Mrs. Haydar had lived in the Middle East for twelve years — and at the time of the Israeli blitz she, with her

303

husband and three children, were living in Jerusalem where her husband was spending his sabbatical year doing research in malnutrition with Arab refugee children at the Augusta Victoria Hospital. Writing some ten days after the Holy City had been strafed and seized by the Israelis (they left Jerusalem June 19), she refers to the long hard pull by Arab Jerusalem after the 1948 Zionist attempt to seize the city (thwarted by Jordan's Arab Legion), and explains how Jerusalem's population had been slowly developing a real taste of growth and prosperity in a climate of peace and hopeful security. In her letter, as they left Jerusalem amidst the terror and disorder, and obviously with some emotional sympathy for the Arab people, she wrote:

"Today Jerusalem is an occupied city, ruled over by an enemy determined to irrevocably change its physical appearance and break the spirit of its people. These objectives are being pursued in many ways with the utmost speed and precision, as we saw very clearly. After a three hours' notice to evacuate their homes, the dwellings of approximately 250 families were bulldozed down in the Moroccan Quarter of the Old City to make way for a paved square in front of the Wailing Wall.

"In like manner the Jewish quarter (prior to 1948) . . . was destroyed so that a road leading directly to the Wailing Wall might be built. This area contained a refugee camp, many small workshops and numerous homes. The 2,000-3,000 people made homeless by these combined operations, all of which was accomplished within 24 hours, wandered the streets with the few possessions they were able to snatch up and carry until, finally, in desperation, most of them had no alternative but to board buses which took them to the banks of the Jordan River where they crossed over into what remains of Free Jordan. The Israeli authorities made absolutely no attempt to find or provide any kind of housing for any of these people.

"Since, up to the day of our departure, there was no international relief agency working in Jerusalem, or in any other section of occupied Jordan, which could report to the world about these violations of all humanitarian principles, the Israeli authorities can pursue their aims unwatched and unhindered . . . all efforts by the people of Jerusalem to organize relief have been thwarted. The Greek Patriarch in Jerusalem called for a meeting of all heads of religious communities in the Old City so that they might make plans to help their people. He promptly received a summons by the office of the Israeli military governor who told him that such meetings were forbidden . . . the Patriarch, a man of about 80 years, was denied the use of his official car and returned to the Patriarchate, a distance of about two miles, on foot.

"The deliberate bombing of hospitals in Bethlehem and Jerusalem, destruction of ambulances clearly marked as such, the strafing of doctors retreating on foot from an army hospital, napalm bombs used on retreating soldiers and civilians, terror tactics such as threatening the use of gas in Bethlehem and the kidnapping of children from the Old City of Jerusalem, are all calculated to drive people out of their homes and country."

NOTE: The Wailing Wall just mentioned is a section (60 feet high and 160 feet long) of large hewn stones, regarded as a remnant of the wall that surrounded Herod's temple (not Solomon's — about 1,000 years earlier). Sometime after the 10th century (roughly 2,000 years after Solomon and 1,000 years after Herod), this section of stone wall, because it was believed to have been near the original temple, became a worshipping or "wailing" place for the few orthodox Jews who inhabited the area. With the rise of political Zionism, it has been raised to the status of a rallying image in the crusade to "return to Zion."

*   *   *

The attempt has been made here to select from this and other reports such references as appear readily verifiable and to avoid the accusation of highlighting the emotional. In cases of great human tragedy like this it is not easy to report the facts without the stirring of passion, for the simple reason that emotion and passion are the woof and warp of the tragedies of war. One fearful and deplorable calamity of the 1967 seizure of the Holy City was the senseless murder of the Christian Warden of the Garden Tomb where many believe that Jesus was buried. When the shelling of Jerusalem began on June 5, Dr. Solomon J. Mattar, his wife and assistant (a German woman named Sigrid) took refuge in the Tomb as a safer shelter than their nearby living quarters. They remained there during that day and night. The next day, in response to repeated knocking on the Garden gate, Dr. Mattar went to investigate. The two women inside heard him say "Good Morning" and they then heard a blast of shooting. The soldiers entered the Garden and shot into the Tomb — fortunately missing the huddled women. The German girl rushed out screaming. The soldiers, apparently abashed at the sudden sight of a non-Arab, directed their machine gunning into the Garden residence and then left the premises. Dr. Mattar's body was not allowed to be removed from where it had fallen for two days. It was later buried in the Garden. This report was obtained for this book in conversation with Mrs. Minerva Mattar, who lived through the frightful tragedy.

It is imposible to make here an extensive report on the damages or the suffering that resulted from this latest Israeli-Arab conflict. It can only be said with certainty that it has added fuel to the flames of bitterness that now, more than ever, threaten the Middle East — and other nations along with it.

The following is quoted from David Holden, in the London Sunday Times (November 19, 1967): "An Israeli soldier with a sub-machine gun on his lap stopped me at the gate of the mosque this week as I was about to enter among the crowd of Israeli tourists, and asked me to cover my head in respect for the Jewish faith. He rejected my suggestion that I should take off my shoes as well out of respect for Islam . . . Most of the place (was) converted into something like a museum."

WHAT ABOUT "FREEDOM FIGHTERS"?

Israel army leaders excuse their expansionism into Jordan and Syria as necessary to meet the challenge of the Arab "Freedom Fighters" who harass them in their recently occupied areas which, before that land was seized, was long the home of the Arabs.

This, say some, brings forward the matter of the Israeli "Freedom Fighters" who harassed the British when they were the legally constituted authority in Palestine — killing British soldiers and statesmen like Lord Moyne and Count Bernadotte. Does "freedom fighting" then become a question of "whose bull is being gored" to make it either righteous or villainous? This seems an interesting question for the court of world opinion.

---

22. WHAT THE ZIONISTS EXPECT OF CHRISTIANS

One question that came to the surface out of the June, 1967 Israel-Arab blitz was the extent to which Zionists have placed a responsibility upon Christians for supporting their Israel nationalistic-adventure:

Very soon after the six-day war was over, American Zionists began criticising Christian leaders for not actively raising their voices on behalf of Israel, presumably to help mold wider public opinion and impress Washington with a duty to be ready to take a pro-Israel position in the Middle East military confrontation, if and when that should become necessary.

Various Zionists have frequently made statements implying that America was pledged to defend Israel. The Chicago (Jewish) Sentinel (February 24, 1967) carried a story that began as follows: "President Johnson told Foreign Minister Abba Eban in Washington that as long as he was President Israel did not have to fear for its existence." Whether or not the President made this extraordinary pledge would not prevent some avid Zionist from reporting it, knowing how difficult it would be for the President to deny it with politics as it is in the United States.

Among other journalistic attempts over the years to impress Washington with its "responsibility" was a release to American papers by the Jewish Telegraph Agency (September, 1956) wherein the first paragraph read: "A powerful campaign against Secretary of State John Foster Dulles for his Middle East policy is being launched by the Zionist Organization of America." The story went on to indicate that the Zionists were unhappy about Washington's lagging interest in Israel and the campaign of criticism was apparently intended to awaken and inform Mr. Dulles. Jumping over many expressions during the years, a New York Congressman named Benjamin S. Rosenthal put a statement in the Congressional Record (January 23, 1967) headed — "United States Has Moral Duty to Protect Israel."

CHRISTIANS TOLD OF THEIR DUTY

Criticism of Christians for not mobilizing on the side of Israel in the 1967 June war began with an article in the New York Times, June 23, 1967, headed: "Rabbis Score Christians for Silence on Mideast." Rabbi Balfour Brickman, director of the Commission on Interfaith Activities of American Reformed Judaism, was quoted as "contending that the 'Christian Establishment' was silent on support for the integrity of the state of Israel." The Rabbi, in his speech before 500 other rabbis, took issue with the American Jewish Committee which had praised "widespread Christian support for Israel's position" as a result of "the growth of Jewish-Christian understanding." He also revealed why so many pro-Zionists are against the U.S. commitment in Vietnam. "There is simply no comparison," Rabbi Balfour Brickman said, "between our long standing and clearly expressed commitment to the state of Israel and the involvement in Vietnam." If, as he states, there is any official defense commitment to Israel on the part of the United States, it can be safely said that there are nearly 200 million people in the United States who are not aware of it.

Another story in the New York Times (June 27, 1967), headed "Rabbinical Leaders Criticize Christians," said in part that Rabbi Pesach Z. Levowitz, President Rabbinical Council of America, "Expressed deep disappointment" over what he described as the failure of "major segments of the world and American Christian community to raise their voices in defense of Israel . . ."

"COWARDICE IN THE CLERGY"

was the heading of an article in the Chicago (Jewish) Sentinel (July 6, 1967) by Rabbi Irving J. Rosenbaum who devoted more than two columns to a story "he knew to be true," where after the June Israel air-blitz, a group of rabbis prepared a statement condemning the Arabs, which they planned to get a list of Christian leaders to sign. Since one of the number had personal acquaintance with "a leading Catholic prelate," it was decided to secure his name to lead the list. They felt sure he would quickly sign. But when the Rabbi tried to make an appointment to secure the signature, he found the prelate (whom he did not name) too busy to discuss the matter. Rabbi Rosenbaum poured out a lengthy critique on the progress of "ecumenism" which he seemed to think should apply to political as well as religious collaboration.

As this pressure on Christians continued, there appeared a full column story in the New York Times (November 8, 1967) titled "Synagogue Group Scores Christians," which began by saying the Synagogue Council of America charged "yesterday" that Christian leaders had been morally lax in failing to condemn Arab threats against Israel. The Synagogue Council's statement, according to the Times, "is the latest and most broadly representative in a series of pronouncements by Jewish leaders on the alleged failure of Christian churchmen to support Israel during the recent Middle East crisis. The resulting tensions have endangered the future of the growing dialogue between Christians and Jews." One Christian leader of some prominence, when asked about this, said — "If the Zionist-Jews want to go into politics and set up a nation, that is their business and they must stand or fall on their own legs. It is a political — not an ecumenical matter."

Rabbi Henry Siegman, executive vice president of the Synagogue Council, was reported in the Times as saying that the cause of the rabbis' concern was a July statement by the National Council of Churches which called for — "acceptance by the entire international community of the state of Israel" — but declared that it could not "condone by silence" Israel's "territorial expansion by armed force."

Some members of the liberal N.C.C. were irritated at what appeared to be an attempt to whip the Christian world into backing the full Zionist "political line" — and some Christians regarded it as poor appreciation of the collaboration that N.C.C. had already extended to such Jewish leadership organizations as the powerful American Jewish Committee where the A.J.C. has established a special task force to offer advice in the Christian field.

ONE WAY ROAD?

In a 38-page booklet published by A.J.C. in 1951, the eagerness of the American Jewish Committee to give Christians counsel was outlined. "We supply Christian religious publications with prepared material, articles and stories," the booklet stated, "depicting Jewish life. Through the newly created Division of Christian Education of the National Council of Churches, the American Jewish Committee and the Anti-Defamation League will jointly have an unprecedented opportunity to aid in the preparation of lesson materials, study guides, audio-visual aids, etc., for use in educational activities sponsored by the Protestant churches and organizations."

The report to their sponsors went on to explain that a correct analysis of films depicting the crucifixion story had been so prepared and other important films and materials were being completed. Meetings on a regular basis with Protestant leaders were arranged for this work in 1952. After all of this, followed by the wide criticism of the rabbis in the Israel conflict, there is considerable puzzlement as to just who is leading whom.

Zionists seem to be emphasizing more and more that Americans and Christians in general must share a one-sided partnership responsibility with them in their nationalistic adventures in the international arena of tooth and claw politics. The eloquent and voluble Zionist leader, Abba Eban, has seemed to emphasize this in numerous speeches. As far back as 1955, the Chicago Daily News (January 11, 1955) reported a speech by the then Israeli Ambassador to the United States, in a story headed "Israel's Birth Called Christian Victory." Eban, speaking at Notre Dame University, South Bend, Indiana, was quoted as saying — "The homelessness, and martyrdom of the Jewish people was not merely a source of international political tensions: it was also a heavy burden upon the Christian conscience."

The trouble with this use of the Zionist shibboleth "the Jewish people" is that it is not acceptable to a growing number of substantial Jewish people in the United States. More than that, this *ad hominem* is that it seeks to create a blame-consciousness where it does not belong and overlooks the first century "heavy burden" of Christian persecution that could as easily be raised in background argument, if there were disposition to do so. Is it not better for each boat to float upon its own bottom?

23. HOW ZIONIST-JEWS COLLECT MILLIONS IN UNITED STATES TO SUPPORT THE "JEWISH STATE"—ISRAEL

During the United Nations' hearings on the June, 1967 war explosion between Zionist-Israel and the Arab States, one of the delegates made the charge that Israel-Zionism had, during the past several years, received around EIGHT BILLIONS of dollars from sources within the United States.

This amount may have been largely speculative, but it does not appear to have had either comment or challenge from Mr. Goldberg (U.S. spokesman at U.N.) or any Israeli authority. Perhaps it was considered the better part of valor not to stir the subject. Without question vast sums have been collected in the United States and poured into the Zionist movement — first, to help turn Palestine into a Jewish State; and next, to support and promote the growth of that State after it was self-proclaimed.

Just how much money has been collected in the United States for these stated purposes is not known, so far as one can discover, but it is quite revealing to take a look at a 1963 investigation of the Zionist-Israel complex and its operational record inside the United States. This investigation was conducted by the U.S. Senate Foreign Relations Committee, with Senator J. William Fulbright (Arkansas) as Chairman.

It is interesting to note that the Chairman was not from one of the big-city states where there are heavy Zionist colonizations. In the bloc-vote pressure system that has developed in the United States since 1933, such a hearing could hardly have been expected if the Chairman of the Senate Foreign Relations Committee had been from New York—

or Illinois — or California, for illustration. These are by no means the only states that could be so mentioned. This is not an astounding revelation. It is simply a well known fact of political life in any country where a Republic (that is definable by rigid constitutional rules of law) allows itself to become a putty-democracy to be squeezed into any interpretation desired by the pressure-groups that are strongest. This sort of federalism produces the seeds of self-destruction.

*　　*　　*

The hearings by the U.S. Senate Committee on Foreign Affairs began on May 23, 1963, in Washington, where the chief executive officers of the two major Jewish-Zionist organizations appeared under subpoena for questioning. They disclosed the visible and the not too visible make-up of the Zionist organization-complex operating in the United States.

Early in the investigation, with Gottlieb Hammer, secretary of the United Israel Appeal on the witness stand, Senator Fulbright showed him a letter that had been written by him (Hammer) to Henry C. Bernstein, executive vice president of the United Jewish Appeal of Greater New York, in which he explained that he had been "authorized by Mr. Aryeh L. Pincus, treasurer of the Jewish Agency, to ask New York U.J.A. (United Jewish Appeal) to pay out on behalf of the United Israel Appeal 67 percent of $50,000 to the Jewish Telegraph Agency for the year commencing April 1, 1962. We understand that the Joint Distribution Committee will likewise ask you to pay out on their behalf 33 percent of the $50,000."

For the average reader, this may require a bit of unraveling and explaining. In the first place, it appears that here are two different money-collecting "Appeal" organizations in New York, with contributions "deductible," getting orders from a Zionist-Israel organization (the Jewish Agency) as to how and where the welfare money was to be distributed. Of the two organizations mentioned in the letter that were to get this particular $50,000, the Jewish Telegraph Agency is a news gathering and propaganda distributing organization, heavily oriented to the Zionist cause.

J.T.A. was organized originally at The Hague, but for years has been headquartered (conveniently) in New York. It supplies "news columns" to various Jewish papers in the United States. The highlight on the Jewish Telegraph Agency came when Gottlieb Hammer, under questioning by Senator Fulbright, was forced to admit that this propaganda agency was controlled through stock ownership by the Jewish Agency for Israel, which is acknowledged by Israel law to be the same as the World Zionist Organization, and that this organization complex is an integral part of the Israeli Government. When the Senate committee chairman asked Hammer whether the Israel ownership of controlling stock in the Jewish Telegraph Agency had been reported to the Department of Justice in Washington, Hammer replied — "I do not recall, sir."

The Zionist-Israel Government in Palestine would allow no other Government to operate inside its borders along the lines that it operates within the confines of the United States. There apparently is no parallel anywhere and the answer is, by many astute observers, attributed to the political influence Zionism now has in Washington. Because of this extraordinary situation, the following note is included to show the origin, function and status of the Jewish Agency in Israel.

MEMORANDUM OF THE JEWISH AGENCY: In 1927, Zionism was in a state of crisis due to lagging interest and dearth of funds. At that time some "non-Zionists" in America, headed by the late Louis Marshall (prominent New York lawyer) and banker Felix Warburg, were then prominent in the Joint Distribution Committee (welfare distributor for overseas) and were in controversy with Rabbi Stephen Wise who headed the Zionist Organization for America) over the collection and distribution of funds collected in America. The non-Zionists had organized a large campaign for Jewish colonization in Russia (before Stalin began to liquidate the Jews who had helped Lenin achieve the revolution). In order to get money for the Zionist cause, Rabbi Wise had organized the United Palestine Appeal as a separate fund-raising unit. This conflict threatened unity of backing for Zionism among American Jews and quickly brought top-Zionist Chaim Weizmann to the United States to ameliorate the threatened peril. Under his charm and strategy, the non-Zionists were persuaded to join in forming the Jewish Agency (for Israel) as a central Jewish organization with wide functions.

One main purpose was to deal with the British government, which had been given a Mandate over Palestine by the League of Nations. This was a period when the Zionists were "fighting in London with the Colonial Office, and in Geneva in the lobbies of the League of Nations for the right

314

of the Jews to establish their National Home in Palestine . . . There were ten years in which the Jewish Agency was headed by the late Dr. Chaim Weizmann, who was later to become the first President of Israel . . . The years 1938-1948 were marked by the evaporation of the non-Zionists from the Jewish Agency . . . The years 1948-1959 were marked by the Agency's taking over the burden of bringing into Israel and settling there about 1,000,000 Jews from various countries" (American Examiner — December 17, 1959).

The Jewish Agency has long been an official alter ego of the World Zionist Organization. After a turbulent period of Zionist activity in Palestine, causing the British to relinquish the Mandate in despair on May 15, 1948, the Zionists immediately (at midnight) announced the self proclaimed State of Israel in Palestine and began to set up a national State. After four years of fighting the Arabs, and consolidating a government structure, the 1952 World Zionist Congress held in Jerusalem (Israel) passed a resolution calling upon the Israeli government to grant a recognized Status to the World Zionist Organization. Consequently and obediently the Israeli Government passed a Law of Status, which reads in part: "The World Zionist Organization which is also the Jewish Agency for Palestine, deals, as heretofore, with immigration and directs the projects of absorption and settlement in the State. The State of Israel recognizes the World Zionist Organization as the authorized agency which shall continue to work in the State of Israel for the development and colonization of the activities in Israel of Jewish institutions and institutions operating in these fields."

This legislation also licensed the World Zionist Organization (being the same as the Jewish Agency) as the agent of the State of Israel to do what "the State neither can nor may do" itself beyond its own borders — in the words of the then Israeli Prime Minister. It does not seem that further documentation need be added to clarify the "foreign agent" status of the Jewish Agency which was shown by the Senate investigation to be directing, in a major way, the distribution of millions of dollars collected annually in the United States.

In the Senate investigation, the Committee Chairman, Senator Fulbright, introduced also into evidence a Budget-Digest report (No. 30-May 1961) of the Council of Jewish Federations and Welfare Funds of New York, which is an agency set up to gather, analyze and evaluate the budgets of beneficiaries of the many individual Jewish Welfare funds — of which there are more than 200. Budget-Digest No. 30 appears to be a report of the budgetary needs for expenditures planned for the ensuing year, by a very important organization in the Zionist-Israeli-complex — the AMERICAN ZIONIST COUNCIL and its nine constituent agencies. Here is a quick look at the Council — its constituent agencies — and the ways in which this complex planned to spend money raised in America through Welfare Funds which were deductible from income tax returns of contributors, thereby put-

315

ting part of the cost on the shoulders of every taxpayer in the United States.

THE AMERICAN ZIONIST COUNCIL (New York) is an organization of organizations. The constituent organizations are:

1. The American Jewish League for Israel
2. B'nai Zion
3. Hadassah Women's Zionist Organization of America
4. Religious Zionists of America (Including Hamizrachi Women and Mizrachi Women)
5. Labor Zionist Movement (Including Farband, Pioneer Women)
6. Progressive Zionist League—Hashomer Hatzair
7. United Labor Zionist Party (Achdut Avodah-Poale Zion)
8. United Zionist-Revisionists of America
9. Zionist Organization of America

The expenditures planned by this one group of operational organizations were substantial. (1) The Information and Public Relations Department required $328,350 to create "a positive understanding of Israel on the American scene" — and to "combat Arab propaganda." To carry this out, $53,300 would be needed for radio, television, films, periodicals, etc.; $72,700 for speakers bureau for non-Jewish and non-sectarian groups; seminars on Israel and the Middle East would cost $67,000. They would need $65,200 for press and research; there would be tours to Israel and many other activities, including "close cooperation with the Christian community." (2) $306,610 for the Youth Department. This was detailed with various sums mentioned. (3) The Organization Department was down for $129,133. (4) The Herzl Foundation wanted $211,336 and the Herzl Press needed $40,160. (5) The Department of Education and Culture needed $161,675 to promote Hebrew culture and modern Israel. (6) The Department of Torah Education and Culture was listed for $75,083; while (7) the Archives and Library requested $67,400. In addition, there was the Headquarters Department needing $138,900 and $45,000 for fund raising. This was for independent campaigns to be conducted in New York and other large cities.

It may be worth emphasizing again here that in most cases of welfare contributions, such as those from which money was to come, the Federal Treasury grants a permit of de-

316

ductibility which enables the contributor to deduct his contribution, in computing his Federal income tax returns. This deductibility concession by the Government is highly useful for those soliciting contributions.

During the investigation into the complicated and mysterious process by which funds were collected in the United States and transferred to the use of the Zionist-Israel State, the Senate Committee chairman, Senator Fulbright, in the process of interrogating Mr. Isadore Hamlin, Executive Director, Jewish Agency for Israel (American Section), asked these questions:

> FULBRIGHT: We had testimony this morning that in the last 25 years a billion and a half dollars have been contributed by this country. Have you had much more than that from any other country?
>
> HAMLIN: I cannot comment on that, but I can say that of our present income in Jerusalem per year, perhaps 35 to 40 percent comes from the United States. The balance comes from other countries.
>
> FULBRIGHT: What other countries?
>
> HAMLIN: Other sources of income.
>
> FULBRIGHT: What other countries contribute as much as 35 or 40 percent?

After more haggling with Senator Fulbright to get a straightforward answer, Hamlin finally admitted that the next largest amount of support came from England and that this amounted to only 5 to 7 percent. The opinion has often been expressed that the State of Israel could never have come into existence — nor could it for long survive without the financial assistance it has had and continues to receive from the United States and its citizens.

PEOPLE WERE AROUSED—
WILL THEY REMAIN SO?

For years prior to the Senate investigation of 1963, the anti-Zionist American Council for Judaism made repeated charges that there was in process a well disguised manipulation in the distribution of money collected in the name of Welfare Funds and then, in a highly complicated manner, switched to cover the cost of operating Zionist activities. The A.C.J. charge emerged from the belief that Jewish welfare contributors had a right to know in what way and for what purpose their contributions were being spent. But that was

317

only part of this masquerade operation. The American people as a whole also had a right to know about it. Even after the investigation and the publicity it received, it is doubtful if many people could make heads or tails of the tricky involved manipulations. More than just an investigation was needed, many have complained, and that would be Federal action — with politics thrown to the winds. There was an investigation — but no Federal action.

At the time of the investigation a story appeared in Newsweek (August 12, 1963) quoting Senator Fulbright as having observed to a witness: "If you can make this report clear, you're a genius . . . It's not clear to me what you gained by all this rigmarole." The Newsweek story went on to say: "The rigmarole, in simplest terms, was the maze of overlapping and interlocking directorates that enabled the Jewish Agency-American Section, Inc., a registered foreign agent, to use the American Zionist Council as a 'conduit' for propaganda funds to create a favorable climate in the United States for Israel and Zionist policies." These "policies" undoubtedly included a "favorable climate" for the sale of millions of dollars worth of Israel bonds. Crafty politics always gets its main support from people with short memories.

A United Press wire-service report of the Senate committee's investigation (appearing in newspapers dated August 1, 1963) stated in part that Isadore Hamlin, director of the Jewish Agency's "American Section" in New York — "agreed with a statement by Committee Chairman (Senator Fulbright) that the Zionist Council (American Zionist Council — also of New York) was 'merely acting as a conduit' for large sums of money supplied by the Jewish Agency to help create a 'favorable image' of Israel among moulders of public opinion in the United States."

Because the American Council for Judaism (a group of highly respected Jewish leaders) appears to be the only organized, outspoken opposition to Zionism in the United States, there are, no doubt, those who think this is merely an ideological squabble between Jewish groups. It is true that A.C.J. is limited largely to the controversial question of religion versus nationality but this has also extended into the misuse of welfare funds and that, in the nature of the problem, has put the spotlight on critical and highly important political angles.

NOTE: In all of this, the American Council for Judaism seems to have performed a useful service for non-Zionists and non-Jews as well (especially for Christians) by putting emphasis upon the matter of keeping religion in its proper place — the place of RELIGION. In all monotheistic religions today there is a rapidly growing tendency toward political orientation. To eliminate any question of prejudice, may we say that the Christianity (in which we were reared) is rapidly becoming ardent in political consciousness — seeking changes that often seem for the mere sake of change. In Christianity the emphasis is on "social acion," while in Judaism the drive is for "Zionism." It is quite impossible, at this particular point, to resist quoting again the chiding of Disraeli when he addressed the great Gladstone to say that he didn't object to his debating opponent having cards up his sleeve, but did disapprove the implication that God put them there.

*　　*　　*

TECHNIQUE OF MONEY COLLECTING

The following excerpts are quoted (by permission) from the address of a prominent Jewish individual, speaking to a group of Jewish citizens in New York a year or so ago, explaining to them the extensive operations of "money collecting" in the United States, through a highly complicated mechanism where much of the money flows into Zionist activities.

"There are," the speaker said, "an estimated 5,666,000 Americans of Jewish faith. At last word, 2,678,175, or nearly half of all U.S. Jews, reside in the Greater New York area . . . Though two-thirds of all Americans live in cities, more than 96 percent of our Jewish citizens are urbanites. There are 777 different Jewish organizations — more organizations than there are Jews in Hawaii, Idaho, Montana, South Dakota, Wyoming or Alaska.

"There are 260 Jewish newspapers. Nearly all are printed in English and virtually all depend upon the handouts — monetary and editorial — from the Jewish organizations. In many cities, the Jewish newspaper is owned and/or controlled by the local welfare fund or community council. The community council is the steering committee composed of representatives of most other Jewish organizations in town. The community councils describe themselves as the coordinators of public relations and other activities of the local Jewish organizations. The welfare funds, on a federated basis, coordinate virtually all of the fund-raising of Jewish organizations in a given city. In some cities, the Jewish federation and the community council are themselves merged into an apex of hierarchies.

"There are 143 different federations, welfare funds and community councils in as many cities throughout the United States. They claim to represent 95 percent of the Jewish population in the United States. All of these local hierarchies are drawn together into a single national summit called the Council of Jewish Federations and Welfare Funds (CJFWF). This important, topmost financial holding company will be described in greater detail next time," explained the speaker. "And, later, we shall also discuss the National Community Relations Advisory Council (NCRAC) which is the national-level holding company for many local community relations councils and some national community relations organizations. It is ironic," stated this Jewish speaker, "that Jews, who regard themselves as the symbol of individualism, have allowed their organizers to build a complex structure of interlocking directorates, that defies clear description and is not responsive to the basic views of most U.S. Jews."

The speaker then continued outlining the broad structure. "There are," he said, "118 organizations which describe themselves as religious or educational in character, over and above the synagogues and temples themselves (there are some 650 Reform, 900 Conservative and 2,400 Orthodox houses of worship). There are 69 Zionist and pro-Israel organizations, 35 social welfare groups, 33 cultural organizations, 26 mutual benefit societies, 21 youth associations, 20 professional groups (these are the organizations of full-time administrators of other organizations — they coordinate whatever has been left uncoordinated through the various inter-organizational directorates). There are 18 women's organizations and 15 groups devoted exclusively to providing overseas aid.

"In summary, the cradle-to-grave structure of Jewish organizations in America, together with its sophisticated financing and staffing, matches the complexity of a small-sized state of the U.S. or a medium-sized country abroad. The Gross National Product of all Jewish organizations in 1963 was conservatively estimated at $680,500,000 (including $55,500,000 in Israel bonds).

"Many small countries in the world have smaller GNP's than the Jewish structure of the U.S. The actual cash income of Jewish organizations in 1963 was $125,000,160 or more than the total budgets of 12 percent of the States of the U.S. Another $55,500,000 was invested here that year in Israel bonds for a total of $180,660,000. 1963 was by no means the year of highest reward for Jewish organizations. Cash income alone topped $200,000,000 in 1948. The total income of U.S. Jewish Organizations since 1939 has been $3,627,333,000 ($627,330,000 in Israel bonds).

"This is truly big business, American style. The money represents more than buying power. When the frail structure was haltingly established some 100 years ago, Jewish organizations were intended to meet limited and rather personal needs of newly arrived immigrant Jews. The organizations provided mainly social service assistance. They labored magnificently to 'Americanize' the new arrivals. There was an economy of manpower and money, both by design and as a matter of harsh reality. There was little or no organization for organization's sake. If there was any personal or political profit to be won by a Jewish layman or a non-Jewish politician, it was limited to the ward level of big-city politics. The implications of Jewish organizational life seldom extended to the state level and — with rare exceptions (such as appeals on behalf of Russian Jews in 1911) — almost never carried national and international implications."

The lecture continued to considerable length, describing the various organizations and their functionary processes, for which detail there is not space here. Of particular importance was his explanation of "the Jewish Agency" which has been the key organization of the Zionist movement (otherwise known as the "World Zionist Organization") since the term "a Jewish Agency" was cleverly inserted in the 1920 Mandate over Palestine when it was given to Great Britain. This two-named organization was the foundation and the capstone of Zionism from the Mandate until it proclaimed itself as "Israel" in 1948. In 1952, the Jewish Agency became legalized as an integral part of the Israel government, with certain duties. It now is registered — with offices in the United States, and is closely allied with the American network of Jewish agencies.

The speaker quoted a revealing statement from a 1950 closed-meeting speech in the Israeli Knesset (parliament) by the powerful president of the World Zionist Organization (Dr. Nahum Goldmann) wherein that gentleman reportedly said, "The Zionist movement must be regarded as the agent for mobilizing and representing the (Jewish) people in its partnership with Israel." A number of charts were used by the speaker to illustrate the interlocking and operating relationship of the various money-collecting organizations.

*   *   *

ISRAEL BOND SALES GROW

In addition to the numerous other ways of collecting money in the United States as just described, the sale of Israel bonds is a main and growing source of revenue to help keep the State of Israel going.

Despite numerous press reports through several months prior to Israel's air attack on its neighboring Arab states, which indicated a very poor condition of economic affairs and unemployment in a country that was consuming more than it produced (New York Times editorial, March 16, 1967), Israel's bond selling network in the United States did a flourishing business.

The Chicago (Jewish) Sentinel (December 22, 1966) carried a story titled — "Chicago Is 'No. 1' Bond City in Nation As Local Purchases Soar." This story states that the Israel Bond sales were $2,000,000 in 1951 (the year the bond sales were started) but by 1961 the annual sales had jumped to $4,028,600. In 1963 the sales rose to $5,900,250 and in 1964 went to $6,593,650. In 1965, the Israel bond sale in Chicago alone rose to $7,215,200 — and "in 1966 sales will establish once again . . . a new record high."

The article went on to tell how these sales were accomplished — five or six "bond dinners" every Sunday evening;

322

trade or professional dinners during the week; innumerable Women's division luncheons; parlor meetings in various parts of the city; synagogue campaigns with most of the congregations holding annual bond dinners; etc., etc. Movie stars and other celebrities often appear at the bond dinners as attractions. Awards are given to top bond salesmen with considerable publicity.

NOTE: The Zionist controlled Jewish Telegraph Agency released a statement appearing in the Chicago (Jewish) Sentinel, June 1, 1967, promoting the urgency of Israel Bond sales. The release was headed — "Need $25 Million In Bond Cash — Now!" This amount was needed immediately (just before the Israel blitz) for Israel's "economic development in a period of crisis." The item said that leaders of 68 "communities" throughout the United States had participated in "a nation-wide telephone conference." A bond sales goal had been set for $115,000,000 during 1967 to meet critical economic needs. "The Government of Israel has addressed an urgent appeal to us," stated Dr. Joseph J. Schwartz, vice president of the Israel Bond Organization.

The tremendous esprit de corps that American Jews have developed in relation to the network of Zionist activities is amazing. One commentator offered the observation that if only in America this same type of enthusiastic effort could be mobilized on behalf of traditional Americanism, what a blessing it would be.

*　　*　　*

In a single chapter, there is not space to detail all the statistical information available on the money-raising apparatus in the United States, but it may be worth taking note of an AP dispatch in the San Jose (California) Mercury in early 1967, which reported that the United Jewish Appeal raised about $935,000,000 from 1948 to 1966. Israeli bond sales amounted to about $900,000,000 from 1950 to 1966. Hadassah, the women's Zionist group, raised about $200,-000,000 for Israel since 1948. These sources total about $2,000,00,000. There are numerous other organizational and individual sources not included in this report. Mentioned, however, was United States Government Aid to Israel, including $3,400,000,000 in loans and credits; and about $1,100,-000,000 through the Marshall Plan.

Early in June, 1967, there was another eruption in the conflict between the Israeli Jews and the surrounding Arab states, with Israel's air assault on Egypt, followed by attacks on Syria and Jordan. The massive Zionist-Jewish organization in the United States went into furious collaborative action with an emotional call for funds in a passion-choked atmosphere, tending to create the feverish excitement that is usually a gold mine for promotion. In this particular case, the campaign dedicated to raising money and glorifying Israel vis-a-vis the Arabs was a huge success — bringing in millions of dollars.

One big affair, staged at Madison Square Garden, New York, June 11, 1967, called "Stars For Israel," paid off with $500,000 (New York Times, June 13). The large ad showed Golda Meir (Israel's Foreign Minister), Senator Jacob Javits, Mayor Lindsay and 56 movie and stage stars listed as guests. The seats sold from $10 to $100. Boxes sold from $1,500 to $2,000. The show was on behalf of the "Israel Emergency Fund of the United Jewish Appeal" and indicia at the bottom of the ad, in very small type, said the money would "insure the continuation of great humanitarian programs." This small type was apparently to insure "deductibility" on behalf of the thousands who "contributed" by attending — otherwise why pass the money through U.J.A.?

The main source of money reaching the United Jewish Appeal flows in from some 200 local Jewish Welfare agencies. These local agencies retain 20 percent of the contributions and forward 80 percent to U.J.A. As "welfare" collections, the money is deductible in computing income tax returns of the donors. From U.J.A. funds flow on to an organization called United Israel Appeal, which is hooked in with the Jewish Agency for Israel (otherwise named the World Zionist Organization) — and from here passes to uses serving the State of Israel.

From 1948-1964, according to the documentation of our Jewish authority (the speaker previously mentioned), the United Jewish Appeal "transmitted more than $600,000,000 to the Jewish Agency for Israel, and another $115,000,000 to the Jewish National Fund." The J.N.F. has an interlocking directorate with the Jewish Agency, and the J.A. is part of the Israel government. We have no estimate on how much the United States government has lost in taxes over the years, through this tricky "welfare deductibility" application to money going directly from the United States for the promotion of a foreign government.

*　　*　　*

IMPRESSIVE? APPARENTLY SO

Throughout America, during June and July of 1967, rallies and meetings of all kinds were held by Zionist-Jewish organizations, wherever there were substantial "Jewish communities." Full page ad-appeals were run in large metropolitan newspapers and the Jewish press — costing multiple thousands of dollars. The official Congressional Record was well loaded with letters favoring Israel by Jewish congressmen, while non-Jewish representatives with substantial Jewish constituencies hurried to make obeisance. Radio commentators, like newspapers who depend largely on retail advertisers, gave all the breaks to Israel. The imbalance of it all seemed to say something about Zionism to Americans.

Every effort, it appeared, was made to get full sympathy and money returns from the "flush of victory" that boomed over the air and filled the headlines. For two weeks immediately following the Israeli "blitz" America was overwhelmed with the melodramatic performance just mentioned (meetings, newspaper advertisements, radio and other demonstrations) that seemed to accomplish well the money-raising and public opinion effects for which it was obviously intended.

In all of this great excitement and furor, there was tremendous silence concerning the tragedy of killed and maimed American sailors resulting from the Israeli attack upon the U.S.S. Liberty which was on duty with the American Sixth Fleet in the Mediterranean. This unprovoked attack happened during the very same fracas about which the money-raising hoop-la for Israel was staged in the United States. Some irate citizens regarded this as irony compounded. (See Chapter 21 about U.S.S. Liberty.)

POSTSCRIPT:

The 1968 drive for Israel bond sales in the United States (where they are principally sold) was announced with a news story in the New York Times (March 3), datelined "Miami Beach, Florida" — a fashionable pleasure resort with a large Jewish community. The story reported a gathering of 3,000 American and Canadian Jewish leaders who were addressed by Louis H. Boyar, chairman of the Board of Governors of the Israeli bond organization. He urged "maximum financial support" and explained that in recent years Israel had depended upon these bond sales to supply one third of that country's "development budget" but this year "we are expected to provide from one half to two thirds of the current budget of $269,000,000" because Israel must devote most of her resources to "prepare her position for peace."

This reference, the Times added, applied to the need for Israel to maintain her military strength. Israel's Premier Eshkol sent a cablegram to the meeting at the grandiose Fontainebleau hotel, urging the greatest possible purchase of Israel bonds by those present. The Times story stated that the Israel bond sales, since they were started in 1951 by the then Premier David Ben-Gurion, had amounted to 1.2 billion dollars. (This is exclusive of all the other money-raising programs described in this chapter.)

Three days later, the New York Times carried a story from the Miami Beach conclave announcing that the gathering had ended with a record sale of bonds — $41,272,000. This volume was 37 percent greater than the sale at the same gathering a year ago.

NOTE: The story explained that Vice President Hubert Humphrey was a principal speaker at the affair, and that included in his remarks was a reference to President Johnson's affirmation at the time of the 1967 Israel blitz against the Arabs that the United States stood for safeguarding "the territorial and political integrity" of all the Middle East states. This, however, apparently did not mean much. Israel, by force, occupied essentially all of Jordan west of the Jordan river, and continues to hold and settle it.

STIMULATION FOR U.J.A.

Encouragement to another unit of the fund-raising machine was given a full page "ad" in the New York Times

(March 12, 1968), headed — "We Are Americans of Different Faiths . . ." — in the form of a "humanitarian" appeal for support of the annual United Jewish Appeal drive for money. This "ad" carried the stimulating endorsement of 200 names of "prominent people" who, in name at least, compose a "Non-Sectarian Community Committee of the United Jewish Appeal of Greater New York." Among these were such political figures as Jacob Javits, Thomas E. Dewey, Robert F. Kennedy, John V. Lindsay, Nelson A. Rockefeller, Franklin D. Roosevelt, Jr., Robert F. Wagner — all of whom function politically in New York.

The record seems to show that year by year the State of Israel becomes more dependent upon money supplied from the United States.

*   *   *

Raising money for the support of Israel seems to be developing into a permanent "emergency" industry in the United States, following the already described pattern of organizational network.

For illustration — after all the emergency calls and appeals made over the last several years — the latest (at publication date) in another "emergency" kickoff drive was a full page "ad" in the New York Times (April 8, 1968) which in big type announced —

"THE EMERGENCY CONTINUES . . . Help Israel's People Again By Meeting Great Humanitarian Needs. Your All-out Support Is Needed For U.J.A.'s ISRAEL EMERGENCY FUND . . ."

The "ad" was sponsored by the United Jewish Appeal of Greater New York — "on behalf" of four other organizations listed in small type including the United Israel Appeal. The same wording was used in an "ad" for the Chicago area with an appeal to "Give to the Israel Emergency Fund of the U.J.A. of the Jewish United Fund of Metropolitan Chicago."

24. POLITICAL MACHINERY AND TRENDS IN ZIONIST ISRAEL

One reason for this brief examination of politics in Israel is the past assurances — from the days of Weizmann to the present — that Israel should be supported as a bulwark of Middle East strength beneficial to the West. There are many who have questioned the durability of this thesis. The Zionist assurances of serving as a defense for British Middle East lifeline, made so ardently during the drive to obtain the Balfour commitment, were most unfruitful, say some of the British soldiers who had to endure the Zionist "underground" war of so-called liberation.

Communism, we are told, entered Palestine on the heels of Zionism. A. B. Magil, in his book "Israel in Crisis" *(already described),* stated that the first Communist organization in Palestine was formed in 1920. This was soon after the Zionists began to use the 1917 Balfour Declaration to push Jewish immigration into that small country. The Communist nucleus mentioned was apparently kept alive through the years, but during the next two decades of British rule there is not much available record to document any particular political party activity.

One main reason for this, outside of World War II, was the all-consuming dedication to Zionist promotion, with emphasis on its one central goal — the creation of a Jewish State as blue-printed by Theodor Herzl (founder of organized Zionism) in his book "Der Judenstaat." Also, during the period of the British Mandate in Palestine (1922-1948), the immigration process of the embryo Jewish State was under the general direction of the World Zionist Organization and its twin entity, the Jewish Agency, with the Zionist goal being expanded more or less clandestinely within a Palestine Government, administered by Great Britain under the Mandate entrusted to it by the League of Nations.

EMERGENCE OF POLITICAL PARTIES

Prior to the self-proclamation of the Zionist State of Israel, there had, in the nature of the forces at work, been many group formations looking toward political existence. Among these were the "underground" groups, labor organizations, the kibbutzim, the cooperative organizations and others. During the eight months or so after the proclamation, while the area "partitioned" by the United Nations as a "Jewish State" was being administered by a sort of "provisional government" and the machinery for a permanent government was being assembled, the many political parties began to spring up around just about everybody who considered himself a "leader" — and this was the beginning of their multi-party system.

At the first real national election (January 25, 1949) there emerged the largest of the multi-party complex — the Mapai or Israel Labor Party, with David Ben Gurion as its principal leader. In a book called "Foundations of Israel — Emergence of a Welfare State" (D. Van Nostrand Co.), Dr. Oscar I. Janowsky (listed as professor of history, New York City College and board member, Hebrew University, Jerusalem), it is stated that Mapai was a "social democratic" development. It was further described as a party seeking to attain its "socialist goal primarily through cooperative ownership of the means of production and distribution rather than through nationalization."

Since the "control of the means of production and distribution" would soon put an end to any essential private enterprise and lead to State Capitalism (or a Socialist State), and since also Mapai is described as a product of the Social Democratic philosophy and purpose, it may be well to take a quick look at the "Social Democratic" movement and its record.

WEBSTER'S New World Dictionary defines the Social-Democratic Party as "a German-Marxist political party founded in 1875 by the merger of the General German Workers Association, founded in 1863 by Ferdinand

Lassalle, with the Social Democratic Workers Association, founded in 1869." Dr. Jacob R. Marcus (outstanding authority on Jewish history), in his book "The Rise and Destiny of the German Jew," says that Social Democracy owed a great deal "both to its founder, Karl Marx, and to its first organizer, Ferdinand Lassalle."

The Social-Democrat movement was the main-stream of "socialism" that spread throughout Europe and Russia during the late 19th and early 20th centuries. The movement in Russia was split into two factions by Lenin. Those who did not go along with his revolutionary plan were called Mensheviki or Utopian Socialists — while those who joined his Communist program were called the Bolsheviki or Scientific Socialists. The distinction between them is not the goal of State Capitalism — but the methods of getting there. The Communists take the road of bloody revolution; the Communists, however, for public consumption, call their movement "socialism" and refer to the Soviet satellites as "socialist democracies" when this description is needed to shield the more frightening word of "communism."

Another major political group to appear early in Israel was the United Workers Party, Mapam, formed in 1948 through a coalition of "three previously existing left-wing socialist groups," states Dr. Janowsky, and he adds that it represents a fusion of Zionism and Marxism and favors a united socialist front. Mapam, according to the Standard Jewish Encyclopedia, "stands left of Mapai, endorsing the Marxist dogma." Another of the major Israeli parties to emerge in 1955 was called Ahdut Ha-Avoda. The Encyclopedia identifies it as "Israel Socialist Party," explaining it was formed by a merger of three or four smaller groups, including Poale Zion of which one of the founders is quoted in the Encyclopedia as saying "There can be no Zionism except Zionist Socialism." An October (1967) news dispatch, by the chief of the Jewish Telegraph Agency in Israel, on party maneuvering referred to Achdut Avodah as a "left of center party."

COLORATION OF ISRAEL PARTIES

Among the movements in the Zionist development prior to formation of the Jewish State, which later formed the nucleus for political parties with seats in the Knesset, was the widely publicized "underground-terrorist" Irgun Zvai Leumi, which played a leading role in the so-called "Freedom Movement" to drive the British out of the Palestine Mandate. Out of the Irgun, when Israel was proclaimed, came the Herut political party, headed by the Polish born

Menachem Begin, who in secret hiding had headed the underground Irgun.

Another similar underground operation, known as the Stern Group, which had splintered away from Irgun, metamorphosed into a political party known as "Fighters" or Lohame Herut Ysrael. Acts of violence (the murder of Lord Moyne and Count Bernadotte) attributed to this group gave it short political life — but it did have one member in the Knesset through 1949-51.

A comparatively new party that has come into the public eye is Reshimat Po'ale Israel, known as Rafi. Its new importance requires some involved explanation which will follow presently in the discussion of 1967 political action. There are in Israel a number of other political parties of lesser significance. Among these is a coalition of religious-based parties, listed in the Israel Government Year Book collectively as the National Religious Party.

Among all the recognized Parties in that little country, comparatively small but highly active, the Israel Communist Party is farthest to the Left. It has had representation in the Knesset from the State's beginning. More is explained about the Communists in Israel elsewhere in this book — mainly because of Russia's increasing activities and influence in the Middle East, and to point up a strange incongruity in the Communist Party functional mechanism vis-a-vis the Jewish State.

POLITICAL PARTIES DOMINATE ISRAEL

Political parties in Israel, under its unique form of government, play an extremely important role in the nature of the State, and for that reason their political philosophies can largely determine the political stability of the country. Israel does not have the guide lines of a restrictive Constitution as does the United States, and the political parties permeate actively all branches of public life. They are dominantly active in the cooperative agencies — the trade unions — the agricultural settlements — housing projects — religion; and consequently great power derives to leaders through party affiliation and proportional representation. With so much socialist orientation in the Parties, there are those who take a dim view of the future. One need only look at France and some of the other multi-party countries to make a determination of the stability of such a system.

NOTE: Despite all the paeans of peace and good-will that are sung to the glory of the reincarnated Israel, it, no less than its Israelite antecedent, is not precisely a paragon of internal peace and tranquility in its experiment of self-government. In the September 9, 1965 issue of the Chicago (Jewish) Sentinel, for illustration, a story under the heading "Mud Flies in Israel" gave the correspondent's picture of an Israel political campaign. After explaining that he had seen many political campaigns in both the United States and in Israel, he said — "but our current one here (in Israel) is the most virulent I have ever witnessed." He gave as one cause the multi-party problem — splitting, coalescing and bickering — citing especially the turmoil in the powerful Mapai "which have turned the campaign into a family mud-slinging match." Aside from being a "dirty campaign," he said it is also "an expensive one." Shalom!

Reporting in the Los Angeles Times (December 14, 1966), the substantial Times' correspondent, Don Cook, had a long story headed: "Israel Elective System Key to Political Unrest — Proportional Representation Seemed Fine 18 Years Ago, Now It Just Confuses." Significant in the article are these observations: "When a country's economy is in trouble, the government usually finds itself in trouble too, and the five-party coalition government of Israel under Premier Levi Eshkol is no exception . . . The simple truth about the Israel political scene is that there is plenty of dissatisfaction, and there is plenty going wrong in the country, but there is no clear-cut, well organized political opposition which stands ready to take over from the present regime."

GOVERNMENT IN ACTION

The Knesset is made up of members who, as political products of some twenty battling parties, frequently changing in nature and purpose through mergers and bartering coalitions, exercise heavy control over the Executive branch. Each party has its "proportional number" of the 120 Knesset seats. It is this rather curious multi-party government system with so many of the parties having pronounced socialistic backgrounds — plus the unique inclusion of governmental international working-tentacles (known as the World Zionist Organization and the Jewish Agency) which appear to point the way of Israel's future and destiny.

Israel's Knesset (parliament) is unicameral. Unlike England and the United States, Israel has only one legislative body — the Chamber of Deputies. At each national election, Israelis choose not only their Knesset but the whole government in one bundle. The President is elected by a majority vote in the Knesset. His duties are mainly ceremonial and nominal — except his one major duty of picking a prospective Prime Minister (chief government executive) from among the Knesset members — and this is routine since he chooses a person from the largest political party in the Knesset. The Prime Minister chooses and submits Cabinet member names to the Knesset for approval.

In Israel the Cabinet is the product of — and responsive to — a working coalition of several Knesset parties. At any time the Prime Minister can ask for a vote of confidence — or the opposition can demand a vote of non-confidence, all of which adds up to a government of political parties — by the parties and for the parties. The ideological character of the parties, therefore, largely determines the essence of the whole government.

ISRAEL'S 1967 POLITICAL POWER-STRUGGLE

1967 was an eventful year for Israel — on the battlefield and in the political arena. In describing the latter, it is important to point out that since the beginning of the Jewish State the dominating political party (usually through coalition with other groups) has been David Ben Gurion's Mapai. To that description might be added that its foundation platform said, *inter alia,* that its historic aim was dedicated to a Jewish nation in Palestine and was devoted to:

"the working class of the world in its struggle for the abolition of class oppression and denial of social rights in any and every form; by the aspiration to transfer natural wealth and the means of production to the control of all workers . . ."

In 1944, a segment of Mapai, Siyah Bet, with proclivity even farther Left than Mapai, broke away and in 1948 helped form the Mapam party which stressed "the Marxist dogma." An article in the New York Times (August 22, 1948) said of Mapam: "Almost all the members are from collective settlements and all are inclined towards radical socialism." The United Nations World (January, 1949) said: "Mapam is a Leftist party and one exhibiting strong leanings toward Soviet Russia . . . the result of a belief that the USSR is Israel's natural ally against Britain." The New Republic (November 29, 1948), in an article about Israel's first election, said: "The overwhelming majority of voters will cast ballots for the two socialist parties, moderate Mapai and pro-Soviet-oriented Mapam."

The most important split of Mapai was the peeling off (in the 1965 heated election campaign) of a prestige group (including Ben Gurion and General Dayan) to create the Rafi party. This was somewhat ironic as Ben Gurion had originally fathered Mapai and through it controlled Israel's government for some fifteen years. All of this leads up to the 1967 power struggle between the Ben Gurion-Dayon group and Premier Eshkol as head of Mapai. To put this picture in focus, a very brief recap of Ben Gurion and his long leadership is inserted here:

> In 1910, David Ben Gurion migrated to Israel from his native Poland. There he soon organized a branch of Poale Zion (the Socialist Labor Party). From 1912 to 1914 he studied law in Constantinople and returned to Palestine in 1914. In 1915 the Turkish government, then in control of Palestine, expelled him. He went to New York and became active in Labor Zionism. He returned to Palestine in 1918, after the Turks had been driven out by the British and the Arabs. He founded the Ahdut Ha-Avodah party (Israelite Socialist Party) and through this and the giant labor organization, Histadrut, of which he was the leader, he dominated the Israel government for some fifteen years. In 1953 he resigned from government duties and settled in a Negev kibbutz, but in 1955 he returned to the Premiership and was responsible for the invasion attack on Egyptian Sinai in 1956.

POLITICS PREGNANT WITH UNCERTAINTIES

In 1963, Ben Gurion helped his old friend Levi Eshkol to succeed him as Premier. Eshkol, born in the Russian Ukraine, had migrated to Israel in 1914, the same year that Ben Gurion returned from Constantinople. Eshkol joined an Israel communal settlement of Russian immigrants — the Kibbutzim movement in which Ben Gurion was a leader. By 1950, two years after Israel was declared, Eshkol was near the top of the Zionist machine — treasurer of the Jewish Agency. Then in 1963, Ben Gurion helped Eshkol succeed him as Israel's top officer. But over the following months, wide differences developed between the two who had migrated from Eastern Europe to become leaders in setting up a Jewish State in Palestine.

1965 was a national election year in Israel. The campaign, basically because of the differences between Ben Gurion and

Eshkol, turned into a violently boisterous affair. A correspondent of the Chicago Jewish Sentinel has already been quoted as saying it was the most "virulent" and "dirty" election campaign he had ever seen. In July, 1965, under the heat of some cutting remarks by Ben Gurion, he was expelled from Mapai — the party he himself had formed in 1930.

Following the heat and fury of the 1965 election campaign, Premier Eshkol was reelected and retained his leadership. He was, however, soon to face new problems evolving out of that bitter election affray. The developments that followed have been described by some observers as a critical turning point where new forces are emerging, who dream of expansion and empire — and a larger posture for the Jewish State in the world of international politics. What all of this may portend for the Middle East and the world only time can tell.

A SHOOTING STAR APPEARS

Early in 1967, prior to the Israel-Arab June six-day war, a picturesque figure with little international identification, General Moshe Dayan, suddenly skyrocketed to world prominence. Prior to the 1966 election, he had been serving as Minister of Agriculture in the Eshkol Cabinet. According to a New York Times story (October 22, 1967) he had felt that, because of his military prominence and 1956 record in the Sinai campaign, he was entitled to a more important post. But, according to the story, Eshkol had his own plans for running the government and General Dayan "followed the dissatisfied Mr. Ben Gurion into opposition in the newly formed Rafi party."

As the June (1967) confrontation of Israelis and Arabs became imminent, a sudden ground swell demand (politically fomented or otherwise) hurtled Dayan back into Eshkol's cabinet lap. He was perforce placed in charge of Israel's defense and the air-blitz outcome made him an international figure "over night."

"General Dayan's military background," reported the Times' correspondent, "his dramatic personal and public life and his general popularity with the Israel public thrust him in the fore in the bleak days leading to the June war. While Premier Eshkol was struggling with a sensitive diplomatic situation, General Dayan was visiting thousands of soldiers in the

Negev and receiving tumultuous greetings. He became the hawk to Mr. Eshkol's dove and was drawn into the Cabinet almost by popular acclaim." The story goes on: "General Dayan rode the crest of the brilliant six-day military success to even greater acclaim and the role of hero has been his since. Premier Eshkol, according to some of his friends, feels cheated in his place in history."

The knowledgeable Times' correspondent goes on to say that "the bad feelings left by the dispute over the conduct of the war" have sharpened relationships between the Eshkol and Dayan groups; and "the feud between Mr. Eshkol and General Dayan is expected to worsen as Israel's political situation remains unclear."

General Dayan is, at this moment of writing, a military hero with an army behind him high in spirit after the recent quick defeat of the Arabs. The urge is high in Israel — and throughout the Jewish diaspora — to keep the land they have taken — and not much interest appears to be shown anywhere for the million and more Palestinian Arab refugees who have been deprived of their homes and country since the 1948 and 1967 wars.

*   *   *

As this book is published (middle 1968) a major merger of three political parties (Mapai, Rafi and Achdut Avodah) has just been accomplished after much bickering and opposition from controversial Ben Gurion and other leaders. This merger will (so long as it holds together) operate and exercise its considerable power in the Knesset as the United Labor Party. The big guns in this party, maneuvering for control of the Israeli Government, are such personalities as the present Prime Minister Levi Eshkol, General Moshe Dayan, Ben Gurion, Mrs. Golda Meir, Shimon Perez and several of the young-bloods who are forging Israel ahead. The formative background of Mapai and Rafi have been sketched in this chapter.

*   *   *

NOTE: The unpredictable David Ben-Gurion, Israel's first premier and largely the architect of its political and economic system, has declared in a letter to a Mapam (political) parley in Tel Aviv that he no longer is a Zionist or a Socialist — according to an item in the (Chicago) Sentinel (March 26, 1968). He says both terms have lost their meanings. In both Zionism and Socialism Ben-Gurion has been a vigorous and aggressive leader. As men grow old and look back, they sometimes reflect wisdom. Another

Israeli news item involving the Ben-Gurion name (which may or may not have any connection with the item just given) is interesting at least in reflecting an aspect of Israeli life. A special report from Tel Aviv (March 28, 1968) explained that when Miss Galia Ben-Gurion (granddaughter of David Ben-Gurion) applied to the Haifa Rabbinate for registration of her forthcoming marriage, Rabbi Moshe Fingling, head of the Haifa Rabbinate's marriage section, required further identification of her "Jewishness" as his duty under Israeli law. Miss Ben-Gurion is the daughter of Amos Ben-Gurion (son of David Ben-Gurion) and his wife, Mrs. Mary Ben-Gurion who is a British born convert to Judaism. As to the question involved, we quote: "So far, the Haifa Rabbinate has had the last word that Mrs. Mary Ben-Gurion became a convert to Judaism before her marriage took place in England . . . but we wish to be sure that an Orthodox rabbi approved of the conversion. We could not possibly accept a Conservative or Reform conversion."

* * *

SUMMARY

One purpose of this book is to present a well formed and comprehensive picture of a special political accomplishment with ample documentation to give both detail and depth that will provide better understanding of the entangling forces and processes involved. After this picture has been thrown on the screen of reason and analysis, there may be some disposition to paraphrase Sherlock Holmes — and ask: "Well, my dear Watson, what do you make of it all?" And when this same question is asked of anyone who has followed the trail of events, it may require some real head scratching to come up with a knowledgeable answer.

Here is a unique case where a tremendous combination of ingenuity, effort and money has been poured into an anomalous religio-politico undertaking; yet, from those we have questioned, there appears to be great puzzlement as to both the cause and the effect of all this striving. It is a phenomenon in political history that obviously even few attempt to understand. The world is too full of problems for many of them to be isolated for serious thought.

Asking questions about the Palestine conflict is an interesting experience in futility. The answers from Jewish people, generally, have been quite different from those of non-Jews. This difference is manifested in both the emotional and intellectual responses. Non-Jews, mostly, know but little about Jewish traditions and ethnic motivations — and have only meager and superficial familiarity with the history of Palestine. There is a difference here that makes not only for a rather wide appreciation gap, but sometimes evolves into anti-harmony in greater or less degree.

True — a new State has been carved out of an already well populated country and a million or so of the former lifetime inhabitants have been displaced to make room for some two million foreigners brought in from great distances to take over the farms, villages, homes, businesses and professions of those who fled the peril of terrorism. But what does this mean to people far away? Distance blurs understanding and dims consciousness of this tragedy for the Western world where, unhappily, most of the drama was planned and financed.

From wide questioning about the present state of affairs in Palestine, it becomes clear that more and more Americans (to some degree because of the growing publicity) are worried about the danger that the United States, where Zionism has such deep anchorage and influence, may be pressured into a confrontation with the powerful Soviet bloc over this tiny, new, unconventional and financially insufficient State which could be a costly and bloody involvement, more disappointing than America's misadventures in Korea and Viet Nam. They point to the obvious folly of America trying to be a world policeman — and call attention to the perilous Federal debt of over $300,000,000,000 which is steadily growing under a world welfare and meddling program. Thinking people are frightened at the thought of a money crisis which is clearly in the offing as a result of extravagant spending.

The appetite of this strange adventure seems to grow. In a quick 1967 air-blitz, Israel took over all of Jordan west of the river Jordan, resulting in an immediate and desperate money-collecting drive in the United States to support this expansionism. This brought wide criticism from many sources, including the United Nations and even an alarmed United States. Surprisingly, New York began to murmur. The New York Times (April 4, 1968) carried a story titled "The West Bank: Israel Occupation Viewed by Some as Risk." The reasoning in this article equated Israel's expansionism into Jordan with the young hero of an O. Henry story where the kidnappers of the youth finally paid the family to take him back because he was too difficult to handle. The Times article dwelt on the Israel difficulties in dealing with the growing Arab guerrilla movement. This activity, motivated undoubtedly by the constant sight of the Palestinian refugee tents and shacks as an irritant-reminder on the one hand — and signs of never ending Israel expansionism on the other — is not likely to diminish while these conditions exist as an open sore.

The Israelis argue that by pushing the Arabs back across the Jordan river and invading the Syrian hills near Tiberias, they can enjoy more safety from Arab resentment. But this rollback, according to one knowledgeable observer, only sets up a new frontier for conflict. It is doubtful, he opined, that the Israelis could ever, through such rollback methods, gain safety from Arab retribution for what they have suffered and continue to suffer until a just and honorable settlement has been made — which is nowhere in sight. The Zionist-Israelis, he said, are only miring deeper into trouble by their tactics. If they continue to push the Arab frontier back in an effort to relieve the tension, it would mean that sooner or later they will be so far extended and deeply involved that it would translate into Armageddon. Israel's increasing dependence upon vast outside financial help could likewise bring disaster if a world money crisis should continue to develop. Empire building has always been a perilous and fateful game — and more so now than ever.

*   *   *

Wide displeasure rippled throughout the world over the 1967 Israeli blitz-expansion into Jordan — a country that has been consistently pro-Western and was established through the friendly sponsorship and financial support of Great Britain. Young King Husain of that struggling country has won the good-will and kindly admiration of people everywhere including Americans — yet this small nation was bludgeoned and emasculated in what has been widely considered as an expansionist grab. The Israelis have suffered a decided decline in world opinion over this display of what many regard as covetous intentions.

*　　*　　*

Reference above has been made to the danger of confrontation with Russia over Israel or any Middle East country. In connection with this, there is one problematical equation that was introduced to our attention by a recent conversation one of our associates had with a well known writer and authority on Zionism and Israel because of his many visits there. He voiced the opinion that a considerable part of Israel's present population feels a strong emotional attachment for Russia, due to their childhood background, and also to the fact that they have relatives still living there. He even went so far as to suggest that, while the material support of the United States had made Israel strong, the balance of Israel emotional loyalty might well be in favor of Russia rather than of America.

We, ourselves, feel that it would be rash to hazard such a conjecture — but coming from a reliable writer and authority on Israel, it is worth noting. The emotional tie with a homeland is always strong. In 1942 the widely known writer, Maurice Hindus (born in Russia), wrote a best seller titled "Mother Russia," and although he came to America in 1905, he closed his 1942 book with this paragraph: "The greatest and most momentous triumph of the Russian pioneering is written large and red in blood and valor on the steppes and in the forests of Mother Russia."

APPENDIX "A"
WHO ARE THE ARABS?

FROM ARABIAN DESERT TO REVOLT AGAINST TURKS

America is a long way from the Arab lands of the Middle East. Americans, in general, know very little about the Arab people. The Arab image, for reasons well known to many, has not been handled too favorably by the American press. To understand the message in this book, it is important to have at least an elementary grasp of Arabic history and to help in that purpose the following quick sketch is presented.

Of the many mixed Semitic peoples of ancient history (Babylonians, Assyrians, Chaldeans, Arameans, Phoenicians, Amorites, Arabians, Hebrews and others) only the Arabs and the Jews (generally considered as Hebrew offsprings) remain as organized religious entities. The only language writings (largely cuneiform) of the groups here mentioned have shown such similarity as to indicate these people all came from a common racial (Semitic) stock or source. Presumably, according to Biblical geneology, they would be descendants of the Old Testament Shem (or Sem), oldest son of the legendary Noah.

The word "Arab" is the Semitic term for one who lives in the desert, but it would be no more correct today to visualize the wandering Bedouin remnants living in their black goathair tents in the desert as representing the present Arab civilization than it would be to equate Yemen Jewish peasantry with modern Jewish communities in America, England or elsewhere.

FROM YEMEN THEY SPREAD

In his book "The Arabs," Anthony Nutting, distinguished British diplomat, gives a quick but lucid picture of Arab origins, with an explanation that the earliest mass settlement of the Arab people took place in the Yemen; and when this small corner of the Arabian peninsula became overcrowded, about 3500 B.C., a migrating tribal group pulled away in search of a new and less crowded area for themselves and their herds. They traveled along the west coast of Arabia, circumventing the Red Sea, via Sinai and into Egypt, where the Arabic Semites and the native African Hamites (descendants of Noah's son Ham) mixed and assimilated "to produce the Egyptians of history and absorbed the elements of science and culture which are the basis of our civilization."

Mr. Nutting further explains that another migration from the early Arabian-Yemen inhabitants, going in another direction, reached the Tigris-Euphrates valley where they (the Semites) assimilated with the Sumerians — the people who populated the early Mesopotamian

341

country, known as Sumer. Out of this union of the non-Semitic Sumerians and the migrating Arabic Semites came the Babylonians who gradually developed their own particular customs, culture and life methods.

A thousand years later, further mixtures of the emerging populations which had spread to Syria and Palestine produced the Amorites and Phoenicians and other groups that were the early settlers of the area between the Jordan river and the Mediterranean coast where, several hundred years still later (roughly between 1500 and 1200 B.C.), the sector known as Canaan was invaded by another Semitic division known as the Hebrews. About the same time, a Semitic grouping known as the Arameans established themselves firmly in Syria with Damascus as their capital. Many of the early ethnical and tribal names, particularly as mentioned in the Old Testament, originated out of the geographical section they occupied.

ASSYRIANS PUSH EMPIRE

Much later, in the ninth century B.C., the Assyrians moved into Syria, and with imperialistic might succeeded in setting up a considerable Empire stretching from Babylonia (the southern Iraq of today) to Armenia and on down to Phoenicia, which roughly is the Lebanon of today. It was the custom of early historians to consider the section we later came to know as Palestine as a geographical part of Syria.

In the wide stretches to the East, during the sixth and seventh centuries (B.C.), the Medians (Medes) ruled a considerable land mass, including ancient Persia and part of what is now Pakistan. In the course of time, this developed into the strong Persian Empire which included the conquered territory that had, in an Empire sense, first been Assyria and then Babylonia.

For historical reasons, it may be useful to mention that the major religion which preceded Islam in Persia (now Iran) was Zoroastrianism. There is no need here to say more than that this was a very ancient religion, originating as early as 1200 B.C., as estimated by some, while certain early Greek historians placed Zoroaster as hundreds, or even thousands of years earlier. One such authority describes Zoroastrianism as "a pure monotheistic concept of God, Ahura-Mazda, the perfect creator and ruler of both the material and unmaterial world." Its adherents were and are called Parsees. Zoroastrianism appears to have become an official state religion with the rise of the Persian Empire, and remained as such until it was dethroned and largely abolished by the great Arab conflict around 636 A.D.

Sir John Bagot Glubb, in his book "The Great Arab Conquests," explains the problem encountered by the Christians, Jews and Parsees in adjusting to the new Moslem masters who, at that time, "had no code of civil law . . . The only inevitable solution was to allow the Christians and Jews to have their own separate judicial systems, administered by their own judges." The Turks took over in this area by conquering the Arabs in the sixteenth century. Today there is a small percentage of Iranians who adhere to Zoroastrian beliefs but the majority are Moslem in faith.

All that is being attempted here is to give a running sketch of Middle East background. To go fully into the play and interplay of countless races, tribes, religions, sects and cultures which spanned thousands of years of history, would require volumes and is not necessary to the basic theme of this book. The main purpose here is to point out how the people we know as Arabs entered the arena of a developing civilization; how they brought a great new religion into being; how they spread in prominence and power to become an extensive empire; how they came to be what and where they are today — and the relation of all of this to the latest conflict (between Jew and Arab) in the eternal battlefield known as Palestine.

One of the earliest onslaughts in this storied battleground, as already mentioned, was when the Semitic Israelites whom, according to legend, Moses led out of Egypt, crossed the river Jordan near Jericho, invaded Canaan, and in Jericho "utterly destroyed all that was in the city, both man and woman, young and old, and ox, and sheep, and ass, with the edge of the sword" (Joshua 6:21).

THE RISE OF ISLAM AND ARABISM

While some of the Semitic groups originating in lower Arabia migrated to other Middle East areas, the basic Arab-stock gradually became a more organized and stabilized form of civilization, with its population colonized largely in two particular areas of the Arabian peninsula, known as Hejaz and Nejd. These will be defined later.

The beginning of the Arab world, as we know it today — and that is where our interest in the Arabs presently lies — came with the amalgamizing of a religio-politico culture through the leadership of the Prophet Mohammed — an accomplishment that has become the outstanding Arab image to the other peoples of the world. The miracle of the sixth and seventh centuries A.D. was undoubtedly the birth of the Islamic religion or faith. Its initiation was solely due to the indomitable will and strong personality of one man — Mohammed. Here is the only one of the great religions that was born in the open view of modern history, where the patriarch was a person of national record with less legend and mystery than that of most of the great religious founders. However, it must be said that Mohammed leaned heavily upon the two other monotheistic religions by interweaving a remarkable system of faith and law, with some cognizance of the mysteries of these two prior religions. What was the urge — the inspiration — that produced this almost miraculous achievement in its time and place?

343

The story of Mohammed's childhood and development to manhood and leadership is well told by Sir John Bagot Glubb (Glubb Pasha) in his most excellent book, "The Great Arab Conquests" (Prentice-Hall, U.S.A.). This book contains many descriptive maps that make General Glubb's story of the Arabs easy to follow and understand. At the end of each chapter, he provides a chronology of "Notable Dates" — a most helpful publishing variation, especially where history is involved.

MOHAMMED — THE MAN

A short sketch of Mohammed should begin with his birth — 570 A.D. His father, who was of an important Meccan tribe (the Quraish), died before the boy's birth. His mother died when the lad was about age six. Young Mohammed was cared for by two or three different people, but was raised mainly by an aged grandfather. It may be mentioned that Mohammed is the most common male name in the Arabic category. Little detail is known of Mohammed's child life. Sometime before the age of twenty-five, however, he was employed in a business conducted by a well-to-do widow (Khadijah) of a Meccan merchant whom Mohammed, at the age of twenty-five, married. She was fifteen years his senior, and as long as she lived, Mohammed was devoted to her. He had several daughters, most of whom died before adulthood.

All known facts, as well as tradition, would indicate that young Mohammed was disposed toward a studious and meditative proneness that placed him in the category of a spiritual intellectual of his time and place, although it is not known whether or not he could write. When he became well married, he had more time for the indulgence of his bent for speculating on the fate of mankind. From the Koran we learn that from his cave retreat near Mecca, where he spent considerable time in reflective solitude, he heard a voice saying— "Recite thou in the name of the Lord who created." Later he received more messages, among which was a command to "Arise and warn." His call to preach was not too dissimilar from that of other prophets and evangelists.

He knew considerable about the Jewish and Christian monotheistic religions and was depressed by his polytheistic environment, where the people worshiped a pantheon of divergent idols. He had become convinced that God is One and all-powerful, having created the earth and all living things. He believed that for the righteous there would be a rewarding paradise and dreadful punishment for the wicked. He had become convinced that his mission was to persuade others to believe. He began to preach about salvation and reform. In the main, he was scorned by the people. Besides the loyalty of his wife and a small group of relatives, the few who were at first converted were mostly slaves and very poor people.

344

The greater number of Meccans liked their ways and pleasures, and regarded Mohammed as a nuisance and menace. Opposition to his activities grew to such threatening proportions that finally, as a measure of safety, he had to restrict his public work in Mecca to a point of essential discontinuance. It was at scme time during his evangelistic travail that, according to legend, Mohammed was miraculously transported on a nocturnal journey to the Holy City of Jerusalem, extending into a celestial visit to the seventh heaven from the Dome of the Rock, astride a winged white horse. The "seventh heaven" concept of the legend doubtless arose from the quite common belief among the ancients in a plurality of heavens.

NOTE: That this legend of Mohammed is still revered was reflected in the serious arguments that arose between Zionist Jews and Moslem Arabs in the 1929 "Wailing Wall dispute" in the old walled city of Jerusalem. This was a harbinger of the growing conflict between these two groups that culminated in the 1948 war in Palestine. Inside the walled city is a segment of an old wall of huge stones which is supposed to be the only remnant of the last Temple — not Solomon's Temple but the one built after the return of the exiles, known as Herod's Temple. It was destroyed in the Jerusalem siege by the Roman general Titus, in 70 A.D. Over the years, since the Jewish dispersion, it had been the habit of the few remaining orthodox Jews to visit and pray at the Wall, especially on the 9th of Av (the Jewish 11th month). This Wall has a certain sanctity also for the Moslems, because: (1) the Mosque of Omar is there; and (2) because of the tradition that it was from the Temple area that Mohammed "took off" on his flight to heaven. The 1929 bitter conflict arose when the Arab Mufti started some construction there that interfered with the Jewish performance at the Wall.

One writer describes Mohammed in adulthood as: "Brooding in the gaunt foothills of Mount Hira in the region of his native Mecca, Mohammed came to the strong conviction that idolatry was criminal folly and that God the One commanded utterance against it." Dr. Kenneth Craig, Professor of Arabic and Islamic studies at Hartford Seminary Foundation (working and traveling out of Jerusalem), gives that opinion in his book "The Call of the Minaret" (Oxford University Press), and goes on to explain in considerable detail that Mohammed's continued discouragement at the moral wickedness and idol-worshipping of his fellow Meccans drove him on towards the mission to preach and transform the people and conditions of his time.

THE THORNY ROAD

Mohammed did not rise suddenly as a preacher or a religious leader — but in the beginning, more as a social reformer. Instead of urging violence and revolution as a cure for the economic and social ills of his time, he took the position that he was called by God to help his fellow men and his country by bringing about moral change. Having some familiarity with Christianity and the prophets of the Old Testament, he took the road of action and persuasion to convince the people that there must be a change in the hearts of men for the judgment of God was at hand.

This led him steadily into the role of a proselyting religious leader, which brought increasing hostility from a large proportion of the people of Mecca who were not anxious to change their way of life. It was this opposition that undoubtedly pushed Mohammed on to crystallizing his ideas of moral reform and Godliness in formalizing the religion that became Islam. The road for Mohammed in Mecca was rough — as it was for Jesus in Jerusalem. After ten years of effort, he had attracted only a small following — but had incurred tremendous opposition. The Meccans were strongly against him.

MOHAMMED, OF NECESSITY, MOVES TO MEDINA

As he was considering a different location where there would be less opposition, a provident situation developed in Medina, a city two hundred miles to the north of Mecca, that offered a solution to the Meccan opposition which had almost destroyed his work and his dream. A long internecine or fratricidal war between two Arab tribes had brought a crisis to Medina. Sir Hamilton A. R. Gibbs, professor of Arabic, University of Oxford (at time of writing), in his book "Mohammedanism" (New American Library — Mentor), explains that the Arab tribes of Medina, exhausted from warring-strife — "and fearing lest their weakness should be exploited by the Jewish tribes under their control, besought Mohammed to come to Medina as arbitrator and peacemaker." After long negotiations for guarantees of personal safety and other conditions, Mohammed in 622 A.D. moved his headquarters to Medina and successfully began the building of a strong Islamic movement which stimulated and inspired not only an Arabic order of religious reformation, but extended its strength into an expansion that finally reached out to build one of the great empires of history.

From the new headquarters in Medina, the power and prestige of Mohammed and his movement spread so rapidly that by 628 A.D. the Prophet was able to lead a march of some 1,500 believers triumphantly into Mecca, the city that had rejected him six years before. By 630 A.D. all essential resistance in Mecca had abated and Mohammed returned with power to destroy more than three hundred idols in the established sanctuary.

Immediately following the smashing of the idols, there began an influx of tribal delegations into Mecca and Medina to pay homage to the Prophet and offer allegiance to his leadership. This was known as "the year of delegations" and while those who came from near and far may not have represented more than half the population of Arabia (due to the difficulties of communication and transportation as well as inadequate missionary facilities), this did, however, represent the great turning point. His jurisdiction flowed steadily on to encompass most of Arabia which then, from the standpoint of population, consisted

346

mainly of Hejaz (the coastal strip of Arabia along the Red Sea), Nejd (a central eastern sector sloping off to the Persian Gulf), and the Yemen.

In the tenth year after Mohammed had moved from Mecca to Medina, he made what was to be his final pilgrimage to Mecca. Within three weeks after his return from the pilgrimage to his home in Medina, he became ill with severe headache and fever and within a few days, on June 8, 632 A.D., succumbed to his ailment.

As the force and influence of Christianity had risen from the catacombs to conquer Rome (through expedient acceptance by the Emperor Constantine) so did the growing power of Islam (a word meaning submission or obedience to the Will of Allah — God), inspired and inflamed by the teachings of Mohammed, go forth to conquer.

Of this the distinguished scholar, Dr. Philip K. Hitti, Professor of Semitic Literature, Princeton University, in his book "The Arabs" (Henry Regnery Co.), says: "One hundred years after the death of Mohammed his followers were the masters of an empire greater than that of Rome at its zenith, an empire extending from the Bay of Biscay to the Indus and the confines of China and from the Aral Sea to the lower cataracts of the Nile."

ARAB 1965 POPULATION

Although the political Empire finally disintegrated into sectional controls, ultimately succumbing to subjugation by the rising Turkish (Ottoman) Empire, the religious solidarity of Arabic Islam has steadfastly remained as the major unifying force largely throughout what is known as the Arab world, which embraces some seventeen or more countries throughout the Middle East and North Africa. Listed below are the approximate population figures for those countries today as given by the Britannica Book of the Year 1965:

Algeria	12,000,000
Iraq	7,039,000
Jordan	1,860,000
Kuwait	333,000
Lebanon	2,150,000
Libya	1,559,000
Morocco	12,700,000
Saudi-Arabia	8,000,000
Syria	4,980,000
Sudan	13,011,000
Tunisia	4,546,000
United Arab Republic (Egypt)	28,500,000
Yemen	5,000,000
Aden and South Arabia	1,000,000
Qatar	60,000
Muscat and Oman	750,000
Bahrein	168,493
TOTAL	103,656,493

347

THE NATURE OF ISLAMIC WORSHIP

The Islamic faith is a monotheistic-type religion. It is dedicated to the universal God, called "Allah" in Arabic. The Jews also use other names for God. The primal tenet of the Islamic faith is to recognize Allah as the One God — and Mohammed as "The Prophet" and "The Messenger of God."

NOTE: The God of the Old Testament was variously referred to as "El" — "Elohim" — "Adonai" — and most used (nearly 7,000 times in the Hebrew Bible) was the tetragrammaton "YHVH." This was at first too sacred to be spoken but later the vowel sounds of Adonai and Elohim were used to represent "the Lord" as YeHoVaM, which the Jewish Encyclopedia says was erroneously misconstrued by non-Jewish users as "Jehovah." The tetragram of four letters has been variously written as YMVA—JHVH—JHWH—and YHWH. Such words as Yahveh—Jahveh — Jahaveh — Yahweh and others have been used in Jewish literature to represent the supposed original intention.

The "Bible" of Islam is the Koran (which is sometimes spelled "Qur'an," also Qoran). Professor Hitti tells us in his book already mentioned, that the first, final and only canonized version of this sacred book "was collated nineteen years after the death of Mohammed when it was seen that the memorizers of the Koran were becoming extinct . . ." That would put the date at 651 A.D.

The Koran draws, to some extent, on the Old Testament for names and epochs. It recognizes both Moses and Jesus as leaders of their respective faiths and as prophets. As the Christian and Hebrew bibles are accepted by their followers as the Word of God, so is the Koran accepted by Moslems as the Word of Allah, dictated to Mohammed through the archangel Gabriel.

FOUNDATIONS OF ISLAMIC FAITH

There are five principal pillars of Islamic devotion: Confession, Prayer, Alms-giving, Fasting and Pilgrimage. These are described in splendid detail by Dr. Kenneth Craig in "The Call of the Minaret" (Oxford University Press). In the matter of confession, Dr. Craig brings forward a close conparison with Christianity, and Dr. Erich W. Bethmann (in Steps Toward Understanding Islam) says: "It becomes apparent that man's relationship to God in Islam is basically the same as in Christianity."

In the matter of prayer, the demand upon faithful Moslems is to pray five times a day as they kneel and face toward Mecca. Prayer time is at dawn, at midday, in mid-afternoon, at sunset and at nightfall. We once witnessed an example of Islamic devotion enroute up the Nile by rail from Cairo to Aswan. In a small area near the rest-room in the rear of our car, we came upon an Arab kneeling and facing east on his small prayer rug, performing his prayer devotion. One sees this often in many open places in Moslem countries. The deep-seated religious persuasion of the Arab is a main reason why Communism has made no headway among the common people in the Moslem world.

Important among the five pillars of Islamic religion is a pilgrimage as often as possible (at least once in a lifetime if it does not cause family hardship) to the Holy City of Mecca. The Arabic name for the pilgrimage is "hadj" and when it occurs (in the spring of the year) vast multitudes of pilgrims from all over the Moslem world congregate in Mecca, where tents and other accomodations are prepared for them. Driving in the desert country between Damascus and Saudi Arabia in March of 1966, we met countless trucks and buses, filled to capacity with devout Moslems returning from their Mecca pilgrimage.

The prayer ritual is in a large way meticulously prescribed — in fact the religion of Islam as a whole places real demands upon the faithful. Prayers, however, are not restricted to the set rituals but may be extempore and at the will of the individual. The official house of Moslem worship is the mosque. In Arabic cities or centers where there is sufficient Moslem (Muslim) population, there are mosques to which are usually attached a tower structure called the minaret. Near the top of this tower on an outside surrounding balcony, the Muezzin appears at the alloted prayer periods, and in loud rhythmic cadence, issues a call to the faithful for prayer. Often now in the larger places, the Muezzin call is recorded for broadcast from the minaret.

The Islamic mosque differs from the Jewish synagogue and the Christian church in architecture, both as to exterior and interior. The fine old Mosque of Umayyads in Damascus (oldest continuous city in the world) can serve as an excellent example. The floor of its huge open interior is covered with some 2,500 oriental rugs. There are no seats as in a synagogue or church. The worshipers stand reverently in self-arranged rows while listening to the leader as he speaks or prays. A special section is assigned to women. The Friday noon prayer is the only public service. The Fridays of Islam correspond, in a worship way, to the Saturdays of Judaism and the Sundays of Christianity. The Islamic Friday, however, is not a day of rest as Sunday is generally considered by Christians. Government offices are closed, but shops and other business places continue as usual, except during the time of the Mosque services.

Basic in Islam, as in many other religions including Christianity and Judaism, is the practice of feasting and fasting. "Another practical commandment," writes Dr. Erich W. Bethmann, "is that of keeping the month of Ramadan (of the Moslem calendar) for a yearly period of fasting. During Ramadan, the Moslem is not supposed to eat or drink or smoke during his daylight hours, from early in the morning, when the light becomes sufficient to distinguish between a white and a black thread, to sunset.

"During the night he may eat and drink as much as he likes . . ." To this it might be added that the heavy Moslem drink is coffee and not alcoholic mixtures. They are total abstainers. Fasting

349

has the value, not only of practicing self-control, but was, when introduced, intended to remind the more affluent of the status of the poor.

One great fast period of the Moslems occupies three days in March. Every Moslem who can afford a sheep buys one and invites his friends to his festive board. We were once in Cairo during this period and on the day prior to the festival it was a common sight to see fatted sheep being led homeward by their proud possessors. The three days are joyful and colorful, with crowds congregated everywhere enjoying the holiday.

While the Islamic faith is the generally accepted religion of the Arab countries, there are also many Christian Arabs. A substantial percentage of the Palestinian Arabs (most of whom are now living in sordid refugee camps — excluded from their former Palestine homes by the conquering Zionists) are Christians. We have talked with many of them and it would be difficult not to sympathize with their grievous plight resulting from a disaster which everybody but the Arabs seems to have forgotten. These Christian Arabs are devout and sincere in their devotion to the same Jesus and Christian traditions to which American and British Christians pay spiritual homage —and yet it seems the ties of Christian brotherhood in this instance, which should produce understanding and sympathy, have eroded under the continuous propaganda blasts that emanate from powerful non-Christian sources.

AMAZING SPREAD OF THE ISLAMIC FAITH

Military expansion of the Moslem (Arab) Empire continued until about 732 A.D. with an amazing record of achievement during the hundred years after Mohammed had set the movement in motion with nothing but a spiritual idealism and a handful of relatives and adherents at the beginning. This greatest of Arabs, with his preaching and dedication, mobilized a following that grew into a vast unbelievable dominion. The fragile bond, before Mohammed, that had held the various Arab tribes of the lower Arabian peninsula together (when it did) was that of tribal kinship. After Mohammed, the far stronger bondage that brought them together for an historic march into world history was the brotherhood of Islam through faith in Allah.

At the death of Mohammed the Prophet in June of 632 A.D., his closest friend and associate, Abu Bekr, was selected as his successor. Abu Bekr chose Khalif (Caliph) as his official title, which merely meant "successor." From that time on the Arabic leaders of Islam were known to the English speaking world as "Caliph" and the official office was called the "Caliphate" until this title was suppressed in 1924 by the new Turkey. This office, which was revered for its designation of civil and spiritual sovereignty through thirteen centuries, is now nonexistent.

Following Abu Bekr's accession to the leadership left open by the death of the Prophet Mohammed, there was considerable temporary tribal and party turmoil in the adjusting process, but the new Caliph's able commander, Khalid ibn-al-Walid, soon had his organized fighting forces ready, not only to handle local disorder, but to start carrying the banner of Islam beyond the limited Arabian borders. Abu Bekr, as a devout believer and disciple of Mohammed, was dedicated to the task of carrying out the late Prophet's desire to spread the Will of Allah throughout the world. These intentions had been sent out of Medina by Mohammed in 628 A.D. to all known monarchs.

The records of the various rulers who followed Mohammed and his immediate successor (Abu Bekr) cannot be detailed in this short sketch. After Abu Bekr came Caliph Umar under whom Moslem expansion moved rapidly forward. He was succeeded by Caliph Uthman under whom the Umayyads (Moslem faction) became strongly entrenched in leadership. Uthman was succeeded as Caliph by Ali (ibn abi Talib) who was the last of the elected Caliphs. The ruling office from then became a monarchal hereditary succession from the House of Umayya and remained so for approximately 100 years.

ARMIES MARCH UNDER BANNER OF ISLAM

The armies that marched from Arabia were not great as to size — at first only small forces of 3,000 to 4,000 men for each field action, according to H. G. Wells, but in all operations, more important than the prospects of material gain that comes from expansionist conquest, these men were fired with the vigor and passion of a new Faith. This must have been the explanation for their remarkable victories. This sort of aggression would, of course, be generally — but not entirely — condemned by the world today. But at that time, as had been true generally since the dawn of history, invasion and conquest was a matter of common practice.

The first aggressive outside move by the Moslem-Arab armies was into nearby Syria, north of the Arabian peninsula. Two separate armies moving north from Medina struck, more or less simultaneously, one at the river Yarmuk, south of Damascus, and the other at Hira on the Persion frontier, near the river Euphrates. They easily defeated the larger armies they met. The Byzantine spirit was low and another advantage came from there being many Arabs (some of them Christianized) scattered through Syria — men who as mercenaries had helped both the Persians and the Byzantines in the wars they had been fighting. The inhabitants of the country didn't seem to care especially whether they paid tribute (taxes) to the Byzantines, the Persians or the incoming Arabs. Wells thinks they may have preferred the Arabs as "the cleaner people, more just, and more merciful." At any rate, it was a quick and fairly easy victory for the Arabs when, in 636, they met and defeated a Byzantine army of 50,000 in the hot and dusty Yarmuk valley with a Moslem army of half that number. The change of rule from Byzantine Emperor to Moslem Caliph in Syria was effected readily with the non-Moslems being left freedom under their own religious leaders and with a legal system of their own.

Operating from Syria with Damascus as the Moslem military capital, the Arab armies moved on into Armenia, northern Mesopotamia, and with acquisitional raids, penetrated Asia Minor. The ruling banner of Islam was planted in country after country until the Arab Empire at its peak included Egypt, Palestine, Syria, Persia, Babylonia, all North Africa, Spain and a small portion of France, where they were stopped by Charles Martel as head of Frankish armies, in a murderous battle (732 A.D.) at a place near Tours in France. This broke the advance of the Arabs into western Europe. They were pushed back into Spain, with the Pyrenees as their demarcation perimeter.

THE BEGINNING OF EMPIRE DISINTEGRATION

The way of great Empires is to enter massively and heroically upon the stage of history — parade their might and flash their glory — and then disappear as their power evaporates under the disintegrating heat of inherent pressures. The great Empire of the Arabs was no exception. The processes of decay began with the Umayyads becoming dominant under the Caliph Uthman. Opposition to the Umayyads was led by the Abbasids, who were led in turn by the descendants of Mohammed's uncle Abbas. By 750 the Abbasids had gained dominant power, having largely exterminated the Umayyads. Following this, the regnant Abbasid dynasty transferred the Moslem capital to Baghdad in Mesopotamia (now Iraq). This was the beginning of political divisions or parties that produced disunity within the Empire — symptoms of coming disjunction.

From 750 to 1500, numerous dynasties spread their shadows of influence over the Arab Empire. Following the Umayyads and the Abbasids, there came the Fatimids — the Timurids (descendants of Tamerlane) — the Mamelukes and other groups that played their roles as Arab history unfolded.

It is not the purpose here to give extended detail concerning the internal processes that, through the centuries, governed and shaped the Arab Empire. All that is being attempted is to present a quick picture of the Arabs as a people — how they came into history — and their status in the present world, especially in relation to the present crisis in the Middle East.

Special mention, perhaps, should be made of the Mamelukes, since this was a "slave" dynasty that dominated Egypt and Syria as sectors of the Arab Empire until 1517. It was the last ruling bloc of the fading Empire. Egypt had come under the control of one of the petty dynasties into which the Empire had been splitting. Following the precedent of the earlier Arab rulers in Baghdad and elsewhere, the Moslem ruler in Egypt had taken in foreign slaves to augment the "national guard." Gradually some of these slaves, through sheer force of competence and ambition, rose to commanding positions of responsibility — especially in the armed guard forces. One of them, known in history as Baybars (who had once been a Turkish slave), rose in power to become the leader of the ruling dynasty. He was an able military man who also had considerable ability as a political leader.

His greatest achievement perhaps was in blocking the Mongol hordes as they came roaring down through Baghdad and Damascus, sweeping all resistance before them in streams of blood. Baybars, who died in 1277, made substantial contribution toward minimizing the threat of the Crusaders in Syria and Egypt. He also advanced progress in Egypt by digging useful canals and developing certain institutions of national character.

Instead of recording further details of the Arab Empire story, it is here more important to show briefly the role of the Ottoman Turks in taking control of that far-flung political structure.

RISE AND FORWARD MARCH OF THE TURKS

Around the beginning of the year 1300, a man named Othman (or Osman) managed to make himself Sultan of a small Turkish principality in the area of Anatolia, where he soon began to menace the neighboring Turks as well as the nearby Byzantines. As he grew in power, his followers became known as the Ottoman Turks, the name deriving from "Othman." He ruled from 1288 to 1326.

Sir Mark Sykes, co-author of the controversial Sykes-Picot Agreement, has described the beginning of the Ottoman-Turks (in "The Caliph's Last Heritage") as "A small band of alien herdsmen wandering unchecked through crusades and counter-crusades, principalities, empires and states. Where they camped, how they moved and preserved their flocks and herds, where they found pasture, how they made their peace with the various chiefs through whose territories they passed, are questions which one may well ask in wonder." The question that Sir Mark raises in connection with these particular meandering and marauding groups is one that frequently perplexes students of ancient history about most of the mass movements of the early periods. "Gradually," wrote H. G. Wells, "the Ottoman Turks became important."

The aggressive Ottomans (by 1400) had taken over much of Asia Minor and invaded Europe, advancing as far as the Danube. They began to purchase firearms from Europe which gave them a great advantage over the armies they met, most of which did not, at that time, possess guns. In 1453 the Ottomans, under Sultan Muhammad II, captured Constantinople thereby decapitating the Byzantine Empire.

After the conquest of Constantinople, Muhammad looked hungrily toward Italy and would doubtless have taken it next but for his death in 1481. His successor was Bayezid who reigned from 1481 to 1512 and pushed the Ottoman Empire on to include Poland and a large part of Greece. Selim succeeded him as Sultan in 1512 and with a stroke of strategy, bought from a helpless Abbasid (Arab) Caliph whom he deposed, not only the title of Caliph (thereby himself becoming the Caliph of all Islam which Empire the Ottoman Turks had steadily been taking over) but he obtained also the relics of the late Prophet Mohammed, including the sacred banner. During his eight year reign he extended the Ottoman rule over Armenia and Cairo. It was in Egypt that the last control remnant of the Arab Empire was toppled when Cairo was captured in 1517.

This "last remnant" was the so-called "slave" dynasty that had ascended to control of Egypt many years after it had become a part of the Arab Empire and after the great Moslem surge had reached its zenith. Now the Ottoman Turks had come in to take control. The new ruler was the Ottoman Sultan Selim who was now also Caliph by reason of having purchased that title, as previously explained. He was succeeded by Suleiman the Magnificent who ruled from 1520 to 1566 and extended the Ottoman Empire by conquering Baghdad, much of Hungary, and all of North Africa except Morocco. Ottoman-Turkish control of the former Arab Empire had now been extended to include North Africa (including Egypt) — a large part of Asia — and in Europe up to Poland and Hungary.

There is no purpose here to give any great detail concerning the Ottoman-Turkish Empire other than to mark its conquest over the Arab Empire and to show that the Turks were for some four or five hundred years in control of a vast land mass — including the strategic Middle East — until they were evicted from that area by the British (with help from the Arabs) in World War I. This book is concerned principally with the events that followed. To further set the stage for the present Middle-East conflict between the Arabs and Jews, it is important to understand the status of the Arabs in the Middle East after the Arab Empire had been conquered by the Ottoman Turks.

STATUS OF ARAB WORLD AFTER LOSS OF EMPIRE

After the Arabs moved out of their original home in Arabia under the Islamic banner of Mohammed (about 634 A.D.) — on through the next thirteen hundred years — the Arabic-Moslem peoples multiplied as they settled and developed in the lands of the Middle East (Iraq, Syria, Trans-Jordan, Palestine, Lebanon, North Africa and, of course, remaining strong in Arabia, the homeland of the two Holy Cities. Islam (which at one time was better understood in America as "Mohammedanism") was also penetrating farther east into countries like Afghanistan and India. The people of what is now Pakistan (which became an independent political State in 1947 by seceding from India) had been Moslem for many centuries, according to Sir John Glubb. The same is true of the Sudan which became an independent

354

political State in 1956. These political changes in 1947 and 1956 were political reorganizations by people who were already predominantly Moslem. The Arab world as we know it today, according to figures listed in this chapter (from Britannica Book of the Year — 1965), has a population in excess of 100,000,000.

Of the Moslem countries listed here, it is especially important to make further quick reference to both Egypt and Palestine as Moslem centers at the time of World War I. This period was also the real beginning of Zionism vis-a-vis Arabism — a confrontation that gradually led to the conflict that has made Palestine the powder-keg of the Middle East — opening the gate for Russia to fish in troubled waters.

BRITISH TAKE OVER IN EGYPT

In approaching the critical question of Zionism in Palestine, it is important to examine quickly the question of how the British happened to be playing a strategic role in the Middle East.

The answer starts with British interests in India. After Britain became dominant in India by ousting the Mongol (Mogol) Emperors in battles at Plassey (1757) and at Muxar (1764) through the instrumentality of its East India Trading Company, her interest naturally was stimulated in maintaining a Middle East passage to India, with Egypt as the vital gateway.

This interest caused Great Britain to maintain a friendly cooperative relationship with the Arab-Mameluke dynasty in Egypt and successively with the rule of Mohammed Ali, founder of the Khedivial dynasty of Egypt, as a vassal of the Ottoman-Turkish Sultan when the Turks took control of that country. This British cooperation involved keeping their soldiers (and Navy) alert in that area. We should add, however, in the words of General Glubb, that Britain was always friendly with the Ottoman Empire, in order to safeguard the route to India. Egypt became vitally more important — many times so — as part of this route after 1869, when the Suez Canal was opened. Before that all shipping had to go around the Cape of Good Hope.

In those early days, England and France were quite continuously and often militantly engaged in competitive colonialism struggles. This happened in India — in America — and now Egypt became the testing ground. Toward the close of the eighteenth century, France received complaint from the French Consul in Egypt that French merchant trading was being hampered by the ruling regime. This gave the French an excuse to intervene in a major design to disrupt the British life line to India. Napoleon Bonaparte (then in his early stages of ascension to power) was authorized to sail with armed forces to "restore order." However, the instructions to Napoleon from the French Directoire (April 19, 1798) commanded him to —

"chase the British from all their possessions which he could reach, and notably to destroy all their stations on the Red Sea; to cut through the Isthmus of Suez, and take the necessary measures to assure the free and exclusive possessions of the Red Sea to the French Republic."

Napoleon sailed from Toulon with his fleet on May 19, 1798. The British knew nothing of his action until he reached Malta and there took possession from the Knights of St. John of Jerusalem. When word reached Lord Nelson, who was in command of the British fleet on the high seas, he immediately divined the purpose and set chase. He missed Napoleon's fleet while it was sheltered at Crete, but finally caught and destroyed it at Alexandria. This left Napoleon stranded in Egypt, and after several dismal and devastating experiences (one of which was a marauding adventure up the Palestine coast as far as Acre) he slipped away, leaving his remnant army in Egypt, and by a narrow margin clandestinely reached France.

NOTE: Napoleon's adversities on this ill fated expedition were: (1) losing his fleet to the British; (2) losing a considerable part of his army in a battle with the Turks at Acre; (3) suffering murderous harassment from the Egyptians and Mamelukes in Cairo and Alexandria.

BRITISH FORCED TO ACTION IN EGYPT

Egypt was, at the time of Napoleon's abortive adventure, a Turkish possession and had been since its capture by them in 1517. Turbulent conditions continued in Egypt on through the years of Turkish control, menacing British freedom of action relative to its route to India. This finally caused the British to establish a considerable amount of security protection which included the sending of Lord Cromer to Egypt in 1883 as British Agent and Consul-General. It is hardly necessary to add that the Suez Canal (opened in 1869) had, during its fourteen years of operation to that time, greatly increased Britain's security interests in Egypt.

During all these troubled years, however, Britain scrupulously recognized Egypt as a Turkish possession and strictly observed all the treaties it had with Turkey. Remarkable restraint, under the circumstances, was maintained by the British. They could easily have annexed Egypt at any time and ended much of the disorder. In 1907, Lord Cromer was replaced by Sir Eldon Gorst who was followed in that office in 1911 by the celebrated Lord Kitchener.

The relationship and the situation in Egypt changed to a critically threatening stage, however, when Turkey joined Germany as an ally in World War I. Britain was at war with Germany and this Turkish action could mean nothing less than that Britain was now at war with Turkey also.

Arthur E. P. Brome Weigall, in his book "Egypt from 1798 to 1914" (Wm. Blackwood and Sons, London) stated the case well for British action in forcibly taking control of Egypt by establishing a British Protectorate in that country in 1914. "The anomalous and utterly irregular situation in Egypt," wrote Mr. Weigall, "was at last brought to an end on December 18, 1914 by a proclamation which stated that 'the suzerainty of Turkey over Egypt is terminated,' and that 'Egypt is placed under the Protection of His Majesty and will henceforth constitute a British Protectorate' . . ."

On the next day the British issued another proclamation stating that His Majesty's Government had deposed the Turkish Khedive of Egypt and replaced him with Prince Hussein Pasha, oldest living prince of the family of Mohammed Ali (who, during his lifetime, had worked diligently for Egypt's welfare) and had bestowed upon Hussein the title of Sultan of Egypt. This seemed to meet the general approval of the Egyptian people. When the British set up an official Protectorate over Egypt in 1914, Sir Henry McMahon, late Foreign Secretary to the Government of India, was sent to Egypt to replace Lord Kitchener and the office title there was changed to High Commissioner.

ARAB IMPORTANCE TO THE BRITISH

It is clear that Britain's situation in the war was precarious. It was tremendously important that she counter the Turkish peril by in some way securing the loyalty and military cooperation of the Arabs. It was to this end in 1915 that the new High Commissioner of Egypt, Sir Henry McMahon, entered into communications with Sherif Hussein of Mecca, whose religious and political leadership at the time made him a foremost spokesman for the Arab peoples. It was after World War I that Hejaz was made a Kingdom and Hussein became its King.

The communications concerning the Arab posture had been started in August of 1914 between the Sherif and Lord Kitchener and now, under urgent circumstances, were resumed by Sir Henry McMahon in the interests of British security. Out of these negotiations, plainly expressed in a series of letters, the British agreed to the demands by Hussein for Arab post-war independence in return for Arab participation in the war effort to drive the Turks from the Middle East. The Arabs, in good faith, fulfilled their part of the agreement by carrying out the famous "revolt in the desert" of which the immortalized Lawrence of Arabia was a leader.

A little later, and without Arab sanction or even knowledge, a different British government (that of Lloyd George and Lord Balfour), in order to appease the Zionist-Jews who had maneuvered their way into the good graces of that particular (and very temporary) coalition government, issued the Balfour Declaration which meant the virtual giving of Palestine to the Zionists.

Here we have the key to the trouble that has followed between the Arabs and the Jews.

APPENDIX "B"

WHO ARE THE JEWS?

Presented here is a short sketch of the people first known as Hebrews — later as Israelites — and still later as Jews — as they appear
in history. The purpose is to establish what may be called a group
identity (or status) of a people who figure prominently, along with
the Arabs and others, in the subject matter of this book.

*　　*　　*

PATRIARCHAL PERIOD OF THE HEBREWS

The beginning history of the ancient Hebrews, of which the present
day Jews are the ostensible offspring, is largely lost in the historical
mists of the ages. Numerous Jewish and some non-Jewish writers have
taken turns at trying to unwrap and explain this ethnological enigma,
but due to time and circumstances all must lean heavily upon misty
tradition and inspired imagination. All writers in this field must depend upon the same general source materials: (1) the Old Testament
as it has come down through the hands of countless scribes, redactors
and others; (2) the Talmudic writings of early rabbis with their tedious
disquisitions and conjectures; (3) a limited number of early Jewish
authors such as Josephus and Philo; and (4) a certain amount of supporting archaeological findings. In this discussion, dependence will
center on the same background sources plus certain help from considerable personal research during various trips throughout the Middle
East.

OPINION OF ONE
OUTSTANDING SCHOLAR

"Like the Babylonians and Phoenicians," wrote the late Rabbi Lewis
Browne in his fascinating book "This Believing World" (Macmillan
Company), "the Hebrews were Semites, for their cradle-land was that
vast wilderness we call the Arabian desert." "Thirty-five hundred years
ago," he writes, "the Hebrews were but half-savage tribesmen who
lived off the bedraggled flocks and herds which they drove from one
oasis to another." Their religion, he explains, "like the religion of all
other primitive peoples, was a barbaric animism. They imagined that
all objects around them were possessed of terrible spirits and their worship was no more than a dark magic-mongering."

From the description given by Rabbi Browne and also by other
writers and historians, it appears that the early Hebrews were not too
dissimilar from other primitive people who sprang from that tumultuous spawning ground of early heterogeneous humanity which we
now call the Middle East. Tribal movements seemed to flow out of the
great Arabian desert area toward the more fertile lands that bordered
the long winding Euphrates and Tigris rivers where life was, perhaps,
a little better. Mixed in with these emerging hordes — from some-

358

where — there came an ethnic grouping which at some unknown time became known as "Hebrews" — a word meaning "from over the river." In any library may be found volumes on this general subject but here is space only for essential highlights.

BACKGROUND SOURCES OF AUTHORITY

The history of the Hebrew people, for all practical purposes, starts with the Biblical account of Abraham in its rather fragmented and somewhat fanciful story of this Patriarch's migration from the ancient city of "Ur of the Chaldees" via Haran (Charran) in Mesopotamia and thence via Damascus down into Canaan — "land of the Philistines" from whom the later name of Palestine came.

The "Ur of the Chaldees," as translated in the Bible, was unknown as to location down through the many centuries of history until archaeological excavations about one-hundred years ago helped identify the site beyond reasonable dispute. It is near the Euphrates river in what is now Iraq, about one-hundred and fifty miles from where that river empties into the Persian Gulf.

Dr. Paul Goodman, in his "History of the Jews" (World Publishing Company), places the date of the Abraham migration at about 2,000 B.C. Other authorities give later dates. Norman Bentwich, than whom there is no more devoted Jewish scholar, in his book "The Jews of Our Time" (Pelican), gives the time as about 1800 B.C., while the noted Jewish historian, Professor H. Graetz, in his multi-volume "History of the Jews", dates the Abraham period at about 1500 B.C. All dates, of course, are largely speculative, as are some other parts of the legend.

Ur was presumably the capital of the Sumerian (not Samarian) Empire with an estimated population of 250,000. About 1900 A.D. a Sumerian stele was discovered at Nippur, another Sumerian town, which described the reduction of Ur by attacking Elamite hordes as an "all invading destruction" wherein the city walls were razed, the city burned and the ground left covered with slain bodies. Among those who may have escaped this catastrophe was an Aramean Semite named Terah, who made his way with his family (one of his sons being the storied Abraham, then called Abram) far back up the Euphrates river to a place called Haran.

The background for the story of Abraham's migration is Chapters 11 and 12 of the book of Genesis, but the record is not too clear. It was put into writing over a thousand years after the events are presumed to have happened and even with our advanced civilization, we of today know how difficult it would be to write about things that happened that long ago — remembering also that for most of that time no records, as we know them, were kept.

ABRAHAM AND RELATIVES

Terah had three sons — Abram, Nahor and Haran. Haran died before the family left the Ur region, leaving a son named Lot. We are told that Terah took Abram and his wife Sarai (later called Sarah)

359

with Lot and his wife and started for a land of which they had heard, called Canaan. En route they sojourned at the town called Haran.

NOTE: A British friend who, some forty years ago, patrolled the north-Syrian border, tells us that Haran (spelled Harran in some atlases) is a small, primitive town just inside Turkey from that border — cold in winter but could have provided grazing in summer for Abraham's flocks. Apparently he did not tarry long there. Our British authority reminds us that this was the general site of the bloody battle of Carrhae where in 53 B.C. the Roman general Crassus was badly defeated by the Parthians who slaughtered 20,000 Roman soldiers and carried 10,000 more away for slavery in Persia.

It was at Haran that Terah died. According to the Old Testament writers, he was a polytheist — a believer in many gods or idols. It was apparently about this time that Abram began having visionary visitations with the Lord who, in turn, began making promises to Abram in the form of covenants which assured him he would become a great "nation" and guaranteed him certain land that would be for him and his seed forever.

No reason was given by these ancient scribes as to why this then unprominent nomadic man was singled out from the multitude of humanity for this singular distinction. A possible explanation is that it served to introduce the priestly theme. Outside of this somewhat visionary relationship with deity, Abraham is also mentioned by these early writers as "a prophet" when they are extricating him from an indelicate predicament involving Sarah and a man named Abimelech (Genesis 20) — an episode that is strangely included in Holy Writ. His further anointed and Judaical status is indicated in the Standard Jewish Encyclopedia when it states that "Abraham . . . is pictured as sitting at the gates of Hell not allowing any circumcised Jew to be brought there."

Abraham, at the age of 75, after the death of his father (Terah) at Haran, accompanied by his wife Sarah and nephew Lot with his wife, departed from that place with a few followers as Abraham had apparently become something of an itinerant preacher. The group traveled on, passing through Damascus and sojourning a bit at a place called Shechem — a site now known as Nablus. Here again we are told that the Lord promised Abraham — "Unto thy seed will I give this land." This is important to remember in the matter of Palestine as Abraham later had two sons who went separate ways — Isaac to be regarded as a patriarch of the Hebrew Semites — and Ishmael, claimed by some to have been a progenitor of the Arabic lineage.

A STRANGE EPISODE

Regardless of this promise, Abraham found the land around Shechem to be well populated with Canaanites, and he moved on to a place called Bethel, about thirty miles north of what later became Jerusalem. After a short stay there he moved on in Canaan where he found "a famine in the land." He wasted no time there but hurried on into Egypt where food and riches were more abundant. When the entourage reached Egypt, Abraham involved his wife Sarah in an episode with the Pharaoh which is difficult to equate with the righteous posture later given him. (See chapter 5, page 84).

After the strange affair had been ended by the Pharaoh inviting them to leave Egypt (Lot and his wife also leaving), they all entered Canaan with their cattle and sheep where strife arose between their herdsmen. Lot moved his flocks and herds to the Jordan plain while Abraham moved on from Bethel south to Hebron. The next we hear of Lot he is in trouble in the wicked cities of Sodom and Gomorrah where his wife was turned into a pillar of salt. Lot then went to dwell in the mountains with his two daughters where an incredible involvement with them is reported in Genesis 19: 31-36.

There must have been many other Hebrews among the wide range of Semitic peoples who were pitching their tents and pushing about in the wide expanse of that part of the Middle East. But those who wrote the Old Testament, having in mind mainly the projecting of a religious legend which would serve as a compelling force of fear and persuasion to perpetuate a theocratic philosophy of Hebrew nationalism, chose to build their narration around Abraham as their chief progenitor — and particularly his "seed." One problem is that the reporting about Abraham is spotty, disconnected — sometimes inelegant and often abstruse.

Here we are discussing Abraham mainly in the significant posture which the Old Testament writers gave him as the first Patriarch and progenitor of the Hebrew people. The Bible narrative has numerous references where Abraham talked with the Lord (perhaps as some of our religious leaders do today) and in these conversations between deity and man the Lord made certain "land covenants" with Abraham. This phase of Abraham's status and the nature of the covenants was examined in chapter five titled "Do the Biblical Covenants Give Palestine to the Zionists?"

In the "land covenants" with Abraham, the Lord, it seems, puts most of the stress upon these promised possessions being "for Abraham's seed" — and yet in Genesis (16) it appears that for a long time there was some question about Abraham having any seed. Up to the age of 86 Abraham's wife Sarah had born him no children. Knowing that Abraham was disappointed she generously suggested that he "go unto her maid." To this suggestion, it appears that Abraham harkened and in due time Hagar, the Egyptian handmaid, conceived and was with child.

Soon, the Bible story goes, Sarah regretted her generosity to Abraham and began to treat the pregnant maid badly. Hagar fled for safety but an Angel of the Lord caught up with her in the desert and counseled her to return, promising that "her seed" would multiply exceedingly. Hagar, accordingly, returned and gave birth to Abraham's first child — a boy who was called Ishmael.

361

BOTHERSOME QUESTIONS

Because of its Old Testament textual proximity, it seems important to interject here a reference to another of the "land covenants" given by the Lord to Abraham as reported by the Old Testament writers some ten centuries after the time. This covenant included a pedigree-symbol qualification involving a priestly ritualistic imperative which was stated thusly: "This is my covenant, which ye shall keep, between me and you and thy seed after thee; Every man child among you shall be circumcised" (Genesis 17:10). There are those who question the source of this "command" — and point to the questions it would raise. They ask its meaning if not intended as an effort to set people apart by marking some as "chosen" and some as not. Where would this leave the vast majority of uncircumcised males in the world who also worship the Lord?

When Abraham was 99 and Ishmael was 13 they were both circumcised — but just how this was known to the writers a thousand years later is not explained. It is stated that at such time the Lord appeared with more covenanting whereby he further instructed that from then on Abram was to be known as Abraham and Sarai was to be Sarah. No reason for this seemingly meaningless change was given. The Lord further informed them that they — Abraham then 99 and Sarah 90 — would be blest with a child. The Lord showed great interest in naming Abraham's two sons — the first one by the bondswoman was to be called Ishmael — and the second one by 90 year old Sarah to be named Isaac.

As time moved on, for Sarah, the sight and presence of Hagar and her child became so annoying and distasteful, that she ordered Abraham to get rid of them. "Grievously," but with strange regard for his moral responsibility, Abraham provided Hagar with bread and a bottle of water and sent her with the child off into the desolate desert waste. The Lord, seeing Abraham's grief, assured him that — "In Isaac shall thy seed be called. And also of the son of the bondswoman (Hagar) will I make a nation, because he is thy seed."

THE BLOOD STREAM DIVIDES

Although Hebrew tradition traces Jewish genealogy down through the Isaac "line," we find in the Old Testament (Genesis 21:13) that both sons are considered by the Lord as "the seed" of Abraham — and thus it appears that the "seed" from Abraham's blood has for some 3,000 years been flowing in divergent directions. One might think that this would be something of a problem for the present-day Zionists — but apparently not.

NOTE: As a matter of satisfying curiosity concerning the fate of Hagar and her son Ishmael (who was probably then around 14) after they had been set adrift by Abraham in the desert "wilderness" with only "bread and a bottle of water" — the Old Testament writers haven't much to say. Hagar wandered a considerable distance in the direction of Beersheba, which is at the edge of the Negev. Their food and drink were gone. She put her son under the edge of shrubs that "she not see the death of the child." As she wept God "heard her voice" and an angel appeared.

With a promise again to make of the boy "a great nation," she was told to open her eyes and there before her was a well of water from which she filled the bottle and gave the boy a drink.

The boy grew up, we are told, became an archer (hunter) and dwelt in the wilderness of Paran where his mother secured for him a wife from her native Egypt. From this point (Genesis 21:21) Hagar is mentioned no more. The very next paragraph (in the middle of a chapter) shifts abruptly to another subject, as often happens in the Old Testament — showing, perhaps, a putting together by many hands. Ishmael is mentioned again only briefly as having died at the age of 137. His twelve sons are mentioned as "the generation of Ishmael."

Since it is the line of the Old Testament writers that the Abrahamic bloodstream must flow only through his son Isaac, this examination will dutifully proceed with "Who Are the Jews?" along that genealogical course.

When he was 40, Isaac took Rebekah as his wife. She was "the daughter of Bethuel the Syrian cf Padan-aram, the sister of Laban the Syrian." This Biblical emphasis cn the word "Syrian" may or may not have a special meaning.

STRIFE MARS BROTHERHOOD

When Isaac was 60, after pleading with the Lord for an heir, Rebekah gave birth to twin boys — Esau and Jacob. While she was pregnant the Lord told her "Two nations are in thy womb, and two manner of peoples shall be separated from thy bowels . . ." (Genesis 25:23). A "two child" problem here — even as with Abraham and Sarah. Isaac was devoted to Esau while Rebekah was partial to Jacob. Esau was born first and therefore became the rightful heir to the traditional parental "birthright" which Jacob very much coveted. In their adulthood Esau became ill and was about to die for want of food. He begged Jacob for pottage but Jacob demanded his brother's "birthright" before giving him food to save his life. Esau, fearful of dying, yielded.

This caused much trouble later between the two brothers but before the Old Testament writers say more about it, they abruptly introduce (with complete irrelevance) a strange Isaac-Rebekah episode similar to the two Abraham-Sarah escapades already mentioned. Even the wording in both cases is similar. Isaac and Rebekah travel to another place to escape a famine where (like Abraham did with Sarah) Isaac passes Rebekah off as his sister when "the men of the place ask him of his wife."

After Isaac and Rebekah had been sojourning for some time with the Philistines the king (Abimelech, who had previously had an experience with Abraham and Sarah) discovered the "sister" deception and demanded an explanation frcm Isaac: "What is this thou has done unto us?" Then Abimelech admonished his people not to "touch this man or his wife." The report shows that when Isaac finally left the place of his sojourn he "had possession of flocks, and of herds, and great store of servants and the Philistines envied him."

When Isaac grew old and nearly blind he asked Esau to go fetch him some venison "and make me savory meat such as I love." Rebekah, hearing this, called her favorite son Jacob and together they worked out a deception to trick Isaac into giving Jacob "his blessing" (which he had intended to give Esau)—the purpose being to validate the birthright transfer which had already been extracted from Esau under duress. The nature of this fraud can be read in Genesis (27). No further details are needed here.

Since the record of the three early Hebrew patriarchs is basic to Jewish history and since further the only record of the patriarchs is what has been given us by the Old Testament writers, it is important to include what may be called the moral substance of the legend. Emphasis is continuously placed upon the close relationship, through dialogue and covenanting, between the Lord and the patriarchs. Their trials and wrong-doings were apparently softened by the intimate counsel and help of the Lord and his angels.

*　　　*　　　*

Jacob, being the third and most important of the patriarchs as he produced the twelve sons who became progenitors of the twelve tribes, it appears important to pursue briefly the embroilment between Jacob and Esau, the twin brothers (sons of Isaac and Rebekah).

The bitterness between the two brothers continued with Esau threatening to kill Jacob for the wrong he had done in fraudulently appropriating his birthright. Rebekah, fearing for her choice son Jacob, sent him away to her brother Laban. There Jacob fell in love with Laban's daughter Rachel, and to have her for his wife he agreed to work seven years for Laban.

INFANT BEGINNINGS OF THE 12 TRIBES

At the end of seven years Jacob demanded his prize. Laban arranged a feast to celebrate the occasion and after an evening of feasting, Laban sent Jacob in "unto her." The abode (tent or whatever) was apparently dark and Jacob did not until morning discover the deception that he had been given Leah instead of Rachel. Upon discovery he demanded an explanation from Laban. He wanted Rachel, the younger and prettier of the two sisters—the one he had been promised. Laban excused the fraud by explaining that it was local custom for the older girls to be married off first. But, said clever Laban, if Jacob would serve him another seven years he could have Rachel also. Jacob consented and seven years later he was given Rachel. She, however, was barren while Leah was fruitful and bore four sons—Reuben, Simeon, Levi and Judah.

Rachel, yearning for a child but seemingly unable to bear one, suggested that Jacob go unto her handmaid, Bilhah, that she (Rachel) might in this way have a child. Jacob dutifully followed her advice and the handmaid bore a son who was called Dan. Then the hand-maiden bore another son who was named Naphtali. When Leah realized she had quit bearing she took her maid (Zilpah) unto Jacob and she in turn bore him a son called Gad. Later this same maid bore Jacob another son and he was named Asher.

In Genesis (30) we may read that Leah chided Rachel over Jacob's attentions and Rachel promised Leah that he could be with her that night. Out of this meeting Leah bore Jacob another son and he was named Zebulun. Then "God remembered Rachel" and she bore a son who was called Joseph. Still later, after Jacob had taken his family to other parts, Rachel gave birth to another son, herself dying in the ordeal. Jacob named this son Benjamin.

It was on this trip, while Jacob was moving his family, that he met a mysterious personage at the brook Jabbok (east of the Jordan) with whom he wrestled all night; and in the morning when neither had won, the mystery opponent (called an angel) blest Jacob and told him that he should "be called no more Jacob, but Israel" (Genesis 32:28). But three chapters later (35) under completely different circumstances "God appeared unto Jacob" and said—"Thy name shall not be called any more Jacob, but Israel shall be thy name." No reason is given for this name change.

This man, still mainly called Jacob by the Bible writers, with his sons settled in Canaan where the boys tended his flocks. The brothers, older than Joseph (born of three different women) were jealous of the younger Joseph because his father "loved him more than all his brethren"—and they hated him the more when he told them of his dreams that reflected his superiority. They schemed to be rid of him and one day when he joined them attending the flocks, they plotted to kill him but Reuben objected and they compromised by selling him to a passing caravan which took him on to Egypt and sold him as a servant into Pharaoh's household.

JACOB AND SONS ABANDON CANAAN—SETTLE IN EGYPT

There in Egypt, the account goes, Joseph grew up and because of his intelligence (when he was 30) the Pharaoh made him his chief administrator of all Egypt. Some time after that, there was again a famine in Canaan and Jacob sent his sons to Egypt to obtain grain. When they met Joseph he perceived that they were his brothers and invited them to bring their father and all the family to sojourn in Egypt. This they did and later Jacob, the father, died there.

From this simplified story of the Hebrew patriarchs—as the storied progenitors of the Hebrew people—comes the legend of how the numerous progeny of the twelve sons of Jacob (the third member of the patriarchs, now named "Israel") multiplied over the years that they sojourned in Egypt. This multiplicity of offspring who, according to the account, were later led out of Egypt by Moses (born as one of them) on a 40-year trek through Sinai and other desert wastes toward a purposeful invasion of Palestine, were known as "Israelites."

It was during this strangely long journey over what, straightened out, should have been a comparatively short distance (300 miles or so) that the Israelites became divided into "tribes"—each named for one of the sons of Jacob—except for Joseph who had died in Egypt. His two sons, Ephraim and Manasseh were included as tribal leaders.

At this point, the history of the Hebrews telescopes into the story of the Israelites—and attention from here on turns more to conquest—assaults—wars with neighbors, nationality ambitions, and internecine conflicts—than with previous emphasis on famines, covenants and patriarchal adventures.

THE ISRAELITE PERIOD

The story of the Israelites is, from here on until the invasion of Canaan, built around and about one central figure called Moses. It begins with his unconventional babyhood, as briefed in the following memorandum:

> The personality of Moses enters the ancient legend as a baby found among the bulrushes along the Nile, floating in a calked basket. According to the Bible writers, he had been placed there by his mother (one of the Hebrews in Egypt) in a strange gesture to elude the Pharaoh's order that all male-born Hebrew children should be killed. He was recovered from the river by the Pharaoh's daughter who had come to bathe in this happenstance spot, who then took the baby and reared him in Egyptian palace environment, until we next hear of him as a grown man. This is, by no means, the first historical story of this character. The Encyclopedia Britannica (and other books) relate the legend of Sargon I (some 1,600 years before Moses) who was set adrift in a similarly constructed ark as a baby among the bulrushes along the river Euphrates. He was rescued and reared by a peasant. Later his true source of omnipotence was revealed and (about 2000 B.C.) he became the king of an Akkadian semitic tribe, very early in the history of the Mesopotamian region.

When Moses became a man, he killed an Egyptian whom he saw flogging "a Hebrew, one of his brethern." Fearing for his life (although he was of the royal household), he fled across the Sinai desert to the land of Midian, where he married Zipporah, daughter of the Midian priest Jethro. Later, while attending Jethro's flocks, Moses had a remarkable encounter with a "burning bush" that did not burn, but out of which came the voice of God, commanding him to return to Egypt and lead the Hebrews there out of that country unto the land of Canaan (see Exodus 3, 4 ff. for colloquy between God and Moses on this).

NOTE: Midian, incidentally, was the name of one of the six sons born to Abraham and Keturah, after Sarah died. These sons of Abraham get only a listing of names — nothing else. They, obviously, did not fit into the pattern of the Old Testament as the writers were constructing it. Only Isaac appears to have served that purpose.

Under these most anomalous circumstances, Moses accepted the odd mission but encountered difficulties when he entered Egypt and was rebuffed by the Pharaoh who refused to grant permission for the Hebrews to leave that country. If Moses was reared from babyhood to adulthood in an Egyptian Pharach's house (by a Pharaoh's daughter), recogniticn of such is not indicated in his reported dealings with this Pharach. The legend states that the Lord had to send a series of terrible plagues upcn the Pharaoh before he would consent to let the Hebrews go with Moses (Exodus 7, 8, 9).

This rendition of the "Jews in Egypt" story, however, is contradicted by another version of the Pharaoh's attitude toward the Hebrews in the very same book of Exodus. This contrarious statement by the Bible writers indicated that the Pharaoh was afraid of the Hebrews and anxious to be rid of them. The Pharaoh is quoted as saying: "Behold, the people of the children of Israel are more and mightier than we: Come on, let us deal wisely with them; lest they multiply, and it ccme to pass, that, when there falleth out any war, they join also unto our enemies, and fight against us, and so get them up out of the land."

Since the Old Testament was written by countless numbers of unknown writers and redactors who gave no dates of events and left badly mixed sequences, as well as contradictions like the above in the record, all effort toward unraveling the age-old mysteries should be welcome. There are many who feel that involved here, in some way is a relationship with the story of the semitic Hyksos people who invaded and ruthlessly ruled Egypt for some three or four hundred years in this general area of time. The Pharaoh who "knew not Joseph" could, many believe, have been the true Egyptian Pharaoh who drove the usurper-Hyksos tribes back into the Sinai desert to free the long burdened Egyptian people from these tyrannous overlords. This question is certainly germane enough to justify further examination.

NOTE: The early Jewish historian, Josephus (ca. 37-95 A.D.), quotes the much earlier Egyptian historian, Manetho, who reported a conquest of Egypt by Asiatic semites whom Manetho called "the Shepherd kings." This invasion and conquest was apparently accomplished by some form of immigration or trickery, as Manetho said no battles were involved. These conquerors who held Egypt in cruel bondage for some 400 years, badly treating the Egyptian women and children, are known in history as the Hyksos people. Certain archaeological research indicates some kind of a relationship with the Hebrews.

In his book "Egpyt and Israel," the late Professor Flinders Petrie (foremost British archaeologist) describes a great earthen fortress near the Nile Delta, built and maintained by the Hyksos, who gained control of Egypt, probably in the 16th or 17th centuries (B.C.). Its interesting structure of walls, (40-50 feet high and 150-200 feet wide, built entirely of dirt), shows that these people (the Hyksos) knew nothing of stone or wood construction, and therefore must have come from the desert country. The Hyksos, on being evicted by a re-strengthened Egypt from its principal areas, took refuge in this fortress. The Egyptians, unable to penetrate its walls, finally allowed the Hyksos to retreat toward Sinai without attack.

A theory has steadily gained support among scholars that the Hyksos forcible occupation of Egypt for some 400 years is related with the entrance of the Jacob family into Egypt as well as the later Israelite exodus from that country under leadership of Moses. One of the great scholars on the Middle East, Dr. E. A. Wallis Budge, in an early book titled "Egypt," expresses the belief that while the Biblical Moses story is based upon some historical event, it—"has been embroidered so much by the later narratives" that the Biblical version which he thinks was written "not later than the time of Ezra . . . is incredible." He points to the highly doubtful conditions under which the Moses entourage left Egypt—the almost overnight mobilization of "600,000 men" and at least that many women and children for a long trek into a grainless, fruitless and foodless desert. "The people took their dough before it was leavened . . . neither had they prepared for themselves any victual." (Exodus 12:34, 39)

NOTE: Dr. William F. Albright, the celebrated Middle East authority, in his excellent Pelican book, "The Archaeology of Palestine," says: "The Middle Bronze Age corresponds to the Patriarchal Age of the Bible, though it is not yet possible to date the migration of Abraham from Mesopotamia or of Jacob into Egypt precisely." He also says that in his present opinion, the Abraham trek may be dated in the 20th or 19th centuries (B.C.) while the Hebrew migration into Egypt may have been in the 18th or more likely the 17th centuries.

The late Dr. H. R. Hall (former keeper of Egyptian and Assyrian Antiquities in the British Museum) in his great 500-page book, "The Ancient History of the Near East," says that Josephus "believed — and he may not have been far wrong — that the episode of the Hyksos conquest of Egypt and the expulsion thereafter was the real Exodus." "We need not identify absolutely Hyksos with Hebrew," says Dr. Hall. "We may perhaps regard the Hebrews as a small Semitic tribe which entered the land at the time of expulsion of their patrons, or shortly afterwards."

More positive on the subject is the well known Jewish scholar and lecturer, Max I. Dimont. In his book, "Jews, God and History," (Signet-New American Library), he says: "It was the Hyksos (usurper) Pharaoh who had invited the Jews and other peoples hard hit by the famine to settle in Egypt." He takes an assured position on this point and asserts that a century and a half later the Egyptians turned the tables on the Hyksos — enslaving both them and their Hebrew guests, which included the sons of Jacob — meaning by this the Israelites. Mr. Dimont says the Hebrews went "into Egypt by Joseph" in the 16th century and left under the leadership of Moses in the 12th century B.C. This is a period, he points out, of some 400 years on which the Old Testament is essentially silent with the exception of a few sentences. This is approximately the number of years that the Hyksos occupied Egypt as overlords and would seem to add strength to the suggested

Numerous scholarly references have been given here to help fill in and strengthen understanding, so much as possible, of a critical four or five hundred years of history (roughly from the dating of Jacob through the period of Moses) which was sadly neglected by the Old Testament writers as well as by the Pharaonic Egyptians, of whom we would expect some recorded reference to the "Jews in Egypt," either on stone or papyri.

NO RECORDS IN LAND OF EGYPT

The lack of Egyptian records may be because the Egyptians were, possibly most of that time, under a despotic alien clique that had, in some way, obtained key control of the operational machinery of the nation. This foreign junto (called Hyksos) probably had no interest in preserving records of their doings. As to the Old Testament authors, it seems clear they were writing more to a theme than to the objective recording of history. It should also be remembered that they were writing about characters and events of which they had no personal knowledge—legends even then covered with the dust of centuries.

Religious legends have a way of requiring time and practice to glorify them. Mostly they must be accepted on faith for, like the trail of a comet their sources fade into the great unknown. But this is no challenge to the true value of faith; on the contrary, it has a quality of giving vibrancy and strength to realistic belief. Judaism, with which this chapter deals, had a long formative record, and did not suddenly appear full-blown as a bolt from the sky; and neither did Christianity—nor Islam—nor any of the other great religions. The history of each has been one of tedious survival through a long period of martyrdom and travail.

To take an example, in our study here, of the long formative stages involved in the growth of religions, it may be pointed out that centuries passed after the time ascribed to Moses before anything that could be called formal Judaism emerged with sufficient strength to make even a feeble challenge to the paganism that flourished far and wide—among Israelites and all. In fact, the Moses story and the Old Testament Book of Kings show the ever recurring problem of idol worship among the Israelites from Sinai through to the end of their national existence.

Today we can hardly conceive of a religion that has no basic book (Bible). During the early days of the Hebrew religion (likewise Christianity) there were no books as we know them now—only scrolls. While Moses, the law-giver, is estimated to have lived sometime in the 12th or 13th centuries B.C., there seems to be no mention of the earlier use of "a book" than the Old Testament reference (II Kings 22:8) to the miraculous finding of "a book" during the reign of King Josiah of Israel (637-608 B.C.).

369

NOTE: When Josiah was eight years old, he succeeded his murdered father, King Amon. At adulthood he assumed the kingly powers of administration. Kings before him, including his father, seem to have been indifferent to the law of Moses, allowing heathenish worship of idols to become widespread in Judah — as Israel had already been destroyed by the Assyrians.

Josiah, more amenable to the priestly party, agreed to allow the priests to repair "the House of the Lord." During the repairs, the high priest (one Hilkiah) suddenly discovered what he called a "book of the law." This seems to be the first mention in the Old Testament of a "holy book" which, of course, would have been a scroll. This reference to a document is quite generally regarded as probably the nucleus of what much later appeared as "Deuteronomy" — one of the "five books of Moses" — otherwise known as the Pentateuch or Sefer Torah.

This finding of "a book" and its compelling effects are somewhat sequential to the experience related of Moses who brought the word of the law down from the mountain to quiet his "murmuring" followers. Years later, the "five books" were completed in scrolls — and many years later came the more expanded Old Testament with its history of "a people" and their religious pattern. Following this, over the long years came the vast proliferation of Talmudic literature — all of which stems from the venerated Mosaic code.

Hilkiah sent the "book" to King Josiah by his assistant Shaphan who told the King of the commandments in it and the awful punishment to be meted out to those who disobey. Josiah, thoroughly frightened, "rent his clothes" and hurriedly sent the document to Huldah, the prophetess, who further frightened him by affirming and emphasizing the commandments and threats. Now, filled with terror, Josiah went into action, ordering destruction of all the "high places," all heathen symbols and gods; and "made covenant with the Lord." (All the things he did to secure safety for himself and his people from punishment are stated in II Kings: 23.)

FOUNDATIONS OF OLD TESTAMENT

It seems important to examine all facets of the "Hebrews in Egypt" story, including their exit from Egypt as reported, for all of this together is the keystone of the Old Testament and its main theses. All important Old Testament events and doctrines (such as tradition and the Law) either lead to this central phenomenon—or flow from it. The summary reason for emphasis on this Biblical tradition and history here is that it is basic background, adopted by the Zionists as justification for their crusade of nationalism in this twentieth century—some 3,000 years after the events presumably happened.

Undoubtedly the most significant event of the Hebrew "Exodus" was the sojourn of the group at Mount Sinai. After a long and tiring trek across the hot and dreary sand and waste of Sinai, it was here that the cornerstone of the Old Testament was laid. Whether it was done by someone named Moses or by a later Priestly hierarchy does not matter—Judaism rests upon this tradition. It was here that the Law of Moses—which was and is the clear demarcation line between doctrinal Judaism and Christianity, between Mosaic Law and Christian gospel—was born.

As the Israelites approached the rugged and melancholy old Mount, dragging themselves through the dismal Wilderness of Sin—"the children of Israel murmured against Moses and Aaron, "and called out" . . . Would to God we had died by the hand of the Lord in the land of Egypt, when we sat by the flesh pots, and when we did eat bread to the full; for ye have brought us forth into this wilderness, to kill this whole assembly with hunger." According to the narrators, there was much lamenting and protesting. The Biblical account indicates that the Exodus was a troubled trip.

Upon reaching Mount Sinai, Mcses departed from his "murmuring" followers and went into the stormy mountain bleakness—where thunder and lightning prevailed. There, we are told, he met the Lord and apparently told him of the troubles he was having with his recalcitrant followers. The Lord then became angry with the Israelites and said to Moses: "How long shall I bear with this evil congregation, which murmurs against me?" The Lord then told Moses to "Say unto them . . . 'Your carcasses shall fall in this wilderness; and all that were numbered of you, from twenty years old and upward, which have murmured against me'."

WHAT LANGUAGE WAS USED?

It was during the experience at Mount Sinai that Moses is credited with bringing down from his encounter with God in the mountain the two stone tablets bearing the lettering that is popularly known as the "ten commandments" and known especially to Judaism as the basis of "the Law." When he emerged from the mountain, Moses was so angered at finding his followers worshipping the Golden Calf rather than the God he was introducing, that he wrathfully broke and destroyed the lettered stones.

NOTE: Throughout especially the first five books of the Old Testament, the reader is repeatedly confronted with puzzling questions which are difficult alike for student and scholar. Typical are the questions raised by the stone tablets containing the "Ten Words" that Moses brought down the mountain wilderness as the commandments of God. What kind of writing was on the stones? The artist-depictions usually show Hebrew characters. Exodus 31:18 tells us that they were written "with the fingers of God." But Exodus 34:28 indicates that Moses "wrote upon the tables the words of the covenant, the ten commandments." The language used on the stones is not described.

History's archives shed no light on Hebrew writing at the time of Moses— supposedly early 13th century B.C. — nor for hundreds of years thereafter. There were two main forms of writing in use at that time: (1) hieroglyphic "picture" writing of the Egyptians; and (2) cuneiform (wedge-shaped characters) used mainly by the various Semitic groupings, stretching from Mesopotamia through Syria and Palestine.

The writing of record closest to the time of Moses seems to be the Tell-el-Amarna clay tablets (some 200 of them), which were letters and reports to the Egyptian Pharaoh from his governors and underlings in the Palestine-Syria area. These were written in cuneiform. Moses, we are told, was raised from babyhood in Egyptian royal household culture, and it would seem that he would have been trained in hieroglyphic writing which was in use at least from 2700 to 700 B.C.

The Moabites, neighbors of Palestine, left a 9th century (B.C.) record of what is called the Moabite Stone, on which is inscribed a message of victory at freeing themselves from slavery under the Israelites — and on this a Canaanitish script is used. The first evidence of distinctive Hebrew language characters seems to be a few letters scratched on the ceiling walls of the Siloam tunnel, which was constructed (it appears) by Hezekiah, King of Judea, 720-682 B.C., to bring water inside the walled city of Jerusalem. Even if the letters were etched at the time the tunnel was built, that was some 600 years after Moses.

It was about this time that Aramaic became the lingua franca (general language) of much of the Middle East and persisted through the time of Jesus. It is still used in at least one small remote village (Malula) in Syria. The New Jewish Encyclopedia says that the Jews used a number of languages during their history, and their first major language was Aramaic and was the language for translating the Scriptures. The Standard Jewish Encyclopedia says that the "collection, arrangement and final redaction of the Biblical books" was accomplished in the Persian Period (6th century B.C.) by men of the Great Assembly (scholars and writers) between the last of the prophets and first of the rabbis — and while the ancient script of the early scrolls was Phoenician, they were later copied in the square Aramaic letters. This is all interesting in considering the colloquies between God and Moses in the wilderness of the Mount.

When Moses (always forbidding anyone to go with him) went back into the mountain to have the Lord replace the stone tablets he had in rage destroyed, the Exodus writers report: "He was there with the Lord forty days and forty nights . . . And he wrote upon the tablets the words of the covenant, the ten commandments." Moses returned to his people—called them together and talked with them— and "gave them in commandment all that the Lord hath commanded, that ye should do them." Moses then proceeded to outline many of the "laws" which he said he had been given by the Lord and which his followers were to obey as they followed him.

SOURCE OF MOSAIC LAW

The "ten words" on the stone tablets of Moses were later expanded into scrolls, which became "the Written Law" as represented by the first five books of the Old Testament, called the Pentateuch. From the "Written Law" there came gradually a massive accumulation of interpretations, known as the Oral Law. This interpretive process by the learned Rabbis down through the centuries became known as the Mishna—which is the core of the Jewish Oral Law.

This accumulation in turn became so massive and complicated as to need further commentary and interpretation of it by succeeding Rabbis, and this documentation is known as the Gemara. Together the Mishna and the Gemara mainly constitute the Talmud—although included in the Talmudic literature are such other contributions as the Midrash (finding new meanings in the scriptures); the Halakhah and the Haggadah (the first dealing with the legal and the second with the non-legal elements of Talmudic literature); and there are two or three other divisions included. All of this stems from the "ten words" as the basic source. Incidentally, there are two Talmuds—the Babylonian and the Palestinian. The first is generally considered as the more authoritative—and more used in Synagogues. Both Talmuds have a range of preparation and completion from the second to the sixth centuries A.D.

There is no purpose here to comment on the Talmudic literature other than to quote a descriptive paragraph from the "Introduction to the Talmud and Midrash" by the late Dr. Hermann L. Strack (Jewish Publication Society of America):

"There are few literary productions on which as contradictory judgments have been passed as on the Talmud. Among orthodox Jews the "holy Talmud' is spoken of in terms of the highest reverence." At this point a note is included, quoting Rabbi S. R. Hirsch as saying that the Talmud "is the sole spring from which Judaism has flowed, the ground upon which Judaism rests, and the soul of life which shapes and sustains Judaism." The Strack comment (after the Hirsch quote) continues: "In the mind of many Christians it (the Talmud) stands for a medley of absurd and coarse statements, as well as of hostile utterances against Christianity." This latter criticism would obtain only with very few Christians of today — for one reason because very few Christians have the time or interest to read these dull, prodigious volumes.

*　　*　　*

It is in no sense disrespectful—nor contrary to the record—to note the fact that the nascent idea of God that was developing in the Israelite period was quite different from the divine image we have today. Through the earliest ages of history, the primitive idea of worship was largely a rulership conception—a system that helped control the ignorant and sometimes rebellious masses. From the recorded circumstances in the Old Testament, it would seem that when Moses brought his "experience" with God down from the wilderness of the mountain, he was also laboring with a problem of rebellion. His people were "murmuring" loudly in discontent.

The God that Moses found in the mountain was not then regarded as a universal Deity—but was considered as the God of the Hebrew people exclusively. It was not monotheism as we now understand it that Moses introduced. It was a caste type of monolatry—a tribal God for a chosen people. This conception in the main continued for centuries—emerging into a wider degree of universality with the more enlightened prophets—and a still wider degree with the birth and growth of Christianity.

ALONG THE ISRAELITE TRAIL

An interesting incident during the long Israelite journey came from one of the strange unconventional colloquies between God and Moses in the darkness of the mountain when Moses was told in considerable detail how he must ask his people for gifts of gold and silver and jewels to help construct an ark and tabernacle in the wilderness

(Exodus 25 ff). The Israelites, according to the Old Testament, were now in flight from a lifetime of slavery, which raises the question as to how they came to possess valuables. We learned earlier that just as the Israelites were leaving Egypt in their hurried flight, they were told by Moses to borrow jewels and valuables from the Egyptians. Two questions arise here: (1) What did the term "borrow" mean? and (2) Why was it important to decorate a simple and temporary place of worship in the wilderness with "gold and silver and brass?"

THE 40 YEAR TREK

The Old Testament says it took the Israelites forty years to go from Egypt to Jericho (about 300 miles) but it reports on only about two of those years. A few highlights of the trip may here be mentioned. In the desert wilderness when the Israelites were crying out for food, Moses promised them the Lord would "rain food from heaven" and the next day they came upon balls of honey-like substance clinging to the grass, stones and twigs. This miracle of "manna from heaven" has been well explained by scientists as a secretion exuded by tamarisk bushes when they are pierced by a certain shell-backed insect which is found in Sinai. It is available there today.

During the Moses-Israelite sojourn at Mount Sinai and during the 40-day absence of Moses (in the mount), the restless Israelites, seemingly ever anxious to return to idol-worship, asked Moses' brother Aaron to "make us Gods . . . as for Moses . . . we wot not what has become of him" (Exodus 32). Aaron, seemingly not hard to persuade, asked the women for their earrings and jewels and out of these he molded a "golden calf" before which the people offered sacrifices and made merry.

God, in some way, learning of this, became wrathful—called the Israelites a "stiff-necked people" (Exodus 32:9) and ordered Moses to ". . . let me alone, that my wrath may wax hot against them and that I may consume them; and I will make of thee a great nation." The God of Moses here is pictured by the writers as a wrathful God— with uncontrollable temper. This seems to strike a discordant note with the now generally accepted conception that God is master of all things—that God is love.

Moses, however, undaunted in the presence of the Deity, took God to task for his wrath, and—"The Lord repented of the evil which he thought to do unto his people." Then Moses went down from the mountain and waxed wrathful himself at finding his people worshipping the golden calf—becoming so angry that he utterly destroyed the commandment stones which the Lord had given him. One gets the impression at this point (in Exodus) that the Lord in the mountain was tiring of the bothersome Israelite problem and he instructed Moses to get these people on to the land he had promised to Abraham, Isaac and Jacob.

The Lord, in giving this order to Moses to proceed with his entourage on to Canaan, promised that he would "send an angel before

374

thee; and I will drive out the Canaanite, the Amorite, the Hittite, the Perizzite, the Hivite, and the Jebusite" (Exodus 33:1-2). As the Israelite story develops, we learn this did not happen. Moses sent spies to try to find a weak spot where he could enter "the promised land," but the spies reported back (after 40 days) that the present inhabitants were too big and fierce to be easily subdued. Finally, at the end of the 40-year journey from Egypt, the Israelites (then under Joshua) did enter Canaan, crossing the Jordan near Jericho; but it required many more years of fighting and turmoil to make any material progress toward conquest. The Lord's promise to drive out the Canaanites and the other native tribes was obviously not fulfilled—nor was the long, hard, trouble-filled journey mystically aided in any way.

NOTE: The number "forty" (as the 40-year journey of the Israelites) is a numeral repeated over and over in the Old Testament. 40 days of rain for the Flood; after 40 days Noah opened the window of the Ark; Moses was 40 days in the mountain with Yahweh, the Hebrew God; Nimrod was 40; the Philistines dominated the Israelites for 40 years; 40 days required for embalming Jacob; and many other examples. It is generally accepted by scholars that "40" was used by ancient Biblical writers when the correct number was indefinite or unknown.

SAD FATE OF MOSES

The unknown writers of the Old Testament were versatile with promises and tragedies. One that touches the heartstrings is the sad terminal fate of Moses. After the burdensome ordeal of leading the querulous Israelites for "forty years" through the most arduous experiences until they were at the very edge of Canaan, Moses is told by the Lord—"Because ye trespassed against me among the children of Israel at the waters of Meribah-Kadesh, in the wilderness of Zin; because ye sanctified me not in the midst of the children of Israel . . . thou shalt see the land before thee; but thou shalt not go thither into the land which I gave to the children of Israel."

"And the Lord spake unto Moses that selfsame day, saying, Get thee up into this mountain Abarim, unto Mount Nebo . . . and behold the land of Canaan . . . and die in the mount whither thou goest up . . ." (Deuteronomy 32:49).

The cause of this repudiation of Moses by God is extremely vague. It appears to have been caused by an incident along the exodus-route where the Israelites became desperate for water and berated Moses for bringing them from their homes in Egypt — "to die to thirst." Moses appealed to the Lord, who told him to smite a certain rock with his stick, and water would flow from it—and the writers say this did happen. Moses called the place Messa and Meribah, because it was where the Israelites had chided—and doubted, by asking "Is the Lord with us, or not?" At this point the Old Testament makes one of its curious sudden switches to another subject; but the inference is left that the Lord became irritated with Moses because he did not proclaim God's presence to the Israelites and explain that they were indebted to the Lord for the water they had received. This may be the lesson the Old Testament writers were trying to convey to emphasize the priestly design.

This seems tragically strange when the Lord, at the time of his urging and commanding Moses to lead the Israelites out of Egypt, reportedly said unto him: "And I will bring you in unto the land, concerning the which I did swear to give it to Abraham, to Isaac, and to Jacob; and I will give it you for an heritage: I am the Lord" (Exodus 6:8).

The early unknown Hebrew writers who put the Hebrew-Jewish story together in the Old Testament tell us that after Moses died— and when the Israelites had reached a convenient place to cross the Jordan river about ten miles east of Jericho and about the same distance north of the Dead Sea—the command of the Exodus movement (consisting of the twelve tribes) was taken over by Joshua who, except for Caleb, seems to have been the only survivor left of the original Israelite exodus from Egypt.

The first order of business here was to plan and prepare an attack on Jericho as the entrance town to Canaan, the country the Israelites had come to take. The invasion was thus begun with the massacre of the citizenry of Jericho. With that in mind, an interesting experience today is to walk amidst the excavation work that has been done by archaeologists at that ancient and storied site—with a modern town building up at its edge.

THE LORD AND JOSHUA
AT JERICHO AND AI

According to the Old Testament scriptures, the Lord gave Joshua detailed instructions as to how to surround the town and take it (Joshua 6:1-6). When the people of Jericho had been surprised and confused by the Israelite-priests blowing their horns, Joshua's "30,000 men" rushed in and took possession. "And they utterly destroyed all that was in the city, both men and women, young and old, and ox, and sheep, and ass, with the edge of the sword" (Joshua 6:21). So began the Israelites' conquest.

The only persons spared, by Joshua's special order, were the harlot (Rehab), and her father and mother, who had sheltered Joshua's spies. Joshua had instructed his men that "all the silver and gold and jewels of brass and iron" should be collected and turned "into the treasury of the Lord." Some of the Israelites concealed the valuables they collected instead of turning them into "the treasury of the Lord." Joshua discovered this and righteously made them disgorge.

In Joshua (6:20) we are told that when the trumpets blew and the Israelites loudly shouted, the walls of Jericho "fell down flat." This is apparently another metaphorical spectacular. The famous archaeologist, W. F. Albright, in his scholarly book "The Archaeology of Palestine," says that the Jericho wall was destroyed in the early Bronze

376

age—long before the Joshua assault. Many old legends "fall" when archaeologist "dig."

After Jericho, the next Canaanite town to suffer a similar fate was Ai—not far distant. The first men sent against Ai failed to smite the people of the town. "The Lord said unto Joshua, Fear not; take all the people of war with thee . . . and thou shalt do to Ai and her king as thou didst unto Jericho and her king; only the spoil thereof, and the cattle thereof, shall ye take for a prey unto yourselves" (Joshua 8:2).

Joshua then sent "30,000 men"—"And it came to pass, when Israel had made an end of slaying all the inhabitants of Ai in the fields, in the wilderness, wherein they chased them, and when they were all fallen on the edge of the sword until they were consumed . . . Joshua drew not his hand back . . . until he had utterly destroyed all the inhabitants of Ai . . . only the cattle and the spoil of that city Israel took for the prey themselves, according unto the word of the Lord . . . and the king of Ai he hanged on a tree until eventide . . ." (Joshua 8:24-29). Some 12,000 were killed. All of which is quoted in an historical sense as to the nature of the opening offense by the Israelites to evict and take Canaan for themselves as reported and sanctified by the Old Testament writers. And after the destruction of Ai and its people, "Joshua built an altar to the Lord God of Israel in Mount Ebal."

Prior to the Israelite invasion, Palestine had been inhabited and divided into several small nation-states (or city-states) including the Canaanites, the Hittites, the Hivites, Jebusites, Amorites and a few of lesser importance. When the Israelites (composed of twelve tribes named for the sons of Jacob) arrived in Eastern Palestine, a first division of land was made east of the Jordan—but it required years of fighting and conquest before the land was finally divided among the twelve so-called tribes. These tribal land possessions functioned governmentally as a loose federation which, from the time of Joshua to Saul, was ruled by a system of Judges—men selected because their qualifications met the needs of the times.

The unorganized Canaanites and other "nationality groups" in the land did not constitute serious opposition for the Israelite tribes but it was a different matter when the fighting Philistines (who had come from such rough places as the hills of Crete) confronted the tribes. The Philistines had much better armament and proved to be superior in battle against the Israelites. This increasing danger—as well as other inadequacies of the system of Judges—caused the "Children of Israel" to demand a monarchal ruler.

ISRAELITES TRY TO BE A NATION

The Israelite elders went to Samuel (the last of the Judges and who was growing old) and asked him to "make us a king to judge us like all the nations." Samuel selected Saul as the first "king of Israel" but soon regretted his choice. Saul insisted on being a king in his own right rather than a puppet of Samuel. In retribution Samuel anointed a young man named David to succeed Saul. After David had married Saul's daughter and had killed the Philistine giant Goliath with slingshot strategy (making him more popular than the king), Saul grew both angry and jealous and by attempting David's life caused the young man to flee for safety.

Although Saul tried to convert the tribal federation into "a nation," he made but little progress, being bothered on the one hand with intertribal problems and on the other with harassment from the powerful Philistines and other border groups. It was after a heavy battle with the Philistines, where the Israelites suffered a crushing defeat, that Saul in despair killed himself.

David, who had been hiding from Saul's wrath in enemy country, heard of the king's death and returned to Hebron where, with a little formality, he became king of Judah, which was the southern part of loosely organized Israel. A little later—after Saul's successor-son was murdered—David was able to get consent of the tribes outside Judah to make him king of the "new nation" (Israel) which had been started under Saul. With his youthful vigor and better military strategy, David began to lead successful attacks against the Philistines (the most powerful of Israel's enemies) which enabled him gradually to widen the new nation's territory—increasing its size some ten-fold over what it had been under Saul.

To David can go the main credit for converting the twelve tribes and their land divisions into the ancient state of Israel—and giving it a momentum of development that blazoned as a bright light for a few years and flared out at the end of his son Solomon's reign. One possible factor in his success against the Philistines was that in winning some early battles, David may have captured the Philistine's secret for molding iron into tools and war implements— a monopoly the more advanced Philistines had zealously guarded from the Israelites.

While David continued his residence for the time at Hebron, there were tribal reasons why that was not the best place for a capital of the whole of Israel. Incidentally, there does not seem to have been an established capital under Saul unless it was at Gilgal or his fortress at Gilbeah. To avoid jealousy and tension among the tribes David took note of a better site not far away—a village called Jebus, regarded as the capital of the Jebusites, a small Canaanite community. He decided he would take and remake this into his capital for Israel.

JEBUS BECOMES JERUSALEM

The Jebusites resisted valiantly—and although they put their maimed and blind into the front as psychological defense, they were quickly overpowered by the greater strength of David's forces. The village of Jebus became later known as Jerusalem but the time of the name change is not clear in the Old Testament. It was here that

David built a palace, having to bring craftsmen and materials from outside Israel (from Tyre).

It was in this palace that David's scandalous affair with Bath-sheba occurred. While walking on the roof of his house, he sighted nearby a beautiful woman washing herself. He made inquiry and found she was the wife of one of his ablest soldiers—Uriah. Then— "David sent messengers and took her; and she came in unto him, and he lay with her" (II Samuel 11:4). Later she told David— "I am with child." The child when born was named Solomon who later, through the dexterous strategy of his mother, succeeded the aged and dying David as king.

As we have already been told (Chapter 5) it was because the David-image served so well the nationality-ideology of Israelism that the Old Testament writers—despite the questionable moral standards of his personal life — practically deified and established him firmly as the great Hebrew religious symbol from whose blood or hereditary stream, later worshippers decided, "the Messiah" must come. He reigned in the era of 1000 B.C.

David had several sons by different women (II Samuel 5:13 ff). "And David took him more concubines and wives out of Jerusalem, after he was come from Hebron . . ." Of his many children only three sons stand out as unusual. One was Amnon, who "forced his sister" (II Samuel 13:11, 14). The second was Absalom, who formed a conspiracy against his father. The third was Solomon (born of Bath-sheba), who succeeded his father as king.

SOLOMON—LAST KING OF UNITED ISRAEL

Of Solomon's reign it could be said that on the one hand he dramatized and glorified the nation—and on the other, by his social policies and extravagance, he engendered schisms that paved the way toward disaster. It is true, by the records, that schisms between north and south existed prior to Solomon, and in fact there is evidence that the northern and southern sections (Judah and Samaria) never were without schism—theological and otherwise.

Under David the powerful Philistines had finally been well reduced, and as Solomon came to rule there was no sign of immediate difficulty with any of the larger nations (Egypt, Assyria, et al.), as most of them had been temporarily exhausted from the strains of war and other problems. The comparatively new state of Israel, with Solomon on the throne, was facing an unusual outlook for peace and prosperity.

This remarkable period of relative quiet gave Solomon a free hand from politics to glamorize his country with a building and spending program that pleased the Judeans (because most of the activity was centered around Jerusalem where he was building a magnificent temple complex)—but it was quite displeasing to the northern Samarian sector. It was the old story—as of ancient Greece and Rome and some of our modern nations—where the disease of spending for the grandiose State inevitably leads to the tax burdens, political dissensions and social disturbances which too often ends in national disintegration.

The idea of a Temple to house the ark (recovered from the Philistines) had been sparked during David's regime—but it was Solomon who gave it life and action in a climate of peace and prosperity. But just as David had to go outside his country for help to build his palace in Jerusalem, so did Solomon likewise have to go to Hiram, king of Tyre on the Mediterranean coast, for architects, skilled craftsmen and lumber. None of these necessary things were available in Israel. Leonard Cottrell in "The Anvil of Civilization" (Mentor) says that the ancient Hebrews were indifferent artists and designers. They left nothing behind that could compare with the art, the literature and the great construction projects of the Egyptians, the Greeks and the Romans.

Solomon liked raising horses which he imported from Egypt and Cilicia and had grand stables in Megiddo and in Jerusalem where they may be inspected today. He pioneered in limited copper mining and smelting with an ingenious blast furnace, as discovered by archaeologist and Bible authority, Dr. Nelson Glueck. He developed sea commerce—with the Phoenicians building and operating his ships. In modern parlance he "put Jerusalem on the map" but in doing so he brought about disintegration of the tribal unity that had made possible the experiment of combining religion with politics and nationality in a state called Israel.

To sum up the Solomon regime—his extravagance in building, his luxurious social living and lavish court, his flare for fine horses and beautiful women and other indulgences—left behind him at death a nation of quarreling dissidents which could not be held together. It is possible that the writers who set down his record may have exaggerated a bit both as to his indulgences and his great wisdom.

JERUSALEM NOTE: The noted archaeologist, W. F. Albright, says he believes the storied Temple built by Solomon was intended as a royal chapel where the worship of Yahweh was to be under the protection of the king. This was more or less a common policy of ancient nations.

Dr. G. Ernest Wright, in his 1960 book "Bible Archaeology," says in regard to excavation and research that "not a single discovery has been made in Jerusalem which can be dated with any certainty to the time of David and Solomon." "We know," he says, "where they lived and built but practically everything other than the city fortifications has been destroyed . . . the first great fortification has been traced around a section of the hill." The city has been occupied by many different peoples over the centuries — as noted in Chapter III.

ANCIENT ISRAEL SPLITS APART

The ten tribes who constituted the northern part of ancient Israel had long been in opposition to Solomon's excesses and other practices in Judah. When Solomon died, the northerners refused to accept his son Rehoboam (who succeeded his father at the Jerusalem capital) as their king. At the conclave where all the tribes were called to approve the new king, a certain Jeroboam (speaking for the northern tribes) demanded a reduction in spending and taxing. Disregarding the counsel of his conservative elders and following that of the younger "liberals," Solomon's son, Rehoboam, angrily warned:

> "My father made your yoke heavy, and I will add to your yoke; my father also chastized you with whips, but I will chastize you with scorpians" (I Kings 12:14).

When the northern tribes heard this, they cried "To your tents, O Israel," and in revolt against the "House of David" (Judah) created their own state Samaria and Galilee and called it "Israel." Its area was almost three times the size of Judah but Judah had the prestige of Jerusalem. Actually there were three other break-offs which we will not consider here other than to name them as Syria, Moab and Edom which had been taken over under David—and the whole consolidation as a strong, unified "Israel" had, for some fifty or sixty years, dominated the land of Canaan.

During the next several years there was more or less continual friction (and sometimes warfare) between the northern and southern groups. One principal bone of contention between them was scriptural—the northern group accepting as its abiding scripture only the first five books of the Old Testament.

After Solomon's death the northern splinter-state limped along, becoming more and more vulnerable to frictional confrontation with expanding Assyria. The country had a rapid turnover of rulers during its 200-year existence where, according to one Jewish encyclopedia, "Idol worship was widespread and frequently encouraged by the kings themselves." Historian Graetz gives a picture of the closing years of the turbulent state when he explains that in 768 (B.C.) King Zachariah was killed by Shallum who took the throne and exterminated the house of Jehu.

END OF ISRAEL

In the same year Menahem killed Shallum and took control. Pekakiah, who had succeeded his father (Menahem), was killed by Pekah who took over in 756 (B.C.) and in 736 Pekah was killed by Hoshea who reigned until 722 when the country was invaded by the Assyrians. These conquerors carried away the cream of the "ten tribes" and transplanted them in Mesopotamian areas where, through assimilation during the centuries—and perhaps some incidental migration—they became the storied "lost tribes." Graetz, in his several volume "History of the Jews," suggests they were "irretrievably lost among the nations." There were some rumors, according to Graetz, that some of their descendants may have been involved with the "Jewish" Chazar (Khazar) nation that flourished in the central part of what is present-day Russia in the 7th, 8th and 9th centuries (A.D.).

381

JUDAH ENJOYS RESPITE BEFORE DOOM

The southern fragment of the Israel of Saul, David and Solomon (Judah) very nearly suffered the same fate as the northern area some ten to twenty years after the "ten tribes" had been carried off by the Assyrians. Another Assyrian ruler came with an army to attack nearby Egypt, with which Judah had some arrangement. But before the Assyrians could deal with the Egyptians as a prelude to dealing with Judah, the Assyrian army suddenly retreated—and Judah gained a new lease on life.

NOTE: As to this sudden and unexplained retreat, there are two historical rumor-conjectures: In Jerusalem, it was rumored that a devouring pestilence of the Angel of Death had destroyed the Assyrian army — while in Egypt, the priests had a story that countless field mice had destroyed army weapons and equipment, leaving the army no alternative but to retreat. The more realistic answer, doubtless, was that internal troubles in turbulent Assyria called for a quick return.

Judah escaped for the time, but in 586 B.C. the country was conquered by the Babylonians who had risen over the Assyrians to new power. The walls were breached—the Temple razed—and the cream of the Judeans were carried off to Babylon. There the "exiles" did not find Nebuchadnezzar a bad master so long as they restrained their aggressiveness in religio-politico objectives. Some chafed at this limitation while others conformed and prospered.

Some forty-seven years passed with the Babylonian empire dominant in the Mesopotamian area until Cyrus, King of Persia, captured Babylon and formed the Persian Empire, of which Palestine was a part. Being religiously tolerant, Cyrus soon, for one reason or another, offered to let the captive Jews return to Jerusalem and rebuild their Temple for which some of the orthodox were wailing. In 538 B.C., a caravan of several thousand, under Persian protection, did return; but as many or more preferred to remain in Babylon rather than go back to the devastation and famine in Jerusalem. Many became prosperous in Babylon. Archives found by archaeologists in Nippur (ancient Babylonian town) mention Jewish bankers there just a little later.

In a climate of considerable freedom in Babylon, the "captives" had developed a lively religious center which, as it grew, later gave birth to the Babylonian Talmud, which continues to serve Judaism as authority for what is known as the Oral Law.

THREE NAMES — LONG STORY

In tracing the continuity of Abrahamic ancestral-lineage (or seed) —define it as bloodstream or religion as you will—there are three of what may be called nomenclature periods: (1) The people involved were known as "Hebrews" from Abraham to the time that his grandson Jacob, with his twelve sons settled in Egypt to escape famine in Canaan; (2) From then on, certainly from the beginning of the Exodus under Moses on to the settlement of the twelve tribes in Palestine, followed by the later formation of a nation called "Israel," these people were called "Israelites," or in priestly vernacular "children of Israel"; (3) Later the Israelites were carried away as captives at two different times. When those taken to Babylon (as explained in the preceding paragraph) were allowed to return to Judah, the word "Jew" began to be—and continues to be used—as the common term designating this ancestral line.

NOTE: Permission by the Persian King Cyrus to allow the exiles to return to Jerusalem to rebuild their Temple, which had been destroyed when the Babylonians had carried the people away in captivity, did not mean granting them independent sovereignty. Judah, in fact all of Palestine, became an integral part of the Persian Empire. As a matter of fact, Judah had not enjoyed political freedom since King Josiah (608 B.C.) had made the mistake of interfering with the Egyptian army watching under Pharaoh Necho along the coastal route to face the Assyrians. Josiah was killed in battle. The Pharaoh established a protectorate over Judah, appointing Josiah's son as the new ruler. Judah was therefore a dependency of Egypt from 608 until Babylonia captured Jerusalem in 586 B.C.

EXILES RETURN — MEET PROBLEMS

The Jews who returned from Babylon to Jerusalem did so infused with a nostalgic and religious fervor which, sadly, soon declined under the conditions they found around the "city of David." They had returned intending to rebuild the Temple as a great shrine to revive the ancient traditions of the Hebrew-Israelite religion.

It is probable that the long 600 mile caravan trek of four or five months across the hot desert and wasteland, combined with the desolation of the scenes at the end of their journey, may have sapped some of their enthusiasm. At any rate all they could build at first was an altar. The Samaritans who were left in what had been the northern segment of Israel offered to join the exiles in rebuilding the Temple— but the offer was rejected. This stimulated old enmity and turmoil again between the two groups of former Israel. The second Temple was not completed until 516 B.C. Palestine continued as a dependency of Persia with the Jews directing their own social and religious affairs through their high priests.

ALEXANDER SMOTHERS
PERSIA—TAKES EMPIRE

Ancient history is a record of empires rising and falling—usually carrying the control and destinies of smaller countries with them in their ups and downs. The great Persian Empire, for a time, gave promise of considerable permanence but it lasted only about 200 years—from 538 to 330 B.C. when a new hurricane of conquest came sweeping into the Middle East out of Macedonia. It was the Grecian-Macedonian army, led by the young man who was to become known as Alexander the Great. He was a dynamic bundle of genius and courage—determined to fulfil his father's (King Philip's) dream of empire and punish the Persians. This daring invasion of the Mesopotamian lands — to confront powerful Egyptian and Persian armies, with the added problem and danger of long distance logistics — would have caused an older leader to hesitate and ponder.

NOTE: While the main purpose of reference to Alexander and his conquest of empire is to pinpoint that part of it that has to do with Jewish history, this note will digress just enough to picture what was probably the highlight of his whole campaign. Alexander with his army was traveling the historic route that bends around the Mediterranean, after leaving Macedonia and Asia Minor, on the way to Tyre, Sidon, Gaza and Egypt. It happened that a huge Persian army under King Darius III was operating inland not too far from this route, and learning of the Alexander invasion, moved to cut in behind them for a rear attack. Alexander, hearing of this, turned and surprised the Persians by hitting them at Issus where his attack was so fast and furious that the Persian army disintegrated like a tornado-hit city. Darius managed to get out of his chariot and escaped on a horse leaving a harem he had brought with him to its fate.

The battle at Issus in 333 B.C. was decisive — except for a final coup de grace delivered to Darius and a reorganized army which Alexander caught up with in late 331. After Issus, Alexander led his army on to take Tyre, Sidon and other places en route, entering Egypt in 332 B.C.

The Egyptians had lived under Persian rule for 200 years and welcomed a change — surrendering without a blow. Alexander was in Egypt for four months, doing many things the greatest of which, perhaps, was creation of the beautiful seaport city of Alexandria, later noted especially for the great Alexandrian library. Leaving Egypt in charge of one of his generals, Ptolomy I, he started on his great Asian crusade which ended with his sudden illness and death in Babylon in 323 B.C. at the youthful age of 33. What is important here is that the great Empire he left included Palestine, which affected the Jews there because of the wide Hellenizing influence that followed.

When Alexander died, his new empire was divided by his generals. The two in whom we are interested here are Ptolomy I who was already appointed in Egypt as Alexander's governor, who then held it for his own. Seleucus Nicator took Persia and the Mesopotamian country with Babylon as his capital. Ptolomy, now the sole ruler of Egypt, also coveted Palestine because it was the gateway between Egypt and the Mesopotamian countries. Although several penetrations into the country were made, the conquest was never consummated.

There was a long line of Ptolomies who succeeded each other in the rule of Egypt, Cleopatra being the last of the line. Egypt is brought into this discussion mainly because of a heavy colonization of Jews in Alexandria, a city that had been established by Alexander in late 332 B.C. Over the years, many Judean Jews had reached Alexandria either as slaves or as immigrants. These Jews had readily adapted to Hellenistic (Grecian) language and culture—so much so that to help keep Hebrew tradition alive, according to legend, Ptolomy arranged to have the Hebrew Bible (Pentateuch first) translated into Greek (by seventy Hebrew scholars) especially for them (between 258-246 B.C.). Ptolomy also wanted a copy for the famous Alexandrian Library.

NOTE: It is to be remembered that "books" in those days were scrolls. This early Greek translation (called the Septuagint) was used by the early Christians as the only literature they had for some time. It was slightly retranslated by the early Christian Father and scholar, Origen, and by others. Because the Christians quoted from it to prove some of their points, this Greek translation was more or less disowned by the Hebrew leaders.

---

*　　*　　*

HELLENISM AND THE JEWS

Taking up now the area of Judah (or Judea) in Palestine as the center then of the Jewish world, a very long story will be condensed into the shortest possible form. After Alexander's death, the Persian part of his empire, taken over by his general Seleucus Nicator, marked the beginning of the Seleucide dynasty. A number of kings followed in this dynastic line, most of them bearing either the name of Seleucus or Antiochus. Many of them favored the development of Hellenistic culture in their kingdom which encompassed Palestine. In that area this type of culture was anathema to the Jewish religious leaders— yet it was a culture towards which many Jews were friendly. This was probably because it was a refreshing break from the boredom of hard-core Judaic orthodoxy.

Graetz tells us that the Jews looked to the Graeco-Macedonian rulers for "protection from their numerous foes," and in order to curry favor with them the Jews tried to become like them in manners, customs and observance. Thus they joined in the Grecian athletic contests which involved many of the richest and most distinguished of the Judeans. Graetz also says "they (the Judeans) took delight in the luxuries" and refinements introduced by the Hellenists and did not wish to have their pleasures limited to the strictness of the Chasidim.

Life for the Jews moved on under the Seleucidean dynasty, irking some of the Judeans and apparently being not too unpleasant for some of the others. Finally in 174 B.C., one Antiochus Epiphanes came to power, who, more than any of his predecessors, was dedicated to imposing Hellenistic culture upon the Judeans. He sought to unify his government with an amalgamation of common religion and Grecian culture under which the demise of the Jewish religion would have been easily predictable.

This led to what is known as the Maccabean revolt, led by Mattathias (an elderly member of the priestly Hasmonean family) and his five sons. The revolt developed gradually into a wide-spread guerrilla type of warfare which, after long fighting, won for the Judeans a considerable degree of religious and civil freedom.

What Antiochus Epiphanes did to the Jews in pressing Hellenism upon them is the kind of thing the Jews have capitalized down through the centuries as "oppression"—and since realism shows that most human problems are two-way streets, it is interesting to contrast the disposition of Antiochus with that of a Jewish leader just a few years afterwards. John Hyrcanus (of the Jewish Hasmonean-Maccabean line) came to power in Judea in 135 B.C. (under the new freedom won by the revolt). He conquered the small country of Edom to the south and (according to Graetz) gave the inhabitants (Idumaeans) "the choice between acceptance of Judaism or exile." They accepted Judaism in order to keep their homes.

NOTE: Edom was just south of Moab. Both were small areas south and east of the Wadi Arabah that stretches from the Dead Sea to the Gulf of Aqaba — a finger point of the Red Sea. The arid scenery though Edom is awesome and breathtaking. Among those in Edom who were forced to convert to Judaism on orders of Hyrcanus were the immediate forebears of Herod the Great, who later was appointed King of Judea by the Romans. It was Herod Antipas of a later generation who was of the time of Jesus. The Jewish leader Hyrcanus was not the only offender in compelling religious conformity. There were Christians in the Middle Ages who tried, for a time, to force Jews to accept Christianity — and those who submitted were known as Marranos.

Compulsion, in one way or another, is an old story in the field of religion; however it can be said that Judaism is one of the least offenders in religious proselyting — outside their own people. A clear distinction, however, can be made between this and aggressive political action, as in Zionism.

Beginning especially with the rule of this man, John Hyrcanus, in Judah there ensued a typical period of turmoil—intrigue and internal conflict—reminiscent of the eternal problems of the old Kingdom of

Israel period, as the little country tried again the experiment of self-government.

Suffice it here to say that the rulership succession in the newly liberated Judah continued through the Hasmonean (Mattathias) line, which had been accepted as something akin to a royal family heirship, until it reached a point of contest between two "royal line brothers." A prolonged and bitter argument as to who should be the ruler engaged these two "rival" brothers—Aristobulus II and Hyrcanus II. The minutiae of that conflict are not important here, other than its tragic outcome.

When the quarrel had reached an insoluble impasse, it happened that the famous Roman general Pompey was traveling nearby in Asia and the embittered brothers agreed to invite him to moderate their differences. To that end they met him in Damascus. This reckless arrangement ended in easily predictable disaster for the battling brothers and for the people of Judah.

Rome was, at the time, rapidly expanding its dominion. Pompey had been in Asia with an army gathering victories for this very purpose—including Syria, where a last remant of Alexander's conquests was being added to the fast emerging Roman empire. Palestine had traditionally been a geographical part of Syria. The greedy brothers played directly into Pompey's plans. He agreed graciously to arbitrate their differences. He decided in favor of Aristobulus—and then ordered the "lucky" brother to surrender Jerusalem to him—Pompey.

Aristobulus tried to comply but the people inside the walls of Jerusalem refused to submit and stood to fight. The great Jewish historian Josephus tells of the stubborn resistance. Pompey, he says, had to bring battering rams from Tyre, over a hundred miles of rough roads from Phoenicia (now Lebanon), to assail the walls. 12,000 Jews were killed in the fighting, but not all of these were killed by Roman soldiers. Internecine warfare inside the walls took a heavy toll, according to Josephus who was reporting this only about two generations after it happened. The siege was a long one. Pompey reduced and captured the city of Jerusalem in 63 B.C., making Judah a Roman province.

One hundred years rolled off the calendar of time with Judah (Southern Palestine) being governed by officers appointed by Rome, among whom were the well known succession of Herods. The Jews, under this rule, were always restive and often rebellious—unable to adjust themselves to taking orders as part of a widespread empire. Inside Judah a militant group known as the Zealots grew in numbers and influence.

They agitated so violently against Roman authority that by 66 A.D. a Jewish revolt had reached such proportions as to threaten orderly government in the whole area. The following year, Emperor Nero sent his top general, Vespasian, to quell the insurrection. After establishing order in the provinces surrounding Judah, to which the trouble had spread, Vespasian was called back to Rome because of the (suicide) death of Nero.

Vespasian, who had been nominated as Emperor by his soldiers, before he left Palestine turned command of the Roman legions in Judea (so called by the Romans) over to his son Titus, with instructions to subdue the revolt and its leaders in Jerusalem. After lengthy preparations, Titus set siege to the walled city—which lasted nearly six months. The walls were finally breached in 70 A.D. with the city and the Temple (which structure was then a main symbol of Jewish religion) being destroyed.

NOTE: It may be an interesting record for some readers that, according to Eusebius (early Christian Bishop and historian) and others, the fairly limited number of Christians in Jerusalem (as the Jewish revolt picked up momentum in 66-67 A.D.) were ordered "by an oracle" to leave. They moved to Pella, a village about sixty miles north of Jerusalem. The main leaders of the new Christian church movement — the apostles and disciples — were already scattered, preaching and organizing throughout the surrounding countries.

MORE JEWISH TROUBLE FOR ROME

After Titus destroyed Jerusalem in 70 A.D., the city lapsed into desolation, but in the hinterlands of Judah the remaining Jews who felt themselves wronged by religious affronts—such as the Temple of Yahweh in Jerusalem being replaced by the Temple of Jupiter and Jews being ousted from the Jerusalem precincts—were restive with anger. This grew in momentum as passions were stirred by agitators, the leader of whom was a fiery man named Ben Kosiba (known as Bar Kokhba) who had been encouraged and acclaimed by the noted Rabbi Akiva as a Messiah to lead the people.

The Jews were further infuriated when, in 131-2 A.D., the Roman Emperor Hadrian visited the area and ordered a new Roman city to rise on the ruins of old Jerusalem—to be named Aelia Capitolina. The agitation led by Bar Kokhba gradually built up in preparation and fury to the status of a revolt aaginst Rome, and became so serious that Hadrian sent an army to Jerusalem to restore order and settle the Judean trouble once and for all. The Jewish revolters were defeated and devastatingly subdued in 135 A.D. A Roman garrison was left to patrol the district and keep order.

NOTE: The name Aelia Capitolina, which Hadrian gave to the town he built on the ruins of destroyed Jerusalem, is symbolized in modern Jerusalem even today (mid-1967) by a Y.M.C.A.-connected hotel named Aelia Capitolina. That name apparently marked the site of the Old City for some 200 years, until changed back to Jerusalem by Roman Emperor Constantine when he and his mother, Helena, gave Roman recognition to Christianity and restored the religious shrines in the fourth century A.D.

WANDERING JEWS BECOME ''DIASPORA''

The Judean Jews dispersed themselves (after the Roman suppression of 70 and 135 A.D.) into other countries—some to Alexandria—some to Rome—some to Asia Minor and elsewhere—with inconsequential numbers left scattered throughout Palestine, Samaria, Galilee and other parts of what is now called the Middle East. There were also the two prior exiles that scattered Jews throughout Mesopotamia, with a heavy colonization in Babylonia. Gradually, over the earlier centuries of the Christian era, propagation and constantly moving migration throughout the commercial world created an ever-growing population of Jewish people, known as the Diaspora.

Over the centuries the scattered Jewish diaspora multiplied and survived as a religious and ethnic grouping by adjusting to a new system of decentralized worship after the Temple of Yahweh in Jerusalem had been destroyed and many of the people exiled to Babylon. There they first learned not to depend upon the once great central sacrificial Temple but to worship in independent groups. This spread from homes to meeting places that gradually became known as synagogues. This change from dependence on the Jerusalem Temple is described by Dr. Maurice H. Harris in one of his earlier books on Jewish history where he says—"The whole world could then become its (Judaism's) legitimate home." There are those who claim that present day Zionism seeks to reverse this trend and go back to the new Israel as the center of Jewish religious—and even political—loyalties.

Another important factor in aiding the survival of Judaism after the destruction of Jerusalem and dispersion of the Jews in 70 A.D. was the development of priestly "academies" (often conducted in rabbinic homes) which spread to the earlier diaspora colonies.

NOTE: Jewish historians verify the legend that during the savage battle when Titus had laid siege to Jerusalem, a Palestinian tanna (teacher) named Johanan ben Zakkai escaped from the internecine holocaust inside the walls where fratricidal leaders (John of Giscala and others) were giving the Romans competition in killing their own people. He escaped by being carried through one of the temple and city gates in a coffin (ostensibly to be buried); then when out he approached the Roman command with a proposition to help secure surrender of Jerusalem in return for one small favor which was that he be given the privilege of starting a rabbinic school (academy) elsewhere in Palestine. The writers say the request was granted and the school (a yeshiva) was later started in the small Mediterranean coastal town of Jamnia (Jabneh) near Jaffa. Some have credited this "academy" plan with saving Judaism from extinction after the Roman destructions and dispersions in Judea. This seems illogical as there were already academies in Babylon, but it does highlight the doubtless value of such rabbinic schools in keeping Jewish religion and culture alive through trying times. All of these early schools were dedicated strictly to the teaching of the "Mosaic Law." Early Hebrew-Jewish scholarship was largely limited to the reading, understanding and

389

interpreting of the Mosaic doctrinology. One writer has said that "only he was regarded as learned" who was completely competent in all rudiments of the Mosaic Law. The record seems clear that what was called "learning" in an educational sense among the early Hebrew-Jewish people—until they scattered from their original habitat and began to rub shoulders with the outside world—was directed to a particularized concept of religion—narrowed to the interpretation of "the Law."

* * *

JEWISH DIASPORA SPREADS AFAR

All that has been said hereinbefore is largely a tracing of Hebrew-Israelite-Jewish history. After the Roman dispersion the Jews, as a people, took on a somewhat new identity as a scattered people, intermixing with other cultures in different countries. The earlier dispersions into Assyria and Babylonia did not change their geographical and cultural environment and outlook very much. Conditions there were still primitive and nomadic.

The Roman dispersion had a different effect. The Jews from Palestine this time moved into countries where Greek and Roman culture was at the moment in the ascendency. This new or changed social climate had a psychological impact upon the Jews, engendering a new consciousness of world opportunity . The new contacts opened a vista upon a previously unknown social and economic world.

NOTE: It is somewhat relevant to mention incidentally that during the first century (A.D.), a new religion (the Christian movement) had reached out from Jerusalem and was spreading amongst the Roman populace and on to places like Antioch and other cities in the Asia Minor region. The birth of this new religion was another repudiation of the old Hebrew orthodoxy from which environment it had emerged. This represented a distinctive new approach to man's relationship with his God and the first step toward a complete break with the Mosaic traditions of Yahweh. The priestly hostility in Jerusalem toward this new religion brought the crucifixion of Jesus through stimulated pressure upon Pontius Pilate, the Roman Governor of Judea.

During the first three centuries before Constantine, however, the Jews had better treatment in Rome than did the Christians. Despite the fierce hostility of the Jews toward the Roman government prior to the revolt that caused the destruction of Jerusalem by Titus, there was general toleration in Rome for the Jews who came there. Josephus, for instance, was given welcome and freedom to write his histories of the Jews. This tolerance hardened under Emperor Hadrian because of the second Jewish revolt in Palestine, but it softened again under succeeding emperors.

After Christianity was recognized and given national status under Constantine in the fourth century, a climate of tension developed where, according to Dr. Jean Juster (historian of the Jews under Roman rule), "the Jews began to quit the Empire for the precarious hospitality of any barbarian king." The Jews were spreading out and taking their chances, just as were the Christians and other peoples.

*   *   *

JEWS IN MIDDLE AGES — AND ON

Problems for the Jews during the Middle Ages throughout European countries, where they had gone and multiplied through the centuries after they left Palestine, came not so much from regular and stated religious leaders—or State authorities—as from mobs easily mobilized and stirred by agitators, typical of the mob-agitation in the days of Christ—and somewhat as of today by Communists and other extremists who employ mobocracy as part of their strategy.

ENGLAND EXPELS THEM

The history of the Jews (their growth and problems) during the middle centuries is entirely too lengthy a story to detail here. The issues involved are too complicated and uncertain for any attempt to assess causes at this late date. For reasons—how good or bad we do not know—England issued an edict for Jewish expulsion in 1290 A.D. Historian Maurice E. Harris in "History of the Mediaeval Jews" describes conditions that led to the British action. Edward I had forbade the practice of usury and this, Harris says, "depriving them of livelihood made their status impossible." He describes some of the things they turned to which apparently were unpopular. The King and the Church began closing the synagogues and imposing further restrictions until finally, according to Harris, "there was only one thing left for the King to do—to expel them."

EJECTED FROM FRANCE

Historian Graetz, writing in 1893, described conditions in France (814-840) as "a golden era for the Jews . . . such as they had never enjoyed, and were destined never to enjoy again in Europe"—yet they were banished from France, first in 1306. Three years later they bargained with the king and were allowed to return. Trouble arose later and they were expelled again in 1322; and from then until 1359, according to historian Harris, there was no record of Jews in France. After some time an arrangement was made for them to return on a twenty year grant—with conditions.

Harris recounts that the Jews were allowed to charge 80 per cent for money lending but that there was a kick-back to the king who "used Jews as means of indirect and hidden taxation." By 1394 certain incidents, coupled with high anti-Jewish feeling sweeping across the Pyranees from Spain, again brought expulsion of Jews from France and their status did not again become tenable there until the seventeenth century.

After the French Revolution (which many Jewish writers consider one of the greatest "liberating" epochs in Jewish history), the political status of the Jews of France improved. Complaints about money lending and other matters caused Napoleon to call a meeting of Jew-

391

ish notables in Paris in 1806, where he asked for an explanation as to whether they (the Jews) considered themselves as "a nation" or as a "religious grouping." They assured Napoleon of their fidelity and agreed to recognize France's civil laws. A temporary moratorium was placed on lending-debts owed to the Jews.

* * *

JEWS DRIVEN FROM SPAIN

In 1492—the year Columbus sailed to America—Spain expelled its Jewish population. Jews had lived there for centuries—probably some were there before the Christians came. Harris, in his "History of the Mediaeval Jews," says that the Jews had dwelt longer in Spain "than Israel and Judah had lived in Canaan." The Jews were not allowed to take with them their gold, silver and money. Some moved to Portugal (from where they were also expelled in 1497) while some remained in Spain and reluctantly became Marranos. Tragic as these expulsions were, a noteworthy contrast with present day Zionism and the Arab refugees is that prior to the 1492 eviction from Spain, the Jews had found asylum and political refuge in Spain when the Moslems controlled it. They also found hospitality in Moslem Turkey in the late thirteenth century.

RISE OF JEWS IN GERMANY

Mediaeval conditions for the Jews in Germany were difficult— especially around the year 1000— and for several years afterward. The eminent scholar, Dr. Jacob R. Marcus (Hebrew Union College) in his scholarly book "The Rise and Destiny of the German Jew," says that the Jews did not take part actively in German political life until after the "outburst of liberalism" that stemmed from the European Revolution of 1848. He also explains that in 1871 the Jews were granted "formal equality" in the (new-1870) German Empire.

The new European political "liberalism" that had erupted out of the 1789 French Revolution gradually spread across the borders into Germany and Austria—and across the Channel into England. As a result, new political movements designed to augment this greater freedom of action were rapidly developing. Dr. Marcus, in his responsible book, describes the rise of European "Social Democracy" that had crystallized into the Social-Democratic Party—the activity of which was a thorn in the side of the great German leader Bismarck. It was the Social-Democratic movement in Europe that split into the Socialist and Communist Party movements. In Russia the split was into Mensheviks and Bolsheviks; in central Europe it was a split into Marxist Communism and Lassalle Socialism; in England it was into Marxism versus Shaw and Webb's Fabianism.

Dr. Marcus tells us that early Social Democracy owed much to "its founder, Karl Marx . . . and its first political organizer, Ferdinand Lassalle," and he goes on to explain that the first steps in founding a Socialist Party in Germany were due "not to Marx, but to another Jew, Ferdinand Lassalle," and that Lassalle was also a "forty-eighter."

This reference is to the 1848 Revolution when the radical leaders, thinking that all Europe was ready to erupt in over-all revolution, commissioned Karl Marx to prepare the "guide-lines" for such an event; and this document that caused the world so much trouble is known as the Communist Manifesto.

*   *   *

After the Jews were granted "formal equality" in Germany in 1871, they began slowly to develop what became the most stable of Jewish communities throughout the world. The German Jew of the nineteenth century was largely conservative and assimilative in the countries to which he migrated. Many of the early well known department stores in America were started by German Jews. In Germany they enjoyed a general and gradual growth of prosperity and prestige in business—in finance—and in the professions. After World War I, with the sudden emergence of Zionist political power, engineered in England by the Weizmann strategy—and the Bolshevik Revolution in Russia (which was also an immediate offshoot of World War I)— there was a penetration of these new forces into Germany that soon began to "make a difference."

Within a year after the Russian Revolution, the Bolsheviks organized the Communist International (Comintern) as its agency for revolutionary activity throughout the world. The most prominent leaders of this movement in Germany were Karl Liebnecht and Rosa Luxemburg, whose agitational activities along with their co-racial followers soon became an alarming issue in Germany. Added to this was the readily acceptable corollary that the assertive-liberalism of certain people was tantamount to Communist sympathy which, combined with a growing resentment of minority penetration in the fields already mentioned, represented altogether a tinderbox that could readily be set afire by the agitational oratory of a man like Hitler and his followers in the nineteen-thirties. It is quite natural to think of Hitlerism and Nazism as a diabolical cataclysm, engineered by one crazy man, but the true answer of how a whole nation could, in the early stages, be mobilized so readily, is probably not quite that simple. Communist activity has to be regarded as one underlying cause.

*   *   *

The purpose here is to give only a highlighted outline of Jewish history and not to dwell in detail upon the tortuous mediaeval experience of these singular people who, according to the Old Testament story, multiplied from the twelve sons of Jacob. To this grouping, once called "a race" but now characterized by some as a religious body and by others as "a nation," goes a great many credits for minority achievements and one of these is the genius for exercising wide influence with comparatively small numbers.

There seems to be no other grouping of intensely cohesive people who have scattered themselves so widely over the face of the earth (concentrating largely in cities) with such strategic effectiveness as to make their distinctively liberal presence felt so tremendously in the three major fields of practical life—social, economic and political.

POPULATION STATISTICS

To complete this historical study of the Jewish people, it would appear germane to examine briefly some present day population statistics as taken from the World Almanac and the American Jewish Year Books. The figures in the World Almanac were supplied by the Jewish Statistical Bureau. The U.S. Government is not able to collect such statistics independently. Each time an effort is made to include the question of "religion" or "religious affiliation" in the Census questionnaire, fierce and effective oppostion from sensitive sources arises to block it. The "new" anthropology-doctrine proscribes classification as ethnic or racial.

The figures upon which we must therefore depend (from the above sources) show the Jewish population in the United States (as of 1966) to be 5,600,000 (Canada—267,000). Accepting this estimate, with no disposition to join those who question its sufficiency, let it be compared with 3,927,200 in all of Europe (same source); 2,438,350 in Asia (which includes 2,316,000 in the new Israel); 732,350 in Central and South America; 72,000 in Australia and New Zealand together; 265,800 in Africa; with a world total of 13,302,700. The figures show that the United States is by far the most favored asylum with a total of considerably more than all of Europe combined— more than any other nation or continent—and more than 42 per cent of the total world Jewish population, according to their own figures.

Until a few years ago, the world Jewish population was mostly heavily concentrated in Russia, Poland and adjacent East-European countries. The World Almanac for 1925 listed 3,300,000 Jews in Poland; 900,000 in Russia and 3,300,000 in the Russian Ukraine; Hungary 450,000; Romania 650,000; Czechoslovakia 450,000;—a total of 9,050,000 for these particular East European nations. The Jewish populations there were materially reduced during the holocaust of World War II. Any figures on this would, in the nature of things, have to be estimates. Factual documentation is hard to come by. The "six million" estimate has been disputed with extensive documentation in a book by the late professor Paul Rassinier in France—and others.

In countries like Poland, Hitlerism took a heavy toll, but many were able also to leave the East European countries and escape the Nazi terror. This is a reference only to statistics and is not intended in any way to minimize that terror-ordeal. There are no words strong enough sufficiently to condemn any type of genocide or anything similiar to it. During that crisis the United States, with special legislation, admitted nearly a half-million refugees in excess of regular immigration quotas. Many Polish Jews, of course, reached Israel where the population has grown from 100,000 in Palestine (1925 World Almanac) to 2,316,000 (1967 Almanac).

While the Jewish population in the East European countries was shrinking from around 9,050,000 total in 1925 to 2,732,000 in 1966, the net increase of Jews in the United States was 2,500,000 (from 3,100,000 to 5,600,000) according to the before mentioned sources. Canada showed an increase of from 100,000 to 267,000; Great Britain from 300,000 to 450,000; France from 150,000 to 500,000; Argentina from 100,000 to 450,000. If this computation were carried on through other countries and added to the nearly 5,000,000 increase in the United States and Israel lumped together, it would account for a substantial portion of the East Europe decrease over the same period—which decrease has been charged largely to World War II.

Throughout the world the Jewish people tend to colonize in cities—especially large cities—for it is there, presumably, they find the greatest opportunities for their talents. The American Jewish Year Book (American Jewish Committee) for 1962 says that after the heavy immigration to America from Eastern Europe up to the 1930's, "some 12 percent of all world Jewry" was then living in New York. This percentage has steadily increased, according to the 1967 World Almanac (source—Jewish Statistical Bureau) where the New York city Jewish population is shown as 1,836,000, which would be roughly 14 percent of the world Jewish population shown as 13,234,000. If the figure of New York city's "environs," given as 545,000 were added, the percentage would be over 17 percent.

Other American cities have also proved attractive for Jewish community colonization as shown by the same 1967 World Almanac. Sunny Los Angeles is second choice with 490,000; Philadelphia is third with 330,000; Chicago comes fourth with 285,000; then Boston with 169,000; Newark lists 100,000; and so on with smaller cities having lesser numbers. The 1955 Jewish Year Book lists some 800 U.S. Jewish communities with populations ranging from 100 to 72,000, in the case of Detroit. The 1966 World Almanac lists 45 cities with more than 10,000 Jewish population, at which time Detroit and Miami are shown with 90,000 each.

In the brief resume of statistics given here, only such computations have been presented as would seem to indicate important angles of growth and distribution in the historical process.

IMMIGRATION RESTRICTED

After the heavy immigration from Europe to America by the hordes who came seeking work in the great American industrial upsurge of the latter part of the 19th and early part of the 20th centuries, genuine problems began to develop. One alarming situation was that of the numerous immigrants, speaking many different languages, very few could either speak or read English and were complete strangers to the "American way of life." They became easy prey for socialist and other radical agitators who had also migrated to America and were hungry for power.

It was around the turn of the century when Socialism became a real agitative factor—and in 1919 that the Communist Party was organized in America out of the "Left Wing" of the Socialist Party, which itself had been formed largely out of immigrants who, because they could not speak English, had been herded into what were called Foreign Language Federations. One of the early principal socialist leaders was immigrant Morris Hillquit, who describes "The Beginning of America Socialism" in one of his books: "Loose Leaves From a Busy Life." He lists as one of his early colleagues the late Professor John Dewey, dean of "progressive education" which led the swing to the Left in American education.

In 1917, the U.S. Congress took its first major step in curbing immigration by passing the "Immigration Act of 1917." The law was strengthened by an amending act in 1924 and strengthened again, after long and careful study of the problem, in 1952 with what was widely known as the McCarren-Walter omnibus immigration and nationality act. The legislation established a carefully devised mathematical safeguard in the nature of a "quota system," based upon previous immigration records, which was fair to other countries and at the same time a protection for the United States.

From the very first immigration-control legislation, the law became the target of pressure-groups operating principally under auspices of New York city minority-bloc leaders who, for political power reasons, wanted to bring in more of their people. This activity is all a matter of record which is not needed in this particular reference other than to point out that the crusade finally succeeded in 1965, under the driving force of the Johnson "Great Society" administration. Flush with reelected power, reinforced by highly active minority and liberal groups, the Administration pushed through Congress its 1965 Immigration Act, which so liberalized and changed the previous legislation in this field as to open the entrance gates to almost limitless numbers.

Mary Barclay Erb has described the changes and present status well in "While America Sleeps—Foundations Crumble" (American Committee on Immigration Policies, Washington, D.C.).

* * *

This chapter has attempted to present with sincerity and candid objectivity a short review of the outstanding episodic events of "the Jewish people" story (with relevance to the thesis of this book) from the earlist historical period on to the present day—with the exception of "the Zionist story" which is scattered throughout the book. "Who Are the Jews?" is included to complement the chapter "Who Are the Arabs?" as a means of presenting the dramatis personae of the general narrative to which this book is dedicated.

An added reason also for these two chapters is that in researching for documentation, it was discovered that the general public has but a limited acquaintance with the historical background of either the Jews or the Arabs—and without some knowledge of these histories, it would be a waste of time to discuss Palestine and the far-reaching implications of the present conflict there.

LATE BUT SIGNIFICANT NOTES:

ITEM NO. 1.   Two Conservative members of the British Parliament (Mr. Dennis Walters and Mr. Ian Gilmer), at a press conference in an early 1968 visit to Kuwait, concurred in a statement that "Britain, with its Balfour Declaration, must bear heavy responsibility for its part in the creation of Israel," — according to the publication of Kuwait's "Permanent Mission to the United Nations." Since the 1967 Israeli blitz into Jordan, the M.P.s continued, "Britain has shown a realistic reassessment of the Arab position." They further expressed the opinion that after World War II — "Israel's existence was the direct result of U.S. pressure but in the U.S. there is a growing conflict of policy on the Middle East." While Britain, they said, could exert some influence on Middle East policy it is the United States that can change the trend there. (This presumably referred to some blockage on the vast flow of tax-free money from U.S. sources into that troubled area.)

ITEM NO. 2.   An article in the Los Angeles Times (5-10-68) headed "U.S. IN MIDEAST — A FUTILE EAGLE," by its highly responsible Middle East correspondent (Joe Alex Morris, Jr.), opened with this statement: "Recent events in the Middle East have served to illustrate the bankruptcy of American policy in this tense region." The story referred particularly to a March 21st "one day" Israeli military invasion into the Jordan Valley ostensibly to attack Arab Commando bases. After discussing the threats to the future survival of Jordan as one Arab nation that wishes to be a friend of the West the article concluded "From an American standpoint, the outlook could hardly be worse. 'I've never been so depressed,' one high-ranking diplomat here (Beirut) confessed."

INDEX

400

401

402

403

404